PATRICK O'BRIAN

PATRICK O'BRIAN

A Life

DEAN KING

AN OWL BOOK
HENRY HOLT AND COMPANY | NEW YORK

For Jessica,

Hazel, Grace, Willa, Nora,

and Betsey,

with love

Henry Holt and Company, LLC
Publishers since 1866
115 West 18th Street
New York, New York 10011

Henry Holt® is a registered trademark
of Henry Holt and Company, LLC.

Published in Canada by Fitzhenry & Whiteside Ltd.,
195 Allstate Parkway, Markham, Ontario L3R 4T8.

Library of Congress Cataloging-in-Publication Data
King, Dean.
Patrick O'Brian : a life / by Dean King.
p.   cm.
Includes bibliographical references and index.
ISBN 0-8050-5977-6
1. O'Brian, Patrick, 1914–   2. Novelists, English—20th century—Biography.
3. Historical fiction—Authorship.   4. Sea stories—Authorship.   I. Title.
PR6029.B55 Z736   2000   99-048495
823'.912—dc21
[B]

Henry Holt books are available for special promotions and
premiums. For details contact: Director, Special Markets.

First published in hardcover in 2000 by Henry Holt and Company

First Owl Books Edition 2001

Designed by Kate Nichols

Printed in the United States of America

1   3   5   7   9   10   8   6   4   2

Patrick ... is sixteen, the son of a London doctor. He began this story when he was fourteen and finished it in March of this year. "I did it mostly in my bedroom and a little when I should have been doing homework."

—*Caesar,* 1930

Patrick O'Brian was born in the West of Ireland and educated in England. During the war he drove an ambulance in London and later joined the Political Intelligence Department of the Foreign Office. Mr. O'Brian began writing at an early age and had already produced four novels before the war, as a kind of literary exercise.

—*The Walker and Other Stories,* 1955

As to the personal side, the *Spectator* for March 1st 1710 begins, "I have observed, that a Reader seldom peruses a Book with Pleasure, till he knows whether the Writer of it be a black or fair Man, of a mild or cholerick Disposition, Married or a Batchelor, with other particulars of the like Nature, that conduce very much to the right understanding of an Author." To gratify this curiosity, which is so natural to a reader, we may state that Mr. O'Brian is a black man, choleric, and married.

—*Lying in the Sun,* 1956

Nothing is more unjust, however common, than to charge with hypocrisy him that expresses zeal for those virtues, which he neglects to practise; since he may be sincerely convinced of the advantages of conquering his passions, without having yet obtained the victory, as a man may be confident of the advantages of a voyage, or a journey, without having courage or industry to undertake it, and may honestly recommend to others, those attempts which he neglects himself.

The interest which the corrupt part of mankind have in hardening themselves against every motive to amendment, has disposed them to give to these contradictions, when they can be produced against the cause of virtue, that weight which they will not allow them in any other case. . . . In moral or religious questions alone, they determine the sentiments by the actions, and charge every man with endeavouring to impose upon the world, whose writings are not confirmed by his life. They never consider that they themselves neglect, or practise something every day, inconsistently with their own settled judgment, nor discover that the conduct of the advocates for virtue can little increase, or lessen, the obligations of their dictates; argument is to be invalidated only by argument, and is in itself of the same force, whether or not it convinces him by whom it is proposed.

—Samuel Johnson, *The Rambler,* no. 14, May 5, 1750

When does one ever know a human being? Perhaps only after one has realized the impossibility of knowledge and renounced the desire for it and finally ceased to feel even the need of it. But then what one achieves is no longer knowledge, it is simply a kind of coexistence; and this too is one of the guises of love.

—Iris Murdoch, *Under the Net,* 1954

Contents

Contents

PART IV: AZURE

PART V: DEEP BLUE

PART VI: GOLD

Introduction

When an American and an English publisher jointly commissioned Patrick O'Brian to write a naval novel in 1967, no one expected it to be a great work of literature, and certainly no one knew that they had set in motion what would become one of the publishing phenomena of our time. The book was the commercial brainchild of an American editor who hoped to find the next C. S. Forester. A master of depicting naval battles, Forester had died the year before, leaving behind ten novels and a companion book about the exploits of Horatio Hornblower, officer of the Royal Navy. These well-written naval tales, published over the course of three decades, had captured the imagination of British schoolboys and statesmen alike—Winston Churchill included—and sold well on both sides of the Atlantic.

Based on O'Brian's previous historical naval novels, *The Golden Ocean* (1956) and *The Unknown Shore* (1959), the editor at J. B. Lippincott, a Philadelphia publishing house, felt that the fifty-three-year-old novelist, whom he believed to be Irish, was well suited to duplicate Forester's success. The editor knew he could expect an entertaining adventure story, including black squalls, weevils in the hardtack, and graphic sea battles, liberally dusted with O'Brian's sprightly humor.

What he got from O'Brian was vastly more profound.

Master and Commander, published in 1969, was the first volume of what would turn out to be a monumental extended novel set during the Napoleonic wars, a roman-fleuve that filled twenty volumes, currently having sold more than three million copies in twenty languages and changed the lives of countless devotees, in the way that only great books can. However, at first, this seemed an unlikely scenario; neither of the publishers that commissioned *Master and Commander* would succeed with the series. Macmillan of England rejected the manuscript out of hand (William Collins published it instead), and Lippincott, after several poorly selling sequels, also dropped the author.

Nevertheless, O'Brian toiled away on the saga of his two fictional characters—the bluff Royal Navy captain "Lucky" Jack Aubrey and his disheveled "particular friend," the naval surgeon and political intelligence agent Stephen Maturin, whose many passions included nature, music, and opium. Each new book was anxiously awaited by a small dedicated group of British intellectuals and naval veterans. O'Brian was routinely praised by scholars for his accurate naval history and his portrayal of Regency England. They also raved about his prose, which evoked the period authentically without the woodenness of so much historical fiction. Ironically, the books suffered from their own success at verisimilitude. Critics classified them as historical novels, a lowly genre that by definition precluded them from serious attention.

But O'Brian, a serious-minded writer, knew that his work was unfairly pigeonholed. His reputation had once briefly flared in the literary firmament in the 1950s when his novel *Testimonies* received a stunning endorsement from Delmore Schwartz. "*Testimonies* makes one think of a great ballad or a Biblical story," the critic wrote. "The reader, drawn forward by lyric eloquence and the story's fascination, discovers in the end that he has encountered in a new way the sphinx and riddle of existence itself." Schwartz placed the book above recent works by Angus Wilson, Evelyn Waugh, John Steinbeck, and Ernest Hemingway.

But O'Brian's reputation had receded as he continued writing tortured novels and short stories. He had turned to translating to make money, doing many of Simone de Beauvoir's books and dozens of others, including the international best-seller *Papillon*. Returning to fiction in the Aubrey-Maturin novels, he had in a sense started writing afresh, with greater distance and less anger, about his former themes—love and friendship.

"The essence of my books is about human relationships and how people treat one another," he later told the *Financial Times*. "That seems to me what novels are for." In fact, he made that clear at the beginning of his naval series. In *Master and Commander*, when Aubrey, newly made captain of the pint-size warship HMS *Sophie*, asks Maturin to sign on as her surgeon, Maturin responds:

> "For a philosopher, a student of human nature, what could be better? The subjects of his inquiry shut up together, unable to escape his gaze, their passions heightened by the dangers of war, the hazards of their calling, their isolation from women and their curious, but uniform, diet. And by the glow of patriotic fervour, no doubt."—with a bow to Jack—"It is true that for some time past I have taken more interest in the cryptogams than in my fellow-men; but even so, a ship must be a most instructive theatre for an inquiring mind." (P. 43)

By 1990, O'Brian, seventy-five and working largely in obscurity in the south of France, where he had lived for the past four decades with his second wife, Mary, had written thirteen novels in the series, in which Aubrey and Maturin circumnavigate the globe, win and lose battles and their fortunes, fall in and out of love, marry, have children and, in Aubrey's case, numerous affairs. While Aubrey's wife, the motherly Sophie, and Maturin's wife, the dashing, impulsive Diana, frequently embellish the narrative, the primary fuel of the series is O'Brian's study of the relationship between Aubrey and Maturin.

Maturin is a philosopher—cold, saturnine, secretive—a careful examiner of man and nature, and at times a shrewd operator. Aubrey is a jovial, sanguine warrior, devoted to the Royal Navy and most proud that he has twice been spoken to by Horatio Nelson, Britain's great naval captain:

> "The first time it was to say, 'May I trouble you for the salt, sir?'—I have always said it as close as I can to his way ever since—you may have noticed it. But the second time I was trying to make my neighbour, a soldier, understand our naval tactics—weather-gage, breaking the line, and so on—and in a pause he leant over with such a smile and said, 'Never mind manoeuvres, always go at them.' " (P. 115)

While Maturin keeps a coded journal and frequently has to decipher his mail, Aubrey lives by Nelson's dictum. He is a straight-shooter. Despite their differences, Aubrey and Maturin find common ground in their shared values (courage, loyalty, honor, and dedication to their careers), in their mutual goal—the defeat of Napoleon—and in the pleasure of each other's company. Nowhere are the two more in harmony than in the captain's cabin in the evening playing a Mozart or Boccherini duet together, Maturin on the cello and Aubrey on the violin. In *Post Captain*, the second Aubrey-Maturin novel, the two happily seek refuge from oppressive shipboard responsibilities in their music:

> The cabin was filled with the opening movement of Boccherini's Corelli sonata, a glorious texture of sound, the violin sending up brilliant jets through the 'cello's involutions, and they soared up and away from the grind of pumps, the tireless barking [of a lunatic sailor], the problems of command, up, the one answering the other, joining, separating, twining, rising into their native air. (P. 236)

Naturally, each also has a selfish and a sometimes self-destructive side, particularly Maturin, who grows moody and volatile and doses himself with increasingly large amounts of laudanum. Aubrey tends to make impulsive and naive decisions ashore, being easily duped by swindlers, gold-digging women, and political enemies. Sometimes the two friends' personalities clash. Twice they come close to duels.

Forty years after O'Brian's fleeting fame with *Testimonies*, the stage was set for a remarkable comeback. The British critic Peter Wishart had once called the intelligentsia's failure to recognize Patrick O'Brian as a literary wonder of the age "as baffling as the Inca inability to invent the wheel." However, that oversight was about to be corrected. The New York publisher W. W. Norton took a gamble and reissued the Aubrey-Maturin series in the United States. In the January 6, 1991, *New York Times Book Review,* the editor of *American Heritage* magazine called O'Brian's Aubrey-Maturin books the "best historical novels ever written." The bullet hit home.

Suddenly, it became apparent that while O'Brian may or may not have surpassed Forester in sea action, he had created great novels that did not look quite like anything that had come before. His evocation of Nelson's Royal Navy was an escapist world as appealing as J. R. R. Tolkien's Middle Earth, as culturally rich as William Faulkner's Yoknapatawpha County, and as intriguingly ritualistic as Umberto Eco's medieval monastery in *The Name of the Rose*. In this setting, almost flawlessly sustained in the more than five-thousand-page opus, O'Brian had examined his two primary themes, love and friendship, from myriad angles, with extraordinary lucidity and a stylistic range to rival the best novelists. Critics no longer compared him to C. S. Forester but to Jane Austen, Leo Tolstoy, Marcel Proust, and Homer.

O'Brian became a literary juggernaut, with a newsletter and Internet sites devoted to his books, companion books to the series, compact discs of the music mentioned in the novels, and even a slew of bumper stickers. He appeared on stage for interviews before sold-out audiences in the United States. One reader drove from South Dakota to Washington, D.C., just to have his book signed. While this new status as both a meritorious and popular writer was gratifying and financially liberating to O'Brian, he bristled at the media intrusion—encouraged by Norton's publicity machine—that accompanied his anointment as a star.

Those familiar with the series now recognized Maturin's secretive nature in the author. His disdain for personal questions made him testy with reporters and fans. Though he had himself written a biography of Picasso that thoroughly examined the artist's personal life and its effect on his painting, O'Brian insisted that his own life had nothing to do with his writing. Maturin's edict in the novel *The Truelove* (in Britain, *Clarissa Oakes*)—"Question and answer is not a civilized form of conversation"— was clearly O'Brian's own.

When freelance journalist Mark Horowitz, writing a profile of O'Brian for the *New York Times Magazine* in 1993, went to interview O'Brian's former editor before meeting the author himself, he discovered that even the editor had no idea where O'Brian was born and confessed that he did not trust much of what O'Brian said about himself, since he had contradicted himself in the past. O'Brian's current editor bluntly warned Horowitz: "Patrick will make you feel . . . odious and wormlike if you look into his private life."

"There is something the English would say was a bit precious about Patrick," another editor who had worked with O'Brian told Horowitz. "His language, his address . . . there's something slightly finicky, and even almost rather colorful about him in that way. He may have been trying to reshape an idea of himself."

In fact, he had. He was not the Irishman he claimed to be, but a Londoner with an intricate personal history. In 1998, a BBC television profile suggested something was amiss in O'Brian's account of his past, and the news of O'Brian's secret identity was soon made public for the first time in an exposé in the London newspaper the *Daily Telegraph*.

———

By the time of this revelation, I was already well into my research for *Patrick O'Brian: A Life Revealed*, seeking the motives that led O'Brian—born Richard Patrick Russ—to begin transforming his life into fiction at a very early age, and eventually also to fictionalize his life. This effort took me first to the west of Ireland, where O'Brian had said he was born, then to a house called Walden, near the town of Chalfont St. Peter, outside London, where he actually was born, and on to various sections of London and the towns of Kempsey and Lewes, where he spent much of his childhood.

Having lived through most of the troubled twentieth century, O'Brian has shared amply in its pain, developing a dualistic relationship with himself, both loving and hating his own life. As a child, he was sickly. His mother died when he was four, and his father was an aloof bankrupt. Patrick was apparently a misfit in his own family. In his foreword to the 1999 reprint of his novella *Caesar* (first published in 1930) and his novel *Hussein* (1938)—books written under his original surname and whose existence, until recently, he refused to acknowledge—O'Brian gazed seventy years back into his life and observed, "I doubt if my present self would have liked the twelve-year-old boy who wrote this tale—he was certainly not very popular among his brothers and sisters." Just before World War II, he would walk out on his wife and two children. At the end of it, he would change his name and cultivate an Irish persona to match it, and in 1964 he would cease altogether to communicate with his only son (he had two granddaughters he never met).

In 1989, O'Brian's brother Barney Russ wrote to their youngest sister, Joan: "I have had the most fearful letter from Patrick. I really think he thinks he is not my brother ... but I have his birth certificate anyway and whether he likes it or not, I claim him as my brother. . . . The tone of his letter is so violent that I think we have to call an end to friendly correspondence."

At age seventy-five, after having long since separated himself from the society of his family and peers—first moving to Wales and then to southern France—O'Brian was still severing family ties.

Though strange, none of this would be noteworthy if it were not for the fact that O'Brian, who failed in the most basic male relationships—son and father, father and son—was writing arguably the most profound literature of the century on the subject of male friendship.

Aubrey and Maturin are, in O'Brian's own words, "variations on a theme of a man and himself." That divided "man and himself"—two parts English, one part Catalan, and one part Irish, with passionate interests in riding and hunting, natural history and astronomy, music and language, wine, medicine, and the Royal Navy—is the author, as he was, as he perceived himself, and particularly as he wished to be.

While neither Aubrey nor Maturin is wholly autobiographical, the effort of examining their characteristics and circumstances through the prism of O'Brian's life is certainly illuminating. Aubrey's loss of his mother at an early age and intermittent poverty reflect O'Brian's experience, while Maturin's obsession with secrecy mirrors the author's, and Maturin's professional preoccupation with venereal disease matches that of O'Brian's father. The ability of Aubrey and Maturin to overcome personal differences and to find and respect the boundaries of friendship creates an ideal relationship, something O'Brian sorely missed in his family.

It was O'Brian's own loss and failure that created Maturin's highest quality and principal goodness—his indignity at injustice and his love for and protection of the weak. When O'Brian twice had Maturin rescue a pair of children in the series, certainly he was thinking of his own two children abandoned in the flatlands of Norfolk.

Perhaps the most telling moment of this interrelationship between O'Brian and the physician-philosopher Maturin comes when Maturin helps save his young daughter, Brigid, from the netherworld of autism. In this he is aided by his giant and near-mute Irish manservant Padeen Colman, a character born of O'Brian's fascination with the blurred border between human and animal spirits. Together, science and nature combine to bring to Brigid a salvation that O'Brian, or Russ, as he then was, could not provide for his own daughter, Jane, who died of spina bifida at age three.

When in *The Hundred Days*, the nineteenth book of the series, O'Brian revealed (in a few cavalier words from a Greek chorus of passed-over lieutenants on the Rock of Gibraltar) the momentous death of Diana Villiers, the searing love of Maturin's life, O'Brian did so knowing of the impending death of his wife, Mary.

While the tortuous route that O'Brian's snubbed novels took to their proper recognition as one of the century's major literary achievements speaks about the nature of an artistic masterpiece and our ability to recognize one, the story of how these novels came to exist, what inner forces drove O'Brian to persevere during those long decades, is one about the sublime act of creation.

In his book *Against Saint-Beuve* (1909), Proust wrote that "a book is the product of a different self from the one we manifest in our habits, in society, in our vices. If we mean to try to understand this self it is only in our inmost depths, by endeavoring to reconstruct it there, that the quest can be achieved." And it is only in knowing the truth about O'Brian's life that we can fully grasp the magnitude and nature of his accomplishment. It is to be hoped that in this attempt to plumb the depths of O'Brian's real life, the reader will come to agree that his genius was largely that he had continually connected with this "different self" to create from disappointing reality—quite magically—extraordinary fiction, fiction that, for so many of us, embodies the sheer joy of reading.

Author's Note to the
Paperback Edition

So much has happened since I submitted the typescript of the first edition of *Patrick O'Brian: A Life Revealed* to my publisher in the fall of 1999. Sadly and suddenly, it seemed, O'Brian died in Dublin on January 2, 2000. He was eighty-five years old and had recently finished his twentieth Aubrey-Maturin novel. His death was veiled in secrecy just as his life had been. In the onslaught of publicity that followed, however, O'Brian's fame reached new heights.

Ironically, as the biography was on the verge of going to press, new sources were becoming available to me.

In the original research and writing of this book, I faced the challenge of assembling the elusive facts of the life of a person who had changed his name and attempted to bury his past. (He did this so assiduously that his own stepson and heir, Nikolai Tolstoy, told *The Times* that he had to figure out for himself that his stepfather was not Irish.) On the subject of his personal history, O'Brian consistently dissembled, or permitted others unwittingly to dissemble for him. His own sinuous autobiographical accounts, usually contrived under pressure from his publisher or his audience, were misleading.

Nor did O'Brian, for obvious reasons, cooperate with this book. In some cases, he instructed friends and colleagues not to talk to me. Thus, uncovering his identity and his life story was a painstaking business. But it was also one with many rewards. Once I found out about and located

O'Brian's son from a first marriage, I had a candid source of the truth, grateful to be heard at last. Likewise, I tracked down other forgotten family members in Canada and Britain, as well as O'Brian's best friend from World War II, a Welsh shepherd boy he befriended after the war, his oldest friend in France, and his principal agents and editors in England, Scotland, and the United States. Using their firsthand accounts as well as public records, letters, manuscripts, and documents from publishers' archives, I slowly pieced together the fascinating, complex life story of the man (some would say the genius) behind the Aubrey-Maturin tales.

In this edition, I have been able to add a few important new pieces of the puzzle. Following the serialization of the book in Britain in February, I was contacted by readers who knew O'Brian in various capacities throughout his life, chief among them a lover from the 1930s whose story told me, among other things, that O'Brian claimed to be Irish long before he abandoned his original surname, Russ. I also had the pleasure recently of talking to Mary O'Brian's family: her brother, H. F. S. Wicksteed; his wife, Dorothy; and their children, Peter, Jane, and Joanna. The latter three spent summers with the O'Brians in France during the 1960s, and their memories and letters shed a warm glow on that period. Peter became the only person to attest to the fact that O'Brian actually could sail.

All of this has helped round out this new paperback edition of the biography, now simply titled *Patrick O'Brian: A Life*, which I offer as a celebration of O'Brian's monumental achievement, the Aubrey-Maturin novels, in the context of his fascinating, troublesome, often beguiling life.

—Dean King, September 28, 2000

London

July 1945

Saturday, the seventh of July, 1945, was a signal day in southern England. For a luxurious fourteen hours the sun bathed village greens and city row houses, visibly parting the lingering miasma of war and revealing the wonderfully immutable aspects of English life. At Eastbourne, Lord's, and Westcliff, joyous crowds watched cricket matches on freshly mown pitches. On the River Thames, the Henley Royal Regatta had resumed, and spectators thronged the riverbanks for the All Comers' Eights. And at Ascot, King George VI, Princess Elizabeth, and the fashionable cheered the Gold Cup sprint of Ocean Swell, offspring of sire Blue Peter.

In 1945, the barley wine had truly made the cuckoo stutter, and Britannia still ruled. Now the swallows of July were joined by the irrepressible din of humanity on the mend. Like the survivors of a shipwreck, those who had outlived Hitler showed an amazing capacity for looking at the bright side of life and moving on. Almost reflexively, England set about the task of righting itself. Committees met to plan the rebuilding of churches and neighborhoods. Military couples reunited or, all too often, faced up to sad truths and parted company. The past and future were now. Forgive or not, but move on, chin up.

Now that the war in Europe had ended and the Union Jack flapped triumphantly over Berlin, things were happening quickly for foreign office intelligence agent and erstwhile fiction writer Richard Patrick Russ. At last, there was a modicum of breathing room from war duties and war worries, and Russ, a slim, dark-haired, wan-complected resident of Chelsea, London's tony, if somewhat bruised, neighborhood of artists and writers, was busy implementing certain changes in his life, preparing for his own new start after the war.

The first change was his marriage, his second, on the fourth of July, to Mary, the pretty English-born Russian countess Russ had known intimately, despite many complications, since the beginning of the war. Now, on the twentieth of July, a little more than two months after VE-Day, he was about to inscribe his signature—the last time he would use that particular one—on an important deed, a bold move but one, given the unpleasant circumstances, that he was determined to make. To take care of this bit of business, Russ traveled to Leadenhall Street in the City.

So much had changed since war had descended on Europe and on the self-absorbed twenty-five-year-old writer of nature and adventure stories he had been. The flood of war had in many ways scoured his slate clean. In the fight against Hitler, Russ had, to a degree, become his own antithesis. As a writer, he had been a revealer of truths—a promising voice, the critics had proclaimed. But the foreign office had needed his skills for other purposes. He had become a broker of secrets. The war had made him proficient at deception.

All of this was in the back—if not the fore—of Russ's mind as he entered London's devastated financial district. At one stretch, during the Blitz of 1940–41, London had been bombed on fifty-seven consecutive nights and some days as well. Waves of German bombers had dropped high-explosive bombs, capable of boring through fifty feet of earth, and incendiary bombs, whose fires raged throughout the city. Each night, Londoners had huddled for cover in underground stations, in brick-and-concrete neighborhood shelters, or in family lean-tos of corrugated steel and earth. Each night, hundreds had been crushed to death and thousands more wounded. An ambulance driver during the Blitz, Russ had seen his share of destruction firsthand.

Just west of Leadenhall Street, St. Paul's Cathedral, a lonely survivor, stood watch over the wreckage. South of the cathedral, between Cheapside and Queen Victoria Street, much was obliterated, although miraculously the ruined church of St. Nicholas Cole Abbey had not been felled. To the east of Cheapside, where Leadenhall Street lay, the devastation was more complete still. On September 29, 1940, during the Blitz, the heart of the

London book publishing industry, on Paternoster Row, near the cathedral, had been destroyed by bombs. The offices of Simpkin Marshall, the wholesaler and distributor for many publishing houses, perished. Six million books turned into pulp or ash in a single night.

How different, how frightening the ruin seemed now that the war in Europe was over. Without the immediate threat and passion of the war with Germany, the evil that caused it was almost incomprehensible. The sight of the destruction sobered him. Nothing, no amount of repair or rebuilding, could mitigate this disaster. Only time could remove its memory.

On Leadenhall Street, the magnificent centuries-old St. Katherine Cree Church had suffered only minor damage from the bombing, unlike the almost equally ancient Chelsea Old Church in Russ's own neighborhood, where a German bomb had destroyed the sacred stone building in 1941, killing five fire watchers. But no matter how unaffected Cree Church appeared to be, Russ knew this was an illusion. No one and no place living through World War II was unaffected, and those directly in the warpath were in many ways changed forever.

Russ, his pulse elevated a notch, to be sure, opened the cut-glass doors of the three-story brick building at 77 Leadenhall Street and entered the offices of Baddeleys and Co. Solicitors. Through the window he could see the bomb craters, where pasts had been erased and where new buildings would soon rise. Anxiously, he awaited his turn to appear before the solicitors' managing clerk, and then he conducted his business: he was there to sign and file the form that would give him, his new wife, and his son by his first marriage a different surname.

Russ was canny enough to sense that this turning point in world history cleared the path for a break in his own history. It was nothing short of a chance to start over, to put his personal failures behind him. He knew the power of a name. Whether "unsoil'd" or "black," as Shakespeare had once qualified, a name had a defining nature.

If the war had encoded a new message on his slate, Russ would now choose which parts to reveal to others. Ironically, for a writer of fiction, and one who would prove to be among the best at his craft, the ultimate act of creating fiction came down to filling out a legal document:

> By this deed which is intended to be enrolled in the Enrolment
> Department of the Central Office of the Royal Courts of Jus-
> tice, I the undersigned Patrick O'Brian of 1 Upper Cheyne

Road, Chelsea, London S.W.3 in the county of London, Foreign Office Official, described in my certificate of birth as
Richard Patrick Russ, a natural born British Subject DO
HEREBY for myself and my wife Mary and remoter issue
absolutely renounce and abandon the use of my said surname
of Russ and in lieu thereof assume as from the date hereof the
surname of O'Brian.

AND in pursuance of such change of Surname as aforesaid
I hereby declare that I shall at all times hereafter in all records,
deeds and instruments in writing and in all actions and pro-
ceedings and in all dealings and transactions and upon all occasions whatsoever use and sign the name O'Brian as my surname
in lieu of the said surname of Russ so renounced as aforesaid.

AND I HEREBY authorise and require all persons to des-
ignate and address me and my wife and remoter issue by such
assumed surname of O'Brian only.

IN WITNESS whereof I have hereunto signed my first
names of Richard Patrick and my assumed name of O'Brian
this twentieth day of July one thousand nine hundred and
forty-five.

SIGNED, Sealed, and Delivered by the above named
Richard Patrick O'Brian in the presence of: E. Rowe, Solicitors
Managing Clerk, 77 Leadenhall Street, London E.C.3.

[signatures] Richard Patrick Russ   Richard Patrick O'Brian
(Legal Seal)

Although the paperwork would take another month, for all practical purposes the deed was done. What the name change signified was this: Farewell, Richard Patrick Russ. You bore your pain. You made your mistakes.
You served your country. Now, thank God, the madness is over.

With a stroke of the pen, he had dumped some of the baggage that
weighed him down. He could now go where he wanted, do what he
wanted, and make a fresh start in life with his new wife.

However, to one so sensitive to the power of words, the act of changing
his name could not have been taken lightly. Symbolically, he was annihi-
lating his past, and there was a taste of death in it. He was burying the
child-writer prodigy he had been along with his problems. Or was he?

Part I

GREEN

Christian Charles Gottfried Russ, my dear Husband and our good Father, died at 27 Clifton Hill, St John's Wood, N.W. on Saturday Nov. 4th at 4:35 p.m.

He was born at Brandis, near Leipzig—on the 10th of February 1842. The fourth child and the second son of Christian Karl Gottfried Russ, citizen, houseowner, furrier and cap manufacturer at Brandis and of his wife Fredericka Wilhelmina geb. Rüdiger; baptized on the 13th of the same month and the following were his godfathers and godmothers:—

1, Gustav Arudt, tanner in Brandis.

2, Eleanor Rost, wife of Karl Rost shoemaker in Brandis.

3, Friedrich Hansmann junr., ropemaker in Brandis.

The above details have been taken from the register of the Evangelical Lutheran Church of Brandis, 16 vol. 1842 according to birth and baptismal certificate[s] sent by M.A. Müller, Pastor, and countersigned and certified by Mr. Döbler, Mayor of Brandis with the official stamp of the Council attached.

He was married January 25th 1872 to Emily Callaway at Albany Street, Regent's Park by Rev. Burrows. She was born in London December 29th 1849. There was issue of this marriage 13 children, four daughters and nine sons; of whom twelve were alive at the day of his death.

—from the ledger of Emily Callaway Russ,
grandmother of Patrick O'Brian

I

A Top Hat, a Clean Collar, and Clean Boots

1850–1900

Thy wife shall be as the fruitful vine:
upon the walls of thine house.
Thy children like the olive-branches;
round about thy table.

—Psalm 128

It was once the custom in Germany that a young craftsman who had apprenticed for four years, usually with his father, took to the road to work for and learn from other masters at his craft. He was then a journeyman, and he carried a "wandering book," which the masters inscribed with testimonials and the dates of his service. Before moving on to a new master to serve and learn in another town, the journeyman also acquired the signatures of the burgomaster and police chief and recorded the travel time to his next destination to prove his diligence. After several years on the road, the successful craftsman returned home or to another town where his services were needed and became a master in his own right.

Carl Russ's good friend Carl Müller, a ropemaker seven years his senior, did just that, wandering from the town of Taucha, six miles northeast of Leipzig, in Saxony, all the way down to Bavaria and back. In 1858, at the age of sixteen, Carl, Patrick O'Brian's future grandfather and the second son of a furrier in Taucha, a town of two thousand people, set his sights a bit higher. He had already worked in Leipzig, one of the fur centers of Europe. He now traveled to Paris, and after honing his skills there, he and an older cousin caught a ship bound for Edinburgh in 1862. Carl's father had perhaps urged his son to go abroad, for he had fallen deeply in debt and would soon have to auction off his property.

As family lore has it, after the two cousins disembarked, they were walking along and saw a sixpence lying on the ground. They picked it up. A little farther along, they found a half crown, which they also collected. "There's money in this city," the cousin said to Carl. "I'm staying. You go down to London." Russ dutifully headed south.

In London, the fur capital of the world, he found a burgeoning industry ripe for an ambitious young man. Pelts of every imaginable sort arrived there from around the globe: those of fur seals encrusted in salt, wrote an industry observer, were "moist, dirty, brown and most repulsive objects"; of beaver, "flat and hard as a board"; and of mink and ermine, "frequently inside out; exhibiting a singularly unpleasing appearance." Sold at auctions in Mincing Lane, they were then transformed by the furrier.

By 1869, Russ had settled in Clerkenwell, a workingman's district just northwest of the City, where he Anglicized his given name to Charles (although, for the purposes of this story, I will continue to call him Carl to differentiate him from his oldest son). Once a breezy hillside known for its spas, Clerkenwell had absorbed wave after wave of immigrants after the Napoleonic wars, creating a quagmire of sweatshops and noisome alleys.

The process of converting a "skin" into a "fur" took hours of tedious, often noxious, labor: blubbering, washing, unhairing, leathering, dying, fluffing, and combing, among other things. Only then was the skin called a fur, ready to be matched, styled, and assembled as a garment. A creative and enterprising sort, Russ fared well at his trade, which he knew thoroughly, from the dullest tasks of transforming the foul hide to the most artful: designing a voluptuous garment to sit on the shoulders of a rich woman. At twenty-six, he established his own business, leasing a residence and shop on Northampton Square for ten years at £50 per year.

Russ would do well both in business and family-making. After pledging his loyalty and fidelity to Queen Victoria and to the United Kingdom, he married Emily Callaway, the twenty-two-year-old daughter of a manager of one of London's old-line furriers. By 1876, Emily, a raven-haired beauty with sparkling black eyes, a deep voice, and a curvaceous figure, had given birth to four of the couple's thirteen children: three daughters and a son, Charles, Patrick O'Brian's future father.

Russ set up a shop on New Bond Street, in London's fashionable shopping district, and he quickly made a name for himself as one of the most innovative furriers of his day. By improving dressing and dying techniques,

he popularized alternatives to expensive Russian sable. His work won a
gold medal at the Paris Exhibition in 1878, and his furs caught the eye of
Queen Victoria. But, as his advertisement indicates, he was not too proud
to appeal to all women:

> [Carl] Russ, court furrier, invites inspection of his Large
> Assortment of all articles of Fashion in Furs, Embracing all the
> newest designs in Jackets and Paletots, lined and trimmed fur.
> Sortie de ball, etc, etc. Specialties. Genuineness of quality and
> excellence of workmanship at manufacturer's prices. 70 New
> Bond Street.

"Never have sealskin jackets been so well and so elegantly shaped, and
for the first time they fit the figure accurately," the *Queen*, a women's
newspaper, wrote about his furs in 1888. And if sealskin was too expensive, one could try his musquash (muskrat), which resembled seal quite
nicely.

Russ was not just good at his trade; unlike his father, he was a shrewd
businessman as well. He owned several London properties and shares in
four merchant ships: *John Redhead, Carl Rahtkens, Fernbrook,* and *Baron
Clyde.* He grew rich and moved the family to St. John's Wood, an upper-
middle-class neighborhood, where nurses watched children playing in gardens and men in bowler hats commuted into the City on horse-drawn
omnibuses. Russ's grand home, Clifton Villa, filled with mahogany and
walnut furniture and brass beds, was a monument to success. Thirty-one
gilt-framed oil paintings and four watercolors decorated the dining room,
which was furnished with a table for twelve, a couch and chairs, a massive
mahogany sideboard, and both a Story and Clark organ from the United
States and a pianoforte. After dinner, Russ and his male guests retired to
the garden and smoked pipes or Egyptian cigarettes of the finest tobacco.

Clifton Villa teemed with children. Nonetheless, Emily, with her piercing eyes and lively manner, always looked the part of an elegant woman
from a fine family. She wore gold spectacles, a sable cape, and diamond
jewelry. She was unflappable, with a firm but pleasant manner that made
the servants prompt and demure.

Carl was a stout, taciturn man, commanding, sometimes stern, but not
unkind. His broad face was defined by an imposing beard, close-cropped
on his square chin but hanging Poseidonlike from his cheeks. A dense

mustache bridged his sidebeards. Naturally, to a man in his field, dress was important. At age sixteen, Fritz Müller, the third son of Russ's boyhood friend Carl Müller, came to stay with the Russes in London, and Carl often admonished the boy, "Never forget, a top hat, a clean collar, and clean boots make a gentleman." But Russ had few words for his children, though he was good at providing for them. With Teutonic precision, he saw to it that they were all baptized at St. George's Church in Hanover Square and given accounts at Westminster Bank. The family went to church twice on Sundays, and grace was said before each meal.

This industrious and happy life was tragically interrupted shortly after Emily delivered Walter, her twelfth and next-to-last child, on July 13, 1886. Five months later—on the evening of December 13—a cinder sparked from the fireplace and caught fire to the linen in his crib. Walter burned to death.

Soon thereafter the eight surviving boys were dispatched to Shebbear College, a long-established boarding school in North Devon. Charles, at age eleven, and his younger brothers Emil, Percy, and Sidney (who was just eight years old) left home in 1888. Ernest, Albert, Frederick, and William soon completed the Russ contingent at Shebbear, a school founded by a Low Church group and later affiliated with the Methodist Church. The brothers often remained at school even during holidays.

Boarding school was primarily a privilege of the rich, but conditions at Shebbear did not betray that fact. The boys took to eating their peach pits to stave off hunger, a habit that little Sidney would maintain the rest of his life. When at home, the brothers proved that they had absorbed their Latin lessons, calling their mother "Mater." But they were not coddled at home either. "Pater" would not tolerate idleness or airs in his boys, who were put to work during holidays learning the furrier trade.

In 1891, the Russes' oldest daughter, Emily, married Otto Müller, Carl Müller's second but more enterprising son. Russ, perhaps feeling the stress of his intense career, retired the following year, and it was soon thereafter, during a trip to the Continent with Emily and Charles, that the first signs of his ill health appeared. On November 2, 1893, while Emily was in Germany helping with the birth of her second grandchild, Carl suffered a stroke. He had just finished celebrating his son Emil's sixteenth birthday. Two days later, at the age of fifty-one, Carl died with his son Charles and Fritz Müller by his side.

Emily received a telegram informing her of her husband's death. Charles, who at seventeen became the male head of the family, met her at Victoria station. "What terrible news," she said, with remarkable composure. They took a cab home and ate supper. Then Emily went to the mortuary to see her husband's body, remained there for an hour grieving, and returned to her home as unruffled as when she had arrived from Germany.

Despite Emily's apparent stoicism, the loss of the almighty Russ patriarch shook the family profoundly. Patrick O'Brian's grandfather was said to have been a spiky, brilliant, driven man, intensely private. He had been proud and showy in his newfound wealth but had never forgotten where he came from. These traits would travel farther in his descendants than the small fortune he had amassed. Russ's children inherited a fair amount of money, and his sons were gratefully freed of the expectation of becoming furriers. But they also found themselves without their father's discipline and practical guidance, which would prove financially disastrous for Charles, whom Mater particularly indulged. At one point, for example, Charles was enthralled with photography and owned twenty-three cameras. Charles's extravagant ways and poor business sense would eventually color the lives of his children, particularly the younger ones, like Patrick.

One last sad event needs to be recounted before moving on to the next century and the next generation. Mater had already suffered the strange death of her youngest son. In June 1898, she lost her second daughter, Paulina, under distressing circumstances that would become a haunting fixture in the family lore.

At twenty-four, Lena, as she was called, was purportedly suffering from long-standing acute indigestion, which had led to low spirits. Her doctor recommended sea air, so she and Mater went to a boardinghouse in Cliftonville, on the coast of Kent. Soon Lena seemed to perk up, and Mater relaxed her vigilant watch over her daughter. One rainy, blustery morning, Lena slipped out of the boardinghouse to mail a letter, or so Mater later rationalized when she discovered the girl was gone. In fact, Lena had wandered out to the edge of the forty-foot cliff at Foreness Point, where she sat wild-eyed in the pouring rain.

Upon seeing Lena, a startled walker cautioned her: "It is a silly thing to sit so near the edge of the cliff, especially on such a day as this is; the cliff has been falling away lately and the cliff might go down and you might go with it." Lena made a show of moving back. The man continued on the path down and around the cliff. But when he was below, Lena called out to him, "Please pick up my umbrella!"

The man found the umbrella lying on the rocky beach beneath the bluff and began to climb back up the path with it. But, at a bend, he looked up and saw a ghastly sight: Lena was teetering on the brink of the cliff, her arms raised in front of her, as if she were being beckoned into the precipice. As he raced up the path, he heard a dreadful scream. At another bend, he caught a glimpse of the girl. She was lying on the ground and slowly pushing herself over the ledge.

The man, Mr. Stephen Brown Balcome, a vacationing stockbroker from West Kensington, continued his frustratingly slow ascent. Jogging around a corner, he lost sight of Lena. When he finally arrived at the top, only the wind and rain greeted him. Lena had fallen to the beach below. Panicked, Balcome ran to a nearby restaurant for help. But when they reached Lena, she was barely alive. She died on the way to the hospital.

Charles, then a medical student, rushed to Cliftonville. At the inquest, Mater testified that Lena was happily engaged and that there had been nothing wrong other than the misery of her physical ailment. "The day prior . . . [Lena] had been for a long walk by herself and brought home a lot of wild flowers," she recounted. "I think she was getting wild flowers and it being such a wet morning she must have slipped over the cliff." But Balcome told the jury he thought the fall was intentional. Charles countered with pointed questions for Balcome: "To what incident in particular do you attribute your belief that she voluntarily went over the cliff? You did not exactly witness the fall of the body to the sands? Do you think it possible she might have become giddy?"

According to the newspaper, the jury ruled that Lena had "committed suicide whilst temporarily insane." Over the years, family lore would go one better. The story passed down that Lena had been madly in love with a Catholic priest, but she could not persuade him to renounce his priesthood for her.

No matter the reason, Mater was devastated to lose "such a dear girl." Once again, Charles escorted his mother home after a family tragedy.

2

Walden

1914–1922

I am struck by the fact that the more slowly trees grow at first,
the sounder they are at the core, and I think that the same is
true of human beings. We do not wish to see children
precocious, making great strides in their early years like
sprouts, producing a soft and perishable timber, but better if
they expand slowly at first, as if contending with difficulties,
and so are solidified and perfected. Such trees continue to
expand with nearly equal rapidity to an extreme old age.

—Henry David Thoreau, journal, November 5, 1860

That the strength of his understanding, the accuracy of his
discernment, and ardour of his curiosity, might have been
remarked from his infancy, by a diligent observer, there is no
reason to doubt. For, there is no instance of any man, whose
history has been minutely related, that did not in every part of
life discover the same proportion of intellectual vigour.

—Samuel Johnson, "The Life of Sydenham," 1742

When Britain entered the Great War in August 1914, Emily
Russ's two youngest sons, Frederick and William, both decided
to serve their country. Frederick, who was still living at home,
volunteered for the army. He would fight in the trenches in Belgium. After
his second bout of pneumonia, however, the army refused to send him
back to the front, so he became a balloonist in the Royal Flying Corps.
William, the baby of the family, joined an artillery unit and was stationed
outside London, not far from the home of his brother Charles, a medical doctor who commuted into London, and Charles's wife, Jessie, and

their seven children. Whenever Willy rode over for a visit, his nephews, eleven-year-old Godfrey, Victor, nine, and Michael, five, raced out to greet him and to lead his horse to the backyard, where it grazed on the Russes' ample lawn.

The house the Russes called Walden lay in a wooded area in rural Buckinghamshire County, halfway between the towns of Chalfont St. Peter and Gerrards Cross. As the house's name would indicate, it was an idyllic place to raise a family. Charles's brother Sidney, also a London medical doctor and scientist, and two servants lived in the big house as well.

Though a quiet man, Uncle Sidney, whom the children called "Beany," was much loved, especially when he arrived home in the evening with pockets full of candy. He usually placed the candy on a tray and held it over the children's heads so that they had to jump up and knock it off, resulting in a mad scramble to see who could retrieve the most. Any sweet the youngest obtained in the melee was a gift from a protector or held in reserve by Beany, who, being a seventh child, understood the plight of the underdog.

By no means did the tranquillity of Thoreau's Walden apply. In the long, bellicose winter of 1914, the house was close with children, and Jessie was again about to give birth. On December 12, in the big bedroom at the back of the house, she clutched her youngest's hand as a roaring bird flew overhead. Through the window, the boy, Bernard, or "Bun," as everyone called him, gawked with fascination. It was the first time he had seen an airplane. Shortly thereafter, Bun was tugged away from his mother and ushered from the room. Though not yet three years old, he sensed a momentous change.

Later that day, Jessie gave birth to a boy, her fifth. At last, Bun was allowed back into the room. He was shown his mother's mysterious new parcel. The miracle being not nearly so wondrous as an airplane, he soon lost interest and was relegated to the floor. Deposed as the baby of the family, he crawled about forlornly on the large sheets of brown paper spread there, perplexed at just why such a small thing had required so much wrapping.

At least that's how Bernard Russ recounted the story of Patrick's birth some three-quarters of a century later in *Lady Day Prodigal,* his autobiography privately published for the family. Whether he could have experienced such consciousness at the age of two is debatable, as are a number of his other colorful recollections. What is certain is that Bun, later known as Barney, could spin a good yarn. Perhaps it was in his blood.

Actually, Patrick was not yet named, and the Russes were in no hurry to do so. In February 1915, when his birth was registered, he remained nameless. Finally, in a special certificate of naming, he was dubbed Richard Patrick. "Pat," as they would call him, was not a healthy youth. He suffered from what was sometimes identified as bronchitis and sometimes as asthma or, as his brother Barney put it, "a weak chest." According to a letter written much later by his brother, Pat would at some point in his younger years, like his mother, suffer from tuberculosis. But Pat proved to be a remarkably resilient fellow, and Walden was an appropriate birthplace for this extraordinary little boy, whose love of nature, literature, and writing arrived early, whose love of solitude would endure, and whose obsession for privacy would infuse his eventual literary tour de force, the Aubrey-Maturin novels.

As with Thoreau's slow-growing tree, life's difficulties would only make Pat sounder at the core, though they certainly would leave their share of knots in the trunk and odd bends to the branches.

Patrick's father, Charles Russ, was a giant of a man, nearly six feet, five inches tall, but thin, boyish-looking, with wavy blond hair. He was exceedingly handsome, and he had a powerful mind to match his looks. He approached an intellectual or mechanical challenge with enthusiasm and a high degree of creativity. When he was not preoccupied with work, he was often tinkering with whatever automobile was in the driveway. These were his passions.

Carl Russ had intended for his sons to be furriers. But his absence and the fortune he left behind, an estate worth more than £40,000 (£2 million in today's numbers), allowed them to choose their own paths. Charles and Sidney both decided on medical school. Whereas Sidney was steady, dependable, intensely private, and deliberate in his personality and career, Charles was prone to enthusiasms (his twenty-three cameras gave way to the cars), assertive, and something of a malcontent. Children, residences, and creative energy would flow willy-nilly.

In 1902, when he had married his sweetheart, Jessie Naylor Goddard, at St. Luke's Church in Hampstead, he was studying medicine at London's St. Mary's Hospital, where Augustus Waller had discovered the electrical reaction of the human heart and Almroth Wright introduced immunization against typhoid fever. It was in this spirit of experimentation and discovery that Russ collected his medical diplomas in 1903 and prepared to make his mark on the world.

Nine months and a week after they had married, Jessie, a fetching brunette with full lips and thick chestnut eyebrows, the daughter of a town legal clerk, gave birth to a son, Charles Godfrey, at the couple's home in West Hampstead. A towhead, young Godfrey barely had time to break in his lace knickers before Victor arrived on the scene in 1905. Olive followed in 1906, Michael in 1909, and, in 1910, twins Connie and Nora. During this time the Russes lived at almost as many addresses as they had children.

Charles, a bacteriologist, worked as one of two qualified assistants in Dr. G. L. Eastes's laboratory of pathology and public health on Queen Anne Street. But after hours, he explored his own ideas, conducting groundbreaking research in electrolysis. In 1910, he demonstrated to members of the Royal Society of Medicine and later to the British Medical Association that an electrical current could kill bacteria suspended in a liquid. The following year he spoke at the International Hygiene Exhibition in Dresden.

The Royal Society encouraged Charles's promising work with a £100 grant, and interested doctors provided him with cases. Charles eagerly applied his techniques to varicose ulcers, cholecystitis, and gonorrhea. As he worked, he improved means and methods. He was inspired. In March 1912, the same month that Jessie gave birth to Bernard, their seventh child, Charles presented a paper on an improved method of estimating the blood's ability to consume bacteria. While conducting his tests, he invented a felt-lined portable radiator for blood cultivations. In August, he published his observations of syphilitic sera.

Perhaps all of this activity left the independent-minded scientist too little time for his assistant duties, for Dr. Eastes eventually fired him. Charles then set up his own lab less than a mile away, on Beaumont Street, igniting a bitter dispute. Claiming Russ had violated a noncompete clause in his contract, Eastes sued his former assistant. The Chancery court sided with Charles, deeming the contract, which he had never actually signed, flawed. Eastes appealed. At the close of 1913, he was rebuffed again. Charles was vindicated, but the case had attracted some unwanted attention in the medical world, and the unpleasant business had cost him a mentor. Now he had to create a practice of his own, and he would prove none too good at it.

While Charles was living the life of a maverick, his quiet younger brother Sidney had taken a more conventional route to unexpected prominence. At the University of Manchester, where he taught physics, he assisted 1908 Nobel laureate Ernest Rutherford, who identified the alpha particle of a helium nucleus that year. In 1910, Sidney moved back to London to become a fellow of the Cancer Research Laboratories of Middlesex College, and in 1913, he became physicist to Middlesex Hospital, evidently the first physicist ever appointed to a hospital staff.

Charles, meanwhile, affiliated himself with St. Peter's Hospital in Covent Garden. His cholecystitis and gonorrhea treatments, despite their apparent potential in curing the diseases, had a serious drawback. They were frightful in their application. In the first, the patient wore a belt of metallic gauze surrounded by layers of lint, and in the second, a lint-covered metal pad was applied to his scrotum. A rubber catheter was inserted up his urethra to his bladder. One end of a platinum wire ran up the catheter, and the other attached to a battery. Another wire connected the battery to the belt or pad, making a complete circuit. The electrical current ran for up to ninety minutes (see illustration, page 4 of insert). After the setup, the procedure was painless, Charles assured his colleagues: "The patients are unaware of the current's flow and recline at their ease, being occupied in reading, and often also enjoy a smoke."

Off to London early in the morning and home late in the day, the doctors Russ played a secondary role in the life of Walden. The household was essentially run by Jessie and a nanny named Nellie Blencowe, whose Hertfordshire dialect sometimes made her difficult for the Russ children to understand, or so they claimed when it suited their designs.

The heavy decor of Walden recalled the splendor of Clifton Villa, Charles's childhood home, but the focus here, as the name suggests, was on the out-of-doors. In front of the brick house, a horseshoe-shaped driveway with large gates opened onto Packhorse Road, where motorcars were occasionally seen and heard. A half acre of land, mostly in back of the house, provided space for Patrick to toddle and the other children to roam. There was much of interest: an orchard of fruit trees, a large vegetable garden, and, the Russes having a fondness for nicknames, a garage called "Toodles," a teahouse called "Beadle," and a garden shed called "Boodle."

On a summer day, with the perimeter Lombardy poplars rustling softly in the breeze, Jessie could be found tending to her garden or sitting behind an easel painting watercolors of her flowers. Here she found a degree of serenity, something that had not come easily in her life. After her parents, Ernest and Mary Goddard, died when she was thirteen, she was sent to a Roman Catholic orphanage and became separated from her remaining sister, Mabel, and two brothers, Cecil and Morse.

But the quiet moments at Walden were rare. The eight children presented their challenges in as many different ways. Some of them, such as little Pat, who suffered from respiratory difficulties, required extra care. One of the twins, Connie, was afflicted with a rare form of muscular distrophy called Charcot-Marie-Tooth disease, which caused her feet to turn in. Sometimes she had to be pushed about in Pat's pram.

Jessie doted on her children. She sometimes dressed her little boys in velvet jackets and lace collars, which made Bun, with his extravagant, golden curls, look like Little Lord Fauntleroy. He endured much teasing by his older brothers before Charles finally demanded that the curls be cut off. Jessie cried as the barber did his work in the nursery, but it was probably a relief for Bun. Likewise, little sympathy was reserved for the sickly young Pat, who, although not of Bun's galling beauty, was the sort to attract a mother's sympathy. A meek little fellow with straight brown hair, he resembled his Uncle Sidney. He had a round, impish face, a thin mouth, and protruding ears. He wore a thoughtful, open expression, which betrayed no signs of mischief, in marked contrast to his older brothers.

In the evenings, Nellie served the children bread and meat drippings or bread and butter and jam for high tea. "Eat it up and be good, or I'll smack you else," she would say, in her thick dialect.

To which Olive, the eldest daughter, would mischievously reply, "I'm not Else, I'm Olive!"

The children were permitted special treats, like doughnuts or sticky buns, at weekend high teas. On one occasion, Olive was asked to set the tea table. Left on her own to perform the task, she secretly nibbled each of the buns and arranged them to conceal her transgression. Her hungry siblings gobbled down their treats without noticing. However, the trick did not fool Jessie, who notified Olive that since she had already eaten her bun, she needn't have another.

The boys had their own way to needle Olive, whose middle name was

Isobel. "Hello, Is-a-bell on a bicycle?" they greeted her, never failing to get her goat.

At last Nellie moved on, though she would keep in touch with some of the children for many decades. Another nanny, Mrs. Mason, signed on and became a close friend to Jessie. The children regarded her as yet another aunt and called her Aunty Mason. But Godfrey soon pegged her as "Hanty Mason," and the name stuck.

Despite Charles's strict Presbyterian upbringing and Methodist schooling, Jessie's stay with the nuns, and their marriage in the Church of England (or perhaps because of this hodgepodge), there appears to have been no time or energy for religion at the Russ household. None of the children seem to have been baptized. The Russes liked to entertain, however, and holidays, especially Christmas, produced more aunts and uncles and cousins, of which there was no shortage, however dispersed they might be. Of Charles's siblings, Edith had married a bank clerk in 1897 and Bertha a Quaker stationer in 1905. Albert worked as a draper and Frederick, following the war, as a civil servant in Her Majesty's Office of Works. Two would become favorite uncles of Charles and Jessie's children: rugged, raw-boned William, who became a geologist and explored Nigeria, and the gregarious Emil, who was said to have had a talent for writing when younger. In 1905, he had moved to India and, as William recorded, became "court tailor . . . and friend of Maharajah X."

Emily and Otto Müller, who had gone bankrupt in Germany, were raising their twelve children in Canada. Other siblings not in attendance at Walden were Percy, a photographer who lived in Hawkes Bay, New Zealand, and Ernest, a soldier who had joined the military at age sixteen and during the Boer War had changed his surname from Russ to Russell to hide the German link. As his nephew Barney later put it, perhaps overstating the case a bit, for this betrayal he was "summarily dismissed with disgust from the family annals."

No matter who came to the Christmas celebration, the Russes threw a lavish feast in their dark-paneled dining room, which glistened with polished silver. Each year, Jessie saved her silver threepenny pieces, and before Christmas she emptied her jar and bought presents to put under the tree. At one Walden Christmas, possibly Pat's first, the younger children came down with chicken pox and then measles. Dressed in their nightgowns, they watched jealously from the second-floor balustrade. Godfrey and Victor, who had escaped both afflictions, taunted them from below.

In warm weather, driving became one of the family's favorite activities. Charles traded in his motorcycle and sidecar, in which he and Jessie had often escaped into the countryside with a picnic basket, for a Globe. The car, which sported large carriage lamps on either side of the windshield, was always in a state of high polish, though its engine performance was not. Frequent breakdowns sent Charles—often in a formal suit and starched wing collar—under the car, while Jessie watched the children play.

One trip took them to Dashwood Hill, where they stopped to watch other cars attempt the steep climb. The failures were pronounced "crocks" by the children in a hail of laughter. "The fact that our car was itself a crock," Barney later recalled, "did not seem to bother our parents at all, and everyone thoroughly enjoyed the fun."

The worst car that Charles bought was a three-wheeler Morgan, a bad idea for a large man with a small wife: while rounding curves, it tipped over to his side. The best was a Wolseley, which, remarkably, could accommodate the whole family.

Patrick would have only the vaguest of memories of this early period of his life. Perhaps what is more important than what he remembered is what he later knew he had missed. For soon this would all be gone, and in the family memory it became almost a mythical time when everything was right with the world. A time when no matter what the trouble was, there was a loving mother there to fix it.

In 1916, Charles Russ, now in charge of the electro-therapeutic department of the Male Lock Hospital ("lock" signifying a hospital for venereal disease) and affiliated with a similar department of Middlesex Hospital, published *A New Treatment of Gonorrhoea*, which argued for his method of treating the disease. Although the *Lancet*, an influential medical journal, remained skeptical based on the lack of general trials, it ran a lengthy article by the doctor detailing four successful cases from the book. He also addressed an unpleasant side effect: "a spasmodic contraction upon the inserted catheter during the flow of the current." Sometimes, he confessed, the urethra clamped onto the catheter and would not let go. He recommended reversing the current for several minutes—but by no means using force.

Charles's treatment might have cured some patients, but his methods were neither proven nor practical. As venereal disease spread among troops stationed abroad—by 1918, as many as 300,000 were being treated (in a day when everyone did their utmost to ignore the problem)—concern for the potential mass infection of Britain's women approached hysteria. Doctors and health officials rang the alarm louder and louder. In 1917, politicians passed legislation to provide treatment at free clinics, using equally dubious but more popular methods. Charles's supply of patients dried up. Professionally and financially, his ruination had begun.

Before the end of the war, lovely Walden had been left behind. The Russes had moved to 10 College Road, Harrow, an address nearer to Mater's house and closer to Charles's work. Sidney no longer lived with them. He married a nurse named Mary Priestley and soon had three children of his own, but Mary disliked her husband's ties to Germany and did her best to sever connections with his family. Some unsatisfactory financial dealings with Charles might also have clouded the brothers' relationship, an early indication that Charles was already feeling the financial strain that would dog him the rest of his life. Sadly, Charles's and Sidney's children would never know each other.

On July 10, 1917, Charles and Jessie had yet another child—their ninth in fourteen years—a girl they named Sylvia Joan. But this birth was accompanied by complications. In August, Jessie underwent surgery for abdominal problems. She had a tumorlike growth caused by tuberculosis of her intestines. She could have contracted tuberculosis as a child when her father died of the disease, which under some circumstances can remain dormant in the body in the form of a granuloma. She never fully recovered.

One day in late March 1918, Hanty Mason gathered the children, and one by one they were taken in to see their mother. Behind the bed stood Charles, Sidney, and the physician attending Jessie, who was propped up in bed. Putting on a brave face and summoning her last ounces of strength, Jessie said good-bye to her children. Three-year-old Pat was lifted up to her, and she hugged and kissed him one last time. On the evening of March 30, with her husband by her side, Jessie, just forty years old, died of tuberculosis.

That night, Hanty Mason came to the bedside of each of the children. Weeping, she hugged them and told them that their mother had left the world for a better place.

The three youngest children, Bun, Pat, and Joan, did not attend the funeral. They were left to play in the nursery. Bun, who was now six, wandered through the halls and into his mother's empty bedroom. Pale blue candles flickered at each corner of the wire bed frame, now stripped of its bedding. The terrifying sight of emptiness where his mother had lain so recently would haunt the boy for the rest of his life. None of the children escaped without a deep, permanent sorrow from the death of their mother. Jessie had been the soul of the family.

The impact on young Pat was clearly immense, and the loss of his mother would be an animus for his fiction. His first book, which he wrote when he was just fourteen, was about an orphaned wild beast. Subsequent stories and novels were peopled by orphans and abandoned children. His great characters Aubrey and Maturin would be virtually parentless, Aubrey having lost his mother at a young age and then suffering the offenses of a troublemaking father and Maturin being an Irish-Catalan bastard, whose childhood remains obscure.

Patrick's first wife would be an orphan, too.

Charles Russ was devastated by the death of his wife. What he badly needed was a reserve of strength and grace. He had nine suffering children crying out for warmth and tenderness and time, but he was not up to providing these essentials. The Russ household was in shambles. Aunts and nannies tried to tame it but found the effort overwhelming. The infant, Joan, was sent to live with Aunt Bertha and Uncle Frank Welch, a Quaker, at their home in Pinner, a section in the far northwest of London. The three older boys—Godfrey, now fifteen, Victor, thirteen, and Mike, nine—attended day school at the John Lyon School for Boys. They had bicycles on which they came and went as they pleased. The rest were left largely on their own.

Charles could not bear to live in the house where Jessie had died, so he uprooted the family once again, moving to a rowhouse at 276 Willesden Lane, in Willesden Green, also a section of northwest London. Although he was desperately trying to evade the painful memories of his wife, he could not bring himself to abandon her beloved plants and flowers. So he instructed Victor to dig up as much of the garden as he could. On his bike, Victor pedaled the plants to their new home and planted them in the small garden in back.

One day, while he was working outside, a remarkable thing happened. He met a man dressed in naval uniform, who was walking about in the next yard. When Victor told the man his name, the man told him that he had a sister named Jessie, who had married a Dr. Russ. It turned out that the sailor next door was their uncle Morse Goddard, Jessie's younger brother, who had gone to sea as a boy after their parents had died. He was now a worldly first mate in the Canadian Pacific Fleet, awaiting the completion of the fleet's new flagship, *Empress of Canada*, which was being built in Glasgow. He had friends and acquaintances around the globe, but he had not seen his siblings for many years.

This fateful convergence had a calming effect on the Russ gang. Though the procession of nannies and temporary arrangements with aunts and uncles continued, now there was family—Uncle Morse, Aunt Grace, and cousin Molly—next door.

If ever there was a perfect inspiration for a young boy's love of tales and the mystery of the sea, Uncle Morse was it. He fascinated the boys. He called the study his cabin, and there, in front of the fire, he told stories about his adventures. Starting out as a cabin boy at the age of twelve and earning a shilling a month, he had come home second in command. He sailed around Cape Horn in a steel-hulled windjammer, learning to insulate his feet from the frigid winds before a trick at the wheel by filling his boots with seawater. Stories of pirates in the China Sea, of storms, and of life on board Canadian steamers, such as the *Empress of Russia*, on which he had served as second mate, carried the boys away from their present sorrow, if only briefly, and gave them dreams for the future. Patrick was about five years old, an age when reality and fantasy engage in a delightful dance and when one's own mythology is seared into the mind.

Uncle Morse would be the source of another bizarre coincidence in Patrick's life. Although none of the Russ children knew it, Uncle Morse was not actually married to Grace. When he finally did marry, in Canada in 1925, it was to Emma Frances Anson-Cartwright, the sole heir of the Anson estates, including that of Admiral George Anson, whose voyage to the Pacific and capture of a treasure-laden Spanish galleon in 1743 became legendary. Ironically, Patrick would later write about Anson's voyage, unaware, apparently, of the family tie.

Grace's marital status notwithstanding, she was a beloved "aunt" and a cool hand at soothing the inevitable domestic squabbles that erupted among the nine motherless children. She kept an eye on the schooling situation, urging Charles to send Bun to kindergarten. He was soon enrolled at the nearby Maria Gray Preparatory and Kindergarten, which Olive and the twins also attended. Still too young, Pat, it seems, was left to his own druthers.

Shortly after moving to Willesden, on October 3, 1918, Charles Russ and family received another blow. At the age of sixty-eight, Mater, the strong-willed and elegant matriarch, who had suffered from diabetes for five years, lapsed into a coma and died.

Mater represented the last vestiges of the rich Victorian Russ family. Although Charles clung to the assumption of wealth and comfort the rest of his life, he did not have it long. Patrick would hear of the family's former lifestyle and have glimpses of it in heirlooms and the indulgences of his father but did not grow up with the blessings of wealth himself. The remainder of the family fortune was now distributed. To Sidney, Mater left Carl's gold medal from the Paris Exhibition of 1878 and a diamond ear-ring, which, she instructed, was to be made into a ring or scarf pin. She left her daughter Bertha a "diamond and pearl earring to be made into a brooch, my sapphire and diamond ring, my gold bracelet with diamond and my gold glasses, and also my case containing a toilet set in cut glass bottles with silver tops." Charles received Carl's diamond ring. And so on down the line went the jewelry, along with instructions for its use.

But what Charles desperately needed was money. His father had left half of his estate to his children, which meant that it was split twelve ways. The other half had gone to Emily, but now she chose to divide all her money—save the £50 that she left to Florence, her servant—between her two sisters, Alice Callaway and Eliza Cooper.

In the space of six months, Charles had been present at the deaths of both his wife and his mother. He was devastated. In the past, he had taken plea-sure in setting up elaborate toy train systems, complete with trestles and several gauges of tracks, with his boys. Godfrey was the master engineer while Victor, a collector of lead soldiers, played commander of the troops, setting up army depots. Mike, Bun, and Pat served as assistants and enthu-siastic spectators. But now Charles grew more aloof, more the master and disciplinarian.

To escape his painful reality, he redoubled his work efforts. He had previously turned his attention to research involving the eye, and, in 1918, he patented an eye-ray instrument set in motion by the human eye—"i.e., by vision," as he described it. "The instrument is the practical embodiment . . . of experiments which I have made to ascertain whether there is a ray or radiation proceeding from the human eye," he explained in his patent description, though he did not suggest practical applications for the instrument. Despite his optimism, it would not be a lucrative invention.

Charles continued to treat gonorrhea patients with electrolysis and carefully measure the results. In 1920, he published *The Conquest of Venereal Diseases,* and in 1922, *Gonorrhoea Treated by Electrolysis: Results in 500 Cases,* which presented evidence to support his work. But it was an uphill battle, and, with expenses mounting at home and his income unsteady, he was struggling financially.

Domestically, the children were in the care of a widow named Mrs. Newton, who had been a colonel in the precursor to the Women's Army Corps and sometimes wore her war ribbons and medals on her large bosom. Her military experience proved handy in the present situation, and she was able to keep the troops mostly in line. Though not altogether approving of her methods, Charles, preoccupied with his work, was reluctant to interfere. So the children rebelled in all manner of bad behavior. Michael proved to be the most creative at tormenting Mrs. Newton when he decided to see how long it would take to fill up the umbrella stand with urine. Mrs. Newton soon caught wind of the caper and put an end to it.

Mrs. Newton eventually gave way to another widow, a Mrs. Ashmore, whose husband, the manager of a salt mine in South Africa, had been overly fond of the bottle. Her style was entirely different from Mrs. Newton's and far more pleasing. She befriended the children, who liked her more than anyone since Hanty Mason. Mrs. Ashmore was appealing in other ways as well. After Uncle William returned from France in 1919, he took a fancy to her. But apparently she had set her sights on marrying her tall, handsome employer.

It was not to be. Mrs. Ashmore was succeeded by Scotch Annie, who was already part of the domestic staff, in charge of doing the shopping. But Scotch Annie did not like to leave the house, let alone go to the market, so she regularly bribed one of the children with a penny to run her errands. Scotch Annie did garden, though, as did the children, each of whom had his or her own plot at Willesden.

Naturally, they competed in every way imaginable, as siblings will do, to see who could produce the prettiest flowers or the largest vegetables and win the praise of their seniors. This competition among the impatient children often led, of course, to an excess of gardening enthusiasm, usually to the detriment of the poor plants, carrots being prematurely uprooted for inspection, new sprouts being greeted with overabundant libations, delicate flowers being pawed.

Nevertheless, their hands-on experience taught the budding young horticulturalists a thing or two about gardening. One costly lesson arrived in the form of a cage of bantam hens, which Charles had received in lieu of cash as payment for his medical services. The boys built a henhouse. But the cunning hens managed to escape en masse and wreaked havoc in the garden. They were soon dispatched.

So, too, were the older children. Godfrey had enrolled at Dean Close School, an evangelical Church of England school in Cheltenham, as early as 1915, and Victor the next year. In 1921, Michael and Bun, who, like his Uncle Sidney, was just eight years old when he left home, matriculated at Shebbear College, the alma mater of the previous generation of Russ brothers. The boys quickly assumed their father's and uncles' collective nickname, "the spindoos," for their long spindly legs and were hazed with boyish brutality, including floggings with knotted wet towels and burns from cigarettes.

Olive, Connie, and Nora attended Edgehill College, just fifteen miles from Shebbear, and so boarded the same train for Devon as Mike and Bun. Although the schools were not far by train from Willesden—the British rail system being probably the best in the world at the time—during holidays all five stayed in North Devon with three spinster sisters, Kittie, Ethie, and Trixie Hill, at London Lodge, a gatehouse of the grand eighteenth-century estate Clovely Court. Though it was not home, they were treated kindly by the Hills, who became substitute aunts.

Despite this breakup of the family and the distance from their father, the children adjusted. Yet they would remain bitter about spending holidays on their own, an understandable complaint since Charles seems to have made a conscious decision to keep them at arm's length. Ultimately they fared better than Pat, who was too young and too sickly for boarding school, and thus remained at home in the now almost empty house, perhaps sometimes staying with aunts or uncles or friends of the family.

Although Joan had been sent away as an infant, she at least had the advantage of living in a stable household with her Aunt Bertha, Uncle Frank, and cousins Margaret and Christine. Even Uncle Morse shipped out in August 1921, on board the *Empress of India*, since the *Empress of Canada* was still not yet ready for sea. With Charles buried in his work at Beaumont Street or in his inventions (in November 1921, he applied for a patent for his improvements on airtight tins), this was a low point for the family.

But there was reason for optimism. The slimmed-down family, namely Pat, had a new governess, Zoe Center, the daughter of a Staffordshire vicar. She proved to be the tonic that the family so badly needed, in more ways than one. She was charming, beautiful, and comfortably situated if not wealthy. She apparently doted on Pat, and she certainly smote his father.

Like Charles, Zoe had suffered tremendously. In World War I, her husband, William Center, a surgeon, had served on board the battleship *Russell* in the heavily mined Dardanelles. So strategic were these waters that First Lord of the Admiralty Winston Churchill had declared to the fleet commander, "The results to be gained [in the Dardanelles] are . . . great enough to justify the loss of ships and men if success cannot be obtained without it." It could not be. Before dawn on April 27, 1916, HMS *Russell* struck two mines, caught fire, and sank. Center died from burns and gas poisoning from flaming cordite.

Patrick's eighth birthday was the most exciting of his young life. A week later he would have a new mother. It had been four years since Jessie's death, four crucial years with a gaping void in his life. But now his father chose well, especially for Pat. Although he would always lament the loss of his mother, this new addition to the family would go far in righting his world, or at least in making it bearable. He would grow very fond of his stepmother, as would all the boys.

On December 20, 1922, at St. Paul's Church in Knightsbridge, Charles Russ, now forty-five, married Zoe Center, a year younger. The two chose to honeymoon in Malta, where they went to pay their respects to the departed William Center at plot 43 in the Malta Naval Cemetery, across the Grand Harbour from Valletta. This act of sentimentality was something of an aberration for Charles, who was never able to open up emotionally to his children.

The trip says much for Zoe's determination to preserve the memory of her first husband, something she would accomplish far beyond her imagination. For Patrick became her dear boy. What favorite son does not dream of fulfilling his mother's most longed-for wish? Patrick's finest fictional character, of course, would be a naval surgeon.

3

The Pen Mightier
than the Pain

1923–1930

We had not been a very close family, emotionally, perhaps
because of my mother's early death and the subsequent
preponderance of housekeepers coupled with my father's
active mind but failing physical health, which necessitated
cutting short some of our schooling.

—Barney Russ, *Lady Day Prodigal,* 1989

A truly good book is something as wildly natural and primitive,
mysterious and marvelous, ambrosial and fertile, as a fungus or
a lichen. Suppose the muskrat or beaver were to turn his views
to literature, what fresh views of nature would be present! The
fault of our books and other deeds is that they are too humane.
I want something speaking in some measure to the condition of
muskrats and skunk-cabbage as well as of men,—not merely to
a pining and complaining coterie of philanthropists.

—Henry David Thoreau, journal, November 16, 1850

Patrick Russ's stepmother was beautiful and unpretentiously stylish.
Her perkiness contrasted markedly with Jessie's wistful demeanor.
In one early portrait, Zoe looks fetching in a dark feather boa over
a simple white dress and a round-brimmed hat decorated with full roses.
In the Russ household, her presence was a source of both joy and resent-
ment, with emotions running more or less along gender lines.

To the boys, she was loyal, steadfast, and passionately kind. Barney, in
a poem written upon Zoe's death in 1964, remembered her as eternally

optimistic that "goodness must prevail." He also wrote that "Zoe certainly had the knack of making everyone feel better." She was especially fond of Patrick, who was young and impressionable enough when she arrived to be essentially hers. She took him to see her sister, who gave the bright boy a copy of the Reverend J. G. Wood's *Natural History*, a hefty mid-nineteenth-century tome filled with information on birds and beasts. The readable prose and vivid engravings of wildlife in their habitats fed his interest in the animal kingdom, an interest already sparked in part by his brother Michael's enthusiasm for birds. Zoe might also have funded Patrick's early education by sending him for a time to prep school (generally for ages six to thirteen in England) in Torbay, where he came to know the coast of Devon. "The Atlantic Fleet used to gather and King George would come down to review them," Patrick later recollected for the London newspaper *Independent*. "The destroyers would tear along. Four funnels they had, with black smoke streaming from them."

Patrick returned Zoe's affection, and perhaps their bond created some jealousy among his siblings. Joan, who came back to the Russ household after Zoe and Charles married, later harbored an astonishing degree of animosity toward Zoe. Joan was something of a ragamuffin, so skinny that she was nicknamed "Bone," and she was always going about with knickknacks stuffed in her pockets. She was perhaps not the sort of girl who would appeal to a fastidious and coquettish mother like Zoe. But Joan lived at home until she was twenty-two, when the war gave her a reason to move out and to establish her independence, and she seemed happy enough during those years. In a wartime letter to Barney, she spoke very affectionately of Charles and Zoe, expressing particular concern for their health. However, later, when she was no longer a dependent of her father and stepmother, she claimed Zoe had been cruel to her when she was a child, locking her in closets and leaving her unclean.

Nora and Connie shared Joan's dislike for Zoe. They complained that she showered attention on the boys while ignoring the girls. They felt unwanted. Zoe was no doubt a target for the girls' anger over their mother's death. They naturally balked at the idea that Jessie could be replaced, and Zoe may have used heavy-handed tactics to affirm her position as the children's mother, ultimately harming the fragile family.

Zoe's insecurity in her new role was probably increased by Olive's decision to live with her aunt and uncle, Bertha and Frank Welch, rather than with her father and new stepmother. Indeed, it appears that Zoe was hurt by this arrangement and may have colored young Joan's memories of her time spent with the Welches. A subsequent letter from Barney to Joan reveals that Zoe suggested that she had saved Joan from an unhappy situation: "I well remember hearing of your being rescued by dear Stepmother from Auntie Bertha and Frank Welch, Margaret and Christine, where you [were] being kept in the servants' quarters or at least were having your meals with the skivvies and I still feel indignant about it, because the rescue by our Stepmother was timely and effective." This portrayal does not seem to be accurate, however. In fact, far from considering Joan an outsider, the Welches had offered to adopt her.

It was a confusing time for the family, which was beginning to disintegrate. Aloof and self-centered, Charles had little talent or will to unite his family. What little he did have he appears to have focused on the two oldest boys, Godfrey, who was mechanically minded and his particular favorite, and Victor, both of whom remained close to him throughout his life. The others repudiated their father in clear ways. Olive stayed with the Welches, never moving back home. Nora took the vows of a Catholic nun, and Joan married into the working class and adopted Catholicism, despite (or perhaps because of) Charles and Zoe's disapproval. Among the boys, Mike would abandon the family name, and he and Barney would move to Australia to escape the dreary conditions at home. But none would fall farther from the tree than Patrick, who would not only change his surname but eventually concoct an entire new persona.

Despite the friction with the girls, Zoe for a time brought a degree of normalcy to the family. One can picture a brief happy interlude before financial and personality troubles beset the family and created more strife, disappointment, and hardship. Christmas of 1923, a year after Charles and Zoe's wedding and two weeks after Pat's ninth birthday, was a special occasion for the Russes. They spent the holiday, the first in which the family was all together in its new form, in the village of Kempsey, four miles south of Worcester in central England. They stayed at Melbury Lodge, a rambling Napoleonic wars–era house in the Regency Gothic style that belonged to Zoe.

One family story has it that when Zoe married Charles, she thought there were just three children. If so, she was soon disabused of the notion as the other six found their way to Melbury for Christmas. Godfrey and Victor, then ages twenty and eighteen respectively, rode their bikes all the way from London to Kempsey for the occasion. Mike, then fourteen, and Barney, eleven, caught the train up from Shebbear College, and their new stepmother, whom they had never met, picked them up at the station in Worcester. When they arrived at Melbury Lodge, six-year-old Joan opened the door to greet her brothers. Mike and Barney, who had been left in North Devon for the past several Christmas and summer holidays, had seen their little sister only once—very briefly at the Welches' home in Pinner—since their mother died five years earlier.

Seventeen-year-old Olive and the thirteen-year-old twins, Connie and Nora, were all there. Between the excitement of the reunion and the anticipation of Christmas, the clamor in the great house must have been terrific.

With its thatch-roofed houses, ancient church, and distant views of the snow-covered Malvern Hills, Kempsey could not have been more idyllic. Together at last, the family, which had suffered so much, enjoyed the wintery weather and traditions of the season: Christmas carolers, the music of the village band, and mince pies from the local bakery. The six-bedroom Melbury Lodge, so named by the previous owner after his childhood home, Melbury Osmond in Dorset, was a delightful hodgepodge of quirky rooms and additions, including glassed-in summer house pavilions on either side of a glassed-in front terrace. Originally called Gothic Villa, the house had south-facing living rooms with pointed stained-glass windows. Each day the boys spent an hour hand-pumping well water up to the hundred-gallon tank on the roof, which also collected rainwater from the gutters. The hard well water, tasting slightly of limestone and salt, made an excellent cup of tea.

The ever-active doctor, perhaps as part of a continuous effort to limit his boys' mischief making, decided that the stagnant pond at Melbury Lodge's greenhouse needed draining. Instead of handing out the water bucket by bucket, Charles thought it an opportunity to demonstrate the interesting physics involved in siphoning. This, however, was a slow process, and as the boys were charged with returning every so often to carry off the full bucket and replace it with an empty one, they grew impatient. When their father was not around, they emptied the pond in the traditional manner, scooping the water up with buckets and unceremoniously dumping it on the ground. This greatly displeased Charles, who was not able to complete his lesson.

At some point, a toy bow and arrow surfaced, probably a Christmas present for Pat. His brothers promptly tied him up to one of the big trees on the property and launched arrows at him. This was a humiliating turn of events, but Barney later recalled that Pat proved his mettle by taking his punishment with no tears and without tattling. When at last it fell his turn, Pat had only one reasonable choice for sibling target practice, his sister Joan. As luck would have it, a well-aimed shot hit her near the eye, cutting her. Pat pleaded with his bleeding sister to tell their father that she had tripped and fallen down. She did. But Charles studied the evidence and knew better, and again poor Patrick suffered from this child's play. His father gave him a sound thrashing.

The Russes stayed on in Kempsey briefly, presumably for its restorative qualities, namely the clean air and medicinal waters for which the area was famous. (Children with respiratory problems from heavily polluted Birmingham were sent to the area to convalesce.) Wheezy Patrick probably benefited from the climate. This might be where he, on bad days, was examined and dosed by medical men, as he later recalled, and lay in bed reading the *Gentleman's Magazine*, for it was most likely here that he discovered in the basement a chest full of copies of the eighteenth-century publication once edited by Samuel Johnson and considered the first magazine in the modern sense of the word, offering a variety of articles and subjects. The magazine brought the manners and wit, the tales and news stories of Johnson's era vividly to life for the curious boy.

On good days, though, Pat could roam around the grounds beneath the large sycamore, wellingtonia, black mulberry, and cedar trees spotting birds and other wildlife. An easy five minutes' walk took him to the ferry crossing of the forty-foot-wide Severn River, where old barges known as trows were tied to the bank. There is no doubt that Melbury Lodge left an impression on him. He later borrowed the name for the "neat gentleman's residence" that Jack Aubrey leases in the novel *Post Captain*.

After the all-too-brief hiatus at Kempsey, the coming year brought more disruption. Charles published another treatise, *Drink Versus Prohibition* and applied for another patent for "instruments set in motion by the human eye," extending research that had already produced a patent in 1918. Although he hoped the eye study would pay off, his practice was failing. He abandoned his office at 25 Beaumont Street, his only consistent address over the previous decade, and set up at 63 Wimpole Street. To save money during school holidays, the boys cleaned the office and washed the glass vessels and the instruments that Charles used in his bacteriological practice. But within a year, he closed this office as well. In June 1924, Zoe sold Melbury Lodge, which became a rooming house. Charles borrowed money.

Despite their worsening financial straits, Charles, conditioned to having what he wanted in his youth, found it impossible to alter his lifestyle. He continued to dine out and attend the theater with Zoe, pleasures they could not afford. In May 1925, with liabilities of more than £4,000 and assests of only about £150, Charles was forced to declare bankruptcy. To make matters worse, he continued to work on his doomed treatment, publishing *Gonorrhoea Treated by Electrolysis: Results in 1,000 Cases* in 1930. His eye-related invention, to which he also dedicated much time and energy, was equally ill-fated. Although he would publish an article, "Magnetic Spectacles for Ptosis," in the *British Medical Journal* in 1936, nothing ever came of it.

Charles toiled in a dark cloud of insolvency for more than a decade, and this had a profound impact on his family. Following the summer term in 1924, he had been forced to pull his older children out of boarding school. Pat would never attend Shebbear, and Joan would never attend Edgehill. Mike and Barney, who had been at Shebbear spring, summer, and fall since January 1921, left at the end of July. Mike and Olive were both distinguished students. He had passed the senior entrance exam for Cambridge with honors and an exemption in mathematics, while Olive, who excelled at art and biology, had passed the junior exam, qualifying her to take the senior exam the next year. Instead, she went to a London secretarial school.

Pat enrolled at Marylebone Grammar School, where Barney, who also attended Marylebone, gave him a hand with his English homework, something Barney would laugh about later in life given his brother's mounting literary achievement. Jerome K. Jerome, the author of *Three Men in a Boat* and other humorous works, was an alumnus (or "old boy," as the English say) of Marylebone. Barney and Pat heard him speak and became fans of his whimsical writing. They shared their enthusiasm with Joan, and the three found a bond in the pleasure of this playful reading.

Patrick, who later wrote that recurrent illness interfered with his education and made his adolescence introspective and frequently lonely, found refuge in books. At times he read almost incessantly, continuing the day's reading at night in bed by flashlight. As can be seen in his early literary efforts, he was moved by Rudyard Kipling's animal stories and his novel *Kim*, set in colonial India, as well as by Ernest Bramah's Kai Lung stories. Zoe's collection of books from the eighteenth and early nineteenth centuries made its impact too. Patrick absorbed the Reverend Walter's account of Admiral Anson's celebrated, if costly, voyage to the South Pacific. More than half the crew perished, but the survivors got to parade the riches of a captured Spanish galleon through the streets of England. Like his Uncle Morse's adventure tales, the chaplain's account touched the boy's imagination. The seed of the writer was taking root in him. During the next decade, he devoured the works of Tobias Smollett, Jonathan Swift, Samuel Richardson, Henry Fielding, Samuel Johnson, Edward Gibbon, and Richard Hakluyt.

In May 1926, the General Strike, organized by the Trades Union Congress in support of mineworkers, paralyzed England for nine days. Troops and teams of volunteers prevented the strike from creating even greater havoc. Godfrey Russ, who was training as an electrical engineer, drove shunting train locomotives. Michael, who worked in a surveyor's office, substituted as a longshoreman and was chased by a mob of armed union men while moving meat from a refrigerated storage area.

Around this time, Charles moved what was left of the family to Lewes in Sussex, a town that must have stoked Patrick's awareness of history. The family lived at 10 Priory Crescent, an arc of adjoining townhouses beside the Parish Church of St. John the Baptist, formerly a Norman hospital and the burial site of a knight of William the Conqueror. A basking shark weather vane topped the church's Georgian tower.

One end of the path behind Priory Crescent opened onto Southover High Street near a sixteenth-century timber-framed house once owned by Anne of Cleves. In the other direction the path led to the ruins of Lewes Priory, founded in 1077 and destroyed by Thomas Cromwell in 1538. A little farther down the path came the Mount, an Elizabethan prospect mound, and the Dripping Pan, a medieval salt pan now used as a municipal gathering spot. In his novel *The Yellow Admiral*, Patrick would borrow this geographic feature, place it in Dorset, and stage a bare-knuckle fistfight there.

Lewes was staunchly Protestant, and on Guy Fawkes Day, a raucous parade with marching bands converged on the Dripping Pan before the townspeople tossed an effigy, not of Fawkes, as was customary in most towns, but of a pope, from the bridge into the River Ouse. Lewes relished the occasion, and Joan, Pat, and Barney never forgot the excitement of the day. Nor, according to Barney, did they forget David Lloyd George, perhaps the greatest orator of his day, "shaking his silver locks" as he spoke to a throng in the Dripping Pan. Unfortunately for the Russes, it was only a visual memory because they were perched too far away to actually hear the former prime minister.

Barney and Pat attended Old Grammar School, which stood next to a Norman castle and traced its roots back to a thirteenth-century school connected to Lewes Priory. Each morning the two brothers walked up a steep cobblestone road to the High Street to reach the school, where it paid to show up on time, for it was well known that the headmaster, the Reverend Griffith, who doubled as the vicar of Glynde, was unsparing in his use of the cane. Barney, who was fond of writing verse, later commemorated the headmaster with these lines:

> *I am the Vicar of Glynde*
> *For a change, it is pleasant, I find,*
> *In my school, full of noise,*
> *To chastise the boys*
> *By dusting them well behind.*

The Russes did not last long in Lewes. They soon moved back to London. But while in the south, Charles seems to have focused on his inventions. On December 12, 1927, he applied for a patent for an electric heater that prevented the water in car radiators from freezing, a device that Barney helped him demonstrate at an exhibition of inventions and that he apparently sold to an automaker, which unfortunately ended up shelving it. In the fall of 1928, Charles would apply for a patent for winding and constructing electrical heating elements, the description of which filled three pages. Three months after that, he patented an "improved protector for venereal discharges." On each of these, his address is listed as 50 George Street, indicating that, even while residing in Lewes, he managed to keep an office in London.

Times were hard for the whole family, and the children received little assistance in moving on with their lives. In 1927, Barney had sat for and passed his Oxford junior exam, with first-class honors in eight subjects: English, history, geography, religious knowledge, Latin, French, arithmetic, and mathematics, and with "distinction" in history and French. He seemed destined to go to college, but Charles could not afford it. Instead, Barney moved to London, and, at fifteen, took a dreary job collecting rents in the East End's slums. There could be no clearer example of Charles Russ's failure to provide for his family.

Like Pat, Barney turned to books to escape this grim reality. He often passed his lunch hour at the Guildhall Library, immersed in Sidney Colvin's *John Keats, His Life and Poetry* and Edmund Spenser's *Faerie Queene*. He discovered Blake, Wordsworth, and Coleridge in an Arthur Thomas Quiller-Couch anthology. During subsequent travels he sought refuge in the anthology, long after it had grown "sweat-stained and ink-blotted, the pages loose and the binding almost all gone"(*Lady Day Prodigal*, p. 65).

Olive, who was still living with the Welches, made the most of her secretarial training. She joined Standard Telephones and Cables, Ltd., in its Aldwych, London, office and became the personal secretary of Sir Thomas Spencer, managing director. At Standard, she soon met and became engaged to Reginald Cole, an electronics engineer with a physics degree from Cambridge. When Olive took "Reg," as he was called, to meet Charles and Zoe, her father heartily congratulated the couple on their impending nuptials but absolved himself from paying by quickly adding, "Oh, well, no doubt Frank Welch will organize the wedding." Charles had little money to spare, and sometimes even less charm.

In preparing for the wedding, Olive decided to be baptized and confirmed in the Church of England. At the same time she anglicized to Elizabeth her middle name, Isobel—the name her brothers had found great mirth in teasing her about. Her decision to change her name incensed Charles. He refused to attend the wedding. Zoe might well have encouraged this break with Charles's oldest daughter, who had performed in a motherly role for her younger siblings after Jessie's death. Though there would be some reconciliation just before Charles's death, decades later, this turn of events caused a permanent rift between father and daughter. Charles Russ had become hard and intolerant.

In April 1927, Michael, fed up with the family and the bleak outlook in London, enrolled in the Dreadnought Scheme, a program (financed by surplus World War I funds originally meant for building a Dreadnought battleship) that sent young men and women to Australia to assuage its manpower shortage. After arriving in Australia, men trained for three months at dairy and vegetable farming, blacksmithing and horse management, and construction, and women worked as nannies, maids, and cooks. In June, Michael boarded a steamer for New South Wales.

Over the next year and a half, he wrote letters home depicting Australia as wide-open, full of opportunity and new companions. He sent Patrick the pelt of an opossum and the sixteen-foot skin of a carpet snake (an Australian python), which had made the mistake of peering at Michael over some crops that he was harvesting. "He took its head off with a machete," a beaming Patrick later recounted to the BBC, "skinned it and so sent it back." In London, Patrick taped the snake skin to his bedroom wall. This was enough for Barney, who decided to join his brother Down Under. He secured a Dreadnought passage at the Australian embassy and landed in Sydney in November 1929, just days after the U.S. stock market crash shocked the world. It would take Barney three years to pay back his Dreadnought fare of £12.

On December 12, 1928, Patrick turned fourteen. Whether or not he had remained at the Old Grammar School for another year is unclear, but it seems he was now living with his parents in London.* He says he was unpopular with his brothers and sisters, perhaps for the pampering from Zoe or perhaps he simply had a low opinion of himself and assumed others did too. He definitely resembled his later fictional character Stephen Maturin, who was paying "serious attention to voles" by the age of seven and often "wandered alone . . . peering into the water-shrew's domain . . . and making a rough inventory of birds" (*The Yellow Admiral*, p. 49). Patrick also kept an aquarium.

It was around this time that he began to write. As he later described in his foreword to the reprint of his first book, *Caesar*, he began writing while spending "long sessions in the incubator room" (p. v) in his father's laboratory, where Charles confined Patrick ostensibly to improve his health. Sitting at a metal table with a glass top, Patrick finished the tasks assigned to him by his tutor, and barred from bringing in a book to read, he began to write his own. At other times, he told the BBC, he wrote when he was confined to bed "rather fanciful things of a person of my own age making surprising voyages and so on . . . wish-fulfillment."

*According to school officials, all early school records were destroyed in 1965.

From his great-grandfather and grandfather he had inherited a keen interest in wild animals; from his father, the curiosity and acuity of a scientist, as well as the fertile imagination of an inventor; and from his mother, a passion for botany and birds. For his first book, Patrick invented his own beast: the offspring of a male giant panda and a female snow leopard, which he called a panda leopard. He wrote in his bedroom, sometimes with a guilty conscience because he should have been doing his homework. He narrated the story from the point of view of the beast, named Caesar by his master. Much of the tale involves Caesar's hunting. He grows to be a lithe, powerful animal, but each potential meal presents its own challenges and sometimes dangers. When he is not hunting, he is often fending off predators, from warrior ants with disproportionate jaws to starving wolves.

Not surprising, given Patrick's childhood, Caesar's coming-of-age story involves much early suffering. Shortly after his birth, he loses a sister to a black bear and a brother to a hyena. While he is still a youth and just learning to hunt, his mother and remaining brother are killed in a forest fire. The loss of his mother haunts him. After one brutal fight, Caesar dreams about the fire that took his mother: "I saw her quite plainly just before the pine killed her," he reports, "and I felt very sad" (p. 17).

When Caesar is grown, his mother appears in phantom form to scare off a large python. "Then the thought that perhaps she had lived through the fire flashed through my mind," Caesar relates, "and I started forward with a purr of delight to meet her, but to my horror and amazement there was nothing there" (pp. 61–62). Clearly, Patrick, who had experienced this kind of pain firsthand, had a gift for writing with detachment.

Left to fend for himself, Caesar at first searches for easy prey, which he finds in domestic livestock. This naturally leads to an encounter with humans. For a fourteen-year-old, Patrick wrote with striking sangfroid in describing the encounter: "With a shriek of fear he struck me with a stick, and missed. We fell together, but his skull was cracked like an egg-shell. It was ridiculously easy to kill him" (p. 10).

Always true to the voice of his carnivore hero, Patrick coolly—and without a hint of sentimentality—described another scene in which Caesar has caught a mountain goat kid and is attacked by its mother:

> She charged with her long horns lowered. I darted to one side,
> and with my paw I got in a blow which ripped her open to the

shoulder-bone. Then wonderfully quickly she turned and gored me in the side. I leaped clear, and we stood panting and looking at each other for a second. Then I charged, and leaping on to her back I broke her neck.

Then I took up the kid again, and set off home. (P. 15)

By now, the Russ family had moved again, to Sutherland Avenue in the Maida Vale section of London. Pat finished his book in March 1930, just four months after his fifteenth birthday. It was a more than respectable effort for a boy of his age, and Charles decided to seek a publisher.

Barney, who turned eighteen the same month, was about to become a farm laborer in Goolgowi, Australia, four hundred miles west of Sydney. He lived in a tin-roofed shack with a dirt floor, slept on a piece of canvas stretched on metal poles, and performed backbreaking labor all day. Despite Australia's claim to egalitarianism, the family for whom Barney worked made him eat alone in the kitchen. He later expressed his outrage at this humiliation: "Now, I had come from a fairly good English home and my father was a professional man. I was totally unused to life among the lower classes. Yet here were these definitely inferior beings treating this son of a gentleman like a common peasant!"(*Lady Day Prodigal*, p. 37).

Though Pat and Barney were less than three years apart in age, how different their lives had become. Barney would remain in Australia for almost a decade, and though his situation eventually improved, he had not hit rock bottom yet. Pat would endure his own dose of demoralizing poverty; however, it came later, and more on his own terms.

Part II

RED

4

Beasts Royal

1930–1934

The ignorant and the weak only are idle; but those who have
once acquired a good stock of knowledge, always desire to
increase it. Knowledge is like power, in this respect, that those
who have the most are most desirous of having more. It does
not clog, by possession, but increases desires; which is the case
of very few pleasures.

—Lord Chesterfield, letter to his son, August 23, 1748

Entering this gray decade in England, Patrick Russ, a shy fifteen-
year-old, was a promising writer of stories, with a mental library far
beyond his years and emotional baggage too ponderous for so
young a man. Leaving the 1930s, he would be a worldly veteran of the air
force and a father of two children. Once again he would find himself in an
unhappy house. Again his health would fail. While life did its best to confuse and cause chaos, Patrick would read and invent. And again his written
words would amaze and delight.

Under the most stable of conditions, the transition from teenager to
adult is trying, and Patrick's life was anything but stable. The boy with a
tumultuous childhood and adolescence became a restless young man. By
now his five oldest siblings were out on their own. Godfrey, an electrical
engineer, and Victor, a bank clerk, were making careers for themselves.
Olive had succeeded as a secretary and married well. Mike and Barney
were struggling in Australia.

Patrick would later claim in an autobiographical essay and in published
interviews some unlikely adventures during this time, including sailing on
an uncle's two-ton sloop. (This uncle was certainly not a Russ, and there
appears to be no Goddard uncle or Blakeway stepuncle who would be a

likely candidate.) He also said that he sailed on a French-built three-masted yacht owned by the wealthy cousin and guardian of a friend named Edward, with whom he shared a tutor. The man loved to sail and to test out his theories regarding new sail configurations. The yacht sometimes moored in Bantry Bay off Cork, and presumably that is where Patrick and his friend boarded her.

According to Patrick, the vessel sailed to the Azores and down the coast of Africa to test her owner's sailing theories on the edge of the trade winds. Shellbacks crewed her, but she also carried a few adventurous schoolboys who performed the lowliest duties, such as deck swabbing and rope pulling. But eventually the boys learned to climb the masts and work on the yards, to hand and reef a sail, and to steer, the skills of an ordinary seaman.

Perhaps Patrick did have such an experience, or perhaps it was a convenient invention when some claim to square-rigged sailing expertise was desirable. In either case, it made no impact on his prewar writing; one friend with whom he would later discuss naval strategy and literature would not recall ever hearing him talk about such an experience; and Barney would later write to Joan that Patrick's "apparent knowledge of seamanship under sail and the naval terminology never ceases to amaze me. As far as I know he has never been to sea in a tall ship or any other for any distance." Such an experience was never mentioned in any of the biographical sketches accompanying Patrick's early stories or sea books. What does infuse his stories from this decade is his continuing fascination with animals and his burgeoning interest in colonial India.

By the end of May 1930, Charles Russ had negotiated a deal with G. P. Putnam's Sons to publish Patrick's first book. Charles and editor Geoffrey Lackstead met at the Press Club in St. Bride's House, near Fleet Street, and signed a contract. Pat's advance on royalties came to £10. He dedicated the book, titled *Caesar: The Life Story of a Panda Leopard*, to his stepmother, Zoe.

With subdued pride, the doctor wrote a foreword, focusing on the nature of the panda leopard invented by his son. "As the author of the story is only fifteen years old," Charles noted, "he may have unwittingly provided zoologists with a small problem in prophecy as to Caesar's distinguishing features. Fortunately the story does not, I think, chiefly rely for its interest or attraction on its zoological aspect." The book's illustrator, Harry Rountree, simply ignored the mixed parentage of the hero-beast, depicting him entirely as a leopard.

Charles concluded his foreword, "I believe the author's immaturity of literary style and method—which are quite unspoiled by any senior pen— may also contribute to its favourable reception." Putnam's Sons published *Caesar* in October 1930.

Charles was correct in believing that his son's prose gained from this ingenuousness. In the first place, few would attempt a story in which the narrator is an animal, let alone a predator, and one who understands the words of men, and fewer still would have gotten away with it. But Patrick did. With the clear conscience of youth, he neither blushed nor blinked nor rationalized. He wrote clean, active prose, and he successfully entered Caesar's mind, as when the captive beast confesses, "I was given at a regular time every day a smelly, stale and bony lump of flesh with no blood in it. That which I missed most of all was the killing of my own food" (p. 47). And when Caesar kills in the wild, whether an animal for food or a man in self-defense, there is no great human moralizing, no struggling with the meaning of existence (though he raises many issues in the reader's mind), but an elegantly straightforward presentation of the story.

In fact, Patrick displayed in his first published work a remarkable number of the techniques of his most accomplished writing, a quarter century away. Already, he deftly undercut potentially melodramatic scenes. He established his authority with pithy facts: many wild animals drink only in the evening; pythons like to eat monkeys; leopards break the necks of their prey; elephants kill their foes by kneeling on them. His narrative style relied on a tight point of view, seeing through the eyes and mind of the beast, while the author remained almost wholly invisible. The story benefited from this immediacy as well as from the animal-narrator's flawed perception of his environment.

Caesar was a worthy first manifestation of Patrick's skill at characterization. Likable and moral, given his own understanding of the world, Caesar is, nevertheless, a killer of men who slays out of rage. "When I calmed down enough to stop the useless killing, I found myself alone covered with blood, with two dead men," he tells us after fighting shepherds. "I dimly felt sorry that I had needlessly killed these two useless things, for though I was hungry I could not bring myself to eat these smelly men"

(p. 20). Yet Patrick did not fall into the trap of trying to impress the reader. Caesar does not become the stereotypical king of the jungle. In fact, he frequently pursues the weak and the young—natural behavior in the animal kingdom, for which Patrick made no apologies.

Another strength Patrick demonstrated was a knack for the telling detail. On a hunting trip after long being caged, Caesar says, "My master gave me a large piece of the antelope's shoulder, and I remembered that I always used to begin my meal at the shoulder of my prey instead of at the haunch, as I had seen some animals doing" (p. 56). Not only does this passage make the reader pause to consider that a ferocious animal might have idiosyncrasies but, more important, it helps define the relationship between Caesar and his master. The man knows things about Caesar that the animal in captivity has himself forgotten. In fact, they become particular friends, a relationship Patrick never ceased to explore in his fiction.

The book was a critical success. In December 1930, the *New Statesman* included *Caesar* in its Christmas recommendations for children. Putnam's sold Danish translation rights in February 1931, and the book reached stores in the United States that summer. In August, the *New York Herald Tribune* wrote, in a generally favorable review, "*Caesar* may be too human—or boylike—in his reactions for complete plausibility, but his sleek, catlike nature, his carnivorous appetite, his ruthless skill in killing for food, all these are clearly pictured in simple, adequate, straightforward narrative."

The *Saturday Review of Literature* commented that the book was written in the "spirit of an explorer relating his adventures.... There is rapid action, copious bloodshed, and later, the extraordinary devotion felt by the mammoth killer for the master who trains it to hunt for him. Boys themselves will love all that." However, the publication warned, "The question in our minds is this: what effect will such a dish of mental food have on the growing boy, and what kind of dreams will it cause the sensitive child to have?"

Before departing for Australia, Barney Russ had harbored a secret (and never realized) dream: to ride his bike from London to Rome to pay homage to Keats at the poet's tomb. Like Barney and their father, Patrick was prone to enthusiasms. He too had a propensity for fantasizing, which might have been in reverse proportion to the family's ability to display emotions. On Joan's fourteenth birthday, July 10, 1931, Pat gave his sister an inscribed copy of *Caesar*, a kind and personal gift, but with the dry inscription "To Joan from Pat." Love was not a topic to be mentioned.

Other subjects were taboo as well. Neither Charles nor Zoe offered advice regarding the facts of life, a matter that affected Joan deeply. Barney was also kept in the dark, though his experiences were more comical. At seventeen, handsome in the mold of his father, but not as tall, he had departed for Australia a sexual naïf. As might be expected, the Dread-nought Scheme attracted the bold and the outcast. At sea, Barney marveled at the hanky-panky in the supposedly strictly segregated bunk rooms. In Australia, when an attractive married woman lured him to her hotel room, he carried on an honorable conversation with her all the while ignoring the fact that she was half naked.

Later, Patrick, too, would find himself the object of an older woman's affection, one whose powers of seduction were more impressive than those of Barney's Australian temptress.

Pat and Joan, it seems, were left to discover the world on their own, and this they did primarily through Pat's passions—"tearing and painful ones," he later confessed to the BBC—which came in waves. Perhaps under the influence of Ernest Bramah's clever mock-Chinese Kai Lung stories, Pat became fascinated by the Far East. He drank exotic teas and ate litchis, and he gave Joan a flat metal Chinese mirror decorated with a dragon on one side and polished to a reflective gleam on the other. He collected Japanese Samurai swords. He also developed a fervor for India, perhaps through Uncle Emil's tales of his years there and certainly deepened by Kipling's writing. Several years later, under the influence of the writings of James Joyce, he developed a passion for Ireland and claimed to be Irish, a charade he maintained the rest of his life.

Books, nature, and music were his abiding interests. When they could afford it, Pat and Joan attended the popular and inexpensive Proms concerts of classical, patriotic, and show music at Queen's Hall. Sometimes Victor, who loved music, joined them. Literature played a big part in Pat and Joan's fantasy lives. They read endlessly, mostly novels and the *Strand*, the magazine whose catchy illustrated articles, political pieces, interviews, and fiction, mainly detective stories and tales of the weird, were originally chosen to appeal to the railway commuter. The *Strand* had launched Arthur Conan Doyle's Sherlock Holmes stories in 1891, and in the 1930s featured the writing of Agatha Christie and Dorothy L. Sayers, among others. The stories combined the clever and witty with the thrilling and sensational, feeding the young Russes' imaginations and love of reading. Patrick was not the only writer in the family. Joan wrote well, and in high school, she won a copy of Somerset Maugham's *Of Human Bondage* as a literary prize. She later published a chapbook of poetry.

But Patrick simply had to write. It was his chief form of expression and a substitute for the physical activities that his delicate constitution so limited. He published his first story in a fall 1931 issue of *Chums Weekly*, a London boys' magazine, which reported that the sixteen-year-old had "produced what may be described as the boys' best-seller" and that he had been "hailed as the boy-Thoreau." Not only had *Caesar* found its way to the United States and Denmark, but it had been translated and published in Sweden, Norway, and Japan. Despite the success, the magazine noted, "he is exceedingly modest about his achievement and is much more interested in watching the behaviour of the dog-fish and cat-fish in his aquarium than discussing his book."

"Patrick is a great lover of Nature and a keen observer, and that perhaps is the secret of his success as a writer of Nature stories," wrote the magazine. "In truth, Patrick is not a book-worm, but prefers to draw his inspiration from the countryside." Or the sea.

His first venture into the deep blue concerned not naval life but nature. The story, "Skogula," follows the rise to adulthood of a bull whale, whose mother is one of the seven wives of the pod leader, a powerful sixty-foot bull who rules "with his ten-foot ivory-clad under-jaw." During a migration south, a whaler harpoons Skogula, but he escapes when a second harpoon, attached to the first by a short length of rope, snags a whaler boat. The force of Skogula's dive rips the harpoon out of his flesh. At their destination, a southern seas lagoon, the behemoth leader of another pod challenges Skogula's father. As they fight, the sea grows pink. Frenzied sharks gather for the kill. The struggle rages out of sight, and Skogula never again sees his father.

The new chief bull is a great traveler, leading the pod to the Indian Ocean, Zanzibar, and the coast of Brazil. He is also a tedious bully. Skogula eventually comes of age while fighting three giant swordfish off St. Helena. One stabs him, causing him to spout blood. He responds with fury. Wrote Patrick, "For the first time, using his full strength, he lashed with his tail hard enough to blind his enemies, and then turning, he bit one right through the middle of the body." Off the Falkland Islands, Skogula finally challenges the leader over rights to an attractive cow named Miska.

The ruthless old warrior rips the blubber from the sides of Skogula's head in long strips and dislocates his jaw before a freak occurrence saves his life. The leader bumps against a contact mine that explodes and destroys him.

In "Skogula," as in *Caesar*, Patrick used a tight third-person narration very effectively, entering the minds of the whales when he chose. What allowed him to do this was his command of the details of their lives and his ability to anthropomorphize with a minimum of human emotion. In his first story published in a magazine, Patrick proved that the success of *Caesar* was no fluke.

England was now in the thick of the global depression, with unemployment surpassing two million people. The Russes were essentially broke, though there does seem to have been a reserve of cash, perhaps coming from Zoe, who certainly at one point loaned her husband money. Somehow Charles and Zoe preserved at least a minimal middle-class lifestyle. Though information about this time is sketchy, they apparently lived for a while south of the Thames, in Putney, close enough to the river to see the start of the Oxford-Cambridge boat races from their house in the summer. Perhaps inspired by Patrick's success, Charles indulged in a literary endeavor of his own. In July and August 1931, Warwick James repertory company performed his four-act play, *Hidden Power,* at King George's Theatre on Great Russell Street.

Intrigued by the potential for doctors to misuse their powers (he noted that in the previous seventy years at least four doctors had been executed for murder in Britain), Charles constructed a love triangle resulting in a murder during surgery and leading to another love triangle. The *Lancet* wrote in its August 1 issue: "It is a drama full of medical interest, for its opening (and only) murder is committed by the anaesthetist during an operation, and his guilt is subsequently discovered by hypnosis. This gives Dr. Russ a good opportunity for discussing, through his characters, some important aspects of mind and body, and he makes suggestive comments on psychological analysis as practised by doctors and clergy."

But the journal conceded that the play "lacks surprises, and it certainly requires ruthless compression." In fact, it was a dubious distinction that during "moments of crisis in the consulting room" the reviewer took great delight in perusing the "names of well-known surgical instrument makers in place of the usual 'wigs by Clarkson' " in the program.

In September 1932, at the depths of the depression, Patrick's oldest brother, Godfrey, now an electrical engineer, married the daughter of a clerk in London. Victor, who had become a bank clerk, witnessed the ceremony. Not present were Michael and Barney, who were still struggling to survive in Australia, which was no better off than England. National income had plummeted by a third, unemployment had skyrocketed, shops lay deserted and factories idle. Ironically, Mike, the grandson of a furrier to Queen Victoria, found himself on the bottom rung of the ladder in the fur trade, and an outlaw at that. Mike had become, among other things, a platypus poacher, killing the aquatic mammals for their valuable pelts.

Since Mike was a bit of a star in the family no matter what he did, Patrick almost certainly heard of his illicit trapping in the wilds of Australia through his letters home. No doubt Mike's exploits sounded romantic to the teenager, who was fascinated by the animal kingdom and who had so often been confined to bed, but perhaps he was saddened by his brother's hunting of such a rare and exotic species. Sixty years later, Patrick would allow the duck-billed platypus a measure of revenge in his novel *The Nutmeg of Consolation*, when a male of the species viciously barbs Stephen Maturin with his venomous spur. Maturin's exaggerated reaction, a near-death coma (the sting would usually require only a painkiller), paid the platypus back with interest.

What Patrick and the others did not know was that Mike was living the life of a scoundrel in other ways too. He had previously impregnated a farmer's teenage daughter, married her a month before she gave birth to a son, Stanley Charles Russ, and then run out on them to Queensland. He also changed his name. Just why he picked the name O'Brien is hard to say. However, the founder of his school, Shebbear College—and indeed of the Bible Christian Church, a tributary of the Methodist Church of England— was named William O'Bryan, and it could have been a name that resonated for him. If so, Mike ironically renamed himself for a very pious man.

In the midst of these oppressive times, when his family, like others, was learning to live on a more down-to-earth scale, Patrick turned, as he always would, to his writing. In March 1933, he published another story. "A Tale About a Great Peregrine Falcon" ran in the Edinburgh-based *Great-Heart: The Church of Scotland Magazine—for Boys and Girls*. The magazine, aimed at the under-fifteen set and costing a penny, noted that "R. P. Russ has made a name for himself by Nature stories, although he is not much older than *Great-Heart* readers."

In this story, as in "Skogula," Patrick described the life of the animal in detail, evoking the female peregrine's flight, her hunt on the downs for food, her battle with a pair of falcons who attempt to steal her prey, and her relationship with her relatively weak mate, who is unable to fend off the human intruder of their nest. The story's mood is rather glum, in part because Patrick did not name the falcons and did not romanticize their plights at all. When a nameless and doomed oologist raids their aerie, placing the eggs he is stealing in his mouth to protect them as he tries to escape, the peregrine attacks him with the passion and determination of a mother defending her offspring—so different from that of the ineffectual father—a theme that Patrick returns to on several occasions in his early work.

As Patrick advanced through his teen years, finding success writing stories, it is not surprising that he developed a bit of a swagger. At times he played the sophisticate, wearing colorful waistcoats and silk dressing gowns à la Noel Coward, whose comedy *Cavalcade* had taken the British stage by storm in 1931. Patrick smoked French or Turkish cigarettes in holders and even acquired a hookah. He continued to smoke for many years, and Joan, his teenage sidekick, never quit.

In 1933, Patrick also published his first story in *Oxford Annual for Scouts*, a publication of Oxford University Press. "Wang Khan of the Elephants" introduced his latest passion: the culture of colonial India. India was Rudyard Kipling's and E. M. Forster's literary turf, but Patrick was not intimidated. He wrote fearlessly.

Young or old, he always wrote best when plunging headfirst into another world, be it the animal kingdom, India, or the Royal Navy of 1800. Freed of the demons of his daily existence, he roamed in each of these fictional worlds with uncanny detachment, examining both its particular minutiae and the eternal truths.

Though it was still an animal tale, "Wang Khan" was Patrick's first work with central human characters. In the hot summer dust, Wang Khan, a three-ton bull elephant in the employ of the Amalgamated Teak Company, carries his mahout, Moti Lal, and Moti Lal's young son, Little Moti, on his back as he roots up stumps with his tusks and drags trees to the river. As Wang Khan labors, the boy chastises the powerful beast, calling him "fat pig" and "sluggard." When a logjam forms in the river, the negligent superintendent orders Moti Lal to fix the problem with his mighty elephant. However, just as Wang Khan, working on the downriver side of the dangerous snarl, frees it and moves to safety on the bank, Little Moti falls into the river. Knowing that his own escape is impossible, the elephant again heaves against the mounting timber and weight of the river. Moti Lal rescues his son, but Wang Khan is lost.

In this relationship between man and beast, Patrick found a rich vein to mine. An elephant often served several generations of a mahout family, allowing for comparisons between grandfather, son, and grandson, each of whom in his turn commanded, cared for, and established his unique rapport with the elephant. The mysterious dynamics of Indian culture—with its outcastes and gods, curses and magic—had also captured Patrick's imagination. It was a world in which the good, intelligent common man had to make his way against the tide of petty tyranny, corruption, and slothful governance that existed in the moral conundrum of English colonialism. For Patrick, harmony with nature and animals was one way for the native to maintain the moral high ground. He would explore this theme in a number of stories and ultimately in a novel.

With "Wang Khan," Patrick began a lasting relationship with the editors of Oxford University Press's story collections *Oxford Annual for Scouts* and *Oxford Annual for Boys*. From 1933 to 1940, he published eight stories in editor Herbert Strang's two annuals, which were run primarily by Charles John Kaberry, a juvenile department veteran and children's book author who encouraged the young, talented writer.

The 1934 Scouts annual included "The White Cobra," an especially noteworthy tale because here Patrick created his first human protagonist, and a complex one. Hussein, a Sufi Muslim snake charmer, is determined to steal from the Hindu village Kurasai a rare white cobra called Vakrishna, considered by the villagers to be an incarnation of the god Vakrishna and a bearer of good luck. Over a period of days, Hussein befriends the village's headman and priest, dupes them into trusting him, and hatches a scheme to steal the snake, which lives in a hole beneath a pipal tree.

Hussein paints one of his own snakes white, feeds Vakrishna a drugged rat, and then swaps the two. He flees with the white cobra, but that evening, the imposter snake sheds its painted skin. Hussein wakes up the next morning in a village ten miles away to face an angry mob that has pursued him overnight. They beat him unconscious and leave with Vakrishna. The priest remains behind, revives Hussein, beats him again, more fiercely than before, and leaves him for dead. It was the first but not the last time that Patrick would turn a story on the hypocrisy of a priest.

Patrick wrote with the sure voice of an experienced tale spinner, as when he succinctly characterized the villagers through their own faction-alism and stereotypes: "It transpired that Hussein was a Sufi—a free-thinker, as opposed to the orthodox Shiites. This at once raised him in the estimation of the villagers, whose neighbors towards the north were strict Shiites, and great cattle thieves." He once again showed an uncanny ability to establish his authority on an unlikely subject and to almost effortlessly transport the reader to another world, one that he had only learned about vicariously. While much is made of the importance of writing from experi-ence, Patrick, even at this young age, showed a genius for the opposite. He could convincingly roam India like a mahout, climb into the soul of a falcon, or hunt as remorselessly as a leopard. This extraordinary capability would find its full fruition years later in the Aubrey-Maturin novels.

It was probably in the winter of 1933–34 that Patrick put the finishing touches on a collection of tales, which included the four he had already published, with minor edits (though he much improved "A Peregrine Falcon" by subtly honing the ending), and eight new ones. His father sold the manuscript, "Twelve Animal Stories," to G. P. Putnam's Sons in May. Patrick's advance tripled to £30. Of the eight new stories, six had animals as main characters, the last Patrick wrote of this sort, and two continued the adventures of the snake charmer and mahout Hussein. Although Patrick had completed the animal-centric phase of his writing career, he maintained a personal devotion to animals, particularly birds, and his eventual literary alter ego, Stephen Maturin, would delight in the discovery and care of animals throughout the Aubrey-Maturin books. While in these early stories Patrick examined the lives of animals very seriously, later he frequently found humor there, particularly in Maturin's animal keeping on board ship. In one amusing incident, the sailors get his potto (a slow-climbing African primate) drunk, and in another, Maturin proudly brings an active beehive into the captain's cabin so that they can have honey on the voyage.

Patrick dedicated the story collection, titled *Beasts Royal* and issued in September 1934, "To my father." To illustrate it, Putnam's chose Charles Tunnicliffe, a budding master at natural history illustration who had recently established himself in Henry Williamson's *Tarka the Otter*. (That book was not illustrated originally, but Tunnicliffe sent Putnam's several aquatints of Tarka that were so exquisite the publisher reissued the book with art.) It was a good match. Both Tunnicliffe, who drew birds that were accurate to within a millimeter, and Patrick cherished detail, and

Tunnicliffe's illustrations stood up reasonably well to Patrick's dense, often brooding tales.

Beasts Royal featured prominently in an omnibus review of nature books in the November 22 *Times Literary Supplement*, where an enthusiastic reviewer called Tunnicliffe's illustrations "very striking" and managed to give away the endings of several of the animal tales. He rightly reserved the highest praise for the Indian stories: "The best things in the book are four Indian episodes concerned with one Hussein, ex-Mahout and elephant-thief, snake-charmer and swindling discoverer of cobras with which he had 'salted' likely bungalows with the aid of the bribed staff. These are very well told, and have every appearance of truth to fact."

This encouraged the nineteen-year-old, who had by no means exhausted his enthusiasm for India.

5

Catching Lightning in a Jar
1934–1939

The day France fell, I was cycling back from T. Wells,
possessed by a deep anger. As I came near Crowborough, the
whole earth seemed spread out at the foot of the hill, bathed in
clear warm sun, green and gold as far as one could see. The
scent of clover was strong from the quiet fields, and the
distances were tranquil blue. England, spread out fair before
the desperate new peril, infused even my cowardly, flinching
heart so that then and now I still feel I could actually, without
hesitation, take part gladly in slaughter and violence against
anyone setting foot on these shores.

—Joan Russ, letter to Barney Russ, August 30, 1941

Four rocky years passed before Patrick's zeal for India led to a
breakthrough novel. In the meantime, life intervened in its own
mysterious way. The worldwide depression caused varying degrees
of desperation in the Russ family. Mike and Barney tried and failed at
tobacco farming in northeast Australia. Barney moved into a shack by himself on the banks of the Barron River, where he attempted to raise corn.
One day in 1934 a cyclone struck. Violent rains followed, and the river
flooded. Clinging to his horse and praying, Barney nearly drowned while
crossing through a torrent of logs and bloated animal carcasses to safety. A
search party of neighbors found him asleep on the opposite bank, where
he had collapsed after the struggle.

In 1933, prospects for European peace had abruptly deteriorated.
Hitler became chancellor of Germany, and Hermann Göring, an air
squadron commander who had won highest honors in World War I, was
made head of Germany's Air Ministry. Germany immediately quit both
the League of Nations and the Disarmament Conference. England turned

a wary eye toward the Continent. Meanwhile, Charles Russ, who had developed a knack for being out of step with the world, worked on improving the teakettle. In January 1934, he submitted to the patent office seven pages of descriptions and diagrams of his improved pot. Instead of whistling to indicate boiling water, the pot's top rattled.

That Patrick had already grown skeptical of his father's inventions is doubtful, and that he thought them humorous is unlikely. But later he certainly came to understand the sad but laughable irony in the fact that his intelligent, creative, and determined father continued to pour his efforts into a series of useless inventions and impractical medical treatments, supported by a series of books, instead of into finding a practical method of providing for the well-being of his family. Arcane books, nonfunctional machines, and ridiculous inventions would litter the Aubrey-Maturin series. Maturin himself is the author of *Tar-Water Reconsidered*. In one novel, Aubrey finds himself in command of an unnavigable experimental ship having two bows and no stern. In another, a Papin's Digester, a pressure cooker designed to soften bones for stock, explodes, sounding "like the firing of a twelve-pounder" and blasting pudding all over the cook and his mates.

With his royalty advance for *Beasts Royal*, Patrick bought himself and Joan tickets to a benefit concert at the Royal Albert Hall. Sir Henry Wood conducted the Royal Amateur Orchestral Society, and Eva Turner, Conchita Supervia, and Richard Tauber sang. The famous Austrian tenor, who, as one story has it, missed his debut at the large hall out of sheer panic at the sight of it, did not disappoint on this night. King George V, Queen Mary, and Princess Mary were also there to enjoy Tauber's selection of Wagner, Puccini, and songs from the Viennese musical comedies of Franz Lehar. Wood capped the evening with his rousing "Fantasia of British Sea Songs." For the moment, despite their inescapable poverty, the two young Russes basked in England's greater glory.

His writing success not being lucrative enough, Patrick searched for a sustainable way to earn a living. With the economy in shambles and the new national focus on preparing for the German threat, it is not surprising that he set his sights on military service. Although he later admitted to having been rejected by the navy, he would never talk about his brief and unsuccessful stint in the Royal Air Force. What he did disclose was that despite his health woes, he had long hoped to attend Dartmouth, the Royal Naval College, on the coast of Devon. He applied but was rejected, as he later told the *Financial Times*, because "I had not enough teeth, an inferior heart, rotten spine and brain not much cop."

In 1934, the Royal Air Force (RAF) had nothing like the prestige of the long venerated Royal Navy. The RAF had been created in 1918, when the army's Royal Flying Corps and the Royal Naval Air Force combined, and the recently formed Air Ministry took control of the new branch of service. But this was to be a watershed year for the fledgling air force. It was now clear that Germany, with the help of Russia, was surreptitiously building a formidable air force. On July 19, Britain announced plans to expand the RAF by forty-one squadrons to meet this growing threat.

New planes required new pilots. Patrick applied to become a pilot officer. He was accepted, and on September 14, he entered the Royal Air Force, mustering with the other trainees at Uxbridge RAF depot, where they were issued uniforms with smart four-button, four-pocket jackets, belted at the waist, and flat-brimmed hats with the crown-over-eagle RAF insignia. The trainees were told what their table manners would be and whom to salute.

After two weeks, Acting Pilot Officer Russ was sent to Sealand, an RAF base northwest of Chester on the estuary of the River Dee, where the weeding out began. Of the thirty-two officers and ten airmen in the twenty-seventh course at No. 5 Flying Training School (FTS), twenty-seven of the former and nine of the latter completed it. Patrick was not one of them, which the literary world can be thankful for. A third of those who did graduate were killed in World War II.

With its red brick buildings, grass landing strips, rows of biplanes, and windowed, sliding steel-door World War I hangars, Sealand made an impressive boot camp. Officers ate in the Virginia creeper–covered mess hall six nights a week, one night in full mess dress, including a short, RAF-blue monkey jacket, tight trousers, and leather Wellington boots, and another in dinner jacket and black tie. Officers had their own rooms, and every three shared a batman, a civilian servant who made their beds, brought them tea in the morning, polished their shoes, and did their laundry. Adding to the romance of Sealand, flights took off over wild marshes and mudflats, giving way to a view of the coast of north Wales and the five distant peaks of Snowdonia, whose ragged beauty later inspired Patrick to try living there.

The training program lasted two semesters over the course of a year, with a junior (first semester) class and a senior (second semester) class.

Discipline was strict. The junior trainees, known as Sprogs, rose at 7 A.M. to prepare for flight training, followed by classroom training in the afternoon, with the schedule reversing on alternate days. During the first three months, Sprogs flew two-seater Avro Tutor biplanes. These light twenty-six-foot-long planes, with open cockpits, stood nine and a half feet off the ground and had wingspans of thirty-four feet. They could reach a top speed of 122 miles per hour. At first a Sprog sat in the fore cockpit, while an instructor sergeant, in the rear, took off and gave orders to the trainee through a gosport. This setup was not foolproof, and minor mishaps were not uncommon. When one trainee got lost with his instructor, they tried to navigate home via the railway lines but failed. Finally, they stopped in a field and asked directions.

After ten hours of flying time, achieved in the first few weeks of the course, Sprogs received their wings, allowing them to fly without an instructor. This increased the opportunity for folly. One advanced trainee, preparing for the Empire Air Day show, practiced a maneuver whereby he was supposed to skip his Avro on the runway and leapfrog another Avro, but he did not quite make it. Instead, he bowled over another trainee and an instructor who were leaning against the stationary plane. The two airmen, stunned though not seriously hurt, dusted themselves off and continued their conversation. Trainees also competed in blind flying, in which a hood was placed over their windshields, and they had to navigate a triangular course by instruments alone.

None of these maneuvers, however, was as daring as the stunt that classmates expected of one another. This foolhardy exhibition required two men to change seats while in flight. To do this, they left their cockpits simultaneously, stepped out onto opposite wings, and climbed into the other's seat. Meanwhile, the control column (known as "the stick") was held with an outstretched hand, and the rudder bar control, in the bottom of the cockpit, was briefly left unmanned.

Instructors trained Sprogs in the use of Lewis machine guns (a rear gunner's weapon), Lee Enfield .303 rifles, and Browning automatic pistols, which might have been the genesis of Patrick's love of shooting. As in all branches of the service, a certain amount of bravado and aggression was tolerated, even smiled upon. The school held boxing and rugby matches in which the airmen proved their grit. These were undoubtedly tough on Patrick, who was among the smallest in his class and physically weak, but at least boxing and rugby had rules. The harshest roughhousing took place after hours. Trainees such as Paddy Cole, a popular Irishman from a good family in Sligo, a jokester and a storyteller, had no problems. But a quiet or loner Sprog such as Patrick had to be constantly on his guard. At least one unpopular classmate had his room blasted with fire extinguishers. However, no one was immune from the inter-class brawls. In the middle of the night, the seniors often raided the juniors' quarters for wrestling and fist-fighting, which sometimes got out of hand. One trainee walloped another with a golf club, sending the victim to the hospital.

After a total of sixty air hours and the performance of certain pre-scribed manuevers in the Avro, a trainee passed on to the next phase of flight training in the bigger, faster Armstrong Atlas bomber and Bristol Bulldog fighter planes, where the stakes and risks rose considerably. On October 26, a chilling accident occurred among the senior class at No. 5 FTS. Acting Pilot Officer Eric Hall took off alone in an Armstrong Atlas plane on a training flight from Sealand. Attempting to land on an official airstrip about four miles away in Hawarden, Flintshire, he crashed and was killed.

Somehow during his first semester at FTS, either Patrick did not make the grade, or he discovered that he simply was not cut out for the air force. The injured and the sick who could not finish the course for that reason were usually simply moved back a class, losing seniority but continuing on. The most likely reason for being bounced from RAF pilot training was for failing the flying course, most often the result of insufficient hand-eye coordination. This seems probable in Patrick's case since Barney Russ later wrote in a letter that he thought Patrick had left the air force after "he had smashed a couple of aeroplanes in the course of his training." Whatever the reason, Acting Pilot Officer Patrick Russ's commission was terminated on the first of December.*

In late 1934, twenty-year-old Welsh poet Dylan Thomas moved to London. While quaffing beer in pubs, he filled exercise books with poetry, and when there was an audience, he practiced his wit and mimicry by the tap. Neither a university man from a wealthy family nor a radical as it was fashionable to be among his contemporary poets, Thomas liked to

---

*The following entry appeared in the *London Gazette* on December 4, 1934: "Royal Air Force: The short service commissions of the undermentioned Acting Pilot Officers in probation are terminated on cessation of duty—29th November 1934: William Ocock Pridham, Douglas George Scott; 1st December 1934: Basil Stuart Francis, Richard Patrick Russ, Thomas Brisbane Yule."

read detective stories, play a pub game called shove-ha'penny, and chase women. He loathed academicians and avoided discussions of art and literature. Still, he caught the attention of the literary establishment, including Herbert Read, Edith Sitwell, Stephen Spender, and Lawrence Durrell.

Thomas was a unique literary force operating on his own deep-seated principles. He was an outsider who mixed with the establishment, although often reluctantly and while drinking self-destructively. Patrick, back in London after his failed RAF stint, was an outsider who did not mix. Although he was intellectual and well-read, he did not have old-boy connections, literary clout, or Thomas's magnetism. However, their paths did cross. Many years later Patrick recalled a conversation with Thomas about the creative process. Thomas had described it as a waking dream, a metaphor that never suited Patrick, though he was hard-pressed to find one that did. He also made the acquaintance of one of Thomas's court of admiring women. Her name was Elizabeth Jones, and she was an independent young Welsh girl with a résumé of personal hardship that surpassed even Patrick's.

Elizabeth was an orphan from the village of Penycae Rhosllaner-chrugog in northeast Wales. Her mother had been killed, probably by influenza, in 1914, when Elizabeth was just three. Her father—a clay miner—died four years later. The girl and her three brothers were taken in by their aunts and uncles. Though she spoke little English, Elizabeth, while still a teenager, decided to attempt to escape the never-ending cycle of poverty in northeast Wales. She made her way down to London, where she found work as a domestic in the home of an American inventor named Converse.

She soon found the fast set in Chelsea, where Thomas was drinking himself green in hangouts like Finches and the Goat in Boots. It was a lively, loose atmosphere, and although Elizabeth was not well educated, her vivacity and charm in addition to her fresh good looks made her popular.

Both Thomas and Patrick might have briefly flirted with Marxism, the young intellect's credo of the day. But Thomas was a hedonist at heart, preferring worldly pleasures to polemics. Patrick, who would later tell one journalist that if he "hadn't been Catholic, [he] would surely have been a Communist in the thirties, believing the world could be changed," changed his own world, instead, by falling in love with Jones, a five-foot-tall brunette, who was devoted to him. While Patrick might not have been Catholic at the time, he did have a fertile imagination.

In 1935 Patrick, whose byline now read "R. P. Russ," published stories in both of Strang's annuals. To the *Oxford Annual for Scouts*, he delivered "The Snow Leopard," a spare hunting vignette set in the Himalayas of Nepal, in which the son of a shikari (a professional big game hunter) proves himself by killing a leopard with his knife, saving the life of a Gurkha officer, an Englishman who comes to the Himalayas each year to hunt with the boy's father. In this story, Patrick displayed two writing characteristics that would serve him well throughout his career. As he would later do so effectively in his Aubrey-Maturin novels, he peppered the story with undefined arcane lingo: "shikar" (hunting), "kukri" (a curved knife used by Gurkhas), "spoor" (a track or droppings). He trusted the power and the poetry of words. Standing alone, they accomplished more, even if only partially understood, than they would with prosaic definitions.

He also revealed for the first time his facility for creating a bond between two human characters. Just before the climax, in which the boy, Dhorgoshi, saves the Gurkha officer (Major Chetwynd), Chetwynd shows his respect for the boy, who like most boys is struggling with his sense of self-worth. As the party scales a sheer rock face in pursuit of a trophy ibex, Dhorgoshi, finding no foothold, verges on panic and slips. Chetwynd reaches up and guides his foot to a ledge. Afterward Chetwynd tells the boy's father that he almost had to turn back himself. Patrick wrote, "Dhorgoshi loved him for not mentioning that missing foothold, and for acknowledging that it was a stiff climb. He tried to look unconcerned, but he felt his heart still hammering." Patrick then coolly delivered the story's climax so that it resonated profoundly but avoided melodrama.

In "Cheetah," which ran in the *Oxford Annual for Boys*, Patrick wrote another episode about Hussein and continued to examine the mysteries and nuances of Indian storytelling, or at least the British version of it. For the first time, he wrote of opium addiction, a subject that would long fascinate him. Patrick suffused the tale, in which he portrays an India where one survives by one's wits and accepts what cannot be controlled, with a subtle, dry humor.

"Cheetah" is a more complex story than "The Snow Leopard." Hired to care for Shaitan, one of the hunting cheetahs of a raja, a task for which he has no training and no lineage, Hussein is ostracized by the other trainers. However, the resourceful mahout learns that an elderly trainer named Yussuf has a weakness for opium and that one of his wives denies him the means to buy it. Hussein supplies Yussuf with opium in exchange for the secrets of cheetah handling. Patrick took pains not to moralize, passing no overt judgments on this relationship or on Yussuf's opium use. "The Prophet never forbade its use," reasons the old man, who, like Hussein, is a Muhammadan in the midst of Hindus, "he only referred to intoxicating liquors."

In the second part of the story, Hussein handles Shaitan in a staged hunt for gazelles in front of the raja. Suddenly a wild leopard appears and begins killing the trained cheetahs who are stalking the gazelles. In the resulting melee, the leopard knocks Yussuf down. Hussein falls on the beast and tries to choke him. Finally, the raja shoots and kills the leopard and is greatly pleased with himself. Yussuf makes Hussein his blood brother for coming to his rescue, and the raja rewards him for his bravery by tossing him a gold and ruby ring and ordering the treasurer to fill his mouth with gold coins. In a final twist, when Hussein discovers that the treasurer has substituted copper coins for gold, he humbly and wisely remains silent, satisfied in a small victory: one gold mohur is hiding among the copper.

In 1936, Patrick published a watershed story in the twenty-ninth edition of the *Oxford Annual for Boys*. In the past, he had written about animals, about men and animals, and about men on unequal terms, such as the young Hussein and the elder Yussuf. For the first time, in "Noughts and Crosses," he introduced two characters on relatively even footing. Sullivan, a tall, thoughtful Irishman, and Ross, a tough, red-bearded Scot, are, despite their personality differences, bound by friendship, though at first it is not apparent.

In the smoking room of a men's club, Sullivan, in Marlowesque fashion, narrates a sea tale of the Great Barrier Reef, in which Ross's contrariness leads to the sinking of their boat and the death of their crew. Following a fierce storm, the duo's whaler is besieged by sharks, which are agitated by the smell of a zinc tank on board that has been used to extract oil from sharks' livers. The sharks ram the whaler and batter it with their powerful tails. Despite the pleas of his mates, Ross insists on continuing to fish. The sharks sink the whaler and eat the mates. Sullivan and Ross escape by climbing into the foul tank. Adrift, they play tic-tac-toe ("noughts and crosses") as they await rescue or death.

The tale seems fairly straightforward, but Patrick again threw in a clever plot twist. After Sullivan finishes his tale and gets up to leave, Ross—who unbeknownst to the others has been sitting with them in the smoking room all along—reveals himself and confirms the story's truth. The reader is compelled to reconsider the two men and their relationship in light of the fact that the tale was told in front of Ross, not in his absence. The implications are entirely different, and the story becomes ingeniously resonant. Four decades later, Patrick told a reporter, "The essence of my books is about human relationships and how people treat one another." The same was true of his stories written long before.

Patrick enjoyed writing the story, and it showed. He found both comfort and creative power in his new characters Sullivan and Ross, so much so that, in 1954, then writing as Patrick O'Brian, he published a novel recounting an elaborate Eastern adventure involving the two, along with a third character, an orphaned boy. It would be Patrick's only obvious crossover writing, where O'Brian continued Russ's work.

In 1935 Patrick turned twenty-one. Although he wrote for youth magazines, he was no longer a youth himself. There is little documentary evidence of events during this part of his life. It is impossible to verify his claims to have continued his quirky education at Oxford and the Sorbonne, concentrating on the natural sciences, the classics, and philosophy. Neither school has any record of his attendance. Lending further doubt is the fact that his older siblings, after Godfrey, had been unable to afford a higher education.

Patrick later said that he researched at the British Museum and other London libraries, at the Bodleian in Oxford, the Bibliothèque Nationale in Paris, and the Vatican in Rome. He clearly acquired valuable research skills; very likely he did come by them sitting in Karl Marx's chair beneath the great dome in the British Library and combing the stacks in Paris. He apparently pursued an interest in St. Isidore of Seville (d. 636) and the Western bestiary, which makes sense given his abiding interest in the animal kingdom. Patrick certainly had a thirst for knowledge. Although it is hard to say how he might have afforded to work on such an unprofitable project in these hard times, he did reveal a considerable familiarity with bestiaries to his friend Walter Greenway during the war.

The lovably pale boy with a large vocabulary was now a slim, handsome man with the last vestiges of a cherubic face. In Chelsea, his love for Elizabeth Jones continued to blossom. Though poorly educated herself, she recognized brilliance in Patrick's demanding conversation. He was serious, resolute. Though physically gentle, he could be petulant. He was an underdog, but so was she. She found herself believing in his determination, and she knew she had found someone who needed to be cared for. He reciprocated, writing her affectionate letters—and sometimes poetry—when he left town to visit Charles and Zoe.

One thing led to another, and Patrick and Elizabeth moved in together at flat no. 2A on tree-lined Oakley Street, running between the King's Road and Albert Bridge in Chelsea, three doors down from where Antarctic explorer Robert Falcon Scott had lived. Perhaps part of what united the two was the discovery that they had in common traumatic childhoods. For Patrick, there was also the appeal of an older woman. Elizabeth was four years more experienced, and they were young enough for that to mean something. With friends José Birt and Edward H. Taaffe witnessing, the two tied the knot on February 27, 1936, at the Chelsea register office.

The marriage could not have pleased Patrick's class-conscious, financially struggling parents. They would certainly be withering in their disapproval of Joan's marriage to a Birmingham mechanic during the war. Two months after Patrick's marriage, Nora stunned the family as well, entering the Roman Catholic convent Franciscan Sisters of Mill Hill. After a trial period, on November 29, 1936, she was admitted as a novice.

Patrick and Elizabeth's marriage would be anything but conventional. Patrick was still too immature for the serious commitment of marriage, let alone children. The two soon moved into another Chelsea flat, at 24 Gertrude Street, and Elizabeth, whom Patrick often called "Cariad," which is Welsh for darling, became pregnant. On February 2, 1937, at St. Mary Abbots Hospital in Kensington, she gave birth to a baby boy. They named him Richard Francis Tudor; Richard after his father, Francis for the couple's good friend Francis Cox, a Chelsea painter, and, because of Elizabeth's pride in her Welsh heritage, Tudor for the royal house of Henry VIII and Elizabeth I, which was Welsh in origin. His mother called him "Ricky."

With a family to support, Patrick took a job with the left-leaning Workers Travel Association, a vacation packager with a youth focus, that required him to spend the summer at a small hotel in Locarno, a lakeside tourist resort in Italian-speaking south-central Switzerland. He greeted the groups of British tourists at the train station, escorted them to the Hotel Quisisana, where he also stayed, arranging day trips and handling complaints and emergencies, until he saw them off again at the end of their stay and greeted the next group.

It was a strange situation for a recently married man with a baby at home to place himself in, a situation rife with potential. And this was especially true for Patrick, a handsome and charming romantic. He soon found himself infatuated with a pair of sisters.

While other girls, almost always escorted by their mothers, stepped off the overnight train with their noses freshly powdered and a new coat of lipstick glistening, Beryl and Joan Ainsworth, twenty-one and eighteen years old respectively, dismounted with sleep still in their eyes.* Patrick, not cut from the usual mold himself, recognized kindred spirits—who happened not to be chaperoned.

The hotel was small. Patrick's room was just several doors down from the sisters', and the three saw each other frequently. Beryl, a London secretary, was pretty but pining over a boyfriend who was driving his parents around Europe that summer. Patrick paid special attention to Joan, a perky graduate of an arty private school, who was fond of the theater and had a job selling theater tickets in London. She was fair-skinned, shapely, and had dark curly hair.

Patrick made for a bright and convincing tour guide, taking the group to see the Milan Cathedral and the Madonna del Sasso, a spectacular hilltop church in nearby Orta, among other places. Sometimes they traveled by bus and other times they puttered across Lake Maggiore by steamboat. On one hot outing he provided the Ainsworths with wine from a wineskin he carried with him. "Do you like it?" he asked.

"No," they replied, wincing at the sour-tasting local red.

"Well, I only paid fourpence for it," he laughed, shrugging.

Although he was supposed to be tending to the entire group, wherever they went he inevitably gravitated to the sisters and they to him. He told them that he was Irish, and, according to Beryl, that he had been an RAF pilot until an accident with a propeller had sent him to the hospital, where, he said, the doctors had put a steel plate in his head.† He also told them that he was an artist and that he had written a book of stories called *Beasts*

---

* I corresponded with Joan and interviewed both sisters in April 2000.

† While there is no evidence to support this claim, it seems that some accident did occur during Patrick's RAF training (he would complain of a bad back), and readers of the Aubrey-Maturin novels will certainly wonder if it is just a coincidence that Stephen Maturin most ingratiates himself with his shipmates by his remarkable ability to save lives by trepanning the skull.

Royal. He raved about James Joyce, and when Joan confessed that she had
not read him, he playfully chastised her, saying that in that case she had not
been educated at all.

He won them over with his animated, unreserved conversation and his
occasional irreverence. He had something of a superior air, they thought,
but, unlike the public school boys they were used to, he was offbeat and
inflamed with ideas. As he got to know them better, he took notice of their
looks and teased them with arch comments. "You know, Beryl, you would
look good in black," he suddenly observed one day, "but not until you are
thirty." Another time he asked her if he could make a mask of her face and
seemed annoyed when she told him no.

In their spare time, the threesome often went to the Lido, a manmade
sand beach with umbrellas and chairs. While Beryl composed forlorn love
letters to her boyfriend, Patrick and Joan lazed on the beach together,
smoking cigarettes, and both being strong swimmers, raced each other out
to the raft on the lake, where they lay side by side chatting and gazing at
the distant snow-capped mountains. Patrick coyly told Joan, who had
never been in love before, that her decadent appearance when she stepped
off the train had captured him immediately. Joan was receptive to her
dark-browed, urbane new friend, even when he confided in her the shocking news that he had a wife at home. According to Joan, he said he had
been tricked into marrying when Elizabeth falsely claimed to be pregnant.

Beryl, who was supposed to be looking after her younger sister, did not
realize just how intense the relationship had grown, and Joan was careful
to keep it that way. At night after Beryl went to sleep, she crept out of her
twin bed and down the hall to Patrick's room.

After two passionate weeks, Joan had to return to London. Patrick had
warned her that their relationship must die on the vine. But they had fallen
in love, and neither was happy to end the affair. They carried on by mail,
Patrick exercising his biting humor when he told her that "a fresh batch of
erect apes" had arrived, and his tenderness when he sent her a sonnet
devoted to her eyebrows. Joan's illicit telephone calls courtesy of her
employer kept the flame lit the rest of the summer.

But when Patrick returned to England and his family in the fall, they
saw each other just two more times, once to see the Irish playwright Denis
Johnston's *The Moon in the Yellow River*, and another time for dinner at
The Bag of Nails, a Chelsea pub, where they said farewell forever.

During this time Patrick continued to write stories and work on a novel set in India, which Kaberry, his Oxford University Press editor, had encouraged him to write on the basis of his Hussein stories. This work was highly disconnected from the life he was leading, demonstrating again just how thoroughly he could escape reality. In "Two's Company," which ran in the 1937 *Oxford Annual for Boys*, Patrick once again wrote a boy's story with greater depth than first meets the eye. This tale stranded Ross, the wide-jawed Lowland Scot, and Sullivan, the garrulous Irishman, in a northern seas lighthouse so remote that even their wireless is useless. During their first three-month tour of duty in the tower above a dangerous reef, the carcass of an immense whale lodges against the lighthouse in a storm. With no hope of removing the mass of rotting blubber, they find themselves at the epicenter of a seabird and shark feeding frenzy, not to mention an atrocious stench.

Finally, they beg some explosives off the destroyer delivering them supplies, and they blow up the carcass. They sign up for another three months in the lighthouse, but now they find the isolation has seriously strained their friendship. As they try to ignore each other, Sullivan turns to his violin and pet sea eagle, while Ross plays a bagpipe and chats with his pet skua. The two train their tamed birds of prey to hunt from their arms, but when the birds attack each other over a herring, the men are destined to come to blows. That evening bitter words at supper lead to a fight. Fists fly until Ross is knocked senseless. No scene of reconciliation takes place. But none is necessary. The violence clears the air like a summer storm.

In "Two's Company," while the setting and action satisfy the reader on a visceral level, another story—the personal relationship—plays out on a deeper plane. One feeds off the other, but ultimately the latter adds profundity to an otherwise innocent yarn. Patrick used this method again and again, as in his 1938 odyssey, "One Arctic Summer," also published in the *Oxford Annual for Boys*. Later, in the Aubrey-Maturin novels, he would enchant the reader with sailing adventures, secret service intrigues, and naval battles, all the while carefully exploring and commenting on the nature of human relationships.

In "One Arctic Summer," an unnamed narrator, a surgeon, searches the Arctic for his plane-wrecked friend, Wetherill. The search stalls at the border between Christian-controlled Lapland and the land of the savage, pagan nomads to the north when the hired Lapps refuse to travel farther. But the surgeon is aided by the timely arrival of Father Sergei, a missionary priest of the Holy Russian Church. An expert linguist with stature among the Christian Lapps, Sergei stands out in the entire Patrick Russ/O'Brian oeuvre as most nearly resembling a perfect man. This is all the more remarkable because in his early writing Patrick rarely attributed positive qualities to a priest of any sort.

In describing Sergei, the narrator says:

> It sounds most unpleasant, but he was easily the best man I have ever known, and I have met archbishops and cardinals: there was nothing obviously religious about him, he never asked any one whether he was saved, or anything remotely resembling it, and he had been known to knock the heads of two impudent Lapps together and kick them each nearly four feet out of his tent, but he also has a way of doing very decent things, and expecting no thanks for them. . . . I think he must have been the nearest approach to the more robust kind of medieval saint that one could find. (P. 92)

Sergei volunteers to accompany the narrator, and his knowledge of the dialects allows them to gather clues. After many days of wearisome marches, they join a group of Eskimo shamans wearing fox skulls and animal bones, who, unbeknownst to the narrator, are traveling north to determine the fate of his injured, captive friend, Wetherill.

At the meeting place, the shamans and their tribesmen, dancing and howling wickedly, surround the search party. While the surgeon fingers his gun, Sergei begins to laugh raucously. The more the shamans dance, the louder he laughs, holding his sides, spilling tears. Exasperated, the three chief shamans attack, snapping their teeth like wild animals. The priest cocks his fist, and with three swift punches lays them out. He then barks out orders to the shamans with such authority that they obey him immediately.

United with Wetherill, the surgeon amputates his friend's arm to save his life. Afterward, they head south together. Sergei remains with the shamans to teach them Christianity. The story could not make plainer the author's notions of the highest qualities a man can have: chief among them, intelligence, civility, quiet piety, loyalty, competence, and courage, virtues likewise extolled in the Aubrey-Maturin novels.

In addition to writing these stories, Patrick wove his Indian tales into a meandering novel called *Hussein: An Entertainment*. One review later claimed that he had been tutored by "Arabian" storytellers. Perhaps the reviewer was referring to Uncle Emil, who had worked as a tailor in India until he won the Calcutta Sweep in 1920. He pocketed £15,800 and hied it back to England, where he liked to swim in the sea and hold court in the pubs. He was also known to spin a yarn or two. Emil lost his fortune almost as quickly as he made it. According to Major H. Hobbs, who wrote *The Romance of the Calcutta Sweep*: "In 1927 the news was broadcasted through the British Empire, possibly right around the world that he, a prize winner in the Derby Sweep, had made his appearance in the Canterbury Bankruptcy Court, where it was stated that he had been living at the rate of £2,000 a year."

Kipling's "great, gray, formless India," as seen in *Kim*, certainly influenced Patrick. But Hussein, being entirely Indian, allowed for even deeper immersion into the culture than did Kipling's half-Irish Kim. Hussein falls in love with a beauty named Sashiya, murders his evil-spirited rival, and thus embroils himself in a vendetta with the dead man's family. As a result, the handsome clean-cut youth with a high-bridged nose is destined to roam India, surviving by his wits.

Like Kim, Hussein is unsuspectingly drawn into what Kipling called "the Great Game that never ceases day and night throughout India" (*Kim*, p. 158). "There is an incidental Secret Service background, which Mr. Russ is too wise to labour in detail," wrote Professor L. F. Rushbrook in his review of *Hussein* in the *South Asian Review*. "Perhaps he has learned wisdom from the single artistic fault in the construction of *Kim*. However this may be, Hussein really knows very little indeed of the inner meaning of what he is doing—which is exactly as it should be in real life!"

As Kipling wrote of colonial India in *Kim*, "This is a world of danger to honest men" (p. 130). Patrick's India, too, is an ethical morass. The good Hussein will win at all costs. Even murder is justified if the murderee is villainous enough and the act is committed in Hussein's pursuit of Sashiya, who represents his highest ideals. As Patrick cunningly wrote, "Hussein's code was an elastic one, and it would stretch surprisingly on occasion; but he did not like making a cuckold of a man whose salt he had eaten, when he was not in love with the woman" (p. 228). Hussein is faithful to Sashiya, but as Patrick put it, "like most men, faithful in his own way" (p. 212).

Patrick had already arrived at a technique that would hallmark the Aubrey-Maturin novels, examining humanity through the friendship of two men. Such relationships provided some of his most humorous and touching passages. One scene in *Hussein* (originally in the story "Cheetah") particularly stands out. In it, Hussein provides the old man

Yussuf with opium pills in return for instruction on training cheetahs. Because of certain constraints and mutual suspicion, the transaction plays out in a wonderful dance. First Hussein deliberately spills opium pills from a brass box in front of Yussuf, making it appear as if it were an accident. Yussuf later tells Hussein he has a beautiful cheetah collar that he no longer needs, making as if he wishes to sell it to Hussein. Hussein confesses that he cannot afford it. Yussuf, praising his modesty, offers to give it to him, but then appraising it, changes his mind: although the collar has some "commercial value" (p. 214), he says, it is not a worthy gift for one so excellent as Hussein. Hussein insists, "Assuredly it would be a royal gift" (p. 214). But, Yussuf counters, it is still unworthy of Hussein. However, he has an idea. To prove the lack of value of the collar, he will trade it for the tacky brass box that Hussein earlier dropped. Hussein agrees, but first he extracts the pills.

Patrick stretched the tactical game to maximum effect. Eventually both characters get what they are after. This scene, where the two gain respect for one another in their witty duel, sets the stage for their friendship, which is later forged through an act of self-sacrifice.

The white cobra, first seen in Patrick's earlier story "The White Cobra," also found its way into the novel. Feroze Khan, Hussein's master in the Great Game, tells a variation of the tale in which he steals the snake from a village by seducing the wife of the priest and lying to her about the direction in which he is headed. Patrick no doubt took pleasure in cuckolding the priest, who at the end of the short story mercilessly beats Hussein.

Patrick would say in his foreword to the 1999 reprint editions of *Caesar* and *Hussein* that he expanded the Hussein stories into a larger work while living in Dublin in a Leeson Street boardinghouse "kept by two very kind sisters from Tipperary and inhabited mostly by young men studying at the national university with a few from Trinity." (Since he married Elizabeth in London in February 1936 and Richard was born there in February 1937 and the book was published in April 1938, it is difficult to fit this into the chronology, unless he spent some time there soon after leaving the air force and nearly three years passed between the time he wrote the book and its publication, which is unlikely.) Whether or not he finished the book on a bench in Stephen's Green "with a mixture of triumph and regret," he had, indeed, refined his craft in storytelling. He had experienced the exaltation of writing well, in a groove, where everything felt just right, and this sense of pleasure, unachievable by any other means, he never ceased to pursue.

In April 1938, two years after Kipling's death, Oxford University Press published *Hussein: An Entertainment*, with a Welsh dedication reading "I fy ngwraig annwyl/a fy mab bychan," "To my dear wife/and my small son." At 2,965 copies, the print run was modest, but this was the first work of contemporary fiction ever published by the prestigious press, a coup that was not lost on the author. Fortunately for Patrick, the book's reputation did not depend on the number of copies printed but on its critical reception. With the magic of a good storyteller around a campfire at night, he had achieved an almost hypnotic effect. Though reverential of *Kim*, Professor Rushbrook could not resist Patrick's spell. "Such a story as this is full of traps for an author who does not know Indian life like the palm of his hand," wrote the professor. "Mr. Russ is to be congratulated on escaping all the obvious mistakes and a good many of the more subtle ones. . . . [His] spelling of Indian names suggests that he has picked up his knowledge by ear unsupplemented by eye. But the quality is undeniable."

The *Times Literary Supplement* called an episode in which wild dogs chase Hussein the "best adventure in the book" and noted that there was an underlying humor to the story that the "author scarcely sets himself to develop." The review added that Hussein's "methods of self-help would scarcely have commanded the approval of Mr. Samuel Smiles." (Smiles, a Victorian, wrote moralizing books such as *Self Help* and *Thrift*.) As evidence, the review pointed out that Hussein "stole the faithful elephant, . . . had a rival for the hand of Sashiya done to death by the arts of a dreadful fakir, . . . [and] finally won through to fame and fortune by murdering the Rajah of Kapilavatthu and stealing the Rajah's money and jewels." The reviewer failed to qualify this by mentioning that, within the context, Hussein in most cases acted justly. The critique was most notable for the fact that this important literary newspaper noticed the book at all.

In the United States, *Hussein* made a much bigger splash. On May 8, both the *New York Times Book Review* and *New York Herald Tribune* extolled the novel. Both reviewers seemed swept away by the author's control of the beguiling genre, his effortless storytelling, his ability to transfix the reader in this mysterious Eastern adventure. In the *Times*, Percy Hutchison wrote:

> If one has no feeling for Kipling's animal stories, and does not enjoy the bloody and sugared picaresque Arabian tales we

devoured so avidly in our childhood *Hussein* is to be passed by. But if a better elephant story has been written between "My Lord the Elephant" and *Hussein* we have had the misfortune to miss it. Moreover, Patrick Russ, who studied his craft with Arabian story-tellers, has mastered the art of spinning an Oriental yarn in that Oriental manner so different from the Occidental that few have mastered it. *Hussein* is gorgeous entertainment not only in the story which it unfolds but also in the manner of the telling.

In his review in the *New York Herald Tribune*, Thomas Sugrue, not to be outdone, was moved to eloquence:

> Young Patrick Russ, the author of *Hussein*, has said to himself, "Let's make an Arabian Nights story, keep the plot structure and sequence, but rewrite it as a modern, realistic novel." He probably didn't quite know what was going to happen when he began. He was like an alchemist, mixing things on chance: Indian politics, fakirs, the lovely maiden in the tower, the elephant who loves and understands, the curse that kills, the bag of gold, the misfortunes sowed by fates, the rescue of the lovely maiden from the tower, and all the minor ingredients that go to make up the old and the new in the East. The result, when he saw it, must have been something of a surprise, for the experiment turned out as fortunately as Ben Franklin's attempt to catch lightning in a jar. The story of Hussein is a swift-moving, well written account of events so fantastic that moonshine was certainly their mother. As the pages move by things become slightly plausible, then credible, then entirely believable. Finally they are living, factual events, and Hussein, in quest of his Sashiya, is a hero as alive and as human as Tom Jones seeking his Sophia.

In the July 9 *Saturday Review of Literature*, a somewhat more ambivalent reviewer nonetheless added to the chorus of American praise for *Hussein*: "This medley of Eastern folk-tales, assembled in the form of a novel ... resembles the entertainment provided by those professional tellers of tales who have, since before the time of Homer, perpetuated the legends of their people for the price of their daily bread. The adventures are set in that pristine world of fiction where magic joins with realism. . . . excellent entertainment for a thousand and second Arabian Night."

Perhaps *Hussein*'s subdued reception in England owed more to the political climate than to the book's lack of merit or the nation's penchant for understatement. The stench of genocide was already wafting from the Continent, as is apparent in Wilfrid Gibson's April 22 *Manchester Guardian* review: "It is a good yarn, rather in the nature of a boys' story, but with more of a love interest than the puerile are apt to find palatable. It is sufficiently diverting, and I found it a pleasantly relaxing distraction from the stress of contemplating the menace of impending catastrophe which threatens to involve all us poor helpless men of goodwill." The same edition of the *Guardian* reported the increasing persecution of Jews in Danzig and the Gestapo's robbery and deportation of Jews in Austria.

Hitler's army had occupied Austria in March. While Prime Minister Neville Chamberlain practiced appeasement, Britain prepared for war.

In the spring of 1938, Elizabeth Russ became pregnant again. But if the birth of Richard had brought the joy every new parent feels, then the birth of this child would bring the weight of the world crashing down on the young couple. On February 8, 1939, again at St. Mary Abbots Hospital, Elizabeth bore a daughter, whom the couple named Jane Elizabeth Campaspe Tudor. The unusual name "Campaspe" came from a Theban captive of Alexander the Great, whom Alexander loved for her beauty and freed, but then lost to the painter Apelles, with whom she fell in love while sitting for a portrait. Her story—recorded in the first century by Pliny in *Natural History* (XXXV, 36) and retold in John Lyly's play *Alexander and Campaspe* in 1584—delighted Patrick, who almost certainly experimented as a visual artist.

Sadly, the daughter named for a famous love story was born with spina bifida, a disease for which there was no effective treatment at the time. Jane, as she was called, would live only three years.

Although the stress of caring for a hopelessly ill child would strain their relationship to the breaking point, something appears already to have been amiss between the Russes, for by the time the birth was registered, just five weeks later, Elizabeth, Richard, and Jane had left Gertrude Street and moved to 301 King's Road, while Patrick remained behind. The two had been rash in choosing each other as partners, the way the young and lonely often are. Whereas Patrick's life centered on literature, writing, and love of language, Elizabeth, though she had plenty of common sense, was nearly illiterate. Her education had been minimal and in Welsh.

Their marriage officially lasted another five years. Following Jane's birth, the entire family moved to the flat countryside of Suffolk, in east-central England. They lived in a terrace house called Gadds Cottage, which shared a chimney with a vacant attached house. Gadds Cottage was remote enough to provide solitude for Patrick's writing and to allow him to hunt for bird and game with a small-bore shotgun. A duck pond on the property was another source of food for the family. The ducks roosted in the backyard beside a tumbledown garden shed, which, following Russ tradition, Patrick named Lazar-house (a hospital for diseased people, especially lepers), for the general squalor and all the feathers shed there.

A loving mother and a capable provider, Elizabeth spoke tenderly in Welsh to her children and her animals (the ducks and a goat kept for milk). She managed the daily tasks of the household, and it was she who tended and disciplined Richard. When he threw the kitchen utensils into the pond or crushed one of the duck eggs they culled for food, she scolded him mildly. But she focused most of her attention on Jane in a vain attempt to prevent the onset of infection, which in those days ultimately killed most children with spina bifida.

Around this time, Patrick's respiratory ailment "returned with greater severity," as he later wrote, and he was left with a lingering weakness. Photographs, however, show him looking fit and healthy, sitting in a hammock with Jane on his lap and Richard by his side, coyly posing like a film noir detective lighting a cigarette, or standing with his single-barrel shotgun before a hunt. That is not to say that he did not experience an occasional flare-up of the tuberculosis or some other problem. He also complained of a bad back. Elizabeth told her son that there were lumps on his father's spine caused by a plane crash at flight school.

In March 1939, as Hitler terrorized eastern Europe and Mussolini invaded Albania, Chamberlain guaranteed British support to Poland, Greece, and Romania, pushing the country to the brink of war. Britain solemnly prepared, conscripting soldiers and erecting radar stations. By August, when Russia and Germany sliced up Poland, London had emptied its hospitals, laid in a supply of quicklime for mass burials, and stockpiled papier-mâché coffins in city swimming pools ostensibly closed for repairs.

On September 1 and 2, the government evacuated a million children and 200,000 women from London, and on Sunday morning, September 3,

Chamberlain announced that the nation was at war. Although the RAF shot down two German bombers over the Firth of Forth in Scotland in October, Britain remained in a state of limbo, at war but not fighting, a period dubbed the Phony War, an uncomfortable time of teeth gnashing, rising prices, disappearing goods, and last hurrahs.

The winter of 1939–40 was bitterly cold, with a North Sea wind that ravaged the Suffolk countryside. The duck pond at Gadds Cottage froze solid, and one day Elizabeth badly burned her hand when she gripped the freezing handle of the outdoor water pump too long. Because of the war, coal and coke were rationed, but at least in the country Patrick could find brush and cut wood for fuel, and he could hunt for food. When snow covered the ground, he buckled on cross-country skis and went in search of hare and partridge.

By Easter 1940, gas rations were exhausted, and private cars essentially ceased to operate. In May, the German army swept into France and the Low Countries, ending the Phony War, and on June 21, France surrendered to Germany. In July, German reichsmarschall Hermann Göring's Luftwaffe began its assault on England's air force in the prelude to Operation Sea Lion, the planned invasion of Britain. Defending England, Spitfires and Hurricanes fought Messerschmitts, just to have a shot at the slower bombers—Heinkels, Dorniers, and Junkers—easier targets but still equipped with deadly machine guns. Growing used to the racket in the sky, the English carried on with life, playing golf and cricket, taking postprandial walks, gardening, and working in the fields.

Charles, Zoe, and Joan now lived in Crowborough, south of London. Joan described to Barney in a letter their first brush with the Battle of Britain, which would determine the fate of Britain and, indeed, of Europe:

> It was about 5:30, a hot afternoon. We'd just finished tea. Mother and Pa were both down the garden. I was messing about in the scullery when a deep droning suddenly began. I went out of the back door, and looking up through the plum trees, saw the planes at a dizzy height looking like minute silver fish twining and swooping round each other. The noise was disproportionately loud, and every now and then a sharp whine would break out and a plane would come down in a low sweep, to climb up again with a roar back to the fight. Ma and Pa came galloping up the garden, and some passers by came in for shelter. The noise grew terrific, and Ma and I crept under the

table! The zooming seemed like bombs, but actually none came down. It was the first of an endless series of dog-fights, which went on, as you know, all that summer.

Deep emotions and atavistic impulses were stirred now, not only by the news from the Continent but by the sight of the enemy overhead. It was a time when an Englishman could no longer take England for granted. It was a time when he had to consider what he would sacrifice for his country.

Whether Patrick walked out of Gadds Cottage after an argument or failed to return after a research trip to London is unknown. What exactly caused him to leave the family in that summer of 1940 is also unclear. An urge to be involved somehow in the war, not to be left out of history while help-lessly caring for a doomed child, might have overwhelmed his sense of responsibility at home. He might have felt guilty about being the father of a crippled child, a stigma in that day since the malady was often attributed to the infirmities or wickedness of the parents. He might have been unable to stand the daily torment of watching and hearing his infant daughter suffer. Elizabeth was emotionally stretched to the limit. Although she was normally happy-go-lucky, her world had changed dramatically. Her focus now was the flaw in her baby's back. The tension exaggerated the person-ality differences between husband and wife and provided many reasons for resenting their current existence. Patrick's creative endeavors suffered.

Regardless of the reason or the method, in a moment of weakness, he left his helpless family, causing permanent bitterness, not only between him and Elizabeth and Richard, but among his disapproving siblings. When they learned what had happened, Patrick's oldest brother, Godfrey, and Connie, his wife, who were living in Thorpe-next-Norwich, drove out to Gadds Cottage and picked up Elizabeth and the two children. Even Richard, just three at the time, sensed the ominous mood and the finality of that ride to Norwich. Connie had packed a bucket of pickled eggs to tide him over, and the sloshing sound they made remained with him as a per-manent reminder of that miserable day.

Not long afterward, Gadds Cottage was plowed under, and its founda-tions were entombed in a sea of asphalt, an airstrip of a U.S. Air Force base. But the Russ familial wound would fester and cause heartache for the rest of their lives.

6

Blood, Sweat, Toil, and Tears

1940–1943

Force, and fraud, are in war the two cardinal virtues.

—Thomas Hobbes, *Leviathan,* 1651

I am bookless, homeless, sans everything but my eyes to weep with. *All* my . . . notes on animals gone—I shall never write that book now.

—Rose Macaulay, letter to Daniel George, May 14, 1941

Before war turned life on its head, Patrick completed one last story. "No Pirates Nowadays," a Ross and Sullivan episode appearing in the 1940 *Oxford Annual for Boys*, was vintage Russ. It introduced Ross's orphaned school-age nephew, Derrick; carried the reader to a remote island, mixing piracy and fur hunting; and turned on a trick of language. The three-part story can be read as a prequel to Patrick's postwar novel *The Road to Samarcand*, which also involves Ross, Sullivan, and Derrick and begins on board the sailing schooner *Wanderer*. But that book would not be published until 1954. In fact, "No Pirates Nowadays" was the last fiction Patrick published for more than a decade, and the last under the name Russ. The following year, both *Chums* and the *Oxford Annual for Boys* published for the last time, and *Hussein* fell out of print.

War organizations soon began to siphon off publishing personnel and resources, not to mention writers. On January 2, 1940, King George VI signed a proclamation extending military service for men up to age twenty-seven. Because of lingering ill health, Patrick was not accepted for active duty. Likewise, his two immediate older brothers struggled to find their niches in the Allied war machine. In 1938, Barney had attempted to enlist in England but was rejected on medical grounds; viper bites and a severed nerve from an accident with a pig-castrating knife had withered his right arm. After moving to Seattle, where he lived with his uncle Cecil Goddard and worked in a sawmill, he attempted to enlist in Vancouver, Canada, but was again rejected. When France fell in June 1940, however, Barney was made a gunner in the Royal Canadian Artillery. The following year, Mike, working as a timber contractor in Queensland, Australia, shaved several years off his age to qualify for the Royal Australian Air Force (RAAF). He reverted from O'Brien to his family name, preferring to fight and die, if necessary, as a Russ.

Victor served in Arabia as an RAF paymaster, and Connie joined the Imperial Military Nursing Service. Later, in Palestine, she met and married Richard Russell, a British policeman, who happened to be her cousin, the son of Ernest Russ, who had changed his name to Russell during the Boer War.

On the night of September 7, 1940, 180 Luftwaffe bombers attacked central London. They dropped more than three hundred tons of high-explosive bombs and thirteen thousand incendiaries, killing and wounding hundreds of civilians, destroying homes and buildings, and snarling roads with wreckage. During the day, three hundred Luftwaffe bombers had struck the city's East End and docklands, flattening blocks of slums and turning ships and warehouses into infernos. In the next week an average of two hundred bombers attacked London each night amid a constant barrage of antiaircraft fire and the sickening wail of air-raid sirens.

The Blitz would last until May 11, 1941. During those eight months, German bombers dropped almost nineteen thousand tons of bombs on London, killing fifteen thousand people and leaving many more homeless. Patrick later described the beginning of the Blitz in his novel *Richard Temple*: "London turned into a uniformed camp overnight, and those who had no uniforms pinned arm-bands on themselves: Philippa had one as an ambulance driver, and she vanished into a fetid underground garage for twelve hours of the day or the night. It was a time of indescribable confusion, excitement and exaltation. . . . The general vitality of the people had been jerked up to an extraordinary level, and it stayed there" (p. 274).

Four days into the Blitz, a jaded Dylan Thomas wrote: "I am trying to get a job before conscription because my one-and-only body I will not give. I know that all the shysters in London are grovelling about the Ministry of Information . . . and all I have managed to do is have my name on the crook list. . . . So I must explore every avenue now . . . because along will come conscription and the military tribunal, and stretcher-bearing or jail or potato peeling or the Boys' Fire League. And all I want is time to write poems and enough money to keep two and a bit alive."*

But England somehow shuffled its talent into the right roles. Thomas, a pacifist, would not end up in jail or at forced labor but flourishing as a broadcaster and a scriptwriter for the BBC and holding forth at the Gluepot, on Mortimer Street in the West End, with other BBC staff and a host of musicians, poets, artists, and British and American journalists. Patrick, too, would eventually find a niche that made good use of his particular skills. But at first he drove ambulances, among the most vital of jobs during the terrifying bombing raids.

To assist the twenty-two stations of the London Ambulance Service, more than a hundred auxiliary stations, each equipped with some six cars and three ambulances, went into action. Eight thousand paid volunteers, mostly men aged thirty to fifty and women aged eighteen to fifty, manned these stations, with women outnumbering men by about two to one. Four stations operated in Chelsea, where Patrick lived and most likely served.

Ambulance volunteers worked eight-hour shifts, six days a week. Racing to the rescue as bombs fell, they faced near chaos in the streets, which were unmarked (the signposts having been removed to confuse invaders), unlit, debris-strewn, and often cratered. Drivers could be deafened by explosions and antiaircraft fire, blinded by blazing buildings one moment and plunged into pure blackout darkness the next, and the ambulances themselves were temperamental. The American Dodges and British Bedfords, many of them converted service vans, stalled easily and required close attention in gear shifting, a task made more difficult if the driver was properly attired in cumbersome gas-proof coveralls and a hard hat.

On the trip out, an empty ambulance rattled and thumped like the inside of a drum, and on a trip to the hospital, it might be loaded down with a dozen severely wounded people for whom each jolt was agony.

Despite these hardships, ambulance driving, with its night schedule,

*From *Backs to the Wall*, by Leonard Mosley, p. 24.

proved most fortunate the night a Luftwaffe bomb struck Patrick's apartment building, perhaps 24 Gertrude Street, where he and Elizabeth had lived prior to the war. The bomb that hit this building on October 20, 1940, did not explode, but it caused serious damage and had to be removed by the bomb disposal services. Patrick, on duty at the time, escaped injury. However, his manuscript in progress, a nonfiction account of St. Isidore and the Western bestiary, was destroyed.

Among the drivers in Chelsea, Countess Mary Tolstoy stood out. A petite dark-haired English society girl from Devon, she had gone to school in Switzerland, been presented at court at age eighteen, and married Dimitry Tolstoy, a Russian count in exile, at age nineteen. Now twenty-five and the mother of two, Mary had recently seen her marriage collapse.

Instead of zipping off to social functions in her sporty Jowett Jupiter, the soft-spoken countess now shifted the testy gears of an ambulance speeding to the aid of bomb victims. Often Miss Potts, her rough-haired dachshund, sat on her lap. (At other times, Miss Potts, who looked something like a mongoose, followed at her mistress's heels so faithfully that she remained unleashed even in city traffic.) Tolstoy—a hill climber, a good shot, and a horse rider from her youth in Appledore—would prove to be of a far tougher nature than her social station might have suggested.

The work took strong nerves. The novelist Rose Macaulay, who also drove ambulances in central London during the Blitz, described in a letter one late-night scene she attended:

> The demolition men worked and hacked away very skilfully [sic] and patiently, and we all encouraged the people inside, telling them they would be out in a short time, but of course they weren't. There was a mother and a crying baby, who were rescued at 10.0 next morning after I had gone. I drove to hospital another mother, who had left two small children under the ruins. I told her they would be out very soon—but they never were, they were killed.*

Such harrowing incidents were not unusual. At one bomb scene where Mary was working, a victim walked by oblivious to the fact that a large shaft of glass protruded from his back.

*From *Rose Macaulay* by Constance Babington Smith, p. 153. Coincidentally, Macaulay also lost a bestiary in progress to one of Hitler's bombs, on May 10, 1941.

In the spring of 1941, Hitler ordered the most violent attacks on London, in retaliation for the bombing of Berlin. The heaviest fell on April 16 ("the Wednesday"), when seven hundred bombers inundated the capital with explosive and incendiary bombs, and April 19 ("the Saturday"), the heaviest of all, with more than seven hundred Nazi bombers blasting the city. Being close to the river, near both government buildings and power stations, Chelsea took more tons of bombs per acre in the Blitz than all but two boroughs.

"Poor London went through a perfect imitation of Hades," Joan informed Barney in an August 30, 1941, letter. "We went out in the garden and really we could not hear ourselves speak for the roar of the planes. That was at nine o'clock. It went on until four in the morning. We were not the target but we stayed awake til the all clear. The earth shook regularly all the time and what they must have suffered I cannot bear to think."

The Wednesday's eight hours of bombing killed or wounded three thousand people. In Chelsea, at 11:30 P.M., a bomb hit the Royal Hospital Infirmary, trapping forty inside and sending as many wandering about the darkened streets. The same blast knocked out the Auxiliary Fire Station on Cheyne Place. Two hours later, a double explosion destroyed Chelsea Old Church, killing five fire watchers in a heap of rubble and broken timbers. On Petyt Place and Cheyne Walk, the blast crumbled houses. The debris made Old Church Street impassable. Gas mains spouted flames like giant blowtorches. The nearby ambulance station was wrecked. Rescue workers searched for survivors in streets reeking of gas. Sirens, antiaircraft fire, and explosions created a hellish din. The dazed and wounded wandered about, as did, disconcertingly, some downed Luftwaffe pilots. Firefighters fought blazes throughout Chelsea.

It was in such madness that Patrick and Mary drove their ambulances. Mary later told her niece, Jane Wicksteed, that she sometimes felt her instincts take over, warning her to avoid certain roads for no apparent reason, only to find out later that they had been bombed out. It was a time of random death and destruction when one could easily believe in the supremacy of fate. And it was on such a night as the Wednesday that, according to Russ family members, a fateful bomb hit a building in Chelsea that provided billets for officers of the Free French Army. French speakers were desperately needed to help the wounded. The "unearthly, Martian" sirens, as Patrick would describe them in his novel *Richard Temple*

(p. 274), called both him and Mary Tolstoy to the scene, and so in the heat of rescue they met.

For Patrick and Mary, both still reeling from unhappy marriage breakups, a love that would last the rest of their lives blossomed amid the bombs. Soon, they were discussing moving in together, an arrangement that would have shocked London society just a few years earlier. But the war had a way of bringing down social conventions.

Patrick soon moved into Mary's Queen Anne house, called "the Cottage," at 1 Upper Cheyne Row. With four bedrooms, a large dining room full of polished silver, and a prim garden, it was spacious and emphatically English. Patrick had never lived anywhere so fine.

Mary had moved into the Cottage in June 1941 after leaving Tolstoy, who, according to one friend of the family, had had an affair with her best friend, but she would pay a heavy price for living with Patrick. Her husband, Dimitry Mihailovich, Count Tolstoy Miloslavsky, the grandson of a principal counselor to Nicholas II, the last czar, was a barrister specializing in divorce. He was a tough, inscrutable man who had survived the Bolshevik revolution as a child, and he determined to use his legal expertise and Mary's relationship with Patrick to prevent her from seeing her children, Nicholas (known as "Nikolai"), age six, and Natalie (known as "Natasha"), four. In May 1942, Tolstoy petitioned for divorce from Mary, naming Patrick Russ as the corespondent. The fact that Tolstoy went on to write the standard textbook on divorce indicates just how formidable an opponent he was.

At Crowborough, in August 1941, Zoe Russ worked hard to put food on the table. Charles's current labor was also, at last, linked closely to that end. He gardened. "There's hardly an inch unused and we have had crops of every conceivable veg. this year," Joan informed Barney in her report. "It doesn't suit him, but he grinds on day after day, hot or cold, rain or snow almost." They were getting by, but Joan worried about her parents. "They are old, and anxious, both have had one War," she wrote. "You know what Mother suffered in that and although that can't happen to her again it is terrible for anyone to see her gently brace herself to endure violence."

But they all had to stay braced for violence. Joan expressed her feelings with an insight and eloquence that indicated that her gift for writing, like Patrick's, was quite substantial:

We have actually survived all this peril and horror, which staggers me. But it does do something to you mentally. The pulling out and stretching of the nerves, the listening and the helpless feeling acts on people I think. One gets more used to it, and able to discriminate between noises that are dangerous and noises that are probably O.K. But they get waves of mental panic, I'm sure, moments of complete horror when they realize their utter defenselessness and the pointless, hazardous way the bombs come. One thinks "*What? Me.* But I *cannot* die." And after a bit it does something to you, in this way. With so many dying all over the country you begin to feel so valueless.

Joan mentioned no other family members in her lengthy letter, perhaps bowing to wartime discretion, or perhaps because the family had become so fragmented. She herself soon joined the Women's Auxiliary Air Force and moved to Birmingham, leaving Charles and Zoe for the first time since returning home at the age of six. In Patrick's case, she very likely had little information with which to work.

Following the Blitz, both he and Mary were recruited into the murky precincts of the intelligence community of London. Jobs in this line were usually filled through the "old boy" network, one friend pulling in another talented and trustworthy friend, and this usually implied extraordinarily good connections. In both cases, Patrick's and Mary's linguistic skills, not to mention their intellects, were valuable resources. They both spoke French and German, Patrick Italian and Mary some Russian.

In March 1942, Robert Bruce Lockhart took charge of the Political Warfare Executive (PWE), a secret intelligence and propaganda organization that used the Political Intelligence Department (PID) of the foreign office for cover. Lockhart, a diplomat and journalist, was charming, capable, and a good leader. In his 1947 book, *Comes the Reckoning,* he described PWE's two main goals approved by the foreign office and the chiefs of staff: "(1) to undermine and to destroy the morale of the enemy and (2) to sustain and foster the spirit of resistance in enemy-occupied countries" (p. 125). To accomplish these ends, the organization produced subversive radio broadcasts and leaflets, often dropped by RAF bombers over occupied territories.

A chief task was to counter the daily broadcasts of Joseph Goebbels's Berlin radio propagandists. To do this, the BBC pumped out 160,000 words in twenty-three languages every twenty-four hours. Operating day and night, the PWE either wrote, vetted, or doctored these broadcasts.

Housed at two locations, the duke of Bedford's estate in Woburn, forty miles northwest of London, and Bush House, Aldwych, in the same building as the BBC offices for European broadcasts, the PWE was organized by regions. Patrick and Mary joined the French Section, run by Dr. Leslie Beck, an expert on Descartes and an Oxford lecturer. Beck, a former Jesuit novice, had taught in India and studied philosophy at the Sorbonne from 1930 to 1934. At the Sorbonne, he had developed a passion for France and perhaps had even crossed paths with Patrick. As chief intelligence officer of the French Section, Beck and his staff maintained close ties with the Charles de Gaulle camp in London.

Patrick and Mary worked, at least part of the time, at Bush House, where Lockhart tried to bring the organization under one London roof, even though it was not nearly as pleasant as Woburn. Lockhart described the layout in *Comes the Reckoning*:

> The offices which we occupied were spacious but strangely un-English, for they were designed on the United States business pattern with a few small rooms and one large central hall in which all the staff could be under the constant watch of the management. We converted this space into cubicles and, to meet the requirements of the security officer, we wired the entrances from the lifts with heavy netting. In this zoo I remained until the end of the war. (Pp. 163–64)

The PWE and the BBC communicated continually, with the PWE having a strong voice in outlining the official BBC programs to occupied territories, which were considered white propaganda. The PWE also created black propaganda, which consisted of radio broadcasts meant to seem as if they were generated from within an occupied country, creating the illusion of a more powerful and organized resistance, as well as other demoralizing and disruptive campaigns, such as creating bogus German stamps that replaced Hitler's head with Heinrich Himmler's (in the hopes of starting rumors that Himmler was vying for power with the führer), and booklets for German soldiers with instructions for feigning injuries and wounds.

During the second half of the war, PWE agents helped draft British directives issued through the BBC to assist in operations in Europe. With the help of the Special Operations Executive (SOE), a secret service formed in 1940 for promoting subversive warfare in enemy-occupied territory, some PWE agents infiltrated Europe for such purposes as helping to establish clandestine newspapers.

Because PWE employees often worked under pseudonyms in compartmentalized offices at scattered locations, their operations are difficult to trace. Agents kept paper trails to a minimum, and many of those that they did keep were destroyed after the war. But according to Mary's niece, Jane Wicksteed, Patrick and Mary were involved in sending communications to the Resistance. Since radio transmissions were constantly monitored by the Germans, and meetings with Resistance agents in France were dangerous, the secret service sometimes found it expedient to mail communications. Agents were dropped into France with envelopes bearing Pétain stamps forged in London and simply placed them in the nearest mailbox. Patrick was involved in this operation. Because of her Continental education, Mary, who worked under him, could address the envelopes like a native. Later, Mary gave Jane some of the bogus stamps she had saved.

Patrick and Mary may also have been assisting in the underground operations of Vic Gerson, head of Reseau Vic, a resistance organization operating in the south of France. In the fall of 1941, Vic, as he was known in the field, had recruited Armand Goëau-Brissonnière, a forty-six-year-old Parisian lawyer and World War I veteran, who represented the French politician Georges Mandel, a Jew, after he was arrested by the Vichy government. Goëau-Brissonnière, known by the pseudonyms "Gerard" in France and "Renelière" in England, had moved to Cannes and set up an independent, pro-Allied intelligence and resistance organization. He specialized in helping prisoners and fugitives escape. Before Vic found him, Goëau-Brissonnière had already masterminded successful escapes from prisons in Nice, Lyons, and Marseilles. Gerson's superiors in London felt that Goëau-Brissonnière's information on France and North Africa was reliable and important, and Gerson took him fully under his command in February 1942.

With the help of Goëau-Brissonnière, Vic decided to proceed with an escape he had been plotting of eight British parachutists being held in Mauzac prison, on the Garonne River, between Toulouse and the Spanish border.

According to Jean Yves Goëau-Brissonnière, Armand Goëau-

Brissonnière's son, Mary Tolstoy visited Cannes around this time. She was probably either delivering money or documents to Goëau-Brissonnière for the escape or conducting some other PWE mission.*

Acting as the lawyer of a prisoner, Goëau-Brissonnière established a legitimate presence in the camp in order to plan the logistics. An associate of his who had already escaped from prison directed the operation, arranging for locals to provide clothes and two trucks. In the middle of July the parachutists escaped from the prison and made their way through the Pyrenees to Spain. From there they flew to England.

Two weeks later, Vichy police arrested Goëau-Brissonnière for his suspected role in the escape, detained him in Toulon, and interrogated him for a week. He conceded nothing, however, maintaining that his only involvement in the affair was as counsel to one of the prisoners. On August 11, Goëau-Brissonnière himself escaped, and a few weeks later, Reseau Vic conceived a plan to smuggle him out of France by submarine, possibly through Collioure, where Patrick and Mary would live after the war. That scheme failed. Instead, agents escorted Goëau-Brissonnière through the Pyrenees to Spain. He flew to London on October 20, 1942.

Goëau-Brissonnière's wife and children were prevented from leaving France by the German invasion of the Free Zone in November 1942. Jean Yves holed up in Nevers, France, with no money and no news of his father's safety, until one day in a BBC broadcast he heard the message "Le Vétou est arrivé et vous embrasse" (Vétou has arrived and sends you a kiss). "Vétou" was the nickname of Jean Yves's sister, Yvette. Jean Yves knew his father was safe.

The extent of Patrick and Mary's role in this undertaking is unclear, but their connection to Goëau-Brissonnière afterward is not. They worked with him in London, and the three became good friends. After the war, Patrick dedicated a story, "The Little Death," to the Frenchman. He sent *The Last Pool,* the book in which it appeared, to Goëau-Brissonnière in Paris with a note saying that he hoped Goëau-Brissonnière and several other of their friends understood what he was trying to express in the story when he described the state of mind of a man who was fed up with killing.

There is no evidence that Patrick left the country during the war, but

---

*Then sixteen, Jean Yves Goëau-Brissonnière distinctly remembers having lunch with his father and Mary Tolstoy in Cannes. He recalls not just her beauty but the fact that her name was Tolstoy, because he was a devoted reader of Leo Tolstoy. He would see Mary again after the war, when she and Patrick visited his father in Paris.

these words show that he, like his fictional character Stephen Maturin, knew intimately the necessary measures sometimes involved in intelligence work and that Patrick and Goëau-Brissonnière, who definitely worked in the field, shared an understanding about such things. O'Brian greatly respected the Frenchman, an intellect who boldly risked his life to fight for his moral beliefs and who, like Maturin, served in the intelligence agency of a foreign nation to fight for the liberty of his countrymen. Few men could have better served as a model for Maturin's most noble qualities.

The year 1942 was surely one of the dreariest of the war for the English. The duke of Kent was killed in a flying accident in August. Not until British general Bernard Montgomery defeated German general Erwin Rommel at El Alamein, Egypt, in October and November did national morale receive a boost.

For Patrick, the lowest point of that year was not a matter of international significance but a personal one.

In February, Richard turned five and Patrick sent him a present. The previous year he had sent one, he admitted, of a "revolting sort": malt and cod liver oil. He admonished Richard to try to enjoy it because it was good for him. He added some silly verse and concluded, "Now be a good lad, Ricky, and look after our women folk."

But this was a sadly impossible task. On March 31, 1942, twenty-four years and a day after the death of his mother, Patrick's three-year-old daughter, Jane, died of complications caused by spina bifida.

While Patrick had embarked on a new life, Elizabeth had coped with Richard and Jane. For nearly two years, they had lived in a state of limbo in the home of Patrick's oldest brother and his wife in Thorpe-next-Norwich. Godfrey and Connie Russ had kindly provided for them. For Elizabeth, Jane's death in the hospital was a particular agony. The doctors had not allowed her to be with her daughter in her last hours of life. Elizabeth's sense of loss was enormous.

A month after Jane died, on the nights of April 27 and 29, the Germans began the massive bombing of England's historic cities dubbed the Baedeker Blitz. The Luftwaffe's explosive and incendiary bombs wracked poorly defended Norwich, killing more than two hundred people. In the middle of the night, Elizabeth and Richard woke up and stared out of a window at the horrific but mesmerizing sight of the flaming city.

London was no longer necessarily the most dangerous place to live, and Elizabeth decided that she and her son might as well move back. They took a cold-water flat in Chelsea at 237 King's Road, not far from Poulton Square, where they had once lived with Patrick. Elizabeth found work assembling electrical parts in a factory in Earl's Court. Richard, who at age six had felt the tremor of tanks as they rolled down the streets of Norwich in a plume of sparks, with their iron tracks clashing against the pavement, now roamed the streets of London with other young boys, gathering and swapping shrapnel after bombing raids and dazzling drivers by reflecting the sun with shards of broken mirrors. While the homeless foraged outside the charred shells of buildings, he chased after Mitsy, his pet Yorkshire terrier, who was prone to getting picked up by the dogcatcher. And sometimes the boy hung out with his father's friend the painter Francis Cox and his wife, who lived in the flat beneath them.

From time to time, a Russ brother called on Elizabeth and Richard to make sure that they were managing. In early 1943, Mike dropped in to meet his nephew. Mike was living life as if he knew he was on a fast track to demise. In March of the previous year, he had embarked with his RAAF unit for Canada, leaving behind a fiancée in Australia, and, by October, when he had sailed from Canada for England, he left behind yet another. Of course, neither knew that he was already a married man.

To Richard, the six-foot-three-inch, sandy-haired flying officer was a rollicking giant. On the floor on his elbows and knees, Mike took the boy's popgun and knocked down the closest things to Wehrmacht he could find, which happened to be cardboard figures of the Seven Dwarfs. Richard cheered him on.

Fun-loving and quick with a smile, Mike had the ability to connect with people, and, in his uniform, straight and powerfully built, he had a presence that inspired confidence. He was, indeed, mechanically adept, competent at practical matters, a natural survivor. He served as a navigator, and soaring through the heavens in a Lancaster bomber—his "sweet kite," he called it—he had "so sound a basis of mathematics," an anonymous eulogist later wrote about him, "that he could laugh at the certainty of navigation under the stars."

However, his farewell that day, a sullen "good-bye," did not cheer Elizabeth. She could read the serious expression on his tan, chiseled face.

"No, not good-bye," she replied.

"Yes," Mike responded, struggling to maintain his composure. He had a bad feeling. He was about to fly his first combat mission, over

Germany, where his Lancaster would be very vulnerable to the Luftwaffe's Messerschmitts and to antiaircraft fire.

Mike went about seeing his family. He tried to dissuade Nora from making her final profession as a nun, which was anathema to the family, but not even her favorite brother could do that. In July of that year, she would dedicate herself to the Feast of the Ascension and take the name Sister Mary Francis of the Ascension.

Mike took the train up to Birmingham to visit Joan, whom he had not seen in fifteen years. By luck, he ran into her at the train station. She was heading out to the countryside with a beau. They chatted for fifteen minutes, and Mike got back on the train.

He visited Olive in Ilminster and then went to see the three spinster Hill sisters, who used to care for him during holidays at Shebbear. From there, he wrote Olive on April 17: "Have been sawing and splitting logs all morning, and weather still perfect. Really think my visit to Ilminster deserves a letter of thanks and appreciated the rest very much. It has been the pleasantest holiday I've yet had on leave in England."

Whether Mike saw Patrick, who had been only thirteen when his brother sailed for Australia, is unknown but probable. It is certain he would never see him again. Mike joined the 460th Squadron at Breighton, Yorkshire. Five days later, in the early morning of May 4, 1943, Lancaster A4878 was shot down over Dortmund, Germany. Among the seven-man crew, all of whom died, was thirty-four-year-old navigator Flying Officer Michael Russ. Charles Russ received a telegram in Crowborough, as did Mike's fiancée in Queensland.

Mike had had his shortcomings. He was self-centered, an unrepentant womanizer, and tough, but he was also capable and spirited. He had had a hard life, and he had fended for himself. But he was much loved and admired by his family, a favorite sibling, and his death rent the family even further.*

---

*Mike Russ was buried in the Reichswald Forest War Cemetery, plot 3, row A, grave 6.

7

An Irishman Is Born

1943–1946

By holding closely to the truth, the British propaganda effort
did more to sustain British influence in Europe than any other
single factor. For five years it brought to the occupied
countries of Europe the only news from the outside world. It
kept alive the spark of hope in victory and was the backbone of
the resistance movement in every country.

—Robert Bruce Lockhart, *Comes the Reckoning*, 1947

Between wartime austerity and secret service work, which demanded
long, sometimes tense hours of concentration, Patrick and Mary
lived a quiet, simple life, maintaining a small circle of friends.

Together the two weathered the storms of their personal lives. In the
course of three years, Patrick had lost a child and a brother and had abandoned his marriage. The Tolstoys' divorce became official in November
1942. According to one Wicksteed family member, Dimitry offered Mary
generous financial terms and custody of the children if she would leave
Patrick. But she would not, and Dimitry turned almost obsessively spiteful.
Ultimately, not only did he keep custody of the children, but he blocked
Mary from even seeing them. This abysmal cloud followed her for the next
thirteen years, until Nikolai came of age and visited her in France. In the
meantime, he and Natasha were sent off to boarding schools, where even
Mary's letters were sometimes intercepted and not delivered. While
Patrick at least had access to his son, Mary faced almost inhumane treatment on that score. The children often spent their holidays with Mary's
parents at Appledore or in London under the condition that they not come
into contact with her.

Six months after the Tolstoy divorce was settled, Elizabeth Russ filed for divorce from Patrick. She, too, was extremely bitter. Still, though she reviled Patrick in front of their son, she did not seek money because she knew he had precious little to spare but also, she told Richard, "for the sake of his art." But Patrick was certainly financially better off living with Mary than he had been, and this Richard could see if not fully understand.

Patrick tried to maintain a relationship with his son. Sometimes he picked him up at the apartment on King's Road and took him for a walk around the Round Pond in Kensington Gardens or took him to the house where he and Mary lived. To Richard, Upper Cheyne Row, though not far from his mother's small, dreary apartment, was a different world, one of splendor, polish, and intriguing objects. He was fascinated by Patrick's gleaming Panther 250 motorbike, kept in the hallway under a sheet, his collection of Japanese swords, and by the air-raid shelter, made of angle iron and steel plate, in the cellar.

At the Cottage, Richard met Mary's parents, Howard and Frieda Wicksteed, who were visiting; both were very upright and proper. In the cellar, Mary's father, a classics scholar, and a retired captain in the Devon-shire Regiment, mixed coal dust with straw and cement in flowerpots to create fuel for the fireplace. Wicksteed was a man of moral rectitude, who made a deep impression. He had been badly wounded in World War I and was invalided out of the army in 1917. But he refused to accept a pension on the grounds that he was a volunteer and had not served for money and therefore would not accept it now. A similar trait would be a hallmark of Patrick's fictional character Stephen Maturin.

It was an odd domestic scene, as the Wicksteeds, very upset by the collapse of Mary's marriage, blamed her for her separation from her children, no matter what the circumstances. But Richard remembers seeing his father on the floor humbly mashing potatoes in a china pot with a big wooden spoon, and hearing the Wicksteeds comment, "Oh, Patrick seems to be a very pleasant young man."

With their friends, Patrick and Mary still displayed their youthful resilience. By and large, Londoners were intent on their jobs and on winning the war. When they socialized, because of the need for wartime secrecy, they kept their working lives to themselves. Among those whom the couple saw regularly was Walter Greenway, a major in the Royal Artillery, who had attended Cambridge with Dimitry and who had lived with the Tolstoys as a paying guest before the war.

Greenway had been appalled at Tolstoy's treatment of Mary and remained loyal to her. He and his wife, Susan, lived in nearby Markham Square, and he worked in the Ministry of Supply, where he approved military equipment changes due to failure in action. A graduate in mathematics, Greenway was a man of technical skills and knowledge, which Patrick admired, while Greenway, in turn, was attracted to Patrick's erudition and his passions. Patrick constantly engaged in a sort of intellectual sparring. Greenway was a good sport and countered with his practical knowledge; he knew more than Patrick about how weights and pulleys functioned, which gave him the edge in one of their favorite pastimes: shopping for and tinkering with clocks.

Patrick, at least in part inspired by a reading of the Irish novelist Laurence Sterne's *The Life and Opinions of Tristram Shandy* (1760), desired to turn his longcase clock (which had no case) from one that needed frequent winding to one that, like Shandy's, needed winding only once a month. To do this, the two friends devised a plan to attach a series of pulleys and a much heavier weight to the clock. They melted lead in a saucepan over the fire to make the hefty weight (on the order of fifty pounds), and they mounted the clock at the top of the stairs, so that the weight could hang down the stairwell. But no matter how they tinkered with the system, they never succeeded because the friction of the rope through the pulleys overrode their improvements to the clock.

Greenway bought his own longcase clock around this time, and Patrick added several interesting clocks to his collection. One, from the eighteenth century, had been converted from verge escapement to pendulum. Another was fourteen inches square, with a set of homemade pulleys; it kept very precise time—as long as the temperature did not vary greatly—and was known as the "Wonderfully Accurate Clock," though that still meant losing a minute or so a week.

Patrick also gave Greenway the bug for naval history. Together, they combed the used bookstores in Charing Cross Road. Patrick later told a story about participating in a book auction one day, when a bomb fell near enough to call off the bidding. The last bid before the blast had been his, and he was delighted to claim his book at an especially favorable price.

The two friends reenacted Lord Howe's famous 1794 naval victory over the French, known as the Glorious First of June, with matchsticks on the rug in front of the Cottage's fireplace. To feed their discussions, they pored over the six-volume naval histories of eighteenth-century historian Robert Beatson and nineteenth-century historian William James. James's

Naval History of Great Britain from the Declaration of War by France in 1793 to the Accession of George IV (1822) remained the definitive account of naval actions during the Napoleonic wars. Another book, Edward Brenton's *Naval History of Great Britain from 1783 to 1822*, provided the two matchstick commodores with the perspective of a naval post captain. These troves of information supplied the details to be hashed out and mar- veled over at tea or while Patrick puffed his straight-apple pipe.

Though their conversations ranged from the mechanics of clocks to the principles of war, there were things they did not speak about, namely, their war occupations. As Britain's internal propaganda emphasized, "Careless Talk Costs Lives." When Patrick spoke about his war work with Greenway, it was only in innocuous anecdotes. For several days, he railed against a lanky Harvard-educated American working at Bush House, per- haps a representative of the Office of War Information (OWI), who in a conversation corrected Patrick's misquotation of some Shakespeare lines. But even when incensed, Patrick remained properly discreet. Though the audacious Yank was forever cursed, he also remained nameless.*

During this period an overwhelming sense of secrecy began to settle on Patrick, who was an effective agent and promoted within his department. He later told a reporter that after being warned during the war not to be photographed, he never again felt comfortable in front of a camera. Fol- lowing the war, he eventually clamped down tightly on the information in his book-jacket biographies and disdained probing questions. In his Aubrey-Maturin novels and in his personal life, Patrick repeatedly showed that he valued few virtues more than discretion, a quality that is personi- fied in Maturin, who guards his shipmates' secrets even when he knows they threaten the authority of his best friend, Captain Aubrey, and the well-being of the ship.

Within the first forty pages of his first Aubrey-Maturin novel, *Master and Commander,* Patrick would poise Aubrey on the brink of an indiscre- tion in his curiosity about Maturin's impressive knowledge of the Catalan language. " 'How . . . ?' " begins Aubrey. "But finding that he was on the edge of questioning a guest he filled up the space with a cough and rang the bell for the waiter" (p. 36). In the fifteenth book in the series, *The Truelove,* the character Clarissa Oakes remarks to Maturin, " 'How

---

*Among the possibilities is the Yale- and Harvard-educated poet Archibald MacLeish. An official in the OWI, MacLeish was in London in 1942 to coordinate efforts for Operation Torch, a planned Anglo-American invasion of North Africa.

pleasant it is to be sitting . . . next to a man who does not ply one with questions' " (pp. 162–63), just before she candidly unburdens her painful story to him. Perhaps the best-known passage in all of Patrick's writing is also found in that novel, when Maturin says, " 'Question and answer is not a civilized form of conversation. . . . It is extremely ill bred, extremely usual, and extremely difficult to turn aside gracefully or indeed without offence.' " Patrick continued: "Stephen spoke with more than common feeling, for since he was an intelligence-agent even quite idle questions, either answered or evaded, might start a mortal train of suspicion" (p. 80).

In early 1943, Patrick and Mary's new colleague at the PWE, Armand Goëau-Brissonnière, a specialist in ancient Greek in addition to being a renowned lawyer in peacetime, became an adviser to Dr. Beck. Goëau-Brissonnière helped maintain the group's dialogue with the advisers of General de Gaulle, preventing potential conflicts between the leader of the Free French Forces and the PWE, whose propaganda had to be to a certain extent coordinated with the often contentious leader in exile.

Goëau-Brissonnière also wrote policy and intelligence reports for Beck's unit and assessed works by other intelligence branches. Among the works that he either wrote or analyzed was a plan for demoralizing German submarine crews. Suggested goals consisted of thwarting the German sailor's ability to rest and enjoy himself in port; weakening his trust in his family's security in Germany; and undermining his faith in German war progress and the Nazi Party. Most of the techniques involved the spreading of propaganda, often through clandestine and BBC radio broadcasts, or directing such groups as Catholic priests, Communists and Socialists, Gaullists, or ship mechanics to perform certain acts, often violent.

German submarine crews tended to frequent private prostitutes or brothels specifically intended for Germans, making the brothels easy targets. The report suggested using "threats and the execution of threats" against the prostitutes, which would not be difficult to carry out because the idea of French women servicing German men was repugnant to the French.

On August 3, a Dr. P. Russ, presumably Patrick, who had reached the position of section head (though why the "Dr." is unclear), wrote a letter politely asking Goëau-Brissonnière to write a series of five-hundred-word articles on the people and countryside of the regions of France for handbooks the group was preparing on Rouen, Rennes, Lille, Laon, and Lyons.

In November, Goëau-Brissonnière critiqued a handbook on France for British officers and wrote a synopsis to help the officers to better use the book and to understand the current psychology of France.

In the spring of 1944, Goëau-Brissonnière was badly wounded in a bombing attack on London. Patrick wrote his colleague an eloquent note in the hospital. With a touch of dry humor, he noted that everyone in the office was sure the Frenchman lay near death until the return of Dr. Beck from a visit dispelled this rumor, and then everyone decided he was ready to waltz out of the hospital. The truth lay somewhere in between. Patrick offered to bring him some books to make his stay less tedious.

Shortly after he was released from the hospital in June, the unlucky Goëau-Brissonnière happened to be riding on a bus during one of the first V1 bomb scares. Trying to maneuver through the panicky crowd on his crutches, he fell to the floor of the bus, reinjuring himself. He returned to the hospital, and Patrick and Mary were again very solicitous. Mary invited him to stay with them at the Cottage when he was released from the hospital, noting that their maid could look after him during the day. She also tried to visit him one day at lunchtime but got lost on the Underground, and by the time she got her bearings, she had to return to work. Patrick and Mary's notes to their "dear colleague" never explicitly mentioned the momentous Allied invasion of France; instead, Mary provided him with a book containing some things she "hoped would amuse him."*

In the summer of 1944, Joan Russ married an RAF mechanic from a working-class Birmingham family. Charles and Zoe did not approve and refused to attend the Roman Catholic ceremony. That fall, a month after German forces in Paris surrendered, setting off a week of celebrations, Patrick's cousin Charles Russ, one of Sidney and Mary's two sons serving in the Royal Naval Volunteer Reserve, was killed in Ceylon.

In February 1945, Allied forces crossed the German border. Barney Russ, now a lieutenant in the Royal Canadian Medical Corps, found himself in a slit trench near Kleve, Germany, where German artillery hit an ammunition dump behind the Allied trenches, setting off a stupendous explosion that killed a number of men and detonated munitions throughout the night. The unit's chaplain had moved up the line, so the next day, Barney was ordered to perform burials. With an icy wind blowing and

*Robert Bruce Lockhart's *Comes the Reckoning* offers a riveting account of the tensions at Bush House before and after D-Day.

German shells raining down, the soldiers wrapped their dead in army blankets and dropped them into graves. They huddled around, as Barney later recalled, while he read the unrehearsed service. But when he reached Psalm 23, the wind blew the loose page into a grave. Opting not to disturb the corpse, Barney carried on from vague memory, which necessitated splicing in lines from *Pilgrim's Progress* and *Paradise Lost* to reach a reasonable length.

Barney, whose war experience, unlike Patrick's, provided him with an arsenal of good—and sometimes far-fetched—stories to tell back home, continued serving with the occupying troops in Germany. One rainy day as he drove back to base, his jeep suddenly spun out of control and hit a tree. His head and right foot were severely injured. Unconscious, Barney was airlifted back to Bramshot, England, where he spent almost a year recuperating. Later he learned that his jeep had been sabotaged by young Germans who made a practice of cutting various control mechanisms in Allied vehicles and adding sugar to the fuel tanks of Allied aircraft.

That spring, despite the fact that war was still being waged in the Far East, life in London started its slow transition back to normal. The last manned air attack on Britain occurred in early March. At the end of the month, the last V1s and V2s hit the city. On May 8, Churchill made his eagerly awaited announcement: the war in Europe was over.

The foreign office, desperately short of staff, needed qualified personnel to fill embassy positions in liberated nations. It turned to the PWE, an organization that would be phased out, for candidates. Patrick was offered the post of a third secretary in the Paris embassy, an indication of the high regard in which he was held as a section leader in the PWE and the strong relationships he and Mary had forged with the likes of Goëau-Brissonnière. He turned down the post, probably due to a combination of factors: To take such a position required personal wealth; self-sufficiency was a requisite. Even with Mary's help, Patrick did not have the money. Though it needed a bit of resuscitation, Patrick still possessed a passion for writing. And lastly, no matter how essential the cause, he had grown somewhat sickened by the service he had had to perform during the war. The secret services at times were necessarily ruthless in achieving their aims. In order to move on, Patrick needed time and self-reflection to reckon with this phase of his life.*

---

*Barley Alison, a friend of Patrick's at the foreign office, from a wealthy Australian family, accepted the post. She went on to become a legendary editor at Weidenfeld and Nicolson and then at Secker and Warburg, where she had her own imprint, Alison Press.

England had sacrificed more than 300,000 military men and 34,000 merchant marines in the war against totalitarianism. German bombing had destroyed half a million houses. In London, returning military men could not find work. Squatters abounded, and others lived in barrackslike temporary housing. The city was physically devastated. Rationing remained in effect. Patrick and Mary decided to leave. But first they had business to finish.

In the Russ divorce case, the court had issued a decree nisi in December 1944; on June 25, 1945, Patrick and Elizabeth were officially divorced. Ten days later, Patrick and Mary married at the Chelsea Register Office, with two friends, Jane Dunn Byrne and May Whitley, as witnesses.* After all that Patrick and Mary had been through, the two still made a nod to decorum. On their marriage certificate, Patrick recorded his residence as "1 Upper Cheyne Row," while Mary listed "The Cottage, Upper Cheyne Row," though they were one and the same.

But the transformation was not complete. On July 20, Patrick signed the document to change his, Mary's, and his son's surname from Russ to O'Brian. So unceremonious was the event that he did not bother to call and inform eight-year-old Richard, who learned of his new name during recess at Southey Hall, his school, when the headmaster tapped him on the head and said, "Right, you're now called O'Brian." No fuss was made, and Patrick never spoke about the name change to his son.

On August 14, Patrick's new literary agent, Spencer Curtis Brown, appeared before the commissioner of oaths to make it official. Brown, the Cambridge-educated son of Albert Curtis Brown, founder of the prestigious literary agency Curtis Brown, Ltd., had served in the Special Services branch of the Intelligence Corps from 1943 to 1945. In 1945, at the age of thirty-nine, he had become the agency's chairman.

Of all people, he was acutely aware of the sacrifice Patrick was making to change his identity. With his third book, Patrick had established a foothold on a solid literary reputation, particularly in the United States. Nonetheless, he was determined to go through with it. To the commissioner of oaths, Brown swore:

---

*At the war's end, the register office was a busy, if not romantic, place. When Patrick's future publisher Rupert Hart-Davis attended his sister's marriage there, after a spell in the waiting room, his father piped up, "Since we seem to have plenty of time, we might as well make arrangements for my funeral" (Rupert Hart-Davis, *Halfway to Heaven,* p. 19).

I have for fifteen years and upwards personally known and been well acquainted with Richard Patrick O'Brian formerly known as Richard Patrick Russ the person who has executed the Deed now produced and shown to me and marked "A."

The said Richard Patrick O'Brian who has executed the said Deed marked "A" and the person referred to as Richard Patrick Russ in the said Certificate of Birth are one and same person.*

The documents were enrolled in the Central Office of the Supreme Court of Judicature on August 20, 1945. It was official. Patrick Russ, now O'Brian, had forsaken his family name. It was an act that would in many ways haunt him for the rest of his life.

Easing back into the realm of literature, Patrick O'Brian decided to produce an anthology of early English travel writing. On December 3, 1945, Spencer Curtis Brown sold the book concept, titled *A Book of Voyages*, to the publisher Home and Van Thal.

But Patrick and Mary could not afford the literary life in London even if they wanted it. The Wicksteeds moved into the Cottage, where they lived for many years. To some degree they may have turned their backs on the couple. Perhaps they frowned on this marriage of passion and Patrick's determination to write, which promised only poverty. They certainly lamented the fact that Mary could not raise her children.

Patrick and Mary had forged a bond under fire. She had sacrificed everything for him, and he would wholly commit himself to this marriage. They were now a steely, independent unit. Emerging from the war, they would create a new life together, different from anything that they had experienced before. They would live as one, work as one, move as one, and the world and their pasts could not interfere with that.

*Deed poll 10/-1060.

Part III

SLATE

8

The Last Approach
to the Mansion of Pluto

1946–1947

> How shall I express my feelings! The dark tremendous
> precipices, the rapid river roaring over disjoined rocks, black
> caverns, and issuing cataracts; all serve to make this the noblest
> specimen of the Finely Horrid the eye can possibly behold: the
> Poet has not described, nor the Painter pictured so gloomy a
> retreat, 'tis the last Approach to the mansion of Pluto through
> the regions of Despair.
>
> —eighteenth-century visitor to Aberglaslyn Pass, Wales*

O'Brian had soured on London, if not on humanity itself. His later fictional character Richard Temple loathed London's hypocrisy and emptiness, with its "hordes of silly and dirty people in search of a literary justification for silliness and dirt" (*Richard Temple*, p. 70). Like Temple, O'Brian was once again a struggling artist, an outsider, broke, and disdainful of the class system, which caused deep personal conflict: he was both sympathetic to the working class and struggling not to be a part of it.

The O'Brians now fled London, just as so many others did after the war. Finances played a part in their decision, but other conditions compelled them to go as well. Patrick and Mary were both on uneasy terms with their families. Patrick's health also factored into the move. The air in the mountains was believed better for keeping tuberculosis and other respiratory problems at bay. Moreover, Patrick craved solitude for writing.

*This passage is taken from *Living in Croesor*, by Philip O'Connor, p. 122, who cites Clough Williams-Ellis's "Snowdonia" in *Britain's National Parks* (ed. H. M. Abrahams, *Country Life,* 1959) as his source.

The O'Brians rented a cottage on a farm in Cwm ("valley," in Welsh) Croesor, in northwest Wales. The jagged 2,300-foot Cnicht Mountain formed the north rim of the high, narrow valley, while to the south and east the 2,500-foot Moelwyn Mawr made for a towering horizon. This mountain and Cwm Croesor were formerly the province of a slate mine that closed during the war. The visionary architect and conservationist Sir Clough Williams-Ellis had bought most of the valley and let the land to tenants, who raised livestock, mostly sheep.

Down the middle of the stone-pocked valley, a shallow river flowed for about a mile to the village of Croesor, which consisted of ten stone terrace houses in two rows, a small shop with a post office and a telephone, and a school at the bottom. A Methodist chapel on the uphill end of town cast its shadow on the rest. The quarry above the village had been electrified at the turn of the century by a hydropower station in the high pass, but the villagers at the time had rejected electricity, which they thought too much like lightning.

When the O'Brians moved into the valley, the locals naturally assumed by their name that they were Irish and by their bearing that they were upper-class, and, indeed, Patrick took on the persona of an Irish country gentleman. He could speak some Gaelic, and the people were gullible. Since Welsh nationalism had begun to root in these parts, when he additionally showed an ambivalence toward the English, it served him well. Mr. O'Brian, as he was always called, possessed other qualities that endeared him to the locals: he was well mannered, reserved, and did not intrude on others. Mary, for her part, was attractive and pleasant, and although obviously from a privileged background, she did not take on airs.

Still, it was a small place, and rumors flew. Upper-class urbanites did not move to such a backwater for no reason. Some thought that O'Brian was a government spy sent to report on the valley, and some said he was an air force bomber pilot who had injured his back in a crash and was living on a pension. Someone suggested that the detail-oriented stranger was a weather forecaster. That idea seemed the most plausible, so it stuck. O'Brian showed the valley-dwellers a book called *Hussein*, which he claimed he had written. But the name on the cover was not his, and the book bore a Welsh inscription to his wife and son. Mary was clearly not Welsh, and there was, at first, no son. While the book could not prove he was a writer, it did manage to start new rumors: There had been a nasty divorce. Mary was not Mr. O'Brian's wife at all but a mistress.

The O'Brians' cottage was called Fron (pronounced "vron") Wen, meaning "white breast," after the hill it sat on, actually a tiny plateau at about six hundred feet on the slope of Moelwyn Mawr. It was virtually a dependency of the farm Croesor Fawr ("Big Croesor"), nearly six hundred acres of pastures on the Mawr side of the Croesor River. Though small, Fron, which cost the O'Brians around £8 a year to rent, had a nice view of the farm and valley. Built of solid slate and granite, the cottage had been lime-washed a cheerful white to seal it from the driving rains of the high valley.

Three generations of the Roberts family lived in Croesor Fawr's stone-and-slate farmhouse, in the flat of the valley about four hundred yards from Fron. Harry Roberts, a powerful, russet-haired man, over six feet tall and broad shouldered, now did the bulk of the work, along with Bessie, his handsome, brown-haired wife, who ran the household, raising their two boys, six-year-old Gynfor and a toddler named Alun. Harry's parents, Robert and Kate, who had settled on Croesor Fawr two decades earlier, still toiled hard. By Croesor standards, the Robertses were well off. They owned a large flock of sheep and a small herd of dairy cows, and Bessie, a sturdy, capable woman, kept a flock of geese, which soared up the hill behind Fron to graze.

For the labor-intensive farm operations, such as lambings, shearings, and harvests, the Robertses needed all the help they could get, and Patrick and Mary soon entered into a cooperative relationship with them. Although there were no written rules, no contracts, the couple pitched in when hands were needed, and, in turn, they shared in the yield, including milk, carrots, and swedes (rutabagas), and the rights to two furrows of potatoes.

Of course, there was no mistaking the O'Brians for natives of the soil. While the tough-pawed Welshmen wore coarse brown corduroy trousers and steel-tipped hobnail boots, the O'Brians worked in leather walking shoes. Patrick wore a country gentleman's tweed jacket and flannel trousers, Mary a knee-length cotton dress. Every morning, Mary applied lipstick, and Patrick shaved with a strop-sharpened cutthroat razor. But Patrick, though slight, quickly made a statement when he slung a hundred-weight sack of coal over his shoulder and hauled it without stopping from Croesor Fawr up the hill to Fron. Mary also proved a hard worker, uncomplaining, consistent, and capable.

The newcomers helped with the tedious hay harvest, and old Mr.

Roberts, who spoke little English, instructed Patrick. After cutting the hay, they spread it to dry in the sun, first on one side then on the other. Sunshine was a valuable commodity in that narrow valley, and not to be wasted. As O'Brian turned one patch of hay with his twelve-prong rake, Roberts gesticulated and grunted in his pidgin English: "That is do! That is do!" O'Brian thought he meant "good" and kept on. Roberts then rattled off some vibrant Welsh to Eric Williams, a student working during his summer break, who told O'Brian that Mr. Roberts was trying to say "That is done!"

In many ways, Patrick and Mary had effectively escaped their chaotic city lives. Here order and duty defined existence. The farmers milked their cows morning and night, seven days a week, and on Sunday, most, including the Robertses, strict Methodists and teetotalers, attended service at Croesor's chapel in the morning, afternoon, and evening. Conditions at Fron were perhaps blessedly spartan for two who had much emotional clutter to straighten up. They relied on a stream-fed pool, some eighty yards from Fron, for drinking water, and this they lugged in buckets several times a day to their door. For other water, a large barrel collected the rain guttered to it from the roof. Their outhouse was an earth closet, with a bucket that had to be emptied, and they bathed in a tin tub in the living room or in the river.

Others might have balked at such a radical adjustment, but Patrick and Mary did not. They were committed to a simple, austere country life. They had brought all of their possessions from London and meant to stay. Their snug three-room abode, with nearly vertical steps to the second floor, held Patrick's half-second pendulum clock, the one he called the Mariner, and the Wonderfully Accurate Clock, as well as their steel air-raid shelter, now used as both a dining room table and a Ping-Pong table.

In the summer of 1946, Patrick's son, Richard, now nine years old and a boarding student at Southey Hall, also resided at Fron. It rained day after day, and the harvest failed, which meant hardship for all. For fresh meat, O'Brian hunted hare with his single-barrel .410 shotgun, known as a poacher's gun because it could be folded and concealed in a coat or a trouser leg. He fished for trout in the Croesor, but they were small. Although food was not always plentiful, Mary proved remarkably resourceful. Cooking over a kerosene Primus stove, she could turn a one-egg pudding into a meal for three.

Mary eased her heartache over her children by caring for Richard, who would have some fond memories of Croesor despite the trying circumstances. Each morning, he fetched fresh milk from the farmhouse. On the way, he stopped at the steep slate-lined pen of a great mash-eating sow, and scratched her back with a stick. He jogged through the pasture of a bull calf after climbing over a slate fence. Then he walked a bit on the road, and a pack of hounds escorted him to the kitchen door while the geese tried to push through the dogs to peck at him. Carrying two pints of milk, Richard then reversed the procedure. But the now alert and famished young bull never failed to think that the tin of milk was his food, so the trip home involved a special challenge: sprinting without spilling the milk.

At home, Patrick demanded silence while he did what he told his fellow farmers was his "paperwork." Rural north Wales would provide the material for a volume of short stories and a novel, much of it based on or inspired by his hunting and fishing experiences and by life and people on the farm. To make money, Patrick also thumped away on a machine that converted books into braille and worked on an anthology, which would be published in 1947 as *A Book of Voyages*. In this collection of seventeenth- and eighteenth-century travel accounts, he tried to preserve the best of the lesser-known voyages, many of which had appeared in dreary encyclopedic geographies and now went unread.

Patrick gave the slender book's eight sections amusingly understated titles; "Unpleasant Voyages" contained tales of shipwreck and cannibalism, while "Inefficient Pirates" paid for it by swinging from the gallows. Among the longer passages that he chose, "Pelham's Voyage to Greenland" recounted the hardships of whalers who survived the winter of 1630 above the ice line after being accidentally marooned by their companions. "Colonel Norwood's Voyage to Virginia" related the misbegotten 1649 expedition in which Norwood was abandoned by his starving shipmates on an uninhabited island off Virginia.

Editing the anthology certainly enhanced O'Brian's understanding of eighteenth-century Europe and of how the world was perceived at the time. He possessed extraordinary powers of retention and integrated this information into his lively ken. One of the characters in the book, an intrepid joyrider named Lady Craven—a great beauty, whose portrait was painted by both Sir Joshua Reynolds and Élisabeth Vigée-Lebrun—fascinated him and later became an inspiration for his character Diana

Villiers, the sensual, free-spirited heroine of the Aubrey-Maturin opus. After giving birth to six children, Craven boldly left home and drove across the Continent in a coach pulled by six powerful horses. She reveled in the brute force of her steeds, at times flying over snow on runners. Craven was also a keen observer, discovering and admiring such Continental novelties as produce inspectors and prescriptions for drugs, both unknown in England.

Half a century later, when asked to explain the creative process, O'Brian would reach back and compare it to Craven's observations on Russian peasants who sang in parts, in perfect harmony, but did not know they were doing it, let alone how they did it. As she described it:

> In the evening in an amazing large hall . . . I heard the national songs of the Russian peasants—which are so singular that I cannot forbear endeavouring to give you some idea of them— One man stands in the midst of three or four, who make a circle round him; seven or eight make a second round those; a third is composed of a greater number; the man in the middle of this groupe begins, and when he has sung one verse, the first circle accompany him, and then the second, till they become so animated, and the noise so great, that it was with difficulty the officers could stop them—What is very singular they sing in parts, and though the music is not much varied, nor the tune fine, yet as some take thirds and fifths as their ear direct, in perfect harmony, it is by no means unpleasing—If you ask one of them why he does not sing the same note as the man before him—he does not know what you mean—The subjects of these ballads are, hunting, war, or counterfeiting the graduations between soberness into intoxification—and very diverting. As these singers were only young Russian peasants, they began with great timidity, but by little and little ended in a kind of wild jollity, which made us all laugh very heartily. (*A Book of Voyages,* p. 32)

The O'Brians soon had a Russian-style winter of their own to contend with, pushing literary endeavors to the background. The monotonous gray north Welsh winters can seem to last forever, but the winter of 1946–47 was far more bitter and long-lasting than usual. Nobody in Croesor could remember a colder one. Even though Fron was built into the notched hillside to protect it from the northeast winds, the O'Brians, like everyone else in Croesor, struggled to stay warm. A coal fireplace in the living room heated the tiny house, but the lean-to kitchen at the back grew so cold that eggs froze solid. A frost formed over the surface of the valley, and a heavy snow followed in January and February, hardening into a brittle crust. The sheep, which, unlike the cattle, remained outside all winter, could not get to the grass, and it became extremely difficult to transport hay to them on the hillsides.

On the Robertses' farm, the ewes became so weak that they had trouble feeding their lambs. Some unidentified nocturnal creature, no doubt starving itself, began to stalk the little ones, which were found dead or dying in the morning, a finger-sized hole bored into their skulls. Many theories were espoused—the predators were pine martens or polecats—but no identifiable tracks were ever found. Farmers patrolled at night with loaded shotguns.

No trucks could climb the roads to the valley to bring up supplies. Instead, groups of men, including Patrick, Harry Roberts, and his fourteen-year-old shepherd Edgar Williams, Eric's slight, brown-haired younger brother, who had moved into Croesor Fawr just before Christmas, walked down the valley together and toted up what they could carry.

The entire community pulled together to combat the brutal winter, which lasted until April. When a village man named Isaac Jones died, Patrick and Mary even took in his two sons, Arvan and Frank, for several days during the family's bereavement.

Spring arrived at last. Life normalized. Once again, Mary could ride her bicycle down the valley for supplies. The stony, winding road began several miles above Fron at the obsolete slate quarry—where gear-grinding trucks now deposited government-surplus explosives for storage—and passed immediately beside the cottage at rooftop level. Mary could reach the village of Gareg in twenty minutes. At a shop made of corrugated steel, she bought groceries and kerosene. She stowed in her wicker basket what she needed right away and then pedaled back up the hill. The balance was delivered by Bob, the shopowner, who conveniently doubled as the mailman.

As hard as the winter had been on the farmers, it was crucial for the O'Brians' acceptance in the valley community. As all returned to the fields, grateful to be outside in the sun again, they felt a new camaraderie for having come through the ordeal together. The ewes would lamb in April and early May, and it was prior to this busy time that the farmers hunted fox with the most devotion. Unlike the gentry, who carried no guns and hunted for sport, the shepherds of Croesor killed foxes to stop them from preying on their lambs. With his runty shotgun, O'Brian joined them, gathering grist for his writing mill.

On each of the mountains, the farmers knew just where to look for fox dens. They frequently trailed a flushed fox over boulder-strewn terrain and along narrow ridges, where O'Brian moved prudently, always, given a choice, searching for the surest, not the swiftest, route. The foxes often went to earth in inaccessible thickets of rockfall and brush, some so labyrinthine that the farmers halted the terriers' pursuit for certainty of losing them. When successful, the hunters cut off the fox's tail and sent it to the farmers' association for a bounty, easily worth a week's wages to a farmhand. The carrion eaters took care of the rest.

Most of the farmers had seen their flocks reduced by half during the cruel winter. Many of the surviving ewes were so emaciated that they did not have milk for their young. The care of the Robertses' weak, suffering lambs, sheltered amid Croesor Fawr's stockpiles of carrots, potatoes, and oats in a row of abandoned quarry-worker houses, fell to the O'Brians. Each morning, Richard fetched two pails of cow's milk, and they fed the hungry little creatures using nippled soft-drink bottles. The work was heartbreaking to Patrick and Mary, who were very sensitive. Many lambs died. The survivors tumbled about the O'Brians' front lawn until they were strong enough to be sent to pasture.

A long, hot summer provided an exceptional growing season. This stroke of fortune helped put the farmers back on their feet. Hay grew all the way to the top of the valley and required a great deal of labor. Edgar Williams, now Roberts's foreman, kept the schedule and ran the work gang. He and O'Brian had struck up a friendship during the winter. O'Brian perceived the intelligence of the young shepherd, who had passed exams to continue his education but dropped out of school to learn the sheep trade. O'Brian expressed concern that Edgar's only ambition was to train sheepdogs and have a position on the farm.

Although O'Brian stood on formality—even Harry Roberts called him Mr. O'Brian—he did not come across as arrogant, the way many Englishmen did to the Welsh, but as sincere. Roberts, a cheerful man, well read and strong-minded, a keen Welsh nationalist, liked to exchange views and argue with him. O'Brian prefaced many tidbits with "I read in a book that . . ." The phrase became a standing joke with the locals, who considered him something of a know-it-all. Although Roberts and others in Croesor secretly admired his authoritative and wide-ranging knowledge, they relished proving him wrong when his theories were at odds with the practical truths of the valley.

O'Brian was well aware that he was considered inept in practical matters. As the semi-autobiographical protagonist Pugh, an intellectual interloper in a fictional setting clearly based on Croesor, would say in O'Brian's novel *Testimonies*:

> "All ornamental knowledge, the arts entire they allowed me; any dead or foreign tongue was mine, and a perfect acquaintance with all things past. But they would not trust me to tell the difference between a horse and a mare, and when I was pottering about the farm they would send the boy to usher and guide me in any operation more complex than closing a gate." (P. 136)

In Welsh and English, which Edgar had learned to some degree in school and from English evacuees living in Croesor during the war, O'Brian and Edgar engaged in a certain amount of banter. Though it was unpopular among the farmers, particularly with Roberts, O'Brian openly supported creating a national park around Snowdon that would include Cwm Croesor, just six miles from Snowdon as the crow flies. "Calling it a park would make it a place where people would come and roam and enjoy themselves," he reasoned, according to Edgar. "What's wrong with that?"

"You can't live on scenery," Edgar countered, reflecting the opinion of most of the locals, who were suspicious of change.

To counter the tedium of work, O'Brian often asked Edgar questions about Welsh farming and geographic vocabulary. When the two discussed the derivation of the name Cnicht, which has no meaning in Welsh, Edgar doubted the common belief that the mountain's name came from the English word "knight" (the top supposedly resembled a knight's helmet). O'Brian observed that the Gaelic word for a similarly shaped hill was *cnut*. He asked Edgar what he would have called Cnicht instead. Edgar replied,

"*Saeth*," Welsh for "arrow," which is the name the mountain eventually took in O'Brian's novel *Testimonies*, set there.

The two also compared Welsh and Gaelic terms for the parts of a horse. Edgar came to think that O'Brian had grown up on a horse farm in western Ireland. Moreover, he was convinced that O'Brian was neither a spy nor a weather forecaster. He was definitely a schoolteacher. "Your grammar is terrible," he lectured Edgar.

O'Brian offered advice on many subjects, which Edgar took to heart. For instance, O'Brian instructed him on the proper way to jump off a cart. "Many parachutists had quite severe injuries from landing improperly," O'Brian told him. "They jumped into enemy territory only to find themselves already disabled. Never land on your heels, always forward on your toes." When O'Brian saw Edgar's sheepdog bitch, Meg, having fits, he wrote down on his pad some ingredients to buy from the pharmacist and handed it to Edgar. O'Brian's prescription cured the dog.

Another time he discoursed on cooking: fish should be fried slowly over low heat, he said, and hare should be hung to make it more flavorful. Edgar protested that he would not want to eat hare that was not fresh. To prove his point, O'Brian soon shot a hare, hung it, and invited Edgar over for properly aged hare soup.

Late summer was a particularly busy time on the farm. Sheep shearing, a cooperative venture, took place from the middle to the end of July. Shepherds from around the area took turns gathering at each other's farms, first to assemble and wash the sheep in the river, which cleaned the thick animal grease away and loosened the wool, and then after three or four days of drying time, depending on the weather, to shear them. The work started at the bottom of the valley, where the sheep were the first to get their spring growth—tender wool that came in beneath the coarse winter coat and was ideal for slicing through.

When it came time for Croesor Fawr to shear, some thirty helpers, mostly men and boys, from half a dozen farms gathered there for an intensive day. About half the workers, the most experienced, actually cut the wool, while the others, including Patrick and Mary, handled such tasks as tying the sheep's legs together, picking up each fifty-pound sheep after it was close shorn (usually in about five minutes), carrying it to another area where its wounds were carefully dressed and the farmer's mark was applied in paint or tar, and then untying and releasing it.

The work was hard. The reward for Patrick was gritty fodder for his fiction. His notes flowed almost directly into his character Pugh's experience at a similar sheep shearing in the novel *Testimonies*. As Pugh describes:

> I had never been so close to a sheep before, and its smell and warmth repelled me, and the give of its paunch against my body and the feel of the bones of its legs under their thin shifting skin as I lifted it. . . . I had never known that men could work so hard. There was no sense of time any more: it was lifting sheep, sheep and still sheep, the awful belly-strain of it and the tottering walk under the weight. (Pp. 65–67)

That book would not be published for several years. The more immediate reward was the princely noon meal, for which Bessie Roberts was famous. Harry had slaughtered a two-year-old wether lamb (a castrated male), considered the best meat, which Bessie cooked and served along with potatoes, carrots, swedes, rice pudding, and apple tart. While the rest of the hungry workers bolted down their food, with tea and buttermilk, and quickly returned to their shears, Patrick and Mary ate at a separate table at a more leisurely pace. But Patrick's mind worked like a sponge, absorbing it all for his depiction of Welsh sheep shearing, one of his most effective scenes in *Testimonies*.

In July and August, the farmhands also hayed up to the top of the steep, boulder-strewn slopes of Croesor Fawr with scythes, work that required skill and practice. In the field, they drank *glastwr*, a concoction of buttermilk, water, and oats, which they kept cool in the river. Because of the blazing sun in the high, thin air, the farmhands drank often, and while they and even Mary, relieved themselves behind a wall, Mr. O'Brian was too modest for that. Instead, he trudged the half mile back to his outhouse, much to the amusement of the others.

Mary was more adept at haying than Patrick. When they reaped on the islands and bends created by a straight property line running along the curving Croesor River, they crossed over the water on a ladder while carrying a fork full of hay. Unlike Patrick, who did not like this aspect of the work, Mary managed the crossing as if she had been reared on a farm. Still, Patrick maintained his sense of humor. When Edgar pronounced "island" as "iceland," O'Brian elaborately explained to him that the "s" was silent and that Iceland was a country far away. After they harvested this difficult section, Patrick needled the young foreman: "Well, we've finished Iceland now. What next, Edgar?"

The hay was gathered with a two-wheeled hay rake, pulled alternately by the Robertses' dappled gray Percherons: Flo, the elder and a steady worker, or Beetws, her full-blooded mare colt, who was testy and prone to bolting. When it came to handling the horses, Edgar valued O'Brian's advice. (Because of his back, according to Edgar, O'Brian never actually drove the cart.) Beetws would not keep to a straight path until O'Brian instructed Edgar to hold the reins lower, giving him better control.

After a broiling day of field work, it seems necessity overpowered modesty for Patrick and Mary. To refresh themselves and wash away the fine dust, they often hiked up the slope to the high river pools, where they bathed—somewhat shamelessly it seemed to the sweaty Methodists below—to the trill of the waterfalls.

That summer, the O'Brians had visitors. The painter Francis Cox, Richard's namesake, came for a month and painted, but most of all he idled and smoked. He received a scolding from Mary when he tried to send Richard to the store in Croesor to fetch tobacco for him during a torrential downpour. At the end of Cox's stay, Patrick and Richard made wooden corner protectors for shipping his canvases safely back to London. Barbara Puckridge, with whom Patrick and Mary had driven ambulances during the Blitz and who was now divorced, brought her son, James, for a month's stay as well. Mary was grateful for the female company and for conversation with a peer. She was also glad for the chance to spend some relaxing time out-of-doors. As a child of Appledore in west England, she had learned to ride and handle dogs and ferrets. She had relished tricky climbs on Lundy Island, once a pirate stronghold with a lofty rampart of rocks, in the Bristol Channel. Her father had also trained her brother, Howard, and her in the care and use of shotguns, always stressing safety. Mary was an excellent shot, though she did not care for hunting.

Croesor was alive with the summer's glory, and Barbara and Mary spent much of their time enjoying it with the boys, especially when Patrick was writing. Intolerant of noise, he shouted at the youngsters for raising their voices. So they stayed away as much as possible, fishing, foraging, and playing games. They liked to walk down the valley to a derelict farmhouse with an orchard of untended plum trees. That golden season, the branches sagged nearly to the ground under the lush fruit, which the boys picked and devoured.

With Patrick, they picnicked on a water-polished boulder in the middle of the Croesor River, where Barbara toasted bread over an open fire on a forked stick. The boys happily ate their beggar's banquet after spending their energy in the river pools. Another day, Patrick led the boys to the top of Snowdon, but it was socked in with fog. They had stowed their lunch under a rock halfway up the mountain, and Richard and James, disappointed at missing the promised panaromic view, were famished by the time they reached it. But O'Brian had ignored the advice of the women and packed a woefully insufficient meal of half a loaf of bread, some cheese, and a few apples. He returned home with two ravenous, dispirited youngsters.

It was an ideal summer for fishing and shooting. O'Brian and Harry Roberts kept up an ongoing debate on fishing techniques. O'Brian insisted on fly-fishing, while Roberts, like other locals, advocated fishing with bait. Roberts knew that the first rain after a dry spell was the best time to fish, a fact he did not divulge to Patrick. One day, he filled his basket with the river's small trout in an hour's time and smugly delivered half his catch to Fron.

James Puckridge had brought his double-barrel shotgun with him, and O'Brian taught him how to shoot, at newspaper targets pinned to the slate fence, emptying one barrel at a time at two different targets. Richard, deemed too young for the shotgun by Mary, used a bow planed by his father from a limb of ash and arrows made of hazelwood, fletched in goose feathers. This they shot on a grassy swell near the house at a target made of a sack on a stick. Aiming with the wrong eye, Richard accidentally shot his father in the buttocks with an untipped arrow, a wound more embarrassing than serious. The incident undoubtedly caused Patrick to reflect on the quality of his instruction, if not to recall his own errant shot years earlier in the garden at Melbury Lodge that had struck his sister Joan near the eye. It did not, however, squelch O'Brian's enthusiasm for archery, and later he made an even bigger bow that he and Mary shot at propped-up turf squares on a flat expanse lower in the valley.

The corn was harvested in September. One day while Edgar was driving a cart full of freshly picked ears, Beetws bolted, flipping and smashing it, but mercifully throwing Edgar onto some soft hay. Later, O'Brian described to Edgar the cruel method used by Irish gypsies to break a rogue cart horse: They tied a rope from the horse's bit to a spoke of the cart's wheel. Then they held a handful of straw lit with fire to its belly. When the horse bolted, the wheel of the cart jerked the horse's head back. This method broke either its will or its neck.

In the fall, as the ewes came into season, the feistiest rams had to be chained together in pairs by the horns to prevent them from leaping the fences and mating too soon. In late October and November, the rams—one for every forty ewes—were loosed among the three hundred or so ewes for mating. Roberts slaughtered a pig around this time each year. Bessie salted and prepared it and hung the hams and sides from the kitchen beams to be carved throughout the fall and winter. She was a superb cook and ran a productive kitchen, where she often chatted with Mary, while making rhubarb and gooseberry tarts, custards, and suet puddings. She also took great pride in her preserved plums, black currants, and blackberries.

The Robertses fit in the valley almost as naturally as did the massive gray boulders. The O'Brians learned by example, though the lessons sometimes came at the expense of pride, particularly for Patrick. One day while they worked in the field, Roberts spotted a fox in the heather on the hillside. O'Brian could not find it and stubbornly disputed the claim. At the end of the day, Roberts told O'Brian that the fox was still lying there in the sun. "We'll go up," the farmer said, getting his shotgun, "and I will prove my point." Up Cnicht he led O'Brian and Edgar, approaching the spot from above. Sure enough, a fox lay there asleep in the sun. Roberts doffed his boots, tiptoed down some scree, and shot it. Humbled, O'Brian nonetheless gamely helped drag the fox down to the farm, so Roberts could use it to train a shy terrier pup. As he went, the heavy carcass rubbed against his trouser legs, embedding its pungent aroma. When he arrived at the farm, the terrier ignored the fox altogether and instead fearlessly attacked O'Brian's leg.

In the fall of 1947, the Soho publisher Home and Van Thal—one of the postwar "mushroom" houses that sprouted up while the paper-rationing system still hampered the industry—brought out *A Book of Voyages*, which, in the spirit of austerity, bore the dedication: "To M. from P. with love." As if to demonstrate the coziness of London literary circles, the back cover carried an advertisement for *Southwards from Swiss Cottage*, a memoir by Beatrice Curtis Brown, the sister of O'Brian's friend and agent Spencer Curtis Brown, covering her youth in St. John's Wood, where O'Brian's father had also grown up, and her social life between the wars in Chelsea.

The 274-page anthology did not attract much notice. Not long after *Punch* reviewed the book in November ("the editor must be congratulated for having kept the extracts brief and for giving us so much variety"), Margaret Douglas-Home and Herbert van Thal sold their business, which soon folded into another publisher.

By now, O'Brian had moved on to writing fiction. In Croesor, he carried a pen and a pad, scribbling down notes, bits of dialogue, scenery, impressions. He asked many questions about the present or former inhabitants of the various farms and huts in the area, and Edgar often filled him in on the local lore. His recent as yet unpublished stories were mostly about fox hunting and fishing, and they drew their animus from the dour valley.

One evening, Patrick found himself hunting a different predator. A sheepdog had turned bad. It was scavenging in the rubbish heaps behind the houses and stalking the sheep at night, a high crime in Croesor. When O'Brian spotted the dog skulking around the Robertses' pasture, he took down his shotgun, chased the turncoat, and shot it in the rear. It caused no more trouble after that.

9

Moelwyn Bank

1948–1949

I know of no redeeming qualities in me but a sincere love of
some things, and when I am reproved I have to fall back on to
this ground. This is my argument in reserve for all cases. My
love is invulnerable. Meet me on that ground, and you will find
me strong. When I am condemned, and condemn myself
utterly, I think straightaway, "But I rely on my love for some
things." Therein I am whole and entire.

—Henry David Thoreau, journal, December 15, 1841

In 1948, the O'Brians moved several hundred yards down the valley
into a larger house, one in need of renovation, which suited them well
since the rent increase came in the form of sweat. Built on the crest of
a hill in the last quarter of the nineteenth century as a residence for the
quarry manager, Moelwyn Bank possessed a view and a large garden. It
had once even had electricity, but no longer. It did boast, however, a lava-
tory with running water provided by a diverted stream.

Like Ybryn, an even grander quarry executive house, Moelwyn Bank
was considered by the locals to be somewhat undesirable, fine in summer
but hopeless in winter. Being so large and having no geologic protection
from the frigid northeaster, it was damp and drafty. Slate shingles covered
the stone walls, but even this armor was not considered sufficient to
combat the driving rain and winds of Croesor. During the war, the house
had been given over to evacuees from the big cities and had fallen into dis-
repair. Now the O'Brians, with the help of Edgar, spent weeks fixing up
the place, peeling old paper off the walls and scraping the ceilings. They
painted and stenciled the interior with a floral pattern. They cleaned the
chimney and replaced broken windowpanes.

Nearby, at Ybryn, the grass tennis court was now grazed by sheep. An English sculptor named Sydney Whitehead Smith and his wife had lived there since before the war. He was a patronizing John Bull with a modern car that was the envy of the valley. O'Brian did not like the man, and the two were barely cordial. O'Brian even wrote a tale, "It Must Have Been a Branch, They Said," with an inimical Englishman whom locals recognized as Smith. Not that O'Brian would have gone out of his way to make friends with the likes of Smith. The fictional Pugh perhaps expresses O'Brian's own somewhat misanthropic feelings in *Testimonies* when, after moving to his cottage in Wales, he states:

> "I had understood that there were practically no gentlefolk within calling distance, and this seemed to me in many ways an advantage. Perhaps, having rubbed shoulders for so long with more people than I liked, I saw it as a disproportionate benefit; but with all allowances there is something to be said for the absence of formal, enforced intercourse. One may be lucky and chance upon a set of amiable neighbors, liberal and informed, who can make life much more pleasant. It is more probable that no such thing will occur." (P. 103)

As the O'Brians prepared for the move, Patrick was struck with an acute case of appendicitis. Harry Roberts and Edgar answered Mary's call for help, and the two carried him semidelirious and spouting oaths (though this was quite out of character) down the steep steps of Fron's loftlike second floor. With his free hand, the powerful farmer lifted the garden gate right up off its hinges as they carried the writhing author out to a waiting ambulance.

The hospital stay for appendicitis lasted a fortnight or so, and by the time Patrick returned, Mary had moved into the spacious new house, which had three bedrooms and a washing room upstairs. On the front porch, they could hang coats and leave Wellington boots. For writing, O'Brian had his own room off the stairway landing, where his special fountain pen and his machine for typing braille were installed. Downstairs, on one side of a center hallway, a large kitchen and dining area led to a small second kitchen and then into a lean-to scullery with a steep corrugated tin roof, resting on a low stone wall, used for cold storage. On the other side of the hallway, in the drawing room, O'Brian drilled holes into the plaster, inserted wooden plugs, and then screwed in supports for shelves. Here he installed his growing library.

Settling into their new home were the couple's three dogs, Mary's particular delight. Buddug (pronounced "Bithig"), a Welsh farmyard terrier, was not pedigreed but admirably tough and smart. Her two corgis went by the names Bronwen and Nan. A cat named Hodge, after Dr. Johnson's "very fine" cat (which Johnson fed oysters), rounded out their family— almost.

Patrick and Mary could no longer afford to pay for tuition, room, and board at Southey Hall, so Richard was brought to Moelwyn Bank. It was a far cry from the manor house at Fulford, where Southey Hall had operated during the war and where in the magnificent dining hall, the boys were forbidden to carry their pocketknives for fear that the oak paneling or the enormous oil paintings might suffer. The move was but another twist in the boy's already overeventful youth. Just eleven, he had seen his parents separate, his little sister die, his city bombed and burned, and he had spent four years away at boarding school. He had lived in rural Suffolk, in Norwich, in London, in Devon, and in Surrey, and now he found himself in remote Wales. At times he grew desperately homesick for his mother and his pet boxer, Sian (Welsh for "Jane," after his sister).

O'Brian's reserve did not help the situation. He perpetuated the parenting attitudes of both his father and his grandfather. Like them, he was not inclined to relate to a child on his level. He never spoke of his own childhood to him. Though warm and sensitive to Mary, he was very much an authority figure, the master and teacher, to his son. He always chose a lesson in fortitude over a sympathetic response, such as the time Richard dissolved into tears after stepping on a drawing pen that jabbed into his heel. O'Brian took him aside and told him the fable of the Spartan boy, who hid a fox cub under his tunic and carried it home. His parents were entertaining guests, and, instead of interrupting them, the boy sat down and waited quietly. Even when the fox began biting him, the boy kept silent. He eventually bled to death rather than interrupt his parents. The moral of the story was not lost on young Richard, but it provided little comfort at a time when it was sorely needed. (O'Brian later put the tale of the Spartan boy to better use in a hilarious rendition in his novel *The Golden Ocean* [pp. 130–31]).

Patrick and Mary were determined not to let Richard's education suffer. Mary instructed him in French, which she spoke fluently from her days on the Continent. In the evenings, she gave him singing and music lessons. Patrick, whose ability to parse a sentence impressed even his son, taught him English, Latin, history, and mathematics. When Richard mixed up his multiplication tables, Patrick made him write out sentences as punishment. He was a demanding schoolmaster, who required learning by rote. Richard also memorized Thomas Babington Macaulay's "Lars Porsena of Clusium," which quite suited him since it was about the heroic Roman Horatius, who with two companions defends a bridge against an invading army and slays its fiercest warriors. Richard also read widely from Patrick's diverse library: from Arthurian legend to Daniel Defoe's *Robinson Crusoe* and George Catlin's *North American Indians*.

O'Brian was perhaps too stern a taskmaster for the young boy, and it did not help that Richard struggled with Latin, his father's pet subject. Patrick found it difficult enough to dole out commendation when it was merited. Without praise to counterbalance it, his criticism stung the boy. As a result, while Richard did emerge with an impressive vocabulary, he had few fond memories of being taught by his father.

However, outside class the boy took pleasure in the constant flow of activity resulting from his father's abiding interests. He developed a life-long fascination with birds. Wheatears, stonechats, flycatchers, ravens, and peregrines graced the Welsh hills. The O'Brians loved nature and treated it with respect, often picnicking in the wild but never leaving behind a trace. Richard learned to make and repair things. When Bessie Roberts, who hand-churned butter and made lovely round pats with a floral design on top, found a crack in her mold, Patrick volunteered to repair it. He carefully applied a delicate strip of brass using tiny screws so that it wouldn't mar the pats.

Richard also learned the basics of gardening from his father. With his usual energy and enthusiasm, Patrick planted a vegetable garden at Moelwyn Bank. To get it just right, he followed the instructions of a wartime government manual from the "Dig for Britain" days of World War II. With the help of Mary and Richard, he sowed seed on half an acre, enriched with the Robertses' abundant farmyard manure. This labor paid off in a harvest of potatoes, leeks, red and black currants, gooseberries, cauliflower, and marrow, which in the cool scullery lasted well into winter. This experience so boosted O'Brian's zeal for farming that he grew keen on becoming the tenant of a little farm, Ynys Giftan, about four miles away, on the estate of Lord Harlech. O'Brian discussed the idea frequently with Edgar, but the property, on a ten-acre island in the River Dwyryd, was let to someone else.

In their spare time, Mary and Patrick and Richard played Ping-Pong on the air-raid shelter and Racing Demon, a card game of hand speed and memory. With so few distractions, the games grew quite competitive. In the evenings, they sometimes listened to a wireless that ran off a battery they charged at the power station up the mountain. Patrick was especially fond of the outlandish comedy *The Goon Show*, in which Peter Sellers, Spike Milligan, and Harry Secombe played multiple roles. Other times, Mary played the accordion and sang songs such as "Barbara Allen" and "Sweet Lass of Richmond Hill." In the hallway, they kept a wind-up His Master's Voice gramophone. Richard cranked the machine and changed the records. To the music of Haydn and Mozart, the three read by kerosene lamps and the light of the fireplace.

Although the valley largely circumscribed the O'Brians' existence at this time, they did venture outside it. In good weather, they rode bikes to the beach to swim. At the insistence of his mother, Richard regularly attended the Roman Catholic church in the coastal town of Porthmadog, a hilly eight-mile walk or bike ride away.

Between Porthmadog and Croesor lay the lowlands estate of the Jones family, called Ynysfor ("Big Island"), where the O'Brians sometimes hunted. Ynysfor sat on a hill that had been nearly an island before the tidal Glaslyn River was dammed at Porthmadog during the Napoleonic wars to create farmland.

While the briny soil of Ynysfor bore salty grass that produced especially savory lamb, the Joneses' reputation rested on their fox hunt, established in 1765. A succession of Joneses served as masters of the hounds until the fall of 1948, when fifty-nine-year-old Captain John "Jack" Jones was killed in a hunting accident. A hound had been lost, and as usual in such a situation, an impromptu hunt took place the following day in the hope that the lost dog would come to the baying of the pack. A fox was raised and went underground in a rockfall. Jones, who was master of the hounds, rolled back some of the large rocks to examine the hideout. The destabilized pile collapsed, crushing him.

This was sad news for O'Brian, who had hunted with Jones, and for some time the accident was the talk of Croesor, where little love was lost for the lowland gentleman farmers. O'Brian comforted himself about his friend's death by telling Edgar that Captain Jones was not the sort of man who would have wanted to die in bed.

No male Jones remained to lead the hunt, so Major Edmund Roche, whose mother had been a Jones, took over. A Sandhurst-educated officer in the famous South Wales Borderers infantry regiment, Roche was an accomplished sportsman who raced horses and played polo while serving in India, Africa, France, and with Viscount Allenby in Palestine. He inherited a farm in disarray, as well as several resident spinster aunts. The gruff forty-year-old half-Irish veteran went about setting the place to rights. He soon installed a wife, Primrose Buchan-Hepburn, the daughter of a Scots baronet, and packed off the aunts to an auxiliary house on the estate. He bought more land and, after a respectful hiatus, returned to the hunt. Hunts typically started after breakfast and ran until teatime, the participants returning to the house for refreshment and gossip presided over by Primrose and Aunts Sybil (a farmer) and Minnie (a justice of the peace), tough but handsome women who hunted fox and spurned suitors.

While the Ynysfor hunt, which took place every Wednesday and Saturday from October through March, was a social event for the local upper crust, it was no picnic. Unarmed but clad in a proper tweed jacket, Patrick, and sometimes Mary too, walked or biked down to Ynysfor and then hiked the ten to twenty miles over brutal terrain, across bogs, over slate walls, up faces of shale, wherever the fox led, keeping pace as best as possible with the hounds. It was the performance and cry of the pack, the teamwork and the reactions of each dog to the combined music, that stimulated the hunter.

Since the hounds often ran out of sight during the chase, the hunter followed their sound and the sporadic visual clues. When the fox—usually a red fox, whose color could be anything from reddish brown to nearly black—finally went to earth, the hounds marked the spot and then most went silent. Only one or two, the most valuable dogs, kept baying so that the hunters could find them.

The first time Patrick took Richard along, the boy was overwhelmed by the stench of the hounds, which fed on the carcasses of livestock (kept in a river pool until needed). The dogs sensed his fear. They forced their wet noses into his coat pockets and tried to steal the two sandwiches that Mary had carefully wrapped in greased paper. But the mugged boy braced up and returned for more. On one hunt, Idwal, the kennel master, put him in charge of a brace of Lakeland terriers, which came into play only if the fox went to earth. Getting them where they had to be was quite a task, though. The terriers would not climb, so Richard had to lift them over the many walls they encountered while he tried to keep up with the pack.

O'Brian enjoyed the strenuous yet exhilarating hunts. On the severe slopes of Snowdon, this exhausting and dangerous activity exposed his fears and weaknesses and allowed him to test himself. He demonstrated courage and perseverance as well as a love of nature and a respect for its brutality. Hunting on Snowdon with Walter Greenway, who was staying at Moelwyn Bank, O'Brian had a chilling experience one bleak winter day. The two became separated on the mountainside as Greenway lagged behind. The shale was slick. On a steep slope, O'Brian lost his footing. He found nothing to grab as he helplessly slid down a face of shale and scree. When he finally came to a halt, well below the ledge he had been walking on, he was scraped and bruised, but he had broken no bones. Badly shaken, he had lost his taste for hunting that day, and as there was no easy way back up to the trail, he headed down. Before walking back to Croesor, he left a message with a local to tell the master of the hounds that he had headed home. The message never made it to Roche, however, and Greenway finally began the long walk back to Croesor by himself with a heavy heart. As far as ne knew, Patrick had disappeared on the mountain, and he had to tell Mary.

When Greenway climbed the last hill to the house, he saw O'Brian anxiously awaiting him in the yard. O'Brian apologized for the misunderstanding. Elated at seeing his friend safe, Greenway forgave him at once. But Roche remained angry about the incident and reprimanded O'Brian for not making sure that the head of the hunt knew of his departure.

Fox hunting at Ynysfor inspired two riveting short stories—perhaps the most successful of all of O'Brian's hunting tales. Both explore the intense emotions the hunters experience as they race over the craggy, desolate Welsh hills in pursuit of a pack of baying hounds. In both, the hunter is an outsider, new to the sport, and loath to prove unworthy. In both, he teeters on the brink of exhaustion, danger, and self-discovery. O'Brian dedicated "The Steep Slope of Gallt y Wenallt" to Major Roche and the ladies of Ynysfor and the "The Long Day Running" to Greenway. In "The Steep Slope," Greenway served as the model for the mildly unsympathetic character Gonville, who has an intellectual disagreement with Brown, the main character, in a conversation on the nature of birds' flight. O'Brian later apologized to Greenway for the unflattering portrayal.

During Greenway's stay in Croesor, he and O'Brian resumed their old conversations on clocks and naval literature. It was then that O'Brian introduced Greenway to C. S. Forester's Horatio Hornblower stories. Forester had begun writing them before the war, producing a trilogy by 1938 and two new titles, *The Commodore* and *Lord Hornblower*, after the war. "You must read this book," O'Brian declared, handing Greenway the red-cloth one-volume trilogy.

In the spring of 1949, the peace of Cwm Croesor was disrupted by repairs to the dam in the hanging valley above. The Robertses' fields served as a landing pad for the helicopter employed in the work. On May 24, the chopper, carrying a load of dry cement in a vessel suspended from a cable, roared up the valley, but it got caught in a downdraft and dropped like a stone, crashing in a cloud of cement dust. Miraculously, the pilot emerged on his own two feet. People came from near and far to gawk, and Richard made a sport of finding pieces of the helicopter's shattered windshield. But a new helicopter soon arrived, hauled off the wreckage, and finished the work. The dam was repaired by mid-June.

It was a fine, sunny early summer, and O'Brian, now thirty-five, polished up his short stories. But he and Mary, no longer so world-weary, also considered moving. Cwm Croesor had offered them the simple, clean life that they had coveted after the war and a degree of freedom within their means. But life in the Welsh valley, which was cold and damp much of the year, aggravating ailments, was remote, harsh, and monotonous. They also had to consider Richard's welfare. So far, his boyish transgressions were minor. Out of boredom he had attempted to pop a tire of one of the quarry trucks by positioning a slate shard on the road, and he had stoned a neighbor's cowshed, creating a minor stampede. (For the latter, Patrick had punished him with a judicious wallop with a walking stick.) But Richard would soon need the company of children his own age, proper schooling, and additional activities to occupy his teenage mind.

After his two-year apprenticeship, Edgar Williams had moved on to another farm the previous November, and now the O'Brians felt the urge to find a more salubrious situation. London seemed to offer little besides more gray skies and financial hardship. Paris promised much the same, but southern France appealed to them, with its sunny weather and low cost of living. The Mediterranean coast would do nicely, and they had a place in mind. Patrick traveled to France as a scout. One day, an envelope arrived in the mail for Mary. In a romantic gesture, Patrick had wrapped inside a glowing letter a tiny glass vial of seawater taken from the bay of a fishing village. He had found their new home: Collioure, the village along the escape route from Vichy France to Spain and the purported departure point for Goëau-Brissonnière's aborted submarine getaway.

Patrick returned full of enthusiasm. The blessed sunshine, the clear sky, and the temperate sea of Roussillon suddenly made Wales look impossibly grim. Food grew abundantly there; wine seemed to spring from the sun-baked rocks; and, though it was far from a major city, Collioure had much of cultural interest. Not the least of the attractions was that it would be even cheaper to live in Catalan France than in Wales. As they prepared to move, Patrick and Mary bubbled with the prospect of a cheerful climate, but until then the slate-and-shale Welsh hills continued to suffuse Patrick's writing.

The major literary achievement of O'Brian's three years on the far side of Offa's Dyke would be his celebrated novel *Testimonies*, published originally in Britain as *Three Bear Witness* in April 1952. The more immediate product was a collection of short stories written in Cwm Croesor, which would eventually be titled *The Last Pool*.

Under the influence of the dolorous north Wales landscape, where abandoned stone huts stood like monuments of lost causes, O'Brian wrote dark, foreboding tales with an edge of horror. Lost and forlorn protagonists fish and hunt in eerie Irish and Welsh countrysides, often possessed of a malevolent spirit. With minimal plots, the tales tell of discontented or damaged men usually from broken families or living with unsympathetic wives. O'Brian's rendition of the human condition was dismal. Thematically, his stories suited the confusing world that followed two global wars and an economic depression, but they seemed more to reflect his own personal disillusion.

One ruined house in Cwm Foel, a particularly solitary high valley, in the pass between Cnicht and Moelwyn Mawr, inspired O'Brian's story "Naming Calls." Dafydd Foel ("Bald David"), a legendary chieftain, who was said to have fought the invading English at the bottom of the mountain, slaughtering many, once lived in the house in Cwm Foel. In O'Brian's tale, his house, Llys Dafydd, is rented out by Abel Widgery for a solitary stretch of reading and bird-watching. But Widgery comes to realize that Llys Dafydd is "unfit for the habitation of any man but a hermit, a man able to struggle with loneliness and devils" (p. 167). Widgery has trouble sleeping and in his mind relives a haunting scene following the death of his father, a "formidable, roaring tyrant," in which his nanny is about to mention his father's name when her sister stops her: "Naming calls, you know. God between us and harm" (p. 168). When a storm blows the roof off the hut, and an ominous rockslide shakes the mountainside, the most terrifying sound to Widgery, who is haunted by this memory of his father's death, is that of the door creaking.

According to Edgar Williams, the hunt in the story "The Drawing of the Curranwood Badgers" had its origin when he, Patrick, and Harry Roberts once hunted for fox in Cwm Foel, the same desolate high valley of "Naming Calls." Unaware that their fox terriers had lit upon badgers, they sent a pup into the underground warren, where it was badly mauled. In O'Brian's story, set in Ireland, he transformed this real event into a scene of restrained horror when Aloysius FitzGibbon, an aging red-faced Irish huntsman, and the protagonist, Gethin Jones, the son of a Welsh gardener, send FitzGibbon's terriers into a badger holt. A furious subterranean battle rages, with the two listening above. When they hear one dog killed, FitzGibbon starts madly digging. What he encounters is not a badger.

In "The Happy Despatch," O'Brian placed Woollen, an Englishman born to lose, in a remote section of County Mayo, where he fishes in a lonely stream for tiny trout. Raised in a foster home by an unloving parson, Woollen had joined the army and emerged with a "glaze of military stupidity . . . and a kind of superficial arrogance—a protective colouring of which he was wholly unconscious"(p. 50). Now broke and living a despairing existence with a "vile" bedridden wife, he finds in the stream a hidden treasure and his doom. Likewise in "The Last Pool," O'Brian pits James Aislabie, another sportsman destined to lose, against his dream fish, a thirty-pound salmon. O'Brian stacked the odds against Aislabie by giving him a rod and reel meant for a two-pound trout. A furious struggle ensues, in which just as an improbable victory is his, Aislabie's courage fails him, leading to a grave injury.

In "The Little Death"—the story that O'Brian dedicated to Armand Goëau-Brissonnière, his French colleague at the Political Intelligence Department—O'Brian offered a glimmer of hope and a clue to what spawned the dismal scenes and hopeless predicaments in his short stories from this period of his life. This story is about a former combat pilot struggling to come to terms with the war. Here again O'Brian's protagonist, Mr. Grattan, has had an abnormal upbringing, living in the "celibate house" of his uncle and aunts. Unemployed and aimless, Grattan has lost touch with reality. While hunting, he relives shooting down a Messerschmitt. He watches the fighter plane plummet and anxiously waits in vain for the pilot to parachute. The chilling memory fuels Grattan's depression. But on this day, while bird hunting, he has an epiphany: he will never kill again.

While these stories, along with the forbidding hunting tales "The Long Day Running" and "The Steep Slope of the Gallt y Wenallt," perhaps best reflected O'Brian's disposition and concerns while he was living in Wales, he was not always quite so saturnine. During this time he wrote at least two other outstanding stories, both mythic and mischievous, something like adult fairy tales, very different from the hunting narratives. They revealed a more supple imagination and a dry wit. In "The Green Creature," he opposed a handsome, powerful would-be priest named Daniel Colman and a fiend in the form of a beautiful woman known only as "the green creature." She drowns fishermen at her lonely mountain lake in western Ireland and drinks their blood because her god, Aog, has led her to believe it necessary to maintain her beauty. But Colman, who is lured into her lake, survives and, in an underwater cave, while naked and dining on kippered trout with his nemesis, squares off with her in a battle of words. It is their gods who lose, as she renounces Aog for Colman, and he abandons his priestly vows for her.

As strange as that story was, O'Brian topped it in "The Virtuous Peleg," which stood out from his other stories like a glorious speckled trout in a goldfish pond. Most of his spare, serious man-in-nature tales relied on detailed physical description. In this tongue-in-cheek parable, O'Brian dropped his guard, let his wit run free, and previewed the humor and nimble dialogue for which he later became famous. When a flawed angel leads two monks—the bungling Peleg and Kevin, his sanctimonious cousin—on a voyage to a heathen shore, they encounter a pack of bloody-minded but charming devils who argue about how to win the monks' souls. In a bit of repartee worthy of Aubrey and Maturin, the angel asks Peleg if he wants to wrestle. "If it would not be too forward in me, sir, I should welcome it of all things," Peleg responds. "To try a couple of falls with your reverence would give me all the pleasure in life." The angel warns him, "I shall dust your jacket, mind" (p. 69).

The decision to relocate and the completion of the collection of tales lifted the heavy yoke of Welsh mountain life, and the O'Brians now ached to run free. To fund the move, they sold some of Mary's family furniture through an auction house in London. Then they packed up their most valued possessions—carefully crating Patrick's books—and offered the rest to their friends in the valley.

Even pets were given away. Edgar's younger brother Gwilym took home Richard's white angora rabbit, and his father conveyed its hutch made from half a cask down the hill in his wheelbarrow. Mary left her two Welsh corgis, Bronwen and Nan, to friendly families, but she would not part with Buddug. She would have to learn French.

Spirits might have been higher had the custody issue for Richard not flared up. In May, Elizabeth Russ had married a widower named John Cowper le Mee-Power, an army veteran, a company executive, and the son of the director of a Ceylonese tea and rubber estate. Word reached her that Patrick and Mary intended to move to France and to take Richard with them. Possibly on Dimitry Tolstoy's advice, Elizabeth went to court to guarantee that Richard, now twelve, would not move abroad.

One day a constable appeared at Moelwyn Bank. Although Patrick told Richard that the visit concerned their dog, Richard later came to believe that the officer delivered papers notifying his father that he had been barred by a court order from taking Richard out of the country. Elizabeth's second marriage would not last long, but she would have her son by her side.

At this point, there was no turning back for Patrick and Mary. Wales had been both a sweet and a bitter phase of their lives, but it was over now. For most of their neighbors, there was no way out of those doleful, inlooking hills. For the O'Brians, there was no way to remain, even if it meant leaving Richard behind with his mother. He would still be allowed to visit them during school holidays.

Before they left, Patrick went to the village and called at the Williams house to invite Edgar to dinner. He told the boy's mother he had a special gift for him. With visions of owning Patrick's shotgun, which he had freely borrowed for hunting, the sixteen-year-old boy showed up for dinner in great anticipation. The .410 was merely a popgun compared with the twelve-gauge shotguns that most farmers used, but it was still a gun.

That night, Patrick presented Edgar with the couple's piano accordion. "You can teach yourself to play," he told him, with a benevolent smile. "I am sure you will get much pleasure out of this." Astonished, disappointed, but touched by Patrick and Mary's kindness and the honor of their attention, Edgar was speechless.

In the summer of 1949, O'Brian submitted his story collection, which he titled *Country Contentments*, to his agent, Spencer Curtis Brown, who sent it on to Fred Warburg at the publishing house Secker and Warburg, one of London's most prestigious literary publishers, the house of H. G. Wells, George Orwell, Thomas Mann, Colette, and André Gide. Brown had recently delivered Warburg a first collection of stories *(The Wrong Set)* from another young writer, Angus Wilson, which would establish his reputation as a brilliant satirist.

On August 18, Warburg wrote back to Brown telling him that several of O'Brian's story endings needed some tinkering and that the title of the book should be changed to *The Last Pool* but that Secker and Warburg would like to publish O'Brian's remarkable collection.

Warburg, from a poor branch of the banking family, believed strongly in promoting good writing and that sales would eventually follow. He suggested a contract similar to Wilson's.

Brown wrote back four days later to tell Warburg that by good fortune O'Brian, who was in the process of moving to France, would be in London for two weeks and could discuss the title change and alterations with him. He told Warburg that while a £50 advance, the same as Wilson's, was acceptable, he did not want to include as many subsidiary rights as he had with Wilson, who was an unknown. O'Brian, Brown reminded Warburg, had already been published by Oxford University Press and Home and Van Thal.

Two days later Warburg took O'Brian out to lunch. They discussed the editorial changes, and Warburg felt O'Brian took the criticism well, so much so that he informed Brown the agent need not be involved with the minor alterations that O'Brian was going to make. Warburg and O'Brian had gotten on well, and O'Brian had told the publisher about his plans to write a novel set in Wales and another about the French Catalans. Warburg was intrigued. He now advanced the planned publication of the short story book from the fall of 1950 to the summer.

This optimism was justified. O'Brian, who was staying with the

Wicksteeds at the Cottage, went straight to work, adding clearer fore-shadowing of the diabolical ending in "The Drawing of the Curranwood Badgers," lessening the obscurity of "The Little Death," and correcting an error in a fishing story. He also cobbled together a promotional blurb for the book and some biographical information. On August 28, four days after having lunch with Warburg, O'Brian submitted to him the revised typescript. In a handwritten postscript, he meekly suggested a new, lyrical title for the book, *Dark Speech Upon the Harp*, which Warburg rejected, preferring *The Last Pool.* But O'Brian had impressed the publisher. In return for additional subsidiary rights on *The Last Pool* and an option on the planned book about the Catalans, Warburg upped the advance by 50 percent. While Warburg and Brown haggled over the details in early September, the O'Brians departed for Paris.

Shortly thereafter, Patrick wrote to Roger Senhouse (though he mistakenly called him "Spenhouse"), who would become O'Brian's primary editor at Secker and Warburg, to continue an ongoing conversation. Senhouse, a former assistant to Lytton Strachey and Warburg's partner, who had kept the house afloat during the lean prewar years by continually raising money from friends, had questioned the name "the Prawn" for the hunt in the story "It Must Have Been a Branch, They Said." The name was a play on "Quorn," the most famous hunt in England, held in the county of Rutland. ("Prawn" and "Quorn" rhyme in English pronunciation.) O'Brian told Senhouse that when he had written the story, he had thought the name droll but now found it unpleasantly facetious. He was not pleased with "the Bagworthy" or "the Wheatsheaf," the alternatives he had thought up. He asked the editor if he would mind coming up with an appropriate name and inserting it for his approval in page proofs.

This was as cavalier as O'Brian would ever be about his work. Perhaps he was intoxicated by the City of Lights and the exciting new life that lay before him and Mary. After all, the note to Senhouse was penned in Paris's Luxembourg Gardens, where, O'Brian noted with delight, there were woodpigeons in almost every tree and children playing—at a suitable distance.

Part IV

AZURE

10

The Last Stronghold of
Poets and Painters

1949–1953

I wish that every human life might be pure transparent
freedom.

—Simone de Beauvoir, *The Blood of Others,* 1946

Mr. O'Brian writes as though the weight of the world were on
his shoulders.

—*The New Yorker,* review of *Testimonies*, September 6, 1952

In 1949, when the bar at Café des Sports in Collioure, France, collapsed under its own weight, René Pous, the owner, hired a carpenter
to build a new one in the shape of a local fishing bark. The carved fig-
urehead of the new thirty-foot bar—a mermaid wearing a round-brimmed
sailor's hat—suckled a babe clasped in her arms. Around her, Pous's
patrons—artists, fishermen, and vintners—drank pastis or Pernod, played
cards, and smoked cigarettes. Offshore, a German boat sunk with all
hands by a British torpedo, served as a silent reminder of the Occupation,
but otherwise Collioure had returned to celebrating its abundant gifts:
wine, weather, art, and anchovies.

That summer, Patrick and Mary arrived in this isolated, self-absorbed
village of sand-colored stone and red-tiled roofs. Lying fifteen miles southeast of Perpignan on a spit of land jutting into the Gulf of Lions, Collioure
inhabited a stunning landscape. On one side of the town, past a seventeenth-
century church bell tower, the sails of fishing boats glowed like tiny day
moons on the azure sea. On the other, beneath Fort St. Elme, a sixteenth-
century watchtower standing guard to the south, the hillsides of the
Albères massif were terraced in vineyards of fat black grapes.

In 1905, Henri Matisse and some fellow painters had discovered the colorful village and its crisp, clear sky. Inspired by what André Derain described as its "clarity and luminosity that is opposed to sunlight" (*Matisse,* p. 16), the artists turned their shocking palette of bright, bold colors to nature and nudes on the beach, creating Fauvism and forever placing the village of three thousand souls on the map of Western civilization.

Thus was launched Collioure's love affair with itself, a narcissism that had justification: at one time or another, the Romans, the Moors, the Francs, and the Spanish had all occupied Roussillon—the region at the eastern corner of the southernmost part of France, roughly equivalent to the sixteen-hundred-square-mile modern-day French department Pyrénées-Orientales.* Each of the conquering peoples contributed to a rich culture, with distinct music, art, food, and wine. Tourists were quickly seduced, or repelled, by a gritty but sensual paradise of sorts. Collioure's most notable architectural feature—irresistible to artists—was the cylindrical pink-capped church bell tower that watched over the harbor and its beaches looking unmistakably like an erect phallus.

World War II had killed fishing as a way of life in Collioure, but the long process of memorializing that passing tradition had just begun. Bright colors and Catalan themes prevailed. The proprietors of Café des Sports, René and Pauline Pous, often accepted art in lieu of cash, which meant that their establishment, where hardy staples included bouillabaisse and boar, was a pilgrimage site for migratory artists and writers. The gregarious abstract painter Willy Mucha, an expatriate Czech who had fought in the Spanish Civil War, was the soul of the place, which was sandwiched between a twelfth-century chateau and the narrow winding hillside streets of the old town, but still with a view of the harbor. Mucha inaugurated the café's guest book with the inscription: "to glorify Collioure, the last stonghold of free spirits, errant poets and painters thirsting for pure colors."

Collioure welcomed visitors warmly, as O'Brian had discovered when he was scouting out the village. He had stayed with a Madame Perpignane, on the Rue du Soleil in Faubourg, a poorer residential enclave outside the town wall. Walking in her garden, he had met a shapely young woman washing laundry in a basin. Odette Boutet, for whom Madame Perpignane had once been a nanny, was the picture of Mediterranean beauty, soft but

---

*The historical name Roussillon is still in use in the region. Roussillon was united with Catalonia in the Kingdom of Aragon in 1172 and still has many affinities with the Catalan region of Spain. Roussillon was acquired by Louis XIV in 1659 in the Treaty of the Pyrenees.

sturdy, suntanned, with bright teeth and a ready laugh. She was the wife of a painter, François Bernadi, whose mural covered a wall in the train station. She was self-assured and open, even to a foreigner. O'Brian and Odette chatted. Their friendship was spontaneous. Odette represented all that was charming and that delighted O'Brian about Roussillon.

O'Brian recognized in Collioure an authentic people and place, with a tolerance for individuality that suited him. Here his poverty, which he was determined to endure in order to write, would not be so degrading as in England. To his later fictional character Richard Temple, who would also move to the Continent, France was like an odd, sometimes unpleasant relative, full of character and vitality, never a bore, as England could be. France was also, in contrast to England, "not a facetious country—a sense of humour was not obligatorily hung out all day long" (*Richard Temple,* p. 183). Far from glum and entrenched Britain and from the postwar cynicism pervasive among European intellectuals, Collioure had a rugged, earthy physicality and raw beauty, the people of Collioure (Colliourenques) a wild, dark attraction.

For Patrick and Mary, the fall and winter of 1949 was a time of adapting to a new rhythm of life. They had seen enough of the dark side of humanity during the war and the dour side of nature in Wales to last a lifetime. They rented a small third-floor apartment in the main part of town (known as "the village"), at 2 Rue Arago, a central thoroughfare that locals called the "route of coffins" for the funeral processions that passed along it on their way from St. Vincent Catholic Church to the town cemetery. Financially, the picture looked good. The French economy was still in shambles from the war, and in mid-September the franc was devalued by 27 percent, dropping to 350 francs to the dollar and 980 francs to the British pound. Though unfortunate for the French, it made living in France even more attractive for the O'Brians, since their scant income continued to originate from abroad and would now stretch even further. But the Pyrénées-Orientales's frolicsome weather, if not the copious stores of red wine, vanished prematurely that year. In early October, heavy rain spoiled the *vendange,* or grape harvest: "How wretched has been the grape harvest of 1949!" read the newspaper headline. "May it draw to a quick close!" Several weeks later, violent winds struck the area from the southeast, followed by a glacial tramontane from the north.

The O'Brians' new apartment lay in the heart of the village, not forty paces from a town gate leading onto the harbor and just several doors from an anchovy factory, whose unctuous aroma filled the street. The priest, a squat, heavy man, lived beside the gate, and in the Mediterranean tradition, parishioners left food and wine outside his door. Three times a day, a uniformed town crier came to the gate, blew his bugle, and announced important news, such as a death or the arrival of goat cheese in the market. In summer, he announced in French, but in winter, his cries were in Catalan. Two dozen steep, uneven steps led from the narrow street to the O'Brians' landing, where Patrick had to duck to avoid cracking his skull on a low beam. The L-shaped apartment had neither electricity nor hot water, but it now possessed the crates of books shipped from Wales, as well as Patrick's treasured clocks.

Three windows faced onto Rue Arago, and from his desk at the farthest window from the door, O'Brian looked out onto the triangular intersection of Rue Arago, Rue Mailly, and Rue de la Prud'homme, broken by the town gate leading onto the quay and the stony harbor beach.

At the end of September, O'Brian received a reply to his letter to Roger Senhouse. Picking up where they had left off, Senhouse (who, in his turn, spelled O'Brian with an "e" and replaced it by hand with an "a") suggested that "the Prawn" be replaced with "the Rutland," which is the county where the Quorn takes place and a name that he felt evoked the Shires. A handsome, affable man, educated at Eton and Oxford, Senhouse had a wide circle of literary friends. At lunch one day, he had run the name by Nancy Mitford, who approved of it. O'Brian, too, thought it was just right. Senhouse also mentioned that Warburg had gone to the United States and was confident that he would sell the book there. This, however, never transpired.

As he worked, O'Brian could watch the carts and townspeople passing through the village gate and heading either toward the church, which Mary attended and whose celebrated clock tower rose straight up from the bay, or toward the Place de La République, near which the couple could buy everything from hand-sewn espadrilles at Jean Palau's store to food at the fishmonger's, the bakery, the grocery, and Boucherie Maillol, the butcher shop operated by Odette Boutet's aunt Alice. Just as he had in Wales, O'Brian absorbed the scene zealously. His trenchant examination of French Catalan culture would infuse a novel and numerous short stories over the next half decade.

By making a concerted effort to get to know their new neighbors and offering sincere friendship—Patrick's reserve notwithstanding—the O'Brians ingratiated themselves in the local society on more than one level. Mimi Atxer, who ran the grocery shop, fondly remembers Patrick bursting into her store one morning, in a writing frenzy, desperate to know the names of the three wise men. He could remember only two of them. As soon as she responded—"Les trois rois mages? Gaspard, Melchior, et Balthazar!"—he thanked her and dashed off again. But it was Mary who especially thrived among the Colliourenques. While both she and Patrick immediately began to speak Catalan, she mastered the language faster, always chatting with the shop owners in Catalan. The first time she took Buddug into Boucherie Maillol, she met Odette, who was a fellow animal lover and doted over the lovably scruffy dog. Just as Patrick had, Mary hit it off with the garrulous young Catalan immediately, and soon she knew all about her.

Despite their many differences, Mary and twenty-three-year-old Odette, who had left school at age twelve to apprentice as a seamstress, became close friends, helping each other in many ways. Odette could make a dress or blouse for Mary from a picture torn out of a magazine. Odette's extended family accepted the O'Brians as if they were their own. There was Alice, the butcher, who always had a packet of meat scraps for Buddug, and another aunt, Fifine Atxer, whose husband, a customs officer in nearby La Nouvelle, would teach O'Brian how to make wine.

Odette frequently ate dinner with Patrick and Mary. Mary often made a pudding, while Odette brought a side dish or a piece of meat from the butcher shop. The three had fun together, though Patrick rarely joined in their carefree laughter. He was working on a novel and often remained preoccupied, thoughtfully smoking his Gauloise in a holder.

By November, money began to grow tight for the O'Brians. England had restricted the export of legal tender to £250 per year, but Patrick did not worry at first because he was convinced that he would be able to have the £75 advance for the planned book on France sent over, above his £250 annual allotment.

Toward the year's end, he wrote Barclays, his bank, requesting the funds, but he could not get them, or even a straight reply. He sent another letter with his questions spelled out in numbered paragraphs and still received vague answers. Then he read in *Le Figaro* that in 1950 the amount that one could export from England would increase to £1,250, and so he relaxed again, feeling certain the money would be sent. The funds never arrived. Another letter to Barclays, when the O'Brians were nearly broke, produced a response telling them that the bank was still unsure of the new regulations. O'Brian finally got the facts from Spencer Curtis Brown: the new allowance applied only to those who left England after January 2, 1950.

The O'Brians were out of money. In early February 1950, Patrick wrote a desperate letter to Roger Senhouse asking him if someone at Secker and Warburg could intercede with the Bank of England or the Treasury, whichever held jurisdiction in the matter. He was beside himself with anxiety. Nonetheless, he managed to return the corrected proofs of *The Last Pool* to Senhouse toward the end of the month, apologizing for having no concrete suggestions for the cover other than that he thought it should be green.

Senhouse wrote back to O'Brian in early March complimenting his careful revisions, informing him of the progress on the cover, which would feature a vignette of a salmon fisherman among the reeds, and making a somewhat preposterous (from this vantage point at least) suggestion for his money woes. He had heard of English fishermen near Pau in the Pyrenees selling their salmon catch to French restaurateurs for large sums of money. O'Brian could travel inland to Pau and fish for a fortnight to earn the money he needed to tide him over.

O'Brian responded to Senhouse that he thought the fishing idea had merit and he would look into it. Whether or not he was serious is hard to say. He informed Senhouse that his most sensational catch so far had come while fishing for *loup de mer* (sea bass) with a spoon. He had hooked an octopus, a small one but an unpleasant business nonetheless. He concluded his letter by asking if Senhouse might return his typescript of *The Last Pool*, not because he wanted it for a keepsake, but because he needed the scrap paper.

For a while it looked as if the O'Brians might be forced to abandon their new life before it really got under way. They cut expenses to the bare minimum and still did not always have enough food to eat. As the news of their situation circulated, however, gifts started to arrive from their new friends: wine from family cellars, vegetables from their neighbors' storerooms, anchovies from the day's catch. The scraps that Odette's aunt Alice always wrapped up for Buddug started getting bigger—big enough for three. On these gifts from their Catalan friends and neighbors, along with rice and olive oil, Mary managed to feed them.

This generosity was not surprising among the Catalans, who had a tradition of looking out for one another. In fact, when the fishing boats came in, the fishermen with a fresh catch from their nets handed out sardines to all those who desired them. The villagers lit fires of vine clippings in the streets, and the smell of roasting sardines filled the air. This was a heavenly scent to the O'Brians, and the food truly a godsend during this desperate year.

As spring broke, the Pyrenees, rising in intervals to the west and to the south until they towered like a wall against the industrialized world, beckoned them. O'Brian had produced more than one meal "out of the hedge," as he once put it, and now the time was ripe for hedge hunting. An abundance of cold mountain streams meant that he could also fish for trout. He and Mary, with Odette, whose husband had run off with an older woman, camped for a month in the mountains southwest of Collioure, in the sloping vineyards near Tour de la Massane. It was wild country, and one morning, Buddug, whom Odette called Pedyc Dea—that's how she heard "Buddug, dear" in Mary's English accent—began to bristle. Patrick muzzled the dog with a hand and whispered, "Quiet, something's coming!" Then he pointed, and they all watched as a family of boars came trotting by, a large grungy male leading, a brood of neat sucklings in the middle, and the engorged mother bringing up the rear.

Back in Collioure, Odette and Mary took their first swim of the season, jumping into the brisk water and swimming the quarter mile from the beach of St. Vincent to that of La Balette. When they reached the rocky shore, each gallantly offered the other the first exit from the cold water. Neither wanted to admit that she could barely walk after the intense descent from La Massane, topped by the long swim.

In the summer of 1950, Richard arrived to spend his school holiday with Patrick and Mary. While in Wales, the boy had wished desperately to be back in London with his mother and his dog. He got what he wanted but found life there not as pleasant as he might have hoped. Le Mee-Power, his stepfather, was a frighteningly big man and a drunk, who could be abusive. Since the end of the war, Elizabeth had struggled to make a living. She had repaired nylon stockings in a shop and then gone into business for herself doing the same. Later, she donned a black-and-white service uniform and worked in the dining room of the Chelsea Arts Club, bringing home leftover pudding, beef, or custard for her son after shifts. Despite scant resources, Elizabeth was scrappy and did her best for the boy. She had persuaded a Roman Catholic priest to help get Richard accepted at the first-rate Cardinal Vaughn Grammar School. And now, though she seethed at her ex-husband—"May that bastard rot in hell," Richard would later hear her exclaim on more than one occasion—she sent Richard to France for his own good.

Little could she have known how inopportune the timing was for him to arrive in Collioure. For several weeks he, Patrick, and Mary ate mostly homemade marmalade on toast. Mary baby-sat to bring in some money and taught English when she could find students. She stretched what little they had, and she never made Richard feel like a burden.

Fortunately, poverty could not prevent a thirteen-year-old boy from London from finding plenty to occupy his mind and body in this fascinating region of France: the mountains, the sea, the bustling village, where even the boisterous garbagemen, with their German shepherd, named Mazoot Diesel, who barked madly from atop the cab of their truck, helped entertain him. Collioure was exotic and communal, never more so than at dinnertime, when fires suddenly appeared in street-curb grills and villagers traded stories and laughs as the day's catch sizzled in the dim glow.

Richard would also get to experience better times in Collioure, returning each of the next four summers. On these visits, he snorkled in the sea and hiked and camped with Patrick and Mary in the mountains of Andorra, where golden eagles big enough to snatch a dog circled overhead. He attended the seaside Catholic church, as he promised his mother he would, and Collioure's dusty bullfights with the nephew of the priest. He fished with the truant artist Bernadi, whose idea of fishing was to throw a net out in the water and then take a nap on the shore. He also came to admire Odette, with her dark velveteen glow, so unreserved, so un-English, as well as the fine spectacle of Yolande Mucha, painter Willy Mucha's wife, who sunbathed with Mary on the beach beside the church in a postage-stamp bikini.

O'Brian found the Catalans agreeably direct, sensitive and discreet, and sincere in friendship. They were also passionate about people and life. They were of a tough, self-reliant stock, devoutly religious and utterly without pretension, and, as the O'Brians had discovered, capable of great generosity even to outsiders. In his fiction, O'Brian would sympathetically portray a Roussillon housekeeper named Fifine, who was strong-minded and worked incessantly without discontent—cleaning, washing, tending to the garden and poultry, cutting firewood, and cooking. She spoke a harsh regional patois and was of some inscrutable age between thirty and fifty. Her religion, wrote O'Brian, trying to capture the ineffable spirit of the people, was "immensely practical . . . and yet it was lit with a fine unself-conscious mysticism . . . a church of Fifines was likely to outlast time" (*Richard Temple,* p. 54).

In their poverty, the O'Brians remained literally down to earth, close to the smell of dust and grapes and salt, and to the sea. For exercise and entertainment, they swam in the Mediterranean. Just as they had lent a hand on their neighbors' sheep farms in Wales, they helped their new neighbor René Alouge, a tall, lean Catalan fisherman and vintner, during the *vendange*, deepening their relationships with the Colliourenques by sweating in the field alongside them.

Under the ferocious sun that parched the area's rocky soil, Patrick and Mary helped pick grapes off the low vines. It was backbreaking work, but wine was the region's lifeblood, and the labor-intensive *vendange*, with its centuries-old rituals, brought the community together just as the communal sheep shearing had in Croesor. Families overcame disputes to work side by side harvesting each other's grapes in a process that had to be well-timed and swift or a year's fruit could be lost.

O'Brian appreciated the act of creating his own sustenance, and, as he had been in Wales, he was fascinated by the cycle of the harvest: man working with nature, and sometimes against it, men working side by side in unison, the very essence of civilization. He cherished the fruit of that labor, the robust southern wine, and would actively take part in this work for many decades to come. He took notes on the atmosphere and the science, the ritual and the superstition of the harvest. There were the rapid, skillful flashes of razor-sharp sickles, the inevitable wounds quickly bandaged. There were, for the sustenance of the laborer, the thirst-quenching Muscat grapes strategically planted at the ends of rows of wine-making Grenache grapes. There were the elaborate dawn and noon meals, including hard-boiled eggs, ham, chops, anchovies, rabbit stew, white and black puddings, bread, and olives. A remarkable amount of wine was quaffed at noon with seemingly no effect. There was the ritual smashing of the grapes at the foot of the last vine to ensure the next year's harvest. These traditions were crucial, he realized, in perpetuating a way of life, and he drew upon them in his fiction, especially in the novel *The Catalans*.

On August 17, 1950, Secker and Warburg published *The Last Pool*,* whose Irish and Welsh landscapes were distant memories now that O'Brian felt so rooted in France. O'Brian dedicated the book: "MARIAE CONIUGI MEAE AMICAE CARISSIMAE HUNC LIBELLUM DEDICO DONUM INDIGNUM": "Mary, my wife, dear love, I dedicate this little book, this insufficient gift, to you."

The September 1, 1950, *Times Literary Supplement* praised the thirteen tales, noting that "unsuspected subtleties lurk beneath their surface of almost Trollopian simplicity" and that those involving the supernatural "are most dexterously handled in the manner of [Sheridan] Le Fanu or M. R. James." The reviewer called them "models of such tales, belonging to an unfashionable but very interesting tradition."

The *Irish Times* and the *Observer* also reviewed the collection enthusiastically. The former admired the stories, which were sometimes "gay ironical variations on old themes" and other times "violent encounters of man and beast with danger." The paper's critic commented, "There is unease at the brittleness of pleasure, the sudden thrust of affinity with the victim, or a wariness when nature averts her face."

In the *Observer*, the London-born Irish novelist, poet, and playwright Lord Dunsany wrote, "This charming book by an Irish sportsman is a genuine collection of tales of the Irish countryside." Like Dunsany, many would be fooled by O'Brian's name (even though it is not a common Irish spelling), and, surprisingly, no reviewer would ever link O'Brian to his former life as Richard Patrick Russ.

Despite their favorable tone, the reviews perplexed O'Brian. He thought Dunsany's review silly, as he wrote in a February 12, 1951, letter to Roger Senhouse, the *Irish Times*'s overwrought, and a short notice that appeared in the *Spectator* foolish. (He had not seen the *TLS* review at the time he wrote the letter.) But even if he did not consider *The Last Pool*'s positive reviews intelligent, they at least provided him with some sense of relief and renewal. With this first work of fiction written under the name Patrick O'Brian, he had finally and successfully, from a critical standpoint at least, emerged after more than a decade out of print.

*The cover of the book bears the title *The Last Pool*, but the title page has *The Last Pool and Other Stories*.

Secker and Warburg had optimistically printed three thousand copies of the book and bound two thousand. Only about a thousand copies sold; the company lost money on the book, and O'Brian ended up £30 shy of earning royalties on top of his advance. However, along with their other resources, the anthology and *The Last Pool* had generated enough money to allow the O'Brians—once the cash flow issue was resolved—to install both hot water and electricity in their small flat. Still, there was little fat on the calf.

Fortunately, O'Brian's pen was hot. He had swept into his next work, which he would finish by the end of the year, showing sections as he went to Mary, whose opinion he valued immensely. Few authors have the opportunity to rewrite their debut as a novelist, but O'Brian was getting that chance. He had achieved much in the first instance, but he had been a very different person then. Richard Patrick Russ had been naive, writing more from his heart and his instinct than his intellect. The impulses and motivations that governed him then did not apply now. He had been oblivious to the possibility of failure. He had been blind to some of the sources of his own pain. Now more thoughtful, more self-conscious, and having a more complex vision of the world, he *was*, in a sense, starting from scratch. With the newly installed electric light, he worked well into the night, scrawling his narrative in longhand.

Although he used a risky artifice—telling the story from the other side of the grave—it seemed to work. In the novel, which he called *Testimonies*, he placed a paleographer and ex-Oxford tutor, John Aubrey Pugh, in a remote farming valley in Wales. Pugh has retreated to the valley to recuperate from ill health and emotional exhaustion and to sort out his future. He hopes that the hiatus will refresh him for his work on a monograph titled *The Bestiary Before Isidore of Seville*. This was the subject that O'Brian later said he had himself been working on before the war, and perhaps this acknowledgment of that stillborn effort was his way of bringing a sense of closure to a lost cause.

In Wales, the weary Pugh finds unexpected complications when he falls in love with Bronwen Vaughn, a provincial farmer's wife. O'Brian played with the tensions and dynamics inherent in this scenario. Having lived so long in London and then in remote Wales and now France, he juxtaposed rural perspective, born of a simple, hand-to-mouth existence and a closeness to nature, with that of his world-weary protagonist.

Vaughn thinks the world is getting better because there are now anesthetics, injections for cows, and health insurance. Perhaps shedding light on O'Brian's own self-sequestration from mainstream society, the jaded teacher thinks the opposite, explaining:

> We are an evolutionary mistake. We evolved too quickly, and now with the instinctive equipment of apes we are faced with a social life as complicated as a beehive. Men cannot live that kind of life; it cannot be done, and I am sure the attempt will kill us as a species.
>
> The root of the unhappiness is that man's instinctive sense of right clashes with that of society: and it is not surprising that it does, when you consider the speed of our evolution. (P. 176)

O'Brian's microcosm for the novel, the remote Welsh valley, functioned as a hothouse, just as the enclosed world of a naval warship would in the Aubrey-Maturin novels. In his fictional Cwm Bugail ("Shepherd's Valley," in Welsh), even small misdeeds grow into oversized problems, creating an often oppressive atmosphere, where the malevolence of a powerful person can mean disgrace, even death, for those at whom it is aimed. After the necessary economy of short story writing, O'Brian reveled in the spaciousness of the novel. His valley was both harsh and lovely, simultaneously liberating and stultifying. He achieved a complexity there that he felt was close to the truth.

O'Brian found his rhythm in the work. He was writing well, and he knew it. He finished the novel late one night, in one final push of nervous, creative energy. The work exhausted him, yet he felt that this fast, intense writing had elevated his life to another level. Just as a mountain climber lives most fully on the face of a challenging mountain, and a sailor craves a strong wind on the sea, he found exhilaration in this fluid act of creation. He savored what he felt was a breakthrough in his writing.

Mary typed up a final, clean version, and they delivered the manuscript to Spencer Curtis Brown, probably during a Christmas trip to England. Early in the new year, 1951, the book landed in the editorial offices of Secker and Warburg, where Roger Senhouse read it. By the end of January, Brown had negotiated a £100 advance for the book. Half was due on signing, and the other half on publication, but Brown went ahead and advanced the second half to O'Brian from the agency, since he knew O'Brian needed it. "Even agents can have kind hearts on occasion," Brown joked in a letter informing David Farrer, an editor at Secker and Warburg, of this arrangement.

On February 4, O'Brian wrote Senhouse expressing his happiness that the editor liked the book and telling him that he had come up with a brilliant idea. His good friend and neighbor Willy Mucha, a well-known artist, was interested in illustrating the jacket of *Testimonies*. O'Brian acknowledged to Senhouse that the jacket was solely the editor's domain, but he felt confident that Senhouse would see the value in having Mucha's work there. Mucha, O'Brian wrote enthusiastically, had recently had a successful show in Paris and was much admired by Matisse, Dufy, Braque, and Léger, with whom he had exchanged paintings.

Senhouse quickly wrote back. His letter of February 8 foretold the eventual demise of his relationship with O'Brian. He was not opposed to using Mucha, whose work he had seen in a show at the Royal Academy, as long as they could agree on a fee and the illustration was abstract, using no more than three colors. Because O'Brian's book was so steeped in Welsh flavor, he did not want Mucha to attempt from afar a representational work, which might differ from O'Brian's authentic description. But if everything could be worked out, he was excited about the possibility. Thereafter in the letter, however, it became apparent that it was the book itself that he was not so excited about, even though he certainly played a major role in acquiring it.

Although friendly and mostly deferential in tone, Senhouse was also frank. He did not believe that the way O'Brian had structured the novel— dividing it into sections from the various points of view of Pugh, Vaughn, and Lloyd (the schoolmaster)—made the deepest emotional impact or the most chronological sense. He found some of the writing—on first and second readings—unnecessarily obscure. He told O'Brian that none of the three readers of the book liked the ending, and he expected O'Brian to work on it. He explained that he had detailed all of his suggestions on the typescript, which O'Brian would soon receive. In the meantime, Senhouse expressed regret that the two could not hash out the editorial process over tea in Chelsea, as they had with *The Last Pool*, and he begged O'Brian to read his notes without mounting exasperation.

O'Brian took the critique well. He responded calmly on February 12, assuring Senhouse that he would read his remarks with interest and that he resented the criticism of only fools and show-offs. He eased Senhouse's concern by admitting that he had been unable to gain enough distance on this book to observe it as a whole and that he had compromised Mary's ability to do the same by having her read the work in progress. O'Brian did not seem in the least dismayed by the extensive criticism. In fact, he spent most of the letter informing Senhouse of his recent conversation with Willy Mucha about the jacket illustration, in a roundabout way telling him that Mucha would take for payment whatever the going rate was.

In the meantime, on February 14, Senhouse sent O'Brian's marked-up typescript to Spencer Curtis Brown. His accompanying letter was perhaps offensively blunt. It stated plainly that no one at Secker and Warburg liked the presentation of the book. He told Brown that the narrative conceit—the account of Bronwen Vaughn's death being delivered as if to a heavenly inquisition—was too artificial and would have been problematic even for a veteran novelist. Senhouse had accumulated many pages of very specific criticism, both his and other readers', ranging from overuse of Welsh names and syntax to chronological difficulties and the unsympathetic nature of Pugh, a hypochondriac cold fish; one female reader found the idea of Pugh in love repulsive. Senhouse's underlying message was unmistakable. He felt O'Brian was caught up in his own cleverness, in both the construction of the book and in the writing, which he called "a false Celtic utterance."

O'Brian received the manuscript before the end of the month. Presumably Senhouse did not include all of the readers' reports and Brown did not show O'Brian Senhouse's letter, for O'Brian remained on friendly terms with Senhouse. O'Brian revamped *Testimonies* with his usual decisiveness, in his usual meticulous hand—but only in small ways. He disregarded Senhouse's structural suggestions and his advice to reduce the use of Welsh words and names. There would be no major overhaul. As he would throughout his career, O'Brian essentially stood by his original work.

That spring, O'Brian was already working on a new collection of short stories, which he would finish in the fall. But money was still tight, and he and Mary also felt the need to get away from their bustling little village. With a tent and Buddug, they took a train west to Andorra, where the high mountains lay covered in snow six months of the year, and the climate, though cold, was said to be salubrious. A remote, independent state sandwiched between Spain and France and largely populated by Catalan-speaking shepherds, Andorra had attracted pilgrims and various other transients for many centuries. With plans to remain for a considerable time, Patrick and Mary established a mail drop, where Patrick could be reached by his publisher into August. The two camped, living off the land and occasionally surfacing at farms for milk and cheese and at small villages for other provisions. Patrick fished for trout, which were plentiful.

They had made plans for Odette to join them after the weather warmed up. At the agreed-upon time, Mary and Buddug went to the train station to meet her and her red-haired rat-terrier, Rubill ("Rusty," in Catalan). They stayed the night in the small town. When a pack of menacing dogs greeted Buddug and Rubill less than politely, the two beautiful but tough women bravely fought off the assault until help arrived. The next day, the four of them hopped on the bus into the mountains, where they met Patrick. For two months, the trio and their two beloved mutts wandered into remote high valleys on dirt roads and hiked on animal tracks. Occasionally they visited the churches and religious shrines of Andorra, a Roman Catholic state where many of the best vistas were occupied by religious edifices. When inspired, O'Brian wandered off by himself and wrote in his journal.

In subsequent years, O'Brian often pointed out that it was through these mountains, the rugged, untamable Pyrenees, that many Allied agents had infiltrated occupied France and a steady flow of escaped prisoners and war refugees, as well as intelligence agents, had, with the help of the locals, eluded the Nazis and fled to freedom. He held a deep emotional attachment to these hills from his war service and they would appear in several short stories, as well as in the Aubrey-Maturin series. In *Post Captain*, to escape imprisonment after Napoleon suddenly declares war in 1803, Aubrey and Maturin desperately cross the eastern Pyrenees to Recasens, Spain, where Maturin's ancestral castle provides a haven.

Back in Collioure, O'Brian spent the fall polishing his short stories. In November, he sent the new collection, titled *Samphire*, after one of the tales, to Spencer Curtis Brown. Brown delivered the typescript to Fred Warburg, mentioning in his cover letter that O'Brian hoped to hear about the collection before Christmas. O'Brian had asked Brown whether a publisher could still make a profit from a book that sold a thousand copies. Brown answered that to cover its expenses, a publisher needed to sell close to three thousand copies. Perhaps neither Brown nor O'Brian expected to sell the stories, for O'Brian asked Brown if he could find him work translating books from French to English, and Brown suggested the idea to Warburg, who had published many significant translations.

At around this time, the final stages of the editing and crucial steps in the marketing of O'Brian's Welsh novel were taking place. Secker and Warburg was still searching for an acceptable title for the book. The editors and sales staff thought *Testimonies* sounded too much like a treatise or codicil and not enough like a novel. They worried that the title might be confusing and cause their "travelers" (salesmen) to have a problem getting orders from bookstores. Someone had suggested titling the book *Bronwen Vaughn*, after the heroine. O'Brian objected to this, however, and the publisher produced the title *Three Bear Witness*.

O'Brian now saw the proofs of his novel, which he received in a package along with his original typescript and a proof copy for Mucha to read before executing the cover illustration. This step proceeded more smoothly than the title selection. O'Brian had only a minor typographical suggestion and a dedication request (he wanted the book dedicated to his friends in Collioure), which Senhouse apparently was not able to accommodate; the book carries no dedication leaf. O'Brian asked if he might keep the dummy of the book that Senhouse had sent for Mucha to look at while doing the cover illustration. O'Brian thought it would make a charming journal.

Senhouse wrote in early December to inform O'Brian that *Three Bear Witness* was, in fact, to be the title of the book. He noted that the detective novel overtone might help sales and that he liked the urgency of the three witnesses. Though he still preferred his original choice, O'Brian must not have objected strongly to *Three Bear Witness*. In the same letter, Senhouse snubbed O'Brian's request for the book dummy. It was too expensive for him to surrender, he said, and so he must have it back as soon as Mucha was finished with it.

Whether prompted by this petty stroke, by his growing belief that in Senhouse he did not have a strong enough supporter at Secker and Warburg, or for some other reason, such as the fact that an illustration by Willy Mucha would not grace the cover of the book after all, O'Brian informed Spencer Curtis Brown that he no longer wished to work with the editor. Brown wrote a confidential letter on December 14 to Fred Warburg saying that O'Brian did not get along with Senhouse and that if he wanted to keep the author on his list, he should deal with him directly.

Brown told Warburg that he had never found O'Brian difficult and that he did not think the writer would be a burden to Warburg.

The last word on the subject, however, many years later, was O'Brian's. In his novel *The Letter of Marque*, Senhouse, the name at least, makes a cameo appearance. While testing a device for preventing a hot-air balloon from rising too high, "poor Senhouse" (p. 27) flies too high and is never seen again. And so the editor who once suggested that O'Brian fish for a living received poetic justice.

But who was to deal with O'Brian became largely a moot point. Five days later, Warburg wrote back to Brown that, according to his staff's editorial report on *Samphire*, some of the stories were quite good while some failed. So he had determined that it was essential to publish *Three Bear Witness* before he committed to *Samphire*. Secker and Warburg, which was itself struggling financially, had lost money on the first short story collection, and he felt that if the novel did not sell well and additionally was not reviewed well, he might have to decline on any more books by O'Brian. Nevertheless, Warburg, a conscientious publisher willing to buck sales figures for authors in whom he strongly believed, told Brown he still considered O'Brian a potentially brilliant author.

In early January 1952, O'Brian received a letter of encouragement from Warburg. Because he had been in the United States at the beginning of the previous year, Warburg had not actually read *Three Bear Witness*. He had finally read it over the holidays, and he was extremely impressed. Although he had criticisms—he found Pugh unappealing, though well conceived—Warburg considered them trivial next to what O'Brian had accomplished in his description of the Welsh hills, the Welsh villagers and farmers, and the eternal cycles of farm life. Vaughn and her husband were exceptionally well done, he thought, and the sheep-shearing scene was magnificent. Despite the fact that Warburg could not currently accept *Samphire*, he wanted O'Brian to know that he thought his mature vision and his powers of novel construction boded well for his future. As it turned out, though, the firm never again published O'Brian.

Secker and Warburg brought out *Three Bear Witness* that spring. The first review from England was not favorable. Bunched with three other titles in the "Recent Books" column of the Saturday, May 10, *Times,* the book suffered at the hands of a pompous unnamed reviewer who set the scene by judging that in "the high and dry pastures of current English fiction it is often hard to choose between the excesses of the visibly experienced writer and the deficiencies of the relatively unpracticed writer." The critic, concurring with Senhouse, then called *Three Bear Witness* "a slight and technically immature piece of work, loose-jointed and clumsy in construction to the point of amateurishness." He sniped that Pugh "is for some reason middle-aged, while in point of fact almost everything he says and does belongs to a man in his thirties," but he also added that the book "is fresh and individual in tone and leaves an impression of genuine talent."

While the May 16 *Times Literary Supplement* called the literary device of the novel "clumsy" as well, it also had positive words, describing the book as "a quiet little story of much merit . . . of unaffected simplicity." The reviewer noted that O'Brian's "old-fashioned style" suited the work.

In the United States, Harcourt, Brace and Company, which had anted up $750 for the rights to the book, used Patrick's original title, *Testimonies,* and published it on August 15.* As had been the case with *Hussein*, the book's reception was quite different west of the Atlantic than it was east.

In the August 24 *New York Times Book Review*, Pearl Kazin called it a "rare and beautiful novel, deceptively modest in tone, never faltering in the unobtrusive skill of its poetry and dramatic dimensions." She especially admired O'Brian's heroine, whom she called "an altogether touching and marvelous woman, so persuasively and sympathetically portrayed that she deserves a place among the great heroines—for all the differences of setting and scale, Bronwen Vaughn has some of the stature of an Anna Karenina." The same day, in the *Herald Tribune Book Review*, Sylvia Stallings observed: "So many 'love stories' are written; so little is told about love. Mr. O'Brian has set a text to learn from; he has also written one of the finest books to come along for some time."

In the August 23 *Saturday Review*, the novelist Oliver La Farge commended O'Brian's "believable characters, not quaint, but at once universal and creatures of their locale, as we all are." La Farge concluded, "Mr. O'Brian has made a story that moves to its end with the rightness and inevitability we think of as Greek." As if to bolster this assessment, the review was anchored by the book's cover photo of the handsome, darkhaired author, clad in a houndstooth jacket, tie, and button-down shirt.

---

*O'Brian continued to prefer this title. In 1994, when a revised edition of *Three Bear Witness* was released in Britain by HarperCollins, it was renamed *Testimonies*.

His fair skin gave him a delicate, alabasterlike quality, while his wide, dark eyes peering out from beneath bushy brows and his unsmiling, thin lips cast him as intelligent and serious. What the photo could not reveal was the extent to which the clean-cut author remained in turmoil with himself and his own identity.

That summer his brother-in-law, Howard Wicksteed, who had been in Africa during the war and whom he had never met, came to France with his wife, Dorothy, and Mary's mother. They only briefly met Patrick before taking Mary with them on a holiday in Spain. According to Wicksteed, Patrick introduced himself as Dr. Patrick O'Brian. Wicksteed asked if he was a medical doctor. O'Brian replied that he was not but that he had been awarded a doctorate from Padua University, the oldest university in Europe. Wicksteed had no reason to doubt this at the time, but he never heard O'Brian called doctor again.

Although the London *Times* review of *Testimonies* had been disheartening, if not infuriating, to O'Brian—how exasperating to receive esteem from abroad and scorn at home, where the emotional and intellectual ties were—the accumulated praise far outweighed that stinging criticism, and the best was yet to come. In the United States, acclaim for *Testimonies* had tangible results, too. Perhaps tipped off by Kazin, a former editor at *Harper's Bazaar*, Alice Morris and Linda Brandi, the magazine's fiction editors, wrote immediately to ask whether O'Brian had any short stories available. He sent them seven. The editors were so impressed that they set a precedent for the magazine by buying two at the same time.

In December, they reprinted "The Green Creature," from *The Last Pool*, along with a brief biography that included the incorrect information that O'Brian was born "in the west of Ireland," an error, perpetuated by the author, that would continually reappear in reviews and even on the back of one of his subsequent books, *The Walker and Other Stories*. O'Brian published four more stories in the American *Harper's Bazaar* (and one in the British edition) over the next three years.*

That month, in the December *Partisan Review*, the literary world read Delmore Schwartz's omnibus review, "Long After Eden." First, Schwartz, a poet, story writer, and the *Partisan Review*'s fearless editor who never blinked before the establishment, leveled the ground, as if before a great monument. He called the heroine of John Steinbeck's *East of Eden* a

*All subsequent references to *Harper's Bazaar* in this book are to the American edition.

"systematic, unrelieved, entirely incredible caricature of villainy," and the book he deemed filled with "bogus naiveté." Of *The Old Man and the Sea*, Schwartz complained that Ernest Hemingway's portrayal of the old man's emotions revealed "a margin of self-consciousness and a mannerism of assertion which is perhaps inevitable whenever a great writer cannot get free of his knowledge that he is a great writer." But mostly Schwartz faintly praised Hemingway's book, concluding that it offered hope that, after the "bluster, bravado and truculence" of *Across the River and into the Trees*, Hemingway was back on track and might yet produce another masterpiece.

Schwartz bulldozed Evelyn Waugh's *Men at Arms* and Angus Wilson's *Hemlock and After*, comparing them to a startling newcomer: "It is only when one reads Patrick O'Brian's *Testimonies* that it becomes apparent how Waugh and Wilson have permitted their subject matter to cripple their point of view and sensibility." With the mountains now flattened, Schwartz erected his monument to the new kid on the block, launching right in with no transition from his pounding of Wilson:

> To read a first novel by an unknown author which, sentence by sentence and page by page, makes one say: he can't keep going at this pitch, the intensity is bound to break down, the perfection of tone can't be sustained—is to rejoice in an experience of pleasure and astonishment. Patrick O'Brian's *Testimonies* makes one think of a great ballad or a Biblical story. At first one thinks the book's emotional power is chiefly a triumph of style; and indeed the book is remarkable enough for the beauty and exactness of phrasing and rhythm. . . . But the reader soon forgets the style as such—a forgetting that is the greatest accomplishment of prose—in the enchantment and vividness of the story.

Schwartz made two other penetrating comments about the beauty of O'Brian's writing, which would hold equally true for the Aubrey-Maturin novels. A plot summary, he cogently observed, did *Testimonies* little justice, "for the comparative simplicity of the action when thus formulated conceals the labyrinthine complexity of attitude, motive and feeling." Schwartz further noted of *Testimonies* that "the reader, drawn forward by lyric eloquence and the story's fascination, discovers in the end that he has encountered in a new way the sphinx and riddle of existence itself." Schwartz concluded his review by comparing O'Brian to the Irish literary lion W. B. Yeats:

> What O'Brian has accomplished is literally and exactly the equivalent of some of the lyrics in Yeats' *The Tower* and *The Winding Stair* where within the colloquial and formal framework of the folk poem or story the greatest sophistication, consciousness and meaning become articulate. In O'Brian, as in Yeats, the most studied literary cultivation and knowledge bring into being works which read as if they were prior to literature and conscious literary technique.

Schwartz had held up *Testimonies* as a reminder that exquisite, profound writing happened on the page and not in social columns. Nothing could make words come alive except the words themselves.

At the age of thirty-eight, O'Brian had reached one of the pinnacles of his literary career. All at once, he was thrust onto the literary landscape with the masters of the day. But, of course, now there was a new question: could he sustain this position? Who was correct in his assessment of O'Brian's writing, Schwartz or Senhouse?

II

The Catalans

1953–1955

I think *The Catalans* one of the greatest books the century has
so far produced. It is so intensely moving, in tragedy, in
comedy, in the poignancy of love, that it is almost hypnotic.

—Hannah Finegold, *Providence Journal,* October 25, 1953

Since the end of the war, O'Brian had maintained a remarkable
writing pace, perpetually making up for that lost decade surrounding World War II. But now, in the wake of the success of *Testimonies*, Patrick and Mary decided to take a break and drive around the
Iberian Peninsula. Modest sums were trickling in from New York, where
O'Brian was suddenly in demand, and modest sums could be stretched
some distance in Roussillon. The couple bought a Beetlelike Citroën 2CV
(said as *deux chevaux*, but never written that way).

Their journey was more than a much-needed vacation. Since their
arrival in Collioure, the summer tourist traffic had been on the rise. The
annual bullfights now produced a mob scene, and the vacationers created
such a din that the O'Brians feared they might not be able to tolerate living
there much longer. They had decided to search for a more remote village.

Like Lady Craven they rejoiced in their trip and the local curiosities
they encountered. Patrick was delighted, for example, to discover that the
customs officials who received them in Portugal wore no shoes, and wherever there were new birds to see and hear, Patrick and Mary were never
bored. Despite a pleasant vacation, however, no new landscape or village
enticed them enough to relocate.

Back in Collioure, Patrick returned to work. He wrote several stories
and some verse and proceeded with a novel involving his new surroundings. Both the praise and the criticism garnered by *Testimonies* pushed him

to bolder efforts, and he plowed the ground swiftly. The new novel, which would be titled *The Frozen Flame* in Britain and *The Catalans* in the United States, dealt again with the nature of love but this time focused on the frightening possibility of losing one's ability to love. Stylistically, O'Brian pushed his writing, daring to take chances and crafting, in the process, three virtuoso scenes.

He set the story in Roussillon, in the fictional town of Saint-Féliu. Dr. Alain Roig, the novel's main character, returns home from Cambodia at the request of his family to derail the intended second marriage of his older cousin, Xavier Roig, a lawyer, the mayor, and the keeper of the family's financial fortunes.

The first of the three remarkable scenes O'Brian penned is a thirty-five-page dialogue between the two cousins. Over cigars and whiskey on a dark terrace, Xavier rationalizes his intent to marry Madeleine Fajal, his beautiful, young typist, but also unwittingly reveals to Alain his coldheartedness. The two talk all night, with Alain dozing off at times while Xavier outrageously lambastes his son, whom he has come to hate to an almost inhuman degree following the death of the boy's young mother, his wife. He tells Alain: "I should have been satisfied with a manly boy, even if he had been affected, untruthful, hypocritical, unaffectionate, cruel, and of course grossly ill-mannered and undisciplined. . . . I looked into his shallow little soul, and I found that in addition to all those disagreeable qualities it had an epicene namby-pambyness that filled me with despair" (p. 113).

The scene seems born of an excruciating pain—the author's. The parallels to his life are clear, not that any of the characters are wholly biographical, just as those in the Aubrey-Maturin series are not wholly biographical but composites of various influences. Since O'Brian's youth was marked by his mother's death, his illness, and his father's aloofness, he came to have a very low self-esteem, so low that he looked back seventy years later and judged that even he could not like the twelve-year-old boy that he had been. These feelings played a role in his own troubled relationship with his son, Richard, to whom he had a hard time showing love. Their relationship would eventually end unhappily as well.

Xavier Roig bears a resemblance to Stephen Maturin that seems to have originated in O'Brian himself. Xavier has "that cold, dispassionate eye" (p. 85) that made Alain feel inferior when they were younger, just as Maturin has a "reptilian" glare when he is offended. Xavier "indulge[s] his superiority and his irritable nature" (p. 107), which clearly both the fictional Maturin and the real O'Brian do. Maturin, though capable of love and deep acts of kindness, also at times, like Xavier, struggles with an inability to feel love. And apparently so, too, did O'Brian.

Through several plot turns, Alain agonized over his new realizations about Xavier, his loyalties and understanding of love, and as it gradually becomes apparent, over his own attraction to Madeleine. At last, in two tight scenes, among the best of his writing career, O'Brian revealed the extent of Alain's new passion and the consequences. In the first, he capitalized on his *vendange* experience to create an electric climax to Alain's sly courtship of Madeleine. The Roig and Fajal families are in the vineyards together for the *vendange*, but the careful synchronization of the work has broken down, and everyone is waiting impatiently for one of the sturdy young men who carry the full bins of grapes down the hill to return. All at once, Alain, who is neither young nor sturdy, snatches up one of the cumbersome loaded bins and staggers down the hill. All eyes watch him. What he carries, a portion of the year's labor, is symbolically precious to the onlookers, but it represents far more to Alain, who has suddenly been compelled to assert his physical manhood. By the strength of his will—and his secret passion—he makes it to the bottom without spilling the load. Returning, he positions himself in the row next to Madeleine's.

Moved by this act of bravado, which she understands was meant for her, Madeleine darts across and cuts Alain's grapes for him so that he can catch up to her. Once he does, she deliberately misses some of her own, triggering an age-old ritual. Alain discovers her "mistake," which is also a challenge. He stops working and whistles sharply, halting the other workers, who all turn to him. Alain then knocks Madeleine to her knees, grabs her head with both hands, places his mouth on her forehead, and crows like a cock. Brilliantly, O'Brian transformed this ritual of humiliation into a savage, open, and dangerous—yet wonderfully ambiguous—act of lovemaking.

O'Brian then set up the novel's climax in a masterful penultimate scene at the post-*vendange* feast of Saint-Féliu, a Mardi Gras–like nighttime festival. The revelers carouse in elaborate costumes, while Alain, who has betrayed his cousin, sports a pig's snout and Xavier a mask with a mawkish smile. In this wild, mysterious setting amid delirious dancing of the *sardana* to a drunken band, Alain, who has betrayed his cousin, watches a sweating chained bear approach Xavier and announce that he is a cuckold.

O'Brian most likely finished the novel that winter. His new British publisher, Rupert Hart-Davis, would publish it in a print run of three thousand copies, binding fifteen hundred to start with, in September 1953. His New York publisher, Harcourt, Brace, which liked *The Catalans* enough to advance $750 against royalties, would bring out the book the following month.

In March, *Harper's Bazaar* published O'Brian's story "Samphire," in which a boorish botanist, overfond of the expression "jolly good," takes a room by the sea with his browbeaten wife. The magazine billed the story as "a disturbingly realistic portrayal of a wife pushed beyond endurance by a nagging husband." But rather than nagging, it is cold indifference to his wife's feelings that provokes her to shove him as he examines the coastal plant samphire hanging on a cliff face. The tale is doubly chilling given the tragic leap of O'Brian's aunt Pauline Russ, which had so scarred the Russ family a half century earlier. If O'Brian based the story on Pauline's, he had twisted history in a satisfying way. He had also perhaps made another sly autobiographical reference in the story by including an incidental couple from "Letchworth" named Jones (Elizabeth's maiden name), with the husband being an influential lawyer (as was Dimitry Tolstoy).

Although O'Brian's novel *The Golden Ocean* was not published until February 1956, he later stated in his autobiographical essay that he wrote the story sometime between the completion of *The Catalans* and the novel's publication in the fall of 1953.* Until this time, he had not written about the Royal Navy, nor had he written a historical novel. But the navy had long been a love of his intellectual and imaginative life. He had read voyage accounts since his youth, assembling his own anthology after the war, and he had long pored over naval history and been entertained by Forester.

Now O'Brian told the story of Commodore Anson's famous voyage of 1740 through the eyes of the fictional Peter Palafox, an ingenuous Irish parson's son who becomes a midshipman on board Anson's flagship, HMS *Centurion*. Peter and his sidekick, Sean O'Mara, the son of Peter's

---

*All references to O'Brian's "autobiographical essay" are to the essay he wrote for *Patrick O'Brian: Critical Appreciations and a Bibliography* (British Library, 1994), which is the only substantial autobiographical essay he ever published. Two other brief autobiographical articles, "Just a Phase I Am Going Through?" (*Weekend Telegraph,* August 27, 1994) and "A Life in the Day of Patrick O'Brian" (*Sunday Times Magazine,* November 5, 1989), are referred to by name.

nurse, take part in Anson's momentous voyage in which he loses four of his five ships to storms and inaccurate sea charts but finally captures a great treasure-laden Spanish galleon. Attrition along the way means added responsibilities for Peter, as a junior officer, and rapid promotion for Sean, a seaman, who soon becomes captain of the foretop and then a petty officer.

O'Brian found himself laughing out loud as his hand raced across the pages of his manuscript. It was the first novel in which the adult O'Brian let his sense of humor take over. Droll passages abound, as when Peter writes home to his father from Funchal, Madeira, and encloses a few gifts: "Please to take great Care in undoing the Packet for between the Tobacco and the Box made of Shells there is a Nest of Curious Serpents and a Scorpion in a Jar of Spirits which a Seaman of my Divisions brought me. They are for Dermot and Hugh to share as they please" (p. 107).

O'Brian finished the work in about six weeks. He later said that he felt almost a guilty pleasure in retelling the tale, which every British schoolboy knew. But it was the pleasure, not the guilt, that shined through. *The Golden Ocean* showed a joie de vivre not present in his earlier works, and in its two seamen friends lay the seed of O'Brian's ultimate tandem, Jack Aubrey and Stephen Maturin. At the time, however, there was no reason for him to suspect that this little book about the sea would change the course of his career.

In the summer of 1953, Richard, now an energetic sixteen-year-old, convinced Patrick and Mary and his mother that he should be allowed to cycle across France to Collioure. They talked him out of carrying camping and cooking gear, at least, and instead persuaded him to stay at youth hostels. He started in Dieppe, northwest of Paris, and made it to Brive, in the Dordogne, before the rigors of the road caught up with him. Skin boils on his backside made further riding impossible. His last francs purchased a train ticket to Perpignan.

That summer was politically tumultuous in France. In June, Joseph Laniel's right-wing coalition took power, facing intense pressure to end the unpopular war in Indochina, to solve France's financial problems, and to resolve the long-standing controversy over German participation in the proposed European Defense Community. The resulting strikes in government services and nationalized industries briefly crippled the French economy.

Richard just beat the great French railway strike, but a group of English schoolgirls became stranded in Collioure. Patrick and Mary came to their rescue, offering them baths and meals.

Later that summer, Collioure welcomed another refugee to the area: Pablo Picasso. At the time living on the Côte d'Azur, Picasso had fled his crumbling relationship with Françoise Gilot, the mother of Claude and Paloma, and stayed at the magnificent Perpignan mansion of the count and countess de Lazerme. Roussillon seemed to be just the tonic for Picasso, who had not been in the area for some forty years. Still a man of vigor and volatile moods despite his seventy years, he basked in the sunshine, the uncrowded cafés, and the Catalan rhythms of Roussillon. Immediately he felt at home again in the narrow streets of Perpignan, where Catalan could be heard all around and where he intrinsically understood the people and they him. Although it took at least nine hours to travel the poor roads from his home in Vallauris to Perpignan, he made several runs between the two towns that summer.

Whether he was simply trying to avoid the mess with Gilot or, as Gilot suspected, having an affair with the statuesque Paule de Lazerme, a thirty-five-year-old society queen, Picasso spent several weeks in Perpignan, and so did his "court," his well-wishers and hangers-on. When the scene finally grew too outrageous, he snuck away to Collioure, which brought him into the sphere of the O'Brians. Perhaps influenced by his friend Willy Mucha, Patrick had taken to attending the fall art exhibits at Café des Sports, which sponsored an annual art prize, and it was here that Picasso stayed, signing and sketching a bull in the guest book, *Livre D'Or,* on August 14. Surrounded by the work of the many painters who had sought inspiration in the charming village, Picasso, like O'Brian, was fond of eating Pauline Pous's famous bouillabaisse.

O'Brian later said he met Picasso at this time, and he certainly witnessed Picasso's rejuvenation on the beach at Collioure, where he lounged in the sun and swam in the sea. The retiring writer developed a sympathy for the charismatic painter. In fact, though at different stages in their careers, O'Brian could feel much in common with Picasso, whose biography he would one day write. They were both uncompromising artists, fond of smart conversation. They were both expatriates with ties to the fierce, proud Basque region, the one a native and the other an adoptive son. O'Brian admired painters and painting, and Picasso had many friends who were writers. O'Brian cherished his privacy, and he felt for Picasso, who now lived his life in a fishbowl.

That fall, the reviews of *The Catalans* rolled out. The book garnered considerable attention, if not consensus. The criticism had a curious quality. It was as if Beethoven's Ninth Symphony were being performed sotto voce: it soared, it sank, it moved, but no one seemed to hear. Despite the extensive reviewing of *Testimonies* just the previous year, O'Brian remained little known, especially in England. As if to emphasize his distance from the London literary scene, the *Times*, the *Times Literary Supplement*, the *New Statesman and Nation*, and the *Observer* all, incredibly, thought *The Catalans* was his first novel. The *Observer* in a laudatory review wondered aloud that the book, "so unselfconsciously French in feeling and atmosphere," was not written by a Frenchman.

Among the most impressed by the new work, Stevie Smith (a pseudonym for the English poet and novelist Florence Margaret), writing in the September 18 *Spectator*, concurred with the *Observer*: "He has something of the French genius in his writing, the prose fresh, supple and precise, the point of view objective without being heartless (a rare thing among those who write in English)."

While reviewers almost unanimously agreed that O'Brian's description of Catalan France was extraordinary, they divided on their assessment of his prose experimentation. Among the most put off was the *Times*, whose reviewer commented on September 12: "The curious thing about this first novel is that while the author is too immature to give it coherent form he is mature enough to have created its central character." On the other hand, the *Sunday Times* (September 27) called O'Brian "lyrical and witty" and praised his writing style, which seemed to originate in its very subject matter:

> The mayor himself, the doctor home from the East whose own heart so unexpectedly flowers, aunts, cousins, shopkeepers and fishermen are all part and parcel of the land they spring from: the streets and quays, the quiet houses vibrating with heat and passion, the town square pulsating and the terraced vineyards echoing during the celebration of the grape harvest, are drawn

with rich yet graceful and economical line and wash. In telling
his story Mr. O'Brian varies his pace with some verbal experiments: but all is smoothly wrought and there is no sense of
straining after effect.

Registering somewhere in the middle of those was the September 18 *Times
Literary Supplement*: "There are moments when his story flags as a more
artificially contrived entertainment might not, yet always it revives with a
gust of new energy that sometimes finds original expression, as for
example the unexpected use of poetry to describe the dancing of a *sardana*. The humorous and kindly, if slightly cynical, character of Dr. Roig
himself sets the tone of the book and would seem also to epitomize the
nature of Mr. O'Brian's talent, a quiet and reflecting one, in no wise sensational, which runs the risk ... of missing much of the recognition it
deserves."

In the U.S., where O'Brian's reputation was stronger, Harcourt, Brace
splashed a moody photo of the author across the back of the book jacket.
The black-and-white shot, taken from the side-rear, showed O'Brian
sprawled on a striped upholstered chair, shirtless and wearing shorts. He
nonchalantly smoked a cigarette while reading a book on his lap. With his
straight, dark hair cropped above the ears and a five o'clock shadow coloring his face, O'Brian cut the romantic bohemian figure, an ironic pose
for a man of such willpower and ambition, and strikingly different from his
previous author portrait.

Harcourt, Brace was sufficiently encouraged by the success of *Testimonies* and the quality of the new book to advertise the latter in the
November 22 *New York Times Book Review*. The ad featured praise from
Malcolm Cowley, chronicler of the American expatriate writers in Paris
after World War I and a former literary editor of the *New Republic*.
Cowley invoked Hemingway: "O'Brian has a gift for telling exactly what is
essential and not a word more. ... His account of the festival of St. Feliu
[*sic*] is the best thing of its kind since the fiesta in *The Sun Also Rises*."

In the *Saturday Review*, an impressed Oliver La Farge wrote, "The
opening casts the storyteller's spell, and soon enough the story marches.
The end result is a fine novel of conflict of character." Comparing this
book to *Testimonies*, he wrote, "*The Catalans*, more direct in treatment
and freer in style, is by far the better of the two."

O'Brian had now clearly established that he possessed a unique, exacting voice that demanded serious attention. He was not afraid to take stylistic risks, and reviewers were not afraid to point out when they thought he had strained the tale. Particularly interesting among the reviews was the high praise of two female reviewers, who found his exploration of love completely convincing. Stevie Smith's *Spectator* review concluded, "The author's sympathy with human frivolity and passion and suffering, his humour that sets things truly in proportion, make this book remarkable and beautiful." Hannah Finegold, writing in the *Providence Journal*, gushed: "I think *The Catalans* one of the greatest books the century has so far produced. It is so intensely moving, in tragedy, in comedy, in the poignancy of love, that it is almost hypnotic."

Even the curmudgeonly critic Orville Prescott—whose reviews John O'Hara is said to have made a point to avoid by always publishing his books on a Thursday, Prescott's day off—praised O'Brian in the January 1, 1954, *New York Times* as "an astute student of human nature in its more outrageous manifestations, the master of a smooth, firm, suggestive prose style, an original writer with an approach to fiction distinctively his own."

Despite these laudatory reviews, O'Brian eventually came to accept the negative opinion. Although he believed the basic concept of *The Catalans*— an exploration of a man's inability to love, a situation he thought not uncommon—to be a good one, he faulted his execution. In the October 24, 1953, *New Yorker,* critic Brendan Gill had perhaps hit the nail on the head. While the book contained some exquisite passages, Gill observed, it was stylistically inconsistent. Gill wrote that O'Brian was "clever by fits and starts and appears easily winded. We keep feeling that we could accommodate ourselves to his gait if he would only settle down to one, but he never does."

That month, *Harper's Bazaar* ran a new story by O'Brian, "The Walker," along with a nightmarish illustration by the young French painter Bernard Buffet of the house in which the dark story takes place. The magazine commented in its editorial note: "A haunting narrative of strange retribution, it was construed differently by every editor on the Bazaar." In an author's note following the story, O'Brian provided the two origins of the strange tale. The first was Psalm 91, which he quoted roughly: "You shall not fear the terrors that come by night; nor the arrow that flies by day, nor the evils prepared in the shadows; nor the demon that destroys at noonday." In the Latin version of the psalm, he noted, the demon walks in the noonday sun, an image he found particularly horrific.

The second source was a legend O'Brian had heard concerning three seamen who rob a priest and then die horrible deaths one at a time on land. O'Brian combined the two, the narrator being the devil, a man possessed but who thinks he acts for God. "The walking, you see," O'Brian explained, "seems to me an essential part of his madness and his possession; and clearly the evil men of the local legend are precisely those who are to fear the horrors of the night, the arrow that flies by day, the wickedness in the shadows and the high-noon demon."

O'Brian would dedicate this story, in the book of the same name, to his gregarious artist friend Willy Mucha, whose popularity in Collioure sometimes led to problems. One time the Muchas were expected for dinner. Mary spent all day preparing, and then Willy showed up and said that he was sorry but he had double-booked and they were not going to be able to come for dinner after all. Patrick was irate.

In January 1954, *Harper's Bazaar* published a fourth O'Brian story, "The Slope of the High Mountain," a revised version of the fox-hunting tale "The Steep Slope of Gallt y Wenallt." Accompanying O'Brian's bio, which flatly stated that he "does not like to be photographed," was a snapshot of the begrudging, self-conscious author wearing a dress shirt and tie and holding a dog on his lap in what he called a pose of "subhuman wariness." This portrait—almost painful to look at—represented a remarkable about-face from his prewar days, when he posed dramatically for Elizabeth's camera, and even from more sober recents shots, providing a vivid example of his quixotic self-projection.

Again an author's note accompanied the story. O'Brian informed his American readers that there were two types of hunting in Britain: the familiar sport of "pink coats on high horses," which was very different from the hunt on foot as practiced in Wales. The latter was a purer sport, he claimed, "ancient and magnificent . . . strenuous beyond belief," and beyond reproach for snobbery, for while a fool might dress up in a coat and buy an expensive horse to make his social statement, "even English snobbery will not induce him to scramble over twenty or thirty miles of wild, perpendicular country on foot, dressed in old gardening clothes and hobnailed boots." Indeed, O'Brian's tale presented a man exhausted, wet, shivering, alone, and tested to the limits of his endurance.

In February 1954 freezing temperatures blasted the Pyrénées-Orientales. On the fifth day of the month, ten centimeters of snow fell in nearby Céret and eight in Perpignan, enough to close schools. By the next day, a meter of snow had smothered the region. Even old-timers had never seen anything like it before. Colliourenques were simultaneously elated by their new white landscape and staggered by the loss of electricity, phone lines, and transportation. On outlying farms and in remote villages, the situation was grave. Teams of volunteers carried food and medicine to the elderly and the stranded.

O'Brian was, however, immersed in a different atmosphere altogether. He had launched into another novel, a fun-to-write adventure tale, probably worked on simultaneously with the more strenuous writing and revising of some of the stories that would form his next collection. In the new novel, *The Road to Samarcand,* he returned to his old friends: the orphan Derrick, his uncle Terry Sullivan, and Sullivan's Scottish pal Ross (whose first name is never given). They cruise the South China Sea on board Sullivan's schooner *Wanderer*, whose crew also includes the Chinese cook Li Han and the faithful Swedish sailor Olaf Svenssen. After weathering a typhoon, they join Derrick's cousin and guardian, Ayrton, an archaeologist, who insists over Derrick's objections that the boy return to England for schooling. As a consolation, Ayrton proposes an adventurous homeward route via Samarcand, seeking archaeological treasures as they go.

They set off across China on the Old Silk Road, traverse the Gobi Desert, climb snow-covered mountains into Tibet, fight brigands, and commandeer a stranded Russian helicopter that they dig out of the snow before they finally reach Samarcand. While the action-packed tale raced along at breakneck speed, stretching the imagination as it went, O'Brian's command of detail and understatement made the improbable events coalesce without a hitch. Again he had written a credible boys' story that any adult could read with pleasure.

In the summer of 1954, Richard moved in with the O'Brians, ostensibly on a permanent basis, though this arrangement lasted only a year or so until he left to fulfill his required national service. Richard had failed several exams, and now Patrick laid down the law: he *would* successfully complete his studies. So Richard, who wanted to be a mechanical engineer and did not relish subjects such as Greek and Latin, enrolled in correspondence courses in mathematics and science to prepare for the General Certificate of Education exam. Every night he studied at the dining room table after dinner, while Patrick and Mary read in the living room.

In August 1954, Picasso, accompanied by his teenage daughter Maya, returned to Perpignan. He drew Paule de Lazerme, a finely featured beauty with a long neck, big eyes, and Roman nose, in Catalan costume, her round bust flattened by the dress and her arm draped with flowers clutched in her hand. She looks slightly melancholy in the portrait, and perhaps Picasso had transposed his hopeless love onto her. He also painted her in a carved high-back chair with griffin-head handles in the position of power that she held as Perpignan's arts doyenne.

O'Brian was pleased when Picasso again took to visiting the beach at Collioure and holding forth at Café des Sports, where he and friends ate, drank, and carried on lively conversations. The extrovert painter looked happy and healthy, despite his recent marital problems. It was a splendidly clear, sunny summer, the likes of which had so enamored the Fauves. Collioure's protected bay, with its architectural montage of many centuries and cultures and its deeply tanned bathers, effected an appealingly sybaritic atmosphere. But it was not Nice or Cannes. It was still a frontier town with hardy food, a workingman's wine, a stony beach, and an infrastructure of peasant families. Colliourenques almost never gawked or interrupted Picasso, but for the brief period that he spent in Collioure, the writer, as well as the village, basked in Picasso's glow. When he swam, O'Brian later wrote in his biography of the artist, he looked "like a benevolent, round-headed turtle" (*Picasso,* p. 420).

Picasso warmed to the Catalan village, where he was so appreciated, and even considered settling down there. He presided over Collioure's August 15 bullfights, with their spectacular fireworks show in honor of the Assumption of the Virgin Mary. Where Picasso went, excitement seemed to follow. That year, one of the three matadores, Coriano by name, was thrashed by the bull and taken to a hospital in Perpignan, but not gravely hurt. The Collioure correspondent of the Perpignan-based regional newspaper *L'Independant* reported on September 5: "We have the pleasure and the honor to welcome in our midst each day the master Pablo Picasso, to whom the town council has made available the chapel of the castle of the Templiers. We are happy about this good news, and we congratulate and thank the town council for this kindness on behalf of the grand master." But as word leaked out that Picasso might stay, his Côte d'Azur friends descended on the fifty-room house of the de Lazermes, overrunning it. Finally, after a love interest rejected Picasso, he went packing back to Vallauris and never returned.

But the artist's presence had made its impact on O'Brian, who later wrote that, through his art, Picasso had given him more than any other creative man. O'Brian knew many of Picasso's inner circle and salted away a slew of memories, which, along with his admiration for Picasso and a handsome advance from an American publisher, would later compel him to write a very sympathetic biography of the artist.

The fact that Picasso did not stay, however, was perhaps for the best. His presence had begun to attract media attention, and, if extended, it would have fed Collioure's swollen tourism industry. The summer crowds were daunting enough without him. Already, in *The Catalans*, O'Brian had lamented the town's "ghastly new hotels and its seething mass of tourists" through the fictional Alain Roig, who passes by on the train. "It had been such a charming little town," Roig observes, peering "round the bulk of the latest hotel at the tiny beach where men and women lay tight-packed on the dirty stones and overlapping into the water where a thousand stewed together in the tideless wash. Sad, sad" (pp. 24–25).

Worried about Collioure's future, Patrick and Mary decided on a long trip to Cornwall with the idea of possibly moving there. They loaded Richard, now seventeen, and Buddug in the car and drove across France. Patrick revved the engine of the little 2CV to pass slow-moving traffic on the winding two-lane roads. Mary could not stand the thought of being without Buddug for Britain's mandatory six-month rabies quarantine, so they dosed him with a sleeping drug provided by a French veterinarian, and before departing the ferry, packed him away in a suitcase in the trunk of the car. However, someone spotted them doing this and reported them. Buddug was confiscated and impounded. Mary, who loved the dog like a child, was distraught.

The ferry arrived in England very early in the morning, and Mary raced along the empty roads, perhaps recalling her days as an ambulance driver. She was exhausted, though, and used to driving on the right-hand side of the road in France. While Patrick and Richard dozed, Mary ended up speeding along in the wrong lane. A morning delivery truck coming around a curve swerved off the pavement to avoid a head-on wreck with the tiny 2CV. Mary pulled off the road too and apologized to the shaken and angry delivery man. They were safe and unhurt, but it would not be the last time that they encountered such a problem.

They headed for the village of St. Buryan, which lay in rough, remote country about halfway between Penzance and Land's End in the very southwest tip of England. Half a dozen miles from the village, they stayed in one of a terrace of otherwise unoccupied cottages about five hundred yards from the coast, which plummeted more than a hundred feet there. Brutal winds and giant rollers dashed against the landmass, creating a cataclysmic landscape. Small boulders were the size of a van, big ones the size of a cottage. On some days, waves crested the headlands.

Nearby, many hidden coves cut into the coast. It was a smugglers' haven, and on some dark nights the O'Brians heard hushed voices outside but dared not look. According to Richard, Patrick suggested that they buy a small sailing dinghy for use near the shore and learn how to sail it. But he must have thought better of the idea; they never did. It was a heartachingly lonely setting, with clannish inhabitants, and life was truly spartan. While Mary cooked and kept house, Patrick and Richard cut firewood. One day while sawing a limb, Richard nearly hacked off a finger. Mary cleaned and bandaged the injury, and they carried on. As summer turned to fall, however, Mary missed Buddug too much. This harsh existence had given them a new appreciation for the relatively mellow state of life in Roussillon. They chose to return to France.

Soon winter was upon them. Few places change as dramatically from summer to winter as the south of France, much of which in another age was the ocean floor. The lush vegetation disappears, revealing the barren and brittle landscape. The fierce tramontane, rushing down from the Alps like a winter train, turns the glassy blue Mediterranean into a boat grinder and howls for days on end.

On February 18, 1955, Rupert Hart-Davis published *The Road to Samarcand*, printing five thousand copies (binding fifteen hundred). But Patrick's satisfaction at having his new book in hand was soon muted. Eight days after its publication, his seventy-eight-year-old father, Charles Russ, died of pneumonia in Ealing, a suburb of London.

While Charles had remained close to his two eldest sons, he had drifted away from his other children. O'Brian's oldest sister, Olive, had been on poor terms with her father for many years. But she had visited him in Ealing during the last two weeks of his life at the insistence of her uncle Sidney. "Who is this nice lady who has come to see me?" Charles had asked her. Their pointless dispute was long behind them, but they were now strangers to each other.

A flood of confusing emotions must have beset O'Brian. There was regret and anger over the family's disintegration after his mother died and his father—preoccupied by work and the struggle to support nine children—divided up the family. The pain of O'Brian's unhealthy youth always lurked near the surface of his mind. His father had been unable to help. In defense of his father, his career, despite a certain genius, had been plagued by poor timing, bad luck, and his own unsteadfast nature. And he had at least possessed the foresight to encourage Patrick's early literary efforts; Patrick had dedicated his book *Beasts Royal* to him.

Nonetheless, O'Brian's overall feelings are clear. There was a rift. He never introduced his son to his father. He never spoke of his father to Richard, and he did not even tell Richard now that his grandfather had just died. The amazing thing is that a man of O'Brian's insight not only was incapable of repairing his relationship with his father but fostered a similar father-son breach in his own house. Whatever O'Brian's emotions were, he did not share them with his son, and he would pay a price for it.

O'Brian had filled, and would continue to fill, his fiction with **negative** father-son relationships. In the forthcoming *Richard Temple*, for example, Llewellyn Temple, Richard's father, is a coarse, insensitive man who flies into rages. He dies when Richard is a young boy. In *The Catalans*, Xavier Roig becomes vitriolic in his hatred of his son, Dédé, whose "shallow little soul" (p. 113) he claims to have examined. "He was my own son, my only son," laments Roig, "and if I could not find a tenderness in my heart even for him, then indeed I was a monster" (p. 109). Yet he could not.

This would all culminate in the Aubrey-Maturin novels—where O'Brian's writing is less raw—in the form of Aubrey's father, General Aubrey, an outspoken, finagling buffoon, with bad taste in friends, politics, and architecture and little time for his son, to whom he is an embarrassment and a career hindrance. When General Aubrey unexpectedly dies offstage, the intelligence director Sir Joseph Blaine asks Maturin what effect this will have on Aubrey's scheduled voyage. Maturin replies, "It would surprise me if he were much affected. The General was not a man to inspire any great liking or esteem" (*The Letter of Marque,* p. 222).

Interestingly, in his biography *Joseph Banks*, O'Brian would note that in Banks's account of his father's last days, "there is no mention of kindness given or received, no emotion of any kind, and it is possible that they were not very good friends." One is tempted to turn the mirror back on O'Brian.

If there was sorrow at Charles Russ's death, and surely there was, it was probably mostly on behalf of Zoe. O'Brian knew this would be a difficult time for her. Surely his father's death dredged up a diversity of memories, and O'Brian had plenty to mull over during brisk walks in the cold dry air among the leafless vines, where even on a mild day it was hard to believe that the landscape of dreary, bent stumps would blossom back to life again in the spring.

12

Voyaging with Commodore Anson

1955–1959

Having in a previous issue, called *The Road to Samarcand* one of the best boys' adventure stories I had read, I am now rather at a loss for superlatives to apply to this book, which is even better. It has humour, brilliant description, pace and wisdom, and I defy any boy to put it down before he's finished it.

—Margery Fisher, review of *The Golden Ocean* for *Housewife* magazine, October 1956

O'Brian channeled his energy and his emotions into his work. He had returned to writing short stories. A perfectionist, he was also still revamping stories from his earlier collection, *The Last Pool,* which had not been published in the United States. By the spring of 1955, he shipped off a manuscript consisting of eighteen new stories and seven from the previous collection to Harcourt, Brace, which paid him $500 as an advance on royalties.

In his search for greater seclusion, O'Brian now decided to look closer to his Catalan home. The solution lay not in Portugal or Cornwall, but just on the other side of Faubourg. In France, land by law is divided equally among children, resulting in smaller lots with each successive generation. O'Brian bought one such curious subdivision, a long, narrow sloping strip dropping down to a gulley that flowed into the south side of the Collioure bay. The property, which belonged to a carpenter who had done some work for Patrick and Mary, lay in the middle of a hillside covered in mature grenache vines, with a well and a water pump at the bottom.

It was here on the slope beneath Fort St. Elme, the round, high-walled lookout constructed in the sixteenth century by King Charles V of Spain,

that the O'Brians settled for good, but not just yet. The land needed some
loving attention first.

The area was known as Correch d'en Baus (Catalan for "Valley of
Mister Baus"). On the far side of the gully at the bottom of Correch d'en
Baus was very fertile land, where a hefty farmer, whom the O'Brians
labeled "Young Fatty," grew beautiful garden crops for the market, and
Patrick made plans to start his own garden and vineyard. He took great
satisfaction in owning land and, as with the garden in Wales, was determined to be systematic in his planting. But even with his *vendange* experience, he had much to learn. He and Mary borrowed a pickax from their
friends the Atxers to work in the vineyard. The stiff handle stung their soft
hands whenever they struck rock.

The relative solitude and view of the sea from the O'Brians' new property offered some compensation for the lack of level ground for building.
Patrick hoped to blast a hole at the top of the slope in which he could con-
stuct a writing grotto. He planned to do the work himself and, in the
nearby town of Banyuls, bought dynamite, which, astonishingly, he kept
under Richard's bed, though he stored the detonator safely elsewhere.

On the day of the big blast, Patrick accidentally used too much dynamite. Rock showered down on father and son, scaring Patrick enough to
compel him to hire two Catalan miners, who knew what they were doing,
to help with future work. These were tough men who made a living ter-
racing mountainsides, and one of them, Richard would always remember,
a squat, powerful man, could hold his arm out to the side while gripping
the butt end of a sledgehammer, also extended, and then bend his wrist,
raising the fourteen-pound hammer head until he could kiss it.

Together, using sledgehammers and chisels, the four of them cut holes
in the rock, inserted dynamite, packed in explosive charges with clumps of
heather, and sealed them with sheet metal weighed down by rocks. They
had decided that it would be too difficult to blast out a grotto; instead, they
aimed at leveling an area big enough to hold a stone writing hut. It was
slow work, and they were only a third of the way through by June, when
Richard had to leave for London to take his exam.

O'Brian and his helpers continued their laborious excavation and
eventually built the hut by hand, something that O'Brian ironically would
be ashamed of and very touchy about later in life when he became more
established. Richard passed his exam in June, and in the fall he began his
national service in the Royal Navy, eventually rising from ordinary seaman

to able seaman during his two-year stint. He never returned to Collioure to see the hut or the house that later grew around it. His relationship with Patrick was not close, even during the busy year they spent together in Cornwall and Correch d'en Baus, and though he felt loved by Mary, he would become more resentful of his reserved father as he grew to be a man, away from Patrick's influence. No grievous final scene or row occurred, but a definite break came later.

Patrick eventually built living quarters of whitewashed wood on top of the hut, and he and Mary moved from the cramped and noisy center of town to the hillside and rejoiced in their quirky little house in the maquis and vineyards. For them, nightingales and black-eared wheatears, cicadas, and tree frogs made the most desirable neighbors. The two would cultivate their sloping garden with grapefruit and orange trees, vegetables, herbs, and flowers. A tall cypress hedge, walling off their private world, would grow thicker and thicker at the same time as Collioure's development encroached ever closer.

In the spring and summer of 1955, reviews of *The Road to Samarcand* trickled in. The naval historian Oliver Warner wrote, in an omnibus review of adventure stories in *Time and Tide* magazine: "It is not very probable adventure but it keeps admirably within its own convention. There is a splendid hurricane for good measure, and it would be a jaded creature who complained of a lack of things happening."

A review in the July 1 *Times Literary Supplement* carped that "the dénouement of *The Road to Samarcand* is as absurd politically as it is geographically." But *Scout* magazine called it "the year's best story-book so far. . . . Filled with real adventure and quick with incident."

In August, Harcourt, Brace published *The Walker and Other Stories* in the United States. (The British edition of this collection, which was slightly different in content and was titled *Lying in the Sun and Other Stories*, was published the following year.) Four of these stories had appeared in *Harper's Bazaar*, which, at the time, was also publishing stories by the likes of Truman Capote and Tennessee Williams.

But the book was not well received; critics found the tales cryptic and excessively bleak. In the September 23 issue of *Commonweal*, William Dunlea relegated his praise to the review's final paragraph, in which he called "The Clockmender" a "startlingly original nightmare," "The Voluntary Patient" a "smart fantasy-satire of auto-suggestive psychotherapy," and "A Journey to Cannes" the "most authentic *story*, à la Maupassant, of all." But, in general, he dismissed the collection, writing that "the human element here is the crucial deficiency, being saturated in a battery of secretive nature symbols. . . . What [O'Brian] lacks is sensibility." In this case, Dunlea was perhaps not entirely off base, but his criticism is ironic in retrospect, given that it is the humanity of O'Brian's writing, and his deeply nuanced sensibility, that would one day elevate his sea novels to high acclaim.

In the *New York Times*, Orville Prescott, who had generously praised *The Catalans*, seemed in a particularly foul mood, baldly stating: "When Mr. O'Brian writes short stories, he omits human character altogether and writes about faceless shadows called 'the man,' shadows whose gruesome or trivial adventures are supposed to have some portentous meaning but which frequently seem flat and a little silly." He added for good measure: "If he would discipline his imagination and devote his verbal dexterity to better purpose, he could write books that would not leave his readers provoked, perplexed and exasperated."

Other reviewers focused on the stories' sometimes forced endings, trying and failing to find great meaning there. In the *New York Times Book Review*, Donald Barr—making the mistake about O'Brian's birthplace that became the assumed fact—wrote, "This young Irish born, English-educated writer can make all the wounds our common humanity suffers turn into speaking mouths." It was a double-edged compliment, one that captured the tone of much of O'Brian's angst-ridden work, but not one that sold books.

Barr's and other reviewers' mistake about the author's birthplace derived from the book jacket and perpetuated O'Brian's dissembling biographical information, dating back to his biography in the December 1952 and March 1953 issues of *Harper's Bazaar*. These stated that he was born in the "west of Ireland." Similarly, the book jacket for *The Walker* declared that "O'Brian was born in the west of Ireland and educated in England." At least one reviewer, in *The New Yorker*, had doubts: "A collection of sensitive and imaginative sketches," the penetrating critic wrote, "related with a poetic intensity whose Celtic cadences do not always have a natural ring."

The book jacket also stated that O'Brian had "produced four novels before the war, as a kind of literary exercise." Who knows how or why this line was crafted or, for that matter, what it means? Who would believe that anyone would write four novels as a "literary exercise"? The fact was that as Patrick Russ, the author had published a collection of short stories, a novella, and a novel.

In the August *Harper's Bazaar*, which featured O'Brian's story "Lying in the Sun," timed to correspond with the publication of the collection in the United States, his brief biography was one of the most candid of his career. Despite repeating that he was born in Ireland, it revealed that he had been living for six years with his wife and son on the Mediterranean coast of France and that he had recently bought a small vineyard.

At least in the United States, O'Brian felt he could recreate himself. In England, where the collection, titled *Lying in the Sun*, was published in the spring of 1956, he remained under wraps. His strange and bitter-sounding jacket biography expressed a discomfort with the world. Perhaps it was an attempt at cleverness. It came across as a caustic jab at an innocent public:

> As to the personal side, the *Spectator* for March 1st 1710 begins, "I have observed, that a Reader seldom peruses a Book with Pleasure, till he knows whether the Writer of it be a black or fair Man, of a mild or cholerick Disposition, Married or a Batchelor, with other particulars of the like Nature, that conduce very much to the right understanding of an Author." To gratify this curiosity, which is so natural to a reader, we may state that Mr O'Brian is a black man, choleric, and married.

From this point on, with few exceptions, O'Brian jealously guarded his private life, and his terse book-jacket biographies revealed little. Never again did they mention his son.

In England, the reviews of *Lying in the Sun* were no better than in the United States. The *Times Literary Supplement* dismissed the collection in one paragraph: "In *The Frozen Flame* the mood of his writing was quiet, controlled, mature, his style as clear as the seas off the Costa Brava that was its setting, but in most of these stories his mood is angry, assertive and adolescent, his style obscure. By comparison they seem unfinished, and although his publishers do not say so, one would surmise that they are mostly earlier work. . . . One tends to look forward to his next work much more than to remember his present one."

Some of these reviews were perhaps overwrought. O'Brian's powers of description, observation, and characterization often glowed. His hunting and fishing stories, particularly "The Dawn Flighting" and "The Last Pool," quite brilliantly evoked those sports. But other stories could be obscure in the body and inscrutable in the ending and had a tendency to bring out the worst in a reviewer, who grew frustrated, like a person feeling along a dark passage and finally finding a light switch that does not work.

The unenthusiastic reviews of this collection set O'Brian back; it would be nearly a decade before he produced another volume of short stories. Nevertheless, he was clearly a writer driven by an inner force, a need to say something about human love and suffering and about nature and adventure. And just as clearly, although he had produced some work of great clarity that stands with the best of his writing, he had not yet found his milieu.

Two months prior to the publication of *Lying in the Sun*, O'Brian had published *The Golden Ocean*, the book he had whipped off as a breather between writing his two wrenching novels—*Testimonies* and *The Catalans*—and the painstaking work of editing and polishing his stories for the collection. Perhaps too drained and elated after finishing up *The Catalans* to take on another emotionally weighty effort, he had cranked out the novel on a whim, indulging himself in his lifelong interest in the sea and particularly in exploration and the Royal Navy.

It is difficult to say why *The Golden Ocean* might have sat around for more than two years before it was published in February 1956, but it seems that no publisher—let alone the author—was expecting this surprising little book. Rupert Hart-Davis had brought out *The Frozen Flame* in the fall of 1953. They were publishing *The Road to Samarcand* in the spring of 1955 and *Lying in the Sun* in the spring of 1956. That is a lot of books by one author. Perhaps it was a question of finding the right publishing slot for the novel.

The Golden Ocean was billed by the publisher as a book for children, but later O'Brian described it as a book for "readers of no particular age," pointing out that works such as *David Copperfield* and *Kidnapped* could be enjoyed whether you were twelve or seventy-two. In fact, his novel did have an ageless quality.

On February 24, 1956, *The Golden Ocean* was published in London by Rupert Hart-Davis, which printed 3,500 copies (binding 2,000). J. Day and Company bought U.S. rights from O'Brian for $750 and published the book the following year. By the critics' estimation, the publishers more than got their money's worth. If the reception of *The Walker/Lying in the Sun* was devastating, then this at least softened the blow.

The May 11 *Times Literary Supplement*—coincidentally the same issue that panned *Lying in the Sun*—led the charge for *The Golden Ocean*, giving O'Brian one of his best reviews ever. It began with the gratifying analogy that *The Golden Ocean* related to Anson's voyage in the same way that *War and Peace* did to the Napoleonic wars. "It is a big, rollicking, joyous book, in no narrow sense a book for children but likely to appeal to any reader who will meet the challenge of its length, its breadth of canvas, its uninhibited vocabulary," wrote the unnamed reviewer. "The story has in it something like greatness. It is naive, matter-of-fact; tragic, richly funny; closely detailed, but with a bold sweeping action."

As if that were not enough, the reviewer complimented O'Brian's realization of Peter Palafox as whole and individual—unlike the many familiar and unrealistic heroes of most adventure stories—as well as the author's convincing portrait of all the crew and his ability to evoke both the drudgery of such a long, difficult voyage and the dramatic storms and battles. He (or she) concluded:

> The story is written with fine restraint, with a proper apprecia-
> tion of the big moments but with no "fine" writing. *The Golden
> Ocean* is indeed that rarest thing in children's books, a highly
> capable piece of professional narrative, allied to a great heroic
> theme, and developed with humour and absolute integrity. It
> goes alongside *Big Tiger and Christian* on that very small shelf
> reserved for the authors who, disregarding fashions, age-ranges
> or reading aptitudes, spin a story out of the heart and soul of
> their experience and the joy of living.

In October, Margery Fisher attested to its sheer readability in *Housewife* magazine: "Having in a previous issue, called *The Road to Samarcand* one of the best boys' adventure stories I had read, I am now rather at a loss for superlatives to apply to this book, which is even better. It has humour, brilliant description, pace and wisdom, and I defy any boy to put it down before he's finished it."

Oddly, O'Brian later said in his autobiographical essay that the book "made no great impression"; he subsequently strengthened the statement in a *Weekend Telegraph* article, calling the public's reception of this book "frigid indifference."* But both his English and American publishers liked the work and encouraged him, so much so that in his next novel, *The Unknown Shore,* O'Brian returned to Anson's epic voyage.

Not only had *The Golden Ocean* allowed O'Brian to indulge in his youthful fantasies of serving in the Royal Navy, but being particularly poor at the time, he savored the voyage's outcome: having suffered severely and lost many men, the survivors grew rich after taking a treasure-laden Spanish galleon. Like a good many of these lucky men once they were no longer bound to the sea for a living, O'Brian took the money he earned from the book's success and bought land—a vineyard, in fact. Soon he was making use of the wine press that Monsieur Atxer had given him upon retiring from winemaking. Patrick would become an accomplished vintner, using and caring for Atxer's press as if it possessed the secrets of hundreds of years of winemaking magic.

The end of the decade brought political turmoil in France. In 1958, while Queen Elizabeth opened the three-hundredth session of Parliament in England, de Gaulle was elected president again and granted a six-month rule by decree as he prepared a new constitution and formed the Fifth Republic. French leftists protested, and the government called for additional gendarmes, press censorship, and a ban on public assemblies in Paris. In northern Africa, French colonial rule continued to deteriorate, with fifteen thousand French troops blockaded by nationalist forces in Tunisia and Frenchmen seizing government buildings in Algeria.

O'Brian, meanwhile, slipped into the warm bath of history, a refuge from adult worldly strife as effective as his animal kingdom had been during his childhood. This time he told the story of the crew of HMS *Wager,* one of Anson's storeships, which wrecked on an island off the coast of Chile in 1741. A grim story of mutiny and starvation, *The Unknown Shore* introduced the stalwart midshipman Jack Byron and his particular friend Tobias Barrow, a brilliant but eccentric surgeon's mate.

O'Brian based these characters on two historic figures: John "Foul-Weather Jack" Byron was a midshipman on board the *Wager.* He published a well-known narrative of the shipwreck in 1768, which his grandson, Lord Byron, used as his source for the description of the storm

---

*O'Brian's article, supporting the publication of *The Commodore* and titled "Just a Phase I'm Going Through?," appeared in the August 27, 1994, *Weekend Telegraph.*

and wreck in his epic poem *Don Juan*. The character Tobias Barrow was based on a hanger-on at the Byron household who accompanied Jack on the voyage.

Whereas in *The Golden Ocean* O'Brian had created two characters, Peter Palafox and Sean O'Mara, who are to his later heroes Jack Aubrey and Stephen Maturin as a caterpillar is to a butterfly, in *The Unknown Shore* his two central characters are unmistakably Aubrey and Maturin in their early forms. Barrow, like Maturin, is largely oblivious to Royal Navy decorum and totally devoted to his study of the natural world. Byron, like Aubrey, is a consummate navy man. Their differences are frequently the source of conflict and humor in the novel: "There were a good many points upon which Jack and Tobias did not see eye to eye, apart from the desirability of chatting with captains and commodores; one difference concerned the proportion of their cabin that could reasonably be devoted to reptiles, and another was about the relative worth of their ship, considered either as a man-of-war or as a home" (p. 203).

The Unknown Shore, indeed, proved to be the seed from which the Aubrey-Maturin series eventually sprang, but not until a decade later. In May 1959, Rupert Hart-Davis published the book, with a Charles Brooking painting of an Indiaman in a fresh breeze on the cover, courtesy of the National Maritime Museum. The publisher printed 4,500 copies, 1,000 more than it had printed of *The Golden Ocean*. However, *The Unknown Shore* did not gain critically from the praise of *The Golden Ocean*. No mention of the earlier book was made in the dispassionate review of *The Unknown Shore* in the July 24 *Times Literary Supplement*, which tepidly praised O'Brian's eighteenth-century London and Royal Navy patronage system and his descriptions of the bleak Patagonia coast. This was sad treatment given the *TLS*'s enthusiasm for *The Golden Ocean*.

The editors at Rupert Hart-Davis had found O'Brian, who dropped into their offices at 36 Soho Square during production on several occasions that summer, a pleasure to work with—punctual, courteous, deferential, and realistic in his expectations. He charmed the three secretaries who worked downstairs in the big house; they were always delighted to see him walk through the door. But for now O'Brian's run at sea was over.

13

Temple and Beauvoir

1960–1966

What third person can give a true account of what is in
its nature secret and often incommunicable, the essential
causes of a divorce? At the most he can only record the
visible effects.

—Patrick O'Brian, *Pablo Ruiz Picasso*, 1976

The O'Brians spent much of 1960 in London, where Mary's son, Nikolai Tolstoy, was hospitalized while undergoing back surgery to correct a painful congenital problem. That year, the literary cause célèbre in England was the plight of the London Library. For its first eighty years, the venerable library, in St. James's Square, had been a tax-exempt charity. Suddenly the Westminster City Council was demanding an annual rate, which the institution could not pay. After several court hearings the library found itself £20,000 in debt and on the verge of being taxed into oblivion. Its president, Tom (T. S.) Eliot, and chairman, Rupert Hart-Davis, O'Brian's energetic publisher, appealed to the public for donations in an editorial printed in the *Times*. They followed up by shaking down their writer and artist friends for sellables.

In June Christie's held a benefit auction, which was a resounding success. E. M. Forster's manuscript of *A Passage to India* alone fetched £6,500, and Eliot's newly handwritten copy of "The Waste Land" (the original manuscript had been lost), complete with a missing line, £2,800. Lytton Strachey's *Queen Victoria* manuscript, Somerset Maugham's *Up at the Villa*, and Henry Moore's bronze maquette of a screen for the Time-Life building on Bond Street were among the other collectibles sold. Although O'Brian's literary reputation had briefly soared, he was not enough of a name in London to even be tapped by Hart-Davis.

Still he worked away in relative obscurity. He was now writing another "serious" novel, a bildungsroman that explored the anguish of an artist's life, the moral dilemmas involved in trying to survive in an often cruel, almost always misguided and unappreciative world, while remaining true to one's art. The book reflected his own struggling career as a writer, his mixed feelings for both England and France, his experience and observations regarding relationships between men and women, as well as his deep interest in painting and the artist's life. The book, *Richard Temple,* would not be published until the spring of 1962.

Though the O'Brians' income flagged during this period, they had to focus on more important matters. During Nikolai's three-month convalescence, Mary and Patrick visited him every day—in a small way compensating Mary for the time with her children that she had been denied—while Nikolai's father and stepmother came to his hospital room only once. Although Nikolai continued to grow closer to his mother and stepfather in coming years and figured out for himself that O'Brian was not Irish, Patrick maintained this facade even within the family.

Around this time, Patrick and Mary, who had married in a civil service, decided to have a religious wedding. Although it might seem bizarre that they chose Russian Orthodoxy, Dimitry's faith, it was also the faith that Mary's children, Nikolai and Natasha, had been raised in. Thus Mary maintained a degree of allegiance to it. Patrick and Mary were evidently practicing Catholics at this time, and the Russian Orthodox Church had close ties to Catholicism without the same prohibitions against divorce and remarriage. So the couple settled on a Russian Orthodox ceremony. The event was intimate, with only about half a dozen people in attendance. James Puckridge, Barbara's son, held one of the crowns over their heads in a Russian Orthodox wedding ritual. Afterward, there was a small party in Chelsea.

Back in France, Patrick and Mary spared themselves certain expenses by cultivating a garden for food and grapes for wine. In their small vineyard, twenty minutes from their house and a thousand feet higher up, they grew enough grapes to produce hearty red wine for family and friends. Patrick harvested honey from a hive of wild bees on their roof.

To augment his income, O'Brian turned to translating, a pursuit for which he was particularly well suited. By now, he spoke, to some extent, Italian, French, Spanish, German, Catalan, and Irish and had a good background in Latin and Greek. After more than a decade in France, he was not only fluent but also well-read in the tongue, and, in fact, he often translated from French to English almost effortlessly as he read. He also had Mary, with her excellent language skills, to assist him.

Although translating was a notoriously low-paying job, O'Brian was able to do it with great speed. His reading of history was particularly useful and made him a favorite translator for rather arcane texts. He took care to be considerate of the writer's style, often—particularly when he thought it an important book—starting to translate about a third of the way into the work to catch the author's language and rhythm in stride. Later he went back to the beginning.

In 1961, Weidenfeld and Nicolson published O'Brian's translation of Jacques Soustelle's *The Daily Life of the Aztecs on the Eve of the Spanish Conquest*. Next he translated Christine de Rivoyre's *The Wreathed Head*, a love story about a young Frenchwoman studying at an American university, for his publisher Rupert Hart-Davis. "Admirably translated," noted the *Times Literary Supplement*. Among O'Brian's three translations to hit bookstores in 1962 was the 512-page *Daily Life in the Time of Jesus*, written by Henry Daniel-Rops (also known as Jules Charles Henri Petiot). While the *Times Literary Supplement* admonished O'Brian for using "the double plural Apochryphas," it praised his translation.

O'Brian submitted *Richard Temple* to his publisher probably in the late summer or fall of 1961. Though he had taken on some of life's challenging questions and created an insightful and courageous novel, *Richard Temple*, published by Macmillan in June 1962 with the inscription "For Mary, with love," was not uplifting and would not become a readers' favorite. No publisher could be found for the brooding book in the United States.

While O'Brian's later novels chiefly concern ethical characters operating in a generally benevolent world, Temple is poor, morally confused, struggling, and living a seamy, grim life, the product of "divided social heritage and a disturbed boyhood," as the *Times Literary Supplement* observed. Even the book's jacket blurb described him as a "misfit" and "anti-hero," who tries in vain to blend into "the even crueller England of the '30s."

On the other hand, Temple is a painter with real creative power who becomes fully alive while painting, much as O'Brian felt he did while writing. O'Brian explored Temple's moral quandary after he falls in love and, in order to travel in his girlfriend's social circle, begins making trendy, facile paintings—"only decorations" (p. 268)—that he sells for large sums.

Just how much of this bildungsroman is autobiographical is difficult to say. But again some parallels between Temple, the painter, and O'Brian, the writer, are evident. O'Brian was to a certain degree a physical and social misfit in his youth. His mother died when he was three, and his father became, in many ways, unavailable to him; Temple's father dies when he is young, and his mother goes insane and sexually debases herself. O'Brian turned to reading and writing; Temple turns to painting. They both fall in love with women in higher social stations, albeit with very different results. They are both "true creative artists." They both have their lives drastically interrupted and forever changed by World War II, in which they serve as intelligence agents.

Of course, one cannot carry such a comparison too far. Temple becomes briefly deranged and homeless and involves himself in art forgery and burglary. After a long career of selfish, sometimes indifferent relationships with women, Temple finally falls in love but is thwarted in his pursuit.

Bleak, and at times obscure, the novel also has a cumbersome structure: a captured British intelligence agent, Temple tells his life story from a prison camp in Vichy France. The novel begins effectively through his present torture and suffering but soon dwells almost entirely on his personal history. Instead of adding suspense to the story, the camp, left behind in the forgotten present, becomes a heavy-handed symbol.

What is most remarkable is that, despite the dark atmosphere, O'Brian keeps the reader wanting more. In Temple's retelling of his life there are some stunning epiphanal moments. After his alcoholic and depressed mother is taken away for treatment, he moves to France to study in the house of a painter. To describe Temple's transition to his new life, O'Brian produced a poignant metaphor from his time in Cwm Croesor, all the more chilling for its matter-of-fact presentation:

> One of the most striking sights upon a sheep-farm is the castration of the ram-lambs; they undergo their mutilation with a few little inward groans and stand as it were amazed for one or two minutes; then they start to graze again. And although they do not play that day, nor the next, after some time they do, almost as if the thing had never been done to them. In any case, after the mingled shock of travel and exhaustion was over, Richard found himself as much at home in this new house as ever he

was likely to be . . . and he was not without taking pleasure from it. (P. 52)

In *Richard Temple*, O'Brian proved that he could plunge deep into the cold, murky bottom of the psyche. When Temple discovers that his friend Torrance has stolen his prize painting and sold it, his reaction is not rage but something far more complex: "He hoped never to have to see Torrance again. For if they did meet he would be ashamed of his moral superiority, and ashamed for Torrance's face; and if they did meet there might well be a fight, and he could not bear it if Torrance turned out to be shy of a fight" (pp. 208–9).

Although different in period and theme, *Richard Temple* presaged O'Brian's Aubrey-Maturin novel series in a number of ways. The works share certain leitmotifs. Both Captain Aubrey, the hero on his square-rigged ship, and Richard Temple, the struggling prisoner of war, use iron bolt heads as touchstones. Their ritual polishing of the bolt helps them maintain sanity and stability. Temple, like the inquisitive Irish-Catalan doctor–natural philospher–intelligence agent Stephen Maturin, is a brilliant polyglot, who fights chemical dependence, struggles to marry a difficult-to-obtain lover, and becomes an intelligence agent operating along the French-Spanish border. Both are captured and tortured by their enemies.

To charge the plot, O'Brian created a headstrong, sometimes out-of-control heroine in both works. Philippa Brett of *Richard Temple* is most certainly Diana Villiers in the bud. Like Villiers, a dark-haired, slender beauty, Brett is passionate and tomboyish. Like Villiers, she drives too fast (meeting Temple after she runs him down in a car) and ends up in the wrong bed. So striking is the resemblance between the two characters that this passage could as easily apply to Maturin thinking about Villiers as to Temple thinking about Brett:

Self-possession was the important word: she might resent being possessed by anything more than affection and he could only pray without any certainty that she would not resent the burden of being loved. She certainly resented any control, and at times she certainly resented being a woman, although she was such an excellent one. . . . She was most affectionate, where her liking

lay; and although she disguised it she had the strongest sense of
duty: but as for love—would she undergo the violation of love?
(*Richard Temple,* pp. 239–40)

Both Brett and Villiers represent O'Brian's archetypal woman of substance, a complex, often perplexing, passionate being, compelled by the demons of womanhood. She wants to behave with the freedom of a man. She survives by her own wit and guile but is also prone to self-destructive behavior.

There are some additional similarities between *Richard Temple* and the Aubrey-Maturin series, mostly superficial but interesting: In both works, the downs of southern England are described as a series of "whale-backed" curves, giving them a sense of grace, liveliness, and mystery. In both, the "marthambles," an invented illness, which O'Brian read about in a quack's pamphlet, appear. He gave Philippa Brett two aunts named Sophie, which is also the name of Jack Aubrey's wife as well as that of his first command.

The June 1 *Times Literary Supplement* applauded O'Brian's ability to portray the two levels on which Temple lives, the often squalid and lonely life of a poor, confused artist and the transcendent life of a genius at work. The reviewer also admired O'Brian's skill at capturing the process of artistic creation:

> Novelists commonly muff it even when they are writing about writers, with whose medium they themselves struggle and whose pangs they have presumably shared. Mr. O'Brian succeeds triumphantly where the medium is paint and canvas— succeeds even in such detail as the satisfactions to be gained from different techniques, or the gambler's throw of adding a single line or stroke of colour that may transform or wreck a picture, as well as in conveying the rare moments of truth when a man paints in a fury of energy, and in the knowledge that this is the justification of his whole life.

Undeniably insightful and nuance-laden, *Richard Temple* was, nevertheless, a tough read, like many of O'Brian's short stories, and with the above exception received only scant reviews in such out-of-the-way places as the *Liverpool Daily Post* and the *South China Morning Post*. In the latter, a reviewer wrote: "A good book, adult and direct. A theme an American writer would have buried in rococo enthusiasms (psychiatrist's couch to the fore). In Mr. O'Brian's hands it becomes a thing of hewn strength."

Dealing with many issues that were clearly of personal relevance, *Richard Temple* appears to have been a cathartic work for O'Brian. Literarily, at least, it seems to a great extent to have emptied him of bile and severe introspection and, perhaps for a time, of motivation. He did not publish another novel for seven years. Nor did he ever write another set in the twentieth century.

That is not to say that work ceased around the O'Brian house. When Barbara Puckridge and her sixteen-year-old niece, Lu Vlasto, visited Collioure in the summer of 1962, Patrick spent each morning working in his office, and Mary could be heard knocking away on an old typewriter. Silence was to be observed during these intense work hours. Patrick was so sensitive to noise that he eventually took to using earplugs when at work.

As Lu later recalled, Patrick did not relish the idea of having a bored teenage girl flopping about the house for two weeks. At dinner on the evening they arrived, he suddenly announced to her, "We've got a lovely treat in store for you." They had friends whose daughter was in a convent near Perpignan. Lu was to join her and the sisters for a five-day bus trip to Montserrat, a Pyrenees pilgrimage site. Lu, who was on holiday from boarding school, was crestfallen, but she dutifully attended the field trip.

Upon her return, she insisted on going to the beach. "The beach?" Patrick sneered. "You want to go and lie there and get all horrible and pink?" Ignoring him, Lu and her aunt snuck down to the seashore one morning. Lu went swimming and promptly trod on a sea urchin. With spines in her feet, she hobbled back to the house in tears. "Come over here, my dear," Patrick instructed her. "Lie down. I don't want to hear a peep out of you." He then found a razor blade and extracted the spines one by one from her foot. Lu bore this courageously, and thereafter Patrick warmed to her. He could be seen showing her the flora and fauna on the hills surrounding the house and escorting her around town to see the sights. She had won him over against his natural inclinations.

Despite their poverty, Patrick and Mary maintained a receptive household, and a steady stream of visitors meant England was never far from their doorstep. Nikolai, whom Mary dubbed a "valiant weeder" of the garden, was now a summer regular. Mary's brother's children, Jane, Joanna, and Peter Wicksteed, who came to adore their free-spirited Aunt Mary and Uncle Patrick, made frequent summer visits as well. They sat on the beach and walked in the hills, where Patrick entertained them with bird-calls. They traveled to Spain and Andorra and picnicked under trees while sitting on the detachable backseat of the 2CV. And they sometimes visited the homes of former Resistance members to check up on them, though whether this was in any kind of official capacity or just out of personal devotion no one seems to know.

In the summer of 1963, James Puckridge, his wife, Justina, and her eleven-year-old son, Charles, were vacationing in Rosas, Spain, when torrential rains caused flooding. They left the Costa Brava and drove up to Collioure, where it was raining only slightly less hard, to see the O'Brians. One day, while it was pouring outside, Patrick had an idea for passing the time: a whiskey-tasting contest. He rustled up four bottles. Two were Spanish whiskeys, one was Scotch, and the other Irish. The idea was to identify which of the four was the Irish whiskey. The reward turned out to be in the effort, not the result. No one could identify the Irish whiskey with any certainty, but they had a fine time trying.

The Puckridges stayed at a little hotel in town and spent their days with the O'Brians, sharing memories and walking in the hills, where the fresh breeze smelled of sea salt and field herbs. Patrick's strong opinions and his ability to speak in detail on so many topics made for lively conversation. Mary conversed more gently but just as broadly. On occasion, Patrick's temper flared up, as when Charles left Patrick's knife, lent to him so that he could idle away a few hours carving wood, on a garden wall, where the rain rusted it. But from his stay in Wales James was accustomed to Patrick's tempests. They soon blew over.

It was probably in late 1963 that Patrick and Mary met Richard's fiancée. Mimi Parotte was the daughter of a Belgian father and an English mother, who, living in occupied Belgium during the war, had hidden downed RAF pilots in their attic. After being discovered, the Parottes had disguised themselves and fled south, Mimi's father, Jean, carrying his four-year-old daughter—shorn of hair and dressed as a boy—on his back over the Pyrenees. Despite the special occasion, the evening with Patrick and Mary at a London apartment was strained. For one thing, Mimi found Patrick cold and intimidating. She was probably not unbiased, for by this time Richard had come to fully realize what a mess his childhood had been and how it had scarred him. "My father had been very, very bad to my mother," he concluded. "You just don't do this to a woman. And you hope like hell it does not happen in your family." In fact, Richard had delayed marrying Mimi for several years to make sure that they would not make the same mistake his parents had.

In the spring of 1964, Patrick and Mary received a letter from Richard, now twenty-seven years old, telling them that before the wedding he planned to change his name back to Russ. Richard did this, he later said, "for the sake of honesty." He reasoned that he was born a Russ, and he wanted to be married a Russ. He did not make the change out of anger or to spite his father, he insisted. Nevertheless, as he had matured, Richard had come to better understand the nature of the breach between his parents, and, in the absence of any conversation with Patrick regarding it, he had drawn his own conclusions. He had not so much sided with his mother as condemned his father's behavior in leaving the family.

As with so many other important events in his life, O'Brian chose to remain silent about Richard's decision. He had virtually dug a hole, put the memory of his first marriage down in it, and covered it up. For him, that phase of life simply no longer existed. But O'Brian's departure from the family was like a tumor in his relationship with his son. The bigger the tumor grew, the more it drained life from the victim. Finally, it had become too much for Richard to bear. Reverting to his earlier surname allowed him to distance himself from his father's illusion and separate himself from this painful episode in the family history.

Mary wrote Richard, saying that she understood. She addressed the envelope to Richard O'Brian, with a scrawled apology and a promise not to use the name again. But Patrick did not respond at all, and he would eventually disown his only child. Inability to express emotion, to work through anger, to swallow pride, and then to heal had caught up with the family once again.

Richard married Mimi Parotte on the first of July. Elizabeth had said she would not attend if Patrick did, so Richard and Mimi did not invite Patrick and Mary to the wedding. The breach was complete. Patrick and Richard never spoke to each other again. In this regard, Patrick relived the sad history of his sometimes perverse family, where injured pride all too often clogged the lines of communication. Was he bitter about it? "Parents are supposed to love their children," he would write in his biography of

Picasso, "yet surely there is the implied condition that the children should be reasonably lovable?" (p. 466).

O'Brian had been in England in April of that year for another reason. The occasion was a sad one. Zoe Russ had died a week after her eighty-sixth birthday, at a hospital in Ealing, and Patrick went to England to attend the funeral. He rode on the train with family members to the city of Stafford, south of Manchester, and then traveled on to the village of Stone for the service. Drifts of daffodils covered the countryside between Stafford and the churchyard where Zoe was buried. Showing no favoritism, she had left them each £50, including Patrick, the favorite son who had changed his name, Joan, who had married beneath herself, and Joan's daughter Frances, who was Zoe's goddaughter. It was the last time so many family members assembled.

After Zoe's death, O'Brian reached almost complete emotional detachment from his Russ family. When Joan tried to initiate a correspondence with him, he wrote back saying that he would rather not be reminded of his youth. Joan's pride was injured, and they never communicated with each other again. If not for Barney's persistence, Patrick most likely would have forever severed ties with his family at this time.

As he always had, O'Brian nursed himself by working. He was now in demand for translating, and he had a new agent to negotiate for him. Nearing retirement, Spencer Curtis Brown had handed over O'Brian to Richard Scott Simon, who had previously worked in publicity for the publisher William Collins. The two agents were completely different. Shrewd but domineering, Brown was emotional and known to be something of a bully. Simon, who had read history at St. John's College, Oxford, was easygoing and well liked, and he was happy to negotiate O'Brian's translation contracts, which could be somewhat tedious. He and O'Brian got along well, beginning a working relationship that lasted for more than a quarter century.

O'Brian now set about translating Henri Noguères's *Munich or The Phoney Peace*. His translation of *Histoire parallèle des États-Unis et de l'U.R.S.S. 1917–1960*, a three-volume, two-author history of the two powers, conceived by Presses de la Cité, was published in the spring of 1964 in England by Weidenfeld and Nicolson and in the United States by McKay. The parallel histories, as they were called, weighing in at more than a thousand pages, were not warmly received by the *Times Literary*

Supplement, which even took a potshot at O'Brian's translation of André Maurois's volume on the United States. But the comment that the "second handicap is a very mediocre translation which cannot possibly do justice to M. Maurois's usually elegant French" may have been a way of alleviating the respected French novelist and biographer of some of the pain of a disparaging critique.

Patrick and Mary devoted that summer to improving their garden, a budding oasis in a terraced moonscape of grapevines. They planted a cypress hedge as a wind block and cultivated mixed beds of pink, red, and white roses. They also visited Avignon, and ate at the nearby three-star restaurant Noves, a lavish meal that Patrick gleefully recounted in a letter to his niece Joanna: "larks baked in a pie and peering out," langoustine, hare stuffed with truffles, cheese galore. "I have resolved to devote the rest of my life, my declining years, to greed," he concluded. "For gluttony is one of those really satisfactory vices that lasts, and France is filled with bloated literary figures that creep slowly from one three-star restaurant to the next, beaming greatly with satisfaction as they go."

In 1965, O'Brian, now fifty, received a minor glorification. His story "The Walker" was published in *The Uncommon Reader* anthology, the best of Alice Morris's twelve-year fiction editorship at *Harper's Bazaar*, arguably the most prestigious publisher of avant-garde stories in the United States at that time. Morris had published 186 stories at the magazine, and "The Walker" was one of thirty-five chosen, joining the ranks of those by Dylan Thomas, Flannery O'Connor, Donald Barthelme, Jorge Luis Borges, Colette, and Eugène Ionesco.

This must have encouraged the writer in O'Brian, but for now, his income depended upon his translations. Though at times he enjoyed the work, he was not passionate about it. He would later remember it as "essentially a bread-and-butter arrangement," noting, "I have a passion for bread and butter."*

O'Brian's reputation as a deft translator was secure, and the work flowed in steadily. In 1966, Farrar, Straus and Giroux published O'Brian's translation of Maurice Goudeket's *La Douceur de vieillir* (*The Delights of Growing Old*) in the United States. *The New Yorker* called the book by Colette's urbane and insightful husband "enchanting" and the translation "ideal." O'Brian's translation was indeed smooth, and the book delightfully-

---

*In an interview on Amazon.com, 1998.

readable. Goudeket came across as self-effacing and likable, honest about his shortcomings. So felicitous is the translation that one might expect that O'Brian liked the book. But his Aubrey-Maturin series could be read as one extended answer to Goudeket's observation about himself:

> I still have a kind of incapacity for forming strong attachments with males of my own species. . . . When I look back, I see that my real friendships have been with women. There is something that I cannot define that separates me from most men: it may be hunting, which I cordially dislike because of my love of animals; or fishing; or that air that they have, like bumblebees stuffing themselves into every flower; or of the commercial traveler's jokes; or the belly laughs. . . . Friendship implies a certain complicity. (Pp. 27–28)*

In 1966, Weidenfeld and Nicolson (U.K.) and Putnam (U.S.) also published O'Brian's translation of Simone de Beauvoir's *Une Mort très douce* as *A Very Easy Death*. "The translation, by Patrick O'Brian, is so good one almost forgets to give it its due credit," wrote the *Times Literary Supplement*. In 1968 and 1969, Collins and Putnam would bring out his translations of her books *Les Belles Images* (which retained its French title) and *La Femme rompue: L'Age de discrétion: Monologue* (published as *The Woman Destroyed*). He highly enjoyed her work, but found it at times uneven. Although she could write, he later commented, "with extraordinary grace, she could also be pedestrian, writing *n'importe quoi n'importe comment*."

As a translator, O'Brian did not believe in "improving" the text independent of the author. However, he and Beauvoir understood each other well. According to O'Brian, when he contacted her with a problematic passage, she listened carefully and often altered the text. He found her both considerate and extremely kind. Beauvoir obviously liked O'Brian's work too. He translated most of her writing after 1960, an opus that satisfied him greatly, with one regret: that he had not been on the scene in time to translate her early monumental autobiographical works, *Mémoires*

*In interviews later in life, O'Brian frequently referred to his translations of Colette's letters, particularly in comparison with his Simone de Beauvoir work. Though he never mentioned it, these few letters were published in the Goudeket book.

d'une jeune fille rangée, 1954 (*Memoirs of a Dutiful Daughter,* 1959), and *La Force de l'age,* 1960 (*The Prime of Life,* 1962).

In 1968, the *Times Literary Supplement* reviewed two O'Brian translations, both initially published in the United States. In March, the *TLS* called his version of French historian Bernard Fay's *Louis XVI, ou, La Fin d'un monde*, published as *Louis XVI, or The End of the World*, "very competently done, the narrative flows as continuously in English as it does in French." And, in May, the *TLS* praised O'Brian's abridgement of French foreign correspondent Lucien Bodard's two-volume *La Guerre d'Indochine*, which had been quite a complex task. O'Brian had cut the 400,000-word history about France's involvement in Vietnam in half. Wrote the *TLS*, quoting from the translator's introduction: "The selection and condensation were done with care and in full consultation with the author: the translator 'traced out the essential themes . . . and then chose typical passages and examples . . . to illustrate the attitudes of mind, the good will and idealism, the incompetence, muddle and plain graft . . . in their true proportions.' He deserves to be congratulated on the succinct, readable English book which is the result."

In all, O'Brian translated a remarkable nineteen books from French into English during the 1960s, including four published in 1967 alone. In 1966, the financial picture, perhaps with a loan from Barney, looked rosy enough for him to push forward with plans to expand his tiny house among the vineyards of Correch d'en Baus. Also that summer, O'Brian apparently took time out to do some sailing with his nephew, Peter Wicksteed, who stayed with them for six weeks. They sailed a borrowed twenty-foot boat off the stony Collioure beach, according to Peter, who is the only person to confirm that Patrick could sail. On a hot July day, as they cruised up the coast to Argelès-sur-Mer, Peter told his uncle "I want to go for a swim."

"Well, you'd better be careful," Patrick warned him, "because you might not think it, but this boat is moving rather fast." They decided to conduct an experiment. Peter jumped in. The boat quickly left him in its wake. Patrick deftly tacked around and rescued him.

14

Master and Commander

1967–1969

In difficult or doubtful attacks by sea—and the odds of 50 men
to 320 comes within this description—no device can be too
minute, even if apparently absurd, provided it have the effect
of diverting the enemy's attention whilst you are concentrating
your own. In this, and other successes against odds, I have no
hesitation in saying that success in no slight degree depended
on out-of-the-way devices, which the enemy not suspecting,
were in some measure thrown off their guard.

—Thomas Cochrane, *Autobiography of a Seaman* (1860)

In the calendar of rural France, the two most interesting months are
August, the month of vacations and fêtes, and October, when the all-
important *vendange* occurs. August 1967 brought record dryness to
France, especially the south and west. Perpignan recorded well less than
half its normal rainfall. Vacationers heading for the seashore jammed the
coastal roads of Pyrénées-Orientales, and there seemed to be a special
madness in the air in Collioure.

Moviemaker Robert Dhéry was filming *Le Petit Baigneur* in the village,
and he brought with him a boat made on Lake Michigan, a hot-air balloon,
fourteen cubic meters of sand, a special tractor for riding above the
grapevines, and the white horse that had appeared in *La Plume de Ma
Tante* in the United States. To complete the spectacle, the director had
requested a police motorcycle escort.

One victim of August's madness was Manolo Gallardo, a twenty-seven-
year-old matador, who was gored in his femoral artery by a bull at the
corrida on August 16. An ambulance rushed him, bleeding, to the hospital in the neighboring town of Argeles, where he was saved. Another victim

was O'Brian, whose tormentor—the infamous French bureaucracy—was even more tenacious than a mad bull.

In March, O'Brian had filed a proposal to build an addition onto his house, complete with blueprints and a list of materials to be used. Although the mayor of Collioure had approved the plans, on August 29 a village policeman showed up at the O'Brians' door with a stop-work order. The departmental administrator in Perpignan had denied the proposal because Collioure's town-planning commission had not yet completed its plan for O'Brian's neighborhood.

In October, the mayor interceded on O'Brian's behalf, informing the departmental administrator that the commission's plan had now been ratified and requesting that O'Brian's building permit be granted. Nevertheless, in February 1968, O'Brian received a notice that his modest plans had again been rejected—this time by the regional urban planning agency—on the grounds that the type of roof O'Brian proposed had never been used in Collioure and thus could not be sanctioned by the town-planning commission.

That May, in Paris, a minor dispute involving students at Nanterre and Sorbonne universities swelled into a major revolt for reform of the centralized, authoritarian educational system. Along Boulevard St. Germain, ten thousand students overturned cars and buses, barricading themselves in. Bonfires smoldered in the streets. Riot police charged students in the Latin Quarter, who responded by heaving cobblestones and café chairs at them.

Given O'Brian's own entanglement with the unbridled French bureaucracy, he might have felt more than a twinge of sympathy for the frustrated students. They refused to take it sitting down, and so did he. Somehow the O'Brians' much-needed house addition, including a new bedroom with a balcony overlooking the garden, a bathroom, and a garage, eventually got built.

Meanwhile, good news had arrived to offset O'Brian's aggravations, and to provide him with some manner of revenge. The Philadelphia-based publisher J. B. Lippincott Company called to suggest that he try his hand at another sea novel. Their rationale was simple: C. S. Forester, whose Hornblower novels were widely popular among adults and young adults, had died in 1966. Lippincott wanted to launch the next Forester. There were, and would be, other writers who tried to follow Forester's lead. In

1965, Lippincott had published Dudley Pope's *Ramage*, introducing his fictional seaman Nicholas Ramage, but Lippincott editor in chief Robert White Hill did not expect Pope to be Forester's successor. Hill had read *The Golden Ocean* and thought that O'Brian might have the talent, so he tracked him down.

Lippincott specifically asked O'Brian to write the book for adults. O'Brian liked the idea. He considered the sea exploits of the Royal Navy during the Napoleonic wars—the age of Horatio Nelson—to be one of the defining moments in the history and lore of the English. It was their Trojan War tale—with heroes such as Richard Howe, John Jervis, George Keith, and Thomas Cochrane and great single-ship and fleet actions, including the Glorious First of June, the battles of Cape St. Vincent, the Nile, and Trafalgar—and it was a story that he wished to explore.

He had read and absorbed much of the great naval histories of Robert Beatson and William James, and he had enjoyed Forester's Hornblower novels. Still, Hornblower left something to be desired. Although O'Brian admired Forester's masterful action scenes, his characters, other than Hornblower, had little depth, and his presentation of the human experience lacked richness. While the era was well documented in contemporary accounts and by historians, no one, aside from Captain Frederick Marryat, who had actually served in the Royal Navy under Cochrane, had yet breathed real life into it, and his pre-Victorian picaresque novels were growing dated. Having thoroughly enjoyed his previous forays into nautical historical fiction, O'Brian was willing to give Lippincott's idea a try.

On September 19, 1967, at the age of fifty-two, O'Brian signed a contract agreeing to submit a manuscript for the new book in a year. Lippincott was to write a check immediately for $2,500. O'Brian would receive the same amount on showing evidence of satisfactory progress and a third installment on delivery of the manuscript. Even better, in London, Macmillan, which had published *Richard Temple*, agreed to jointly commission the book for British publication.

O'Brian decided to base the novel on a historical episode involving the Scotsman Thomas Cochrane, later the tenth earl of Dundonald. An outsider and an idealist, Cochrane was the Nelson of frigate commanders, fearless, cunning, and admired by his men, whom he enriched with prize money as a result of their victories at sea. Like Nelson, Cochrane was not afraid to ignore or expand orders when he believed he could strike a blow for England by doing so. His first command resulted in one of the great single-ship actions in Royal Navy history. In the fourteen-gun brig *Speedy*, which Cochrane called "a burlesque on a vessel of war," with a crew of 54 men, he fought and defeated the thirty-two-gun Spanish xebec frigate *El Gamo* and her crew of 319.

Although O'Brian modeled the book's action on Cochrane's cruise, he deviated from the Scotsman's character in creating his fictional captain, Jack Aubrey. Cochrane was at times rash, confrontational, and disagreeable, particularly when it came to politics. O'Brian wanted his captain to be a thorough Englishman, reflecting the good qualities of the English. At least in part, he visualized his brother, Mike, a tall, powerful, and spirited man of action, and a sociable one.

O'Brian already had the rough forms of the two main characters he would create for this book, and whose lives he would write about for the next three decades. Peter Palafox, midshipman, and Sean O'Mara, surgeon's mate, from *The Golden Ocean*, were the first incarnation of his fictional seafaring friends. The *Unknown Shore*'s Jack Byron and Tobias Barrow, the one orphaned, the other sold by his parents for a philosopher's experiment, were even better models. In Jack Aubrey, a bluff, likable officer in the Royal Navy, and Stephen Maturin, an odd, frequently irascible, and almost always rational surgeon and natural philosopher, O'Brian crystallized his two archetypal characters, whose lives and friendship would allow him to express a great deal about the world and the nature of friendship and at the same time to maintain the dramatic tension necessary to engage readers throughout what would become a multivolume series. Eventually, Aubrey and Maturin would be compared to the great literary tandems: Holmes and Watson, Quixote and Panza, Achilles and Patroclus.

Maturin was "a good old Irish name," according to Somerset Maugham, who used it in *The Razor's Edge*, with "a bishop in the family, and a dramatist and several distinguished soldiers and scholars." Charles Robert Maturin (1780–1824), an Irish novelist and dramatist, wrote half a dozen Gothic romances during the Napoleonic wars and after, as well as several tragedies. O'Brian's Maturin was a medical man, and O'Brian certainly had models from whom to work. His father for one, but also his uncle, Dr. Sidney Russ, who had conducted radiobiological studies of tumors and was so preeminent in his field that the King Edward's Hospital Fund, which held the main supply of radium for London's hospitals between the wars, was placed under his care.

O'Brian would explore the most complex moral themes—love and fidelity, the nature and boundaries of loyalty, the importance of being discreet, drug dependence—primarily through Maturin, who by all accounts closely resembled the author in many ways. But it was Aubrey's naval career—albeit as the series progressed more and more shaped by Maturin's secret political missions and influence at the Admiralty—that would drive the novels.

O'Brian combed logbooks, official letters, memoirs, and period published accounts for details. In addition to Cochrane's memoirs, he studied Admiral Sir James Saumarez's dispatches and reports of Saumarez's famous naval battles at Algeciras and in the Strait of Gibraltar—actions the fictional Aubrey observes, but unhappily cannot take part in, late in the novel. Meticulous by nature, O'Brian consulted with officials at the Public Record Office in London and at the National Maritime Museum in Greenwich and even with the current commanding officer of Nelson's ship HMS *Victory*. He also traveled to Port Mahon, Minorca, a Royal Navy base for the Mediterranean Fleet at the time of his novel, to see for himself that strategic, long, narrow harbor and the island's Spanish fortifications.

The result was *Master and Commander*, the novel that led off O'Brian's magnum opus, a twenty-novel series that would become one of the longest and perhaps best-loved romans-fleuves of the twentieth century. O'Brian's epic of two heroic yet believably realistic men would in some ways define a generation—but not for two more decades.

O'Brian set *Master and Commander* in the western Mediterranean, where Cochrane's famous cruise on board the tiny sloop *Speedy* took place. While visiting Port Mahon, where Cochrane was based, O'Brian conceived what became one of the series' most famous scenes: Aubrey and Maturin, both down on their luck, meet for the first time at the Governor's House during a concert of Locatelli's C major quartet, Lieutenant Aubrey, passionately beating time with his fist, irritates Maturin, a small, unfriendly-looking man in a grizzled wig, and the two exchange harsh words. It appears they are headed for a duel the following day, but before that can happen, Aubrey is promoted to the rank of master and commander and given command of the brig *Sophie*. In his joy, instead of fighting Maturin, Aubrey apologizes to him, and Maturin invites him for a pot of chocolate. Aubrey soon asks the penniless Maturin to be the

Sophie's surgeon and then sets about attacking Spanish merchant vessels, which makes him rich in prize money but also induces the Spanish merchants to hire a powerful xebec frigate, the *Cacafuego*, to hunt down and destroy the *Sophie*.

While Cochrane's exploits served as a framework for the novel and provided the obvious plot, O'Brian constructed a subplot around the divided loyalties that resulted from the failed Irish Uprising of 1798. Aubrey's first lieutenant, James Dillon, a wealthy Irish aristocrat, played a part in that armed rebellion against Britain, as did Maturin, both having belonged to the United Irishmen. Although their exact roles in the event remain obscure, both must hide elements of their past lives and certain of their deeply held beliefs while they serve in the Royal Navy.

In addition to Aubrey and Maturin and the saturnine Dillon, a man bent on self-destruction, O'Brian introduced some intriguing shipmates, who would live on in the series. Among them were the master's mates Thomas Pullings, an elder midshipman who has passed his lieutenant's examination but has yet to be promoted, and the cheerful, versifying James Mowett. Barrett Bonden, coxswain and captain of the maintop, is a powerful seaman with long pigtails and gold earrings. The young midshipman William Babbington, who is described to Aubrey as a blockhead but not a blackguard, becomes a protégé of the captain. And the grumbling, back-talking steward Preserved Killick, hilarious in his peculiar form of solicitousness, also proves to be a loyal follower of Aubrey, and equally devoted to Maturin, who brings the ship honor in his surgical skills if not in his frequently slovenly appearance and ineptness at sea and in naval customs.

The writing, less angst-ridden than that of his previous non-naval novels but still intended for adults, came fast. For O'Brian, the heat of writing was like taking a hedge on a horse. You don't fret or ponder, he would explain. You simply take the fence, or not. For him, the creative process was largely an inexplicable one, some magical combination of conscious and subconscious, of instinct and intellect, all clicking at once. Fiction writing involved a welling up of one's life experience into a separate entity, a child of sorts. The act of creating that child was exhilarating. But there was a personal transformation too. "The man at his desk is another being," he would later tell a reporter.*

*The *Sunday Telegraph*, "A Man from a Better Age," December 15, 1996.

The drawback of choosing Cochrane's cruise on the *Speedy* would not become apparent until O'Brian decided to carry on with his characters in subsequent books. Cochrane's improbable defeat of the *El Gamo* had occurred in May 1801, near the end of the War of the French Revolution, making it impossible to use earlier events of this war and still remain chronologically correct. So O'Brian was limited to setting future tales in the Napoleonic War, which lasted from 1803 to 1815, and the War of 1812, until finally, with his twentieth novel, he superseded these wars.

Although to begin with he had no idea how much pleasure he would take in writing about Aubrey and Maturin and did not foresee the lengthy series to come, O'Brian purposely left the book open-ended. He thrived while writing it, and he felt that he had engaged in the work as in nothing else since *Testimonies*. In fact, he had connected the two, perhaps subconsciously: the surnames Aubrey and Maturin both appear in *Testimonies*.

O'Brian delivered the typescript to his agent, Richard Simon, who sent it to the two publishers. But before it even got to Lippincott, Simon had to report bad news to O'Brian. Robert Hill, the editor who had commissioned *Master and Commander*, had left the company, which meant the book would have a tougher time finding acceptance there. It was the literary equivalent of an orphan looking for a foster parent to shepherd it through the various editorial, production, promotion, and marketing processes necessary to turn a typescript into a viable book—after ensuring that it did not disappear altogether, a victim of the contentious interoffice politics so common in publishing houses after a new editor in chief has assumed the helm.

The typescript of *Master and Commander* landed on the desk of Lippincott newcomer Wolcott Gibbs, Jr., the son of the witty and urbane *New Yorker* drama critic, and a former publicist at Doubleday. Tony Gibbs, as he was known, was a Princeton graduate and a passionate sailor who had read and reread Forester's novels, not just the Hornblower books but also *The Gun* and *Rifleman Dodd*. He much admired those books and was skeptical of Hornblower imitators. However, nobody at Lippincott would force him to accept an unwanted book, commissioned by a past regime, so he read *Master and Commander* with an open mind, knowing his word would probably either scuttle or float the project.

Gibbs was bowled over by the quality and perceptiveness of O'Brian's writing. He was behind the book. The only question at Lippincott—raised by O'Brian himself—was whether there was too much explanation of square-rigger terminology too early in the book. Gibbs, however, defended O'Brian's novel as it was. He thought that the information had to be given and that it might as well be dealt with early on. He also felt that O'Brian had accomplished the difficult task quite gracefully.

In England, Macmillan did not reach the same conclusion. Richard Garnett, a former Hart-Davis editor and the grandson of Edward Garnett, who had helped discover John Galsworthy, D. H. Lawrence, and Joseph Conrad, found *Master and Commander* too loaded with nautical jargon. Garnett admired O'Brian's *The Golden Ocean* and could still quote the closing line of *The Unknown Shore*, when Tobias, the returning sailor, says to Georgiana, the girl for whom he has been pining, "Come and sit by me, and let us talk of bats." But Garnett was disappointed by *Master and Commander*. He became bored while reading it, and a colleague concurred. Macmillan rejected the book.

Richard Simon had to find another British publisher, but he already had an idea. The forte of William Collins, where he had worked for six years as a publicity manager, was popular, not literary, books, but one editor there might take a special interest in O'Brian's novel. Richard Ollard was a World War II Royal Navy veteran who had taught at the Royal Naval College in Greenwich for a decade before joining Collins in 1960. If anyone could appreciate *Master and Commander*, he was the one.

Before the typescript reached him, Ollard knew little of Patrick O'Brian other than that he had published a children's book with Hart-Davis and a novel with someone else, both well received. Philip Ziegler, another Collins editor, spoke enthusiastically of O'Brian's recent Simone de Beauvoir translation. Ollard respected Simon's opinion, and on his recommendation, he was willing to take a look at the 110,000-word novel. To his great surprise and joy, he quickly grasped that he was reading a challenging work by an exceptionally talented author. *Master and Commander* possessed both the action of Forester's Hornblower books and the literary legs of a Mary Renault novel. He could not put it down.

As at most serious publishing houses, it was customary for editors at Collins to circulate among their colleagues reports of books they wanted to acquire. The report generally contained a brief synopsis of the book, the pros and cons of acquiring it, special information about marketing the title, and the suggested print run.

Although he had a pleasantly retiring manner, Ollard, an Oxford graduate with expressive hands and intellectual authority, was a convincing man. In his March 13, 1969, editorial report addressed to the chairman of the company, William Collins, known as Billy, Ollard wrote: "It is a novel of the C. S. Forester/Dudley Pope type, done with originality, gusto, and a really astonishing knowledge of the sources. . . . What he *has* got is first-class narrative power. . . . This is a book of high literary quality and I think we could sell it well. It is more of the Mary Renault . . . type of historical novel than the Graham Shelby, which is quintessentially popular."

Ollard's only caveats were that "very occasionally the author's expertise in the technicalities of sailing ships or his fondness for parodying 18th century turns of phrase leads him into faint tiresomeness, but these are the most minor blemishes, easily removed." Ollard added that O'Brian's female characters "do not seem to me up to much." But, he noted, women had only a small role to play in a book about Nelson's navy.

Ollard pointed out, in the book's favor, that O'Brian was willing to write more of this kind "if sufficiently encouraged." Ollard further enticed his publisher with the news that Aubrey was to be made the commander of a third-rate in the next novel. He speculated that Captain Aubrey might even be present at Trafalgar, a topic with considerable appeal to book buyers in Britain. This only proved that Ollard, like everyone else, had much to learn about this surprising "new" author, who possessed an inveterate tendency to deviate from the obvious path.

Ollard concluded his report with calculations relevant to the print run and the author's royalty advance: "If we were to offer royalties of 12 ½ to 5 [thousand copies], 15 percent thereafter, an advance of £750 would be earned on a Home sale of 4,000 which seems to me a conservative target." Ollard knew Simon wanted £1,000 for the book. The editor wanted to try to get it for £750, but he suggested that Collins pay the asking price if necessary. In either case, in hindsight, O'Brian's book was one of the great publishing bargains of our time.

Stamped at the top of the first page of Ollard's report was his overall opinion on whether the house should publish *Master and Commander*: "Emphatically yes," he wrote. Collins okayed the purchase. Ollard telephoned Simon and bought the rights to publish the book in the United Kingdom. Ironically, a year after the launch of the Tet Offensive in the Vietnam War—to the West the epitome of demoralizing modern warfare—

O'Brian's novel about sailing ships and the formal, comparatively civilized combat of the Napoleonic wars was put into production at Collins.

In a stroke of deft marketing, Ollard sent a set of *Master and Commander* page proofs to Mary Renault, whose novel *The King Must Die* (1958) recounted the story of the Greek hero Theseus and had been dubbed the best historical novel of modern times. Although Ollard did not know her personally, he had reviewed her work anonymously in the *Times Literary Supplement*. He thought her an extraordinarily talented writer, and in his experience, good writers were usually generous in their praise of other good writers.

The proofs reached Renault in South Africa. She loathed writing such appraisals, which inevitably tended to be glib and self-serving. Nonetheless, she looked at the proofs. Soon she was hooked, and, like Ollard, she was floored by what she read. She knew immediately that O'Brian had jumped directly to the front of the pack of historical fiction writers.

Renault's passion for reading good literature overcame her concern for privacy. Not only did she fire off an enthusiastic line for the book jacket, but she also wrote O'Brian a letter acknowledging her admiration for the novel. The two began a regular correspondence. No doubt Renault's support helped sustain O'Brian when the ill-informed and condescending reviews that followed rankled. For her part, Renault, who had studied under and much admired J. R. R. Tolkien at Oxford, now found great literary inspiration in O'Brian. On her deathbed in 1983, she was anxiously awaiting the arrival of his next novel.

Ollard set about promoting the book among the ranks of his knowledgeable friends as well, including Sir Francis Chichester, the famous sailor and author who lived near Collins's offices in St. James's Place. Chichester, who had recently published a book about his remarkable 226-day circumnavigation of the world on a fifty-three-foot yacht, provided a clean assessment of the book: it was the best sea story he had ever read. The naval historian Tom Pocock, whom Ollard had met at Haslar military hospital during the war, also received a copy. "The book is frightfully good," Ollard told Pocock. "I urge you to read it."

In the United States, *Master and Commander* was critically well received, though not unequivocally. Gibbs had drawn up a clever press release based on a poster recruiting hands for the warship HMS *Sutherland* at the beginning of the Hornblower novel *Ship of the Line* and garnered some attention for the book. The October 1, 1969, *Kirkus Reviews* advised, "lively and very much i' the eighteenth century vein. A welcome treat for sea hounds who care more for belaying pins than ravaged bodices below decks." And the *Chattanooga Times* wrote that the book "will enthrall the aficionado from first to last page, and leave him waiting expectantly for the next adventure of Captain Jack." The December 14 *New York Times Book Review*, by Martin Levin, called it a "sophisticated sea story [that] belongs to the blue-ribbon category." But the December 15 issue of *Library Journal* found that "despite O'Brian's gift for dialogue and his inclusion of many excellent details taken from carefully researched sources, his book suffers in comparison [to C. S. Forester's work]."

On the strength of these mostly favorable reviews, *Master and Commander* sold well enough to effect a second hardcover printing and to interest Lippincott in a sequel. In England, the book—with Renault's heartfelt jacket quote: "A spirited sea-tale with cracking pace and a brilliant sense of period. In a highly competitive field it goes straight to the top. A real first rater."—fared well too, and Ollard's assessment was affirmed. The first printing in January 1970 was quickly followed by another in February. Also in February, Lippincott rewarded O'Brian with a contract to write another Aubrey-Maturin novel on the same terms.

For O'Brian, the 1960s, a decade of the inglorious and underpaid labor of translating and of sliding into middle age—he had turned fifty-six—ended on an encouraging note. But the future could have looked even brighter had he not relinquished his paternal role. Though he probably did not know it, toward the end of the decade Patrick had become a grandfather twice over. Richard and Mimi Russ had given birth to a daughter, Victoria, in June 1967, and another daughter, Joanna, in March 1969.

15

An Epic Is Launched

1970–1973

Great books should tell of good, noble characters and show
them in the real trials and sorrows of life, for God knows
there are enough in every life, and every one of us wants help
to face them.

—Joyce Cary, *Herself Surprised,* 1941

Nervous irritation is the secret desolator of human life; and for
this there is probably no adequate controlling power but that
of opium, taken daily, under steady regulation.

—Thomas De Quincey, *Confessions of an English Opium-Eater,* 1822

A s the reviews of *Master and Commander* came out in British publications in January 1970, O'Brian tackled an extraordinary literary
project of a different sort, one that far outshined his own, at least
for the moment. In fact, O'Brian later called it "a phenomenon almost
unparalleled in the annals of publishing."*

He had been hired by Rupert Hart-Davis to translate *Papillon,* the
memoir of Henri Charrière, a Frenchman who in 1931 was sentenced to a
life of hard labor in a penal colony in French Guiana for the murder of a
pimp he claimed he did not commit. Tough and cunning, "Papillon"—
Charrière was so nicknamed for his tattoo of a butterfly (*papillon,* in
French)—told a mesmerizing story of life in inhuman prisons and of his
almost unbelievable escapes. Though he appears shady to start with, his
courageous tale reveals a moral and likable, even admirable, man.

In his "Translator's Introduction," O'Brian wrote that the book was

*In the "Translator's Introduction" of *Banco: The Further Adventures of Papillon,* p. 9.

one of the most difficult to translate that he had ever worked on.* Stylistically, Charrière "could not get into his stride" (p. 12), O'Brian wrote, and his vivid underworld slang and prison argot defied simple translation, so O'Brian sometimes drew on American slang. He also had to mitigate the use of obscenities, which would be more jarring in English than in French. "I have tried to steer between unnecessary grossness and inaccurate insipidity" (p. 13), he explained.

Charrière had survived fourteen years of hellish prisons and hopeless escapes. Six weeks after arriving in Guiana, he and two companions floated down the Maroni River and sailed across the sea to Trinidad. Captured and imprisoned in Colombia, Charrière escaped again and lived with pearl-diving Indians before setting out once more. He was recaptured by the Colombians, who imprisoned him in an underground cage that flooded with the tides, bringing in sludge, centipedes, and rats. The Colombians eventually handed him back to the French, who imprisoned him on Devil's Island. Charrière made his final break by fleeing on two sacks of coconuts through shark-ridden waters.

In 1970, the *phénomène Papillon*, as O'Brian termed it, was in full swing. Readers bought 850,000 copies of the book in the first several months. O'Brian's version appeared in England in 1970. What really fascinated him was not just the sheer volume of readers, but that they came from all levels of the literary world. *Papillon* was an action story that broke through genre barriers to be considered a serious work of literature even by the Académie Française. The *Times Literary Supplement* called O'Brian's translation "a scrupulous version, more accurate than the American translation."

Best of all, the publisher had agreed to pay O'Brian a royalty for his work on *Papillon*, rather than a flat fee. On this he made a tidy sum, which pushed the wolf farther from the door, as he liked to say, freeing him to pursue his fiction writing.

While *Papillon* scorched perceived publishing barriers (even before the hit film, starring Steve McQueen and Dustin Hoffman, came out in 1973),

---

*In an interview in the *Independent* (March 15, 1992), O'Brian said, "You could type [it] in English as fast as you could read it in French." But in his "Translator's Introduction" to the book, he called it "one of the hardest I have undertaken" (*Papillon*, p. 12) and convincingly described why.

Master and Commander did not. The book did find a sustaining audience in Britain and the United States, but O'Brian learned a hard lesson. The "historical novel," a term that to him had little validity, was an acceptable platform for young adults but not in favor among the literati for serious work. What's more, with the Woodstock generation producing the likes of Tom Wolfe, who published *The Electric Kool-Aid Acid Test* (1968) and *Radical Chic and Mau-Mauing the Flak Catchers* (1970) on either side of *Master and Commander*, and Colombian Gabriel García Márquez captivating readers with his brand of magical realism in *One Hundred Years of Solitude* (1967, English translation 1970), O'Brian's novel—published in the United States several months after the horrifying Manson murders—seemed, in comparison, quaint, even antediluvian. The result was that, despite its popularity, *Master and Commander* went virtually unnoticed by serious critics and scholars.

Those who did read and review the novel were mostly hung up on Forester. In a begrudging recommendation, *Library Journal*'s critic advised that "mourning Hornblower fans may prefer to read a good if disappointing new book rather than to reread one of the master's epics." "Probably the best of many good novels about Nelson's navy since the loss of C. S. Forester," sniffed the *Observer*. O'Brian's supposed roots held no sway with the *Irish Press*, whose reviewer judged the book "not, I think, memorable, at least in the Hornblower way."

In defense of the Hornblower diehards, C. S. Forester's hero held—and still holds—a unique spot in England's literary firmament. Appealing to young and old across social and educational spectra, Hornblower had entered Britain's psyche on a broad brush, a mythic hero. Winston Churchill was an admirer. The navy historian and business scholar C. Northcote Parkinson even wrote a tongue-in-cheek biography of Hornblower (which one poor American admiral reviewed thinking that Hornblower was a real person). Most readers drawn to *Master and Commander* had probably been reared on, or at least had read, the tales of the swashbuckling Hornblower. Having laid claim to many of the basic plotlines of Nelson's Royal Navy, Forester's books would not easily be dislodged as the genre's heavyweight champion.

A reviewer in the *Sunday Mirror* at least recognized that *Master and Commander* was "not secondhand Forester, but a really fine piece of writing." O'Brian knew he had written a sound book—he had satisfied history and avoided the pitfalls of sentimentality and enthusiasm—and *Master and Commander* generated enough sales to justify another volume along the same lines. That in itself was encouraging.

Most important, in Gibbs, Ollard, and Renault, he had found true believers, whose opinions he respected. Removed as he was from the literary world, O'Brian found that Renault provided a useful reality check and a welcome encouraging voice. Gibbs was a supporter in the United States, while Ollard would become a friend and O'Brian's most trusted reader other than Mary. Ollard, who would himself become a noted naval biographer and an officer of the Navy Records Society, could comment with authority on both literary and historical points. He would nurture O'Brian's career for more than a decade, promote him socially, and become a friend. Prior to *Blue at the Mizzen*, Gibbs, Ollard, Renault, and O'Brian's agents, Richard Simon and Vivien Green, were the only people, other than Mary, to whom O'Brian would dedicate an Aubrey-Maturin novel.

O'Brian plunged into the sequel to *Master and Commander*. He found himself highly content working on his new opus. In subject matter he had discovered a deep well of material that was quite removed from the personal turmoil that had fueled his earlier novels and short stories. He was happy in this place, with two characters in whose lives he could infuse his personal interests and beliefs, as well as his joys and sense of humor. He had, at last, found the vernacular for his life's work, and in this new book he decided to give Jack Aubrey and Stephen Maturin a fuller world.

Outside the window of Patrick's writing room, golden orioles and nightingales frolicked in the O'Brians' Mediterranean garden, as, inside, he transferred the southern England of his imagination to paper. His pen sped over the pages, forming his compact, orderly script in black ink. Not far into the manuscript, his personal shorthand quickened the pace: "with" became "w"; "said," "sd"; "Mrs Williams," "Mrs W". When details escaped him, he left spaces to be filled in later. The pages piled up. Notes were added in the margin and, eventually, edits in red ink.

In O'Brian's first draft, *Post Captain* began: "~~Portencarry~~\Polcarry Down . . ." and presented a detailed microcosm of southern England. But he thought better of opening the book there and later inserted a clever eight-page scene on board the homeward bound HMS *Charwell*, on which Aubrey and Maturin are passengers. The year is 1802. All eyes are on Captain Griffiths as a superior enemy ship of the line bears down on the *Char-*

well. Griffiths must issue the order either to fight or to flee. Before he gives the command, however, a barrage of signal guns blasts from the pursuer. Suddenly, the threat of a furious battle evaporates with the shocking news of peace.

O'Brian then foreshadowed events on land. Given a copy of the *Sussex Courier* on board the *Charwell*, Aubrey and Maturin read a classified ad for a gentleman's house for rent and also a notice for an upcoming fox hunt at Champflower Cross, to be held on November 6. Both figure in their immediate future.

This self-contained opener gave those who had not read *Master and Commander* a taste of the sea. But they had to wait to return there while O'Brian constructed his turn-of-the-century southern England, setting up the dynamics of more complex personal lives for Aubrey and Maturin. O'Brian then carried the duo through the French port of Toulon, during the peace, and overland to Maturin's ancestral home in Catalonia. No sea battle occurs in the first hundred pages.

In O'Brian's Sussex, Aubrey and Maturin set up at Melbury Lodge, the house that they saw advertised in the *Sussex Courier*. There they meet their neighbors living at Mapes Court, the Williams family, who are destined to play an important part in their lives. A small-minded and formidable widow of "unprincipled rectitude," O'Brian's Mrs. Williams could have stepped straight out of a Jane Austen novel. Like Austen's Mrs. Bennet from *Pride and Prejudice*, Mrs. Williams is "a woman of mean understanding, little information, and uncertain temper" and the business of her life, like that of Mrs. Bennet, is "to get her daughters married; its solace . . . visiting and news."*

Tenacious, manipulative, and greedy, Mrs. Williams scrutinizes all bachelors and targets the ones who pass muster for her spinster daughters: Sophie, a reserved beauty of twenty-seven; Cecilia, several years younger and a frivolous goose; and Frances, long-legged and tomboyish. Mrs. Williams's lowest priority is for her resident niece, Diana Villiers, an orphan of about Sophie's age who she is most concerned should not become a rival to her daughters.

Initially, O'Brian described Mrs. Williams in detail: She came from a "banking, brewing, army-contracting family" that had earned its riches in the City in Dutch William's day (William III, who reigned from 1688 to

---

***Pride and Prejudice,* p. 5, The Oxford Illustrated Jane Austen.

1702). The family had lived in the south for three or four generations, "doing nothing heinously wrong & taking great care of their capital." Mrs. Williams had married a cousin, George, combining the Champflower and Midden properties. In the final version, O'Brian trimmed and sharpened the description, ultimately calling her "a vulgar woman . . . although her family, which was of some importance in the neighborhood, had been settled there since Dutch William's time" (p. 19).

At first, Diana Villiers was the daughter of Mrs. Williams's brother or half brother; in the end, O'Brian decided she was the daughter of Mrs. Williams's sister. Because she was born in India, Diana was known in the talkative parish as the "Blackamoor," which became the "Black Lady" in the first typed draft, replaced in red ink with "the Ranee" (a Hindu queen or a raja's wife), obviously in this case a facetious title.

For all his speed in writing, the drafts reveal a meticulous and exacting reviser. O'Brian honed, refined, and authenticated. On page 27 of the manuscript, he changed the make of the piano from "Spohr" to "Clementi." On page 28, he penned in "Hummel" as the composer of the sonata in D major. In the typed version of page 33, in red ink in the left margin by the word "extrapolate," he wrote a note to check the *Oxford English Dictionary* to make sure that that word existed in 1800; later, in green ink, "extrapolate," which according to the *OED* was first used in the mid–nineteenth century, was stricken and "go too far" replaced it. He also fine-tuned the language for meaning. For example, on manuscript page 1 of chapter 6, he replaced the word "tension" with "nervous excitement."

O'Brian's novel was largely written in the first draft. Still, as he carefully refined the prose—a process in which his natural sense of reserve served him well—he elevated his storytelling. For example, on page 36 of the typed version, he toned down an amorous scene involving Maturin and Villiers. Maturin's diary entry for February 15 originally stated: "Then when she suddenly kissed me, with her virtually naked body pressed against mine, the strength left my legs, my knees, and I could scarcely follow her into the ball-room with any sort of countenance." In red ink "virtually naked" was stricken. In the published book, "with her body pressed against mine" was also deleted, and following "my knees," he added the phrase "quite ludicrously" (p. 56).

O'Brian revised the book to rid it of physical description unsuitable to the tenor of the period. He might also have sensed that following the sexual revolution of the 1960s, his original language seemed melodramatic. Even more important, he made Maturin harder to fathom and more intriguing. In many instances, he shrouded actions and relationships in a veil of obliqueness, leaving the reader's imagination room to play. O'Brian later explained why: "Outside the exact sciences," he wrote, "scarcely anything worth saying can be said except by indirection" (*Picasso,* p. 327).

These drafts and adjustments were all made with astonishing speed. A little more than a year after the publication of *Master and Commander,* Mary typed up the final draft of *Post Captain,* Patrick's longest work yet and one that eventually came to be considered the single most important volume of the Aubrey-Maturin series. The new novel brought the duo's adventures to more than 750 book pages. With the introduction of the Williams family, *Post Captain* painted a much broader social picture, with a Jane Austen–like attention to the manners of early-nineteenth-century England.

O'Brian had also opened a door to the Admiralty and the inner workings of the Royal Navy, allowing for a more complex plot. Sir Joseph Blaine, the fictional chief of naval intelligence, an intellectual and a natural philosopher, becomes devoted to Maturin, just as Maturin becomes a trusted and, importantly, unpaid intelligence agent and adviser on Catalan and Spanish affairs. O'Brian later told one journalist off the record that Blaine was based in part on his unit director at the Political Intelligence Department during the war. Leslie Beck was a worthy model. With his Jesuit religious training, Beck had brought to his job a combination of theological scrupulousness and a practical ruthlessness for motivating his people to perform strenuous feats in the office and dangerous tasks in the field.

Just as O'Brian raised Maturin's presence and his stature in this manner in *Post Captain,* he also created an Achilles' heel for the doctor. Maturin becomes and remains through much of the series a heavy user of opium, in the quicker-working liquid form, tincture of laudanum, one of the few effective medicines he has on board ship. He struggles with but defends this habit, much as Thomas De Quincey did in his famous *Confessions of an English Opium-Eater,* serialized in the *London Magazine* in 1821. While the 1960s hippie culture had made the subject of drug use timely, O'Brian's fascination with Maturin's use of opium and later of coca ran deep and would endure for many decades.

As he would throughout the series, O'Brian again used historical events as a framework in *Post Captain*. However, he left the charted path more often in this book than in the first. In an amusing and somewhat magical episode, he even had Aubrey trek from Toulon to Maturin's ancestral home near Barcelona while disguised as a bear. Subsequent books would occasionally enter this realm of quasi-believability as well.

O'Brian introduced another significant humorous moment, one that became a running joke in the series. He surely found Maturin's famous dog-watch pun in Admiral William Henry Smyth's *Sailor's Word-Book* (1867). Smyth's definition of "dog-watch," which is one of the two evening half-watches of two hours (a normal watch lasted four hours), informed readers that "Theodore Hook explains this as cur-tailed." Brilliantly, O'Brian seized upon Aubrey's delayed but uproarious response to the pun to create one of his character's defining moments. Later, Aubrey's side-splitting guffaws upon retelling the pun—his face turns pinched and crimson—give the joke many hilarious lives that dwarf the original humor. One can easily imagine O'Brian sitting in his writing studio chortling to himself each time he resurrected this witticism over the next three decades.

In addition to his fiction writing, O'Brian continued to translate, though not at the pace he had maintained in the previous decade. Among the books he worked on during this period were Simone de Beauvoir's *La Vieillesse* (1970), which appeared in 1972 as *Old Age* in Great Britain and *The Coming of Age* in the United States. Although he enjoyed most of her work, he found this book, about growing old, a bit on the depressing side.

He also translated Henri Charrière's *Banco: The Further Adventures of Papillon*, the sequel to Charrière's international blockbuster. With a degree of vicarious pleasure, O'Brian had watched Charrière bask in *Papillon*'s success—sleighing with Brigitte Bardot, wielding an enormous cigar in his diamond-studded fingers, donning a dinner jacket to party in Paris. But to O'Brian's relief, Charrière's rawness and simplicity, among his chief assets as a writer, had not been spoiled.

In the new book, O'Brian must have taken a particular interest in Charrière's remembrance of his childhood. During World War I, he and his mother used to visit a hospital together to look after patients. She caught a contagious disease and died. In his deep sadness and anger, Charrière grew violent. He frequently picked fights, always with bigger and stronger boys, and he fought recklessly, until finally, at the age of seventeen, he stabbed one boy with a protractor just below the heart and had to join the navy to avoid prosecution. Charrière explained his rage:

> I really could not control it; ever since my mother's death, when I was nearly eleven, I'd had this red-hot iron inside me. You can't understand death when you are eleven: you can't accept it. The very old might die, maybe. But your mother, an angel full of youth and beauty and health, how can she conceivably die? (P. 223)

O'Brian's own sadness had played out differently; still, he could empathize with Charrière's fury.

Although thoroughly at home in France now, the O'Brians would always need periodic doses of England, to see Mary's family, to maintain ties with friends and colleagues, and for Patrick, at least, to fill up on fish and chips and suet pudding. In October 1971, Patrick and Mary traveled to Radlett, a village northwest of London, to attend Nikolai's Protestant wedding. His fiancée, Georgina Brown, was a member of the Church of England, so they were having two ceremonies. This was fortunate for all involved because Dimitry, who refused to be in Mary's presence, attended the Russian Orthodox ceremony, and the O'Brians attended this one.

Patrick had delivered the manuscript of *Post Captain* to Richard Simon in August, and he certainly used this time in England to meet with both Simon and Richard Ollard. Things were afoot with Simon, who would soon leave Curtis Brown, which had been bought by a City banking firm. Although he was being groomed for the managing director position, Simon had decided against a life of personnel and finance meetings. Before the end of the year, he would set up his own agency in Covent Garden, and O'Brian would go with him.

Ollard was thoroughly pleased with *Post Captain* and even more impressed than before by O'Brian's writing. This was essential for their budding relationship, for O'Brian, the man, could not be separated from O'Brian, the fiction writer. In his September editorial report, Ollard informed his colleagues that the new 135,000-word manuscript was "an even better book than the author's brilliantly successful debut."

"The author's understanding of the Napoleonic navy, its ethos as well as its ships and guns," Ollard wrote, "is effortless and profound. Altogether this is a very remarkable historical novel and I have no more than a few minor alterations to propose." He suggested a first printing of between ten thousand and twelve thousand books, a healthy increase over the print run for the first title. The price would rise as well, to £1.80.

When it appeared in 1972, however, *Post Captain,* like its predecessor, could not escape the skepticism of condescending reviewers. "Maturin is a charmer and Aubrey an amiable bear of little brain—good company on a pleasant voyage for addicts of this genre," *Kirkus Reviews* reported in the United States. "The author obviously knows the details of life in the British Navy in the early 19th century, but that's the best that can be said for this novel, overwritten for so little plot, which consists mainly of adventures at sea and the friends' feuding over their rather tedious women," sniped the July 17 *Publishers Weekly*.

In England, the *Observer* assessed the book more positively: "The hero of *Post Captain* . . . is vigorous flesh and blood, one of Nelson's ardent disciples who needs the firm hand of his sage and saturnine Irish surgeon. . . . There is substantial character drawing as well as liveliness and expertise." In distant New Zealand, one clear-eyed reviewer, writing in the *Taranaki Herald,* actually saw *Post Captain* as Ollard did: "one of the finest seafaring novels of the Napoleonic wars."

While Hornblower still tended to cloud reviewers' judgments, O'Brian operated under another disadvantage: bad timing. Forester's novels came out before and after World War II, with nationalism and support for the military at a peak, whereas O'Brian's series was launched during the Vietnam War, with the West angrily divided over its role in world politics and the military scorned by a large segment of the population. Among the intelligentsia, as Kevin Myers of the *Irish Times* later explained, "The radical chic opinions of the late 1960s were inclined to view the revolutionary tyrants of the world—Napoleon, Lenin, Trotsky, Stalin, Mao Tse-tung, Ho Chi Minh—as essentially forces for good who had gone off the rails a little. . . . The founding father of the technique of the totalitarian state was Bonaparte; yet the chic historical perspective of the bien pensant viewed him and the abominable events which produced him, namely the French Revolution, as being essentially good things." As O'Brian's two main characters were thorough enemies of Napoleon, they were "desperately unfashionable at the time they made their appearance."

Sales in the United States were as lukewarm as most reviews. Lippincott was having a hard time marketing the books, as evidenced by the jacket illustration for *Post Captain*. In the scene, a short-haired, white-toothed Aubrey, sword in hand, crouches for action while a brown-haired beauty gripping a shawl to her breast gazes dreamily at him. The pair resemble Robert Redford and Jane Fonda. Meanwhile, an enemy ship fires a broadside at them from an impossible angle. The back cover features a somewhat less-than-stirring description of *Master and Commander* from the *New York Times Book Review*: "It re-creates with delightful subtlety, the flavor of life aboard a midget British man-of-war plying the western Mediterranean in the year 1800, a year of indecisive naval skirmishes." This created a confusing package. The swaggering art belied the rich, often subtle content of the book, while the jacket copy excited adventure-novel addicts about as much as the writing on the back of a cereal box.

O'Brian wasted little energy fretting about reviews or American sales, however. He was in deep harmony with his own imagination and too driven to let the critical opinions of upstart colonials and Forester diehards bog him down. He set to work immediately on the series' third book, *H.M.S. Surprise*. When engrossed in a novel, he was rarely seen around Collioure and remained aloof, so much so that on the street or at the post office, he would walk right past friends without uttering a word. Some of the local peasant women were sure that the "Anglais" did not speak French. But friends knew that he was only absorbed in his work. At home, he narrowed his focus, ceasing to read new books, instead perusing the newspaper for diversion and rereading favorites from his youth, which informed his own writing.

Mary, meanwhile, ran the household, put the meals on the table, and maintained the normal social connections. She and Odette chatted on the telephone daily at three in the afternoon, by which means Mary satisfied her need for a sympathetic ear and kept up on the local gossip.

O'Brian now sent Aubrey and Maturin to the East Indies on board HMS *Surprise*, a historical French-built frigate, formerly known as *Unité* and captured by the British in 1796. It was the beginning of a long love affair between ship and captain. More so than any place on land, the twenty-eight-gun *Surprise* became Aubrey and Maturin's home. Though old and small for a frigate, she was both a sweet sailor and exalted in battle. In 1799, under Captain Edward Hamilton, she had daringly entered a

Spanish port and recaptured the infamous thirty-two-gun frigate *Hermione*. (In 1797, the *Hermione* had been turned over to the Spanish after the bloodiest mutiny in Royal Navy history.) *The Surprise* had been sold out of the service in 1802, so O'Brian could appropriate her for his fiction without trampling upon history.

In her, Aubrey is to deliver Mr. Stanhope, the king's envoy, to Kampong for a diplomatic mission. While the *Surprise* is en route, O'Brian took the opportunity to debunk Samuel Taylor Coleridge's peculiar belief that killing an albatross was considered bad luck by seamen. Aubrey tells Maturin that "people have fished for albatrosses and mutton-birds ever since ships came into these seas" (p. 166). Former South Sea whalers among the crew fish for albatross with baited lines, and the large birds "come flapping in, to be converted into tobacco-pouches, pipe-stems, hot dinners, down comforters to be worn next the skin, and charms against drowning—no albatross ever drowned" (p. 165).

In Bombay, India, where the *Surprise* stops on her eastward voyage, O'Brian created a scene charged with tension, leading to violence. Living with a wealthy Jewish-British merchant named Richard Canning, Diana Villiers plays the femme fatale, thrusting an anguished, jealous Maturin onto center stage. Maturin deceives Aubrey, with much self-disdain, in order to prevent him from taking a renewed interest in Diana. Maturin also causes two deaths, one intentional—he shoots Canning in a duel—the other not. The latter unfolds in a heartbreaking chapter in which Maturin befriends a poor Indian girl named Dil, whose mother tries to sell her to him as a prostitute. Maturin comes to love Dil for her wise innocence and her solicitous concern for his health, but he also knows that she is fated to end up in a brothel. He ponders what he can do for her but tragically blunders by giving her valuable jewelry. On the street, thieves murder Dil while robbing her.

The proud, innocent Dil represents a variation on an Aubrey-Maturin series theme. She is by no means the only desperate child whom Maturin attempts to aid. Indeed, tenderness for children is one of Maturin's most endearing qualities. He later rescues orphaned native sisters from the smallpox-devastated Sweetings Island in the Pacific (in *The Nutmeg of Consolation*) and Mona and Kevin Fitzpatrick, Irish twins who have been captured and enslaved by Barbary pirates (in *The Hundred Days*). It is not a coincidence that Maturin, the character most based on O'Brian himself, somehow finds and helps these children. Both O'Brian and his wife, to various degrees, had suffered the loss of their children. What O'Brian failed, or was powerless, to do in his own life, he was able to do in his fiction.

O'Brian later explained Dil's fate as a repercussion of Maturin's betrayal of Aubrey, to whom Maturin offers advice concerning Sophie under the pretense of friendship but in reality to divert him from taking a renewed interest in Diana. "The point of the death of Dil is that [Maturin] had done a wholly dishonorable thing that has its image in the death of that child," O'Brian stated in an unpublished conversation with free-lance reporter Mark Horowitz. "You do something profoundly dishonorable and you've killed something, you've killed a part of your honor."

Another passage of the novel, as the writer and reviewer Francis Spufford later pointed out in the *Independent*, was most telling regarding O'Brian's focus throughout the series:

> Without turning his back on the horrors of the age, he insists that the good things were as real as the bad. There is no choice to be made between the amputees howling beneath Maturin's saw, and the splendid candour of the conversations in the wardroom; but he does choose to develop the latter, while the corpses heaved over the side after a battle soon drop away from the mood of the story too. A passage from early in the series is revealing. For although a novel containing a theory, Proust wrote, is like a hat with the price ticket still on, novelists are allowed a sly reflection or two on their own art, and in *HMS Surprise* O'Brian has Aubrey wondering how to describe a sea-battle to his fiancée. He has come to his letter-writing fresh from cutting French throats, and the memory "sickened him with his trade . . . all at once it occurred to him that of course he had not the slightest wish to convey it."

In other words, O'Brian had made an unfashionable decision to emphasize the positive aspects of life, one that often prevented his work from being considered "serious fiction," a criticism that he was long in overcoming. But this decision ultimately helped make his fiction eminently popular and influential far beyond the psychological scourges written by many "serious" modern novelists, including himself in earlier years.

With Mary's assistance in reading, making suggestions, and typing, O'Brian set a breathtaking pace for his new oeuvre. In September 1972, he landed in London with another fat typescript, some 110,000 words, to hand over to Ollard. Barely more than a year after his last editorial report to Billy Collins, Ollard wrote: "This novel . . . is well up to the standard of its predecessors . . . very good indeed. There is, in particular, a long account of a storm in the Roaring Forties which is the best account of a sailing ship in a storm that I have read since Conrad's *Nigger of the Narcissus*."

Over the next decade, O'Brian frequently delivered typescripts in person, as he did now. Ollard read them immediately, and while he did, O'Brian had time to research at various libraries and to stop in at some of his favorite shops for items not easily found in Collioure or Perpignan. He also made sure to visit his agent, Simon, who, following the gentrification of Covent Garden, had moved his offices to the more affordable neighborhood of Islington.

Ollard suggested to O'Brian some small cuts to tighten up certain passages of the third Aubrey-Maturin installment, but little else. The two also had the opportunity to discuss the cover design. O'Brian wanted the new cover to better capture the flavor of the period than had the previous two, with their 1960s-style illustrations. He suggested Nicholas Pocock's painting of the action between the thirty-six-gun HMS *Amethyst* and the forty-gun French frigate *Thetis*, one that he had used as an illustration in *Men-of-War*, a book he was writing for the children's department of Collins. Ollard agreed. O'Brian returned to France with the marked-up version of the typescript, which he was to revise and resubmit in six weeks.

In February 1973, Patrick and Mary traveled to England to be with Mary's father, who was dying. Whatever the family tension had been when her marriage to Tolstoy had collapsed and her union with O'Brian had begun, it was long since behind them. On February 19, Mary bravely held the hand of her eighty-three-year-old father as he died. Mary's mother would live to be ninety-nine, mentally sharp until the very end, and Mary continued to visit her each year.

In the United States, O'Brian's Aubrey-Maturin series was in danger. Lippincott's staff continued to turn over. Editor in chief George Stevens had left in 1970, and now Tony Gibbs, whom O'Brian had never met but much admired from their correspondence, left to pursue a magazine writing and editing career at *Motor Boating and Sailing*. The staff who had dreamed up the idea for the series and nurtured it through the first two books was gone, and, with weak sales, the publisher hesitated to bring out the third Aubrey-Maturin title. It finally opted to go ahead and publish the book but at a reduced advance. This proved to be Lippincott's last book in the series; the publisher with the foresight to encourage O'Brian to write *Master and Commander* would not benefit from the series' eventual success.

Two reviews of *H.M.S. Surprise*, one in the *Sunday Times* of London and the other in the *New York Times Book Review*, indicate the contrasting fortunes of O'Brian's "naval tales," as he liked to call them, on either side of the Atlantic. In the August 19, 1973, edition of the former, Julian Symons wrote: "The language is just right, with a full late eighteenth century weightiness that is still free from any trace of strain or affectation. . . . In their own field, that of the adventure story which remains faithful in its feeling for place and period, I don't see that one could wish for anything better than Mr. O'Brian's sea stories." Though qualified, the review amounted to high praise.

In the United States, on the other hand, *H.M.S. Surprise* took one in the hull—below the waterline, as it were. "Mr. O'Brian is constantly becalmed in his own diction, which can take a disturbingly giddy turn. Men-of-war with names like *Belle Poule* and *Caca Fuego* just don't inspire confidence," wrote a cranky and ill-informed reviewer in the December 9, 1973, *New York Times Book Review*.*

As O'Brian's fortunes sagged in the United States at the hands of such misinterpretation, his work was beginning to gain real credibility in Britain. At least the debate was on a higher plane. O'Brian was becoming the first serious challenger to Forester's predominance in the genre. In the *Spectator*, a crime-books reviewer, admitting that O'Brian's "virtues as a scholar and story-teller are displayed to considerable advantage" in *H.M.S. Surprise*, nonetheless took the Forester stand, writing:

> I cannot see the force of Mark Kahn's judgement (of an earlier book, *Post Captain*) that "This is not second hand Forester." The loneliness of the captain, the specific working out of problems of command, the deliberate distance the hero creates

---

*California rare-books dealer Stuart Bennett later pointed out in "Four Decades of Reviews" in the British Library's *Patrick O'Brian: Critical Appreciations and a Bibliography* that "O'Brian's research had been, as usual, meticulous: the French quite certainly possessed a ship called the *Belle Poule*— she was captured by HMS *Amazon* on 13th March 1806. Furthermore, the Spaniards often named their men-of-war *Cacafuego*: one formed part of the Invincible Armada"(p. 171).

between himself and others—all the psychological features of the Hornblower novels, which re-create in the reader's stomach the same knot as there is in that of the hero as ships sail to battle, are here at a lesser level of tension. When Aubrey tells his men they are not to try to rescue him from a land operation in Port Mahon his words . . . almost exactly recall Hornblower's instructions to Brown when he is preparing to land to face El Supremo in *The Happy Return*, and there are many such echos.

The unimpressed *Spectator* reviewer concluded that O'Brian "simply labours under the ineradicable handicap of dealing with exactly the same number of limited facts that Forester milked dry over his long career."

The battle lines were drawn. The contest would endure. But one thing was clear: C. S. Forester and Patrick O'Brian were the heavyweight writers of fiction inspired by Nelson's navy.

The next bout had to wait for more than three years, however. An extraordinary opportunity to pursue another subject fell now into O'Brian's lap. Bill Targ, a senior editor at Putnam who handled O'Brian's Beauvoir translations, telephoned Richard Simon from the United States to suggest a new book idea. Targ knew that O'Brian spoke French and Catalan, that he was interested in art, and that he was acquainted with the great painter Pablo Picasso. Targ wanted to know if O'Brian would be interested in writing a biography of the Spanish genius. What's more, he was offering something O'Brian had not seen before: a generous budget for the project.

16

Becoming Picasso

1973–1976

I am not concerned with making a case for or against Picasso;
my aim is to see him whole, as far as ever I can; and to do so
one must get the evidence as straight as possible.

—Patrick O'Brian, *Pablo Ruiz Picasso: A Biography,* 1976

O n April 8, 1973, not long after O'Brian had agreed to write a
biography of Pablo Picasso, whom he both respected as a man
and admired as an artist, the ninety-two-year-old painter died.
Europe mourned Picasso's death. The filmmaker Georges Clouzot,
director of *The Mystery of Picasso*, eulogized, "With Picasso goes the
greatest explorer of forms since the beginning of the Renaissance." Maurice
Druon, French minister of cultural affairs, reflected, "He filled his century
with his colors, his forms, his research, his audacity, and with his vivacious
personality."

During the next week, Picasso dominated French news with drama
that befit him. His family announced the donation of his art collection to
the Louvre. And his distraught twenty-three-year-old grandson, Pablito
Picasso, the son of Paulo, tried to commit suicide. "He felt abandoned,"
his mother, who had been divorced from Paulo since 1953, claimed. "He
didn't have either a father or a grandfather." As Spain and France absurdly
disputed their claims to Picasso, Céret, about twenty-five miles inland from
Collioure, announced that it would be the first village in France to make
Picasso an honorary citizen, to name a square after him, and to build a
monument in remembrance of the time he spent there.

The outpouring of affection for Picasso made clear just how big
O'Brian's biography could be. Richard Simon signed up Collins as the
book's British publisher, and all parties agreed that O'Brian should submit

the manuscript first to Ollard, his trusted editor. In London, Simon and O'Brian lunched with Bill Targ at the Connaught Hotel, where the editor stayed and entertained on his frequent visits to London. "You better choose the wine," the deferential American said to O'Brian, the wine-maker.

"We ought to have the family wine," O'Brian, in a festive mood, replied audaciously, making a play on his name and that of the oldest great château of Bordeaux, "Haut-Brion." Targ never blinked. They drank the expensive red wine, and the two hit it off. When the O'Brians landed in New York on their way to Philadelphia to study the Barnes Foundation's Picassos, Targ and his wife, Roslyn, took them to Coach House, an American-style steak house in the West Village, for another feast.

Before O'Brian launched into the life of Picasso, he put the finishing touches on a volume of seventeen short stories titled *The Chian Wine and Other Stories*. Only six were new. Some had already appeared in both of his previous collections, and many of these he had reworked yet again. O'Brian was relentless. "The Walker" had a new ending and was renamed "The Valise," and "The Curranwood Badgers" had a more graphically terrifying ending. He delivered the collection to Ollard in the fall of 1973.

O'Brian's stories were dense, atmospheric, mysterious, at times lyrical, like James Joyce's *Ulysses*, reading almost like music. Sometimes they were obscure, and often they were grim, painful to read. "The Chian Wine," a new, nightmarish tale, was, like many of O'Brian's short stories, about the dark side of human nature, almost antithetical to the Aubrey-Maturin novels. In the somewhat inscrutable vignette, Alphard, an old man of Saint-Féliu, a fictional walled village that O'Brian modeled on Collioure and also used as the setting for *The Catalans*, befriends Halévy, an Avignon Jew who has set up an art gallery for tourists in Saint-Féliu. Alphard lives in the past and laments the modernization of the village and the "rough, aggressive, ill-mannered" (p. 66) children raised since the village grew rich from tourists. But he argues with Halévy that "the spirit of the place is quite unaltered" (p. 63). Halévy demurs: "These people have lost their sense of beauty. . . . Here too the past has died: two thousand years of tradition have died! There is no bridge between the jet-age and the past" (p. 63).

Seeing a priest, Alphard counters: "There is your bridge—one of your bridges. The Church has not changed" (p. 63). Alphard plans to share with Halévy a bottle of Chian wine, an ancient bottle pulled up from the sea by the village fisherman, who gave it to Alphard. However, first he attends vespers. The priest's anti-Semitic sermon, one that he delivers year in and year out, suddenly incites a youthful mob to storm Halévy's gallery. Alphard tries to stop them, to no avail. The mob burns Halévy alive.

The story calls to mind Shirley Jackson's "The Lottery," a sinister tale of ritual murder in a rural community. As he did in *Testimonies*, O'Brian employed a priest as the catalyst for evil. Though he rarely depicted children sympathetically, in "The Chian Wine" he magnified their disagreeable qualities to monstrous proportions.

"As in every good collection of short stories," Ollard assessed in October 1973, "there is an immense variety of mood and tone between the tales that compose it. 'The Virtuous Peleg' is enchantingly funny; 'A Passage of the Frontier' and 'The Chian Wine' both in their different ways exciting and terrifying; 'The Rendezvous' and 'On the Wolfsberg' disquieting and faintly eerie; 'The Curranwood Badgers,' 'The Long Day Running' and 'The Last Pool' notably good in a setting of hunting and fishing, and the emotions that these sports kindle."

Ollard, once again, trenchantly praised O'Brian's writing in his editorial report to Billy Collins: "All of [the stories] are distinguished by a felicity of language, a visual sense and a true originality that distinguish the really good writer from the competent journeyman." Ollard recommended "certainly to publish" and suggested a printing of seven thousand copies at a price of £2.75. Based on those numbers, he added, "I do not anticipate any difficulty with the agent over terms as O'Brian is not a grasping author."

These last words of Ollard's highlight one of O'Brian's admirable traits. Although he was overjoyed to have a healthy advance for the Picasso biography—one that allowed Mary and him to travel to see Picasso's paintings in museums in Philadelphia and Moscow—neither Patrick nor Mary was overconcerned about money. Together they had sheared sheep, picked grapes, and grown their own vegetables. Patrick had typed braille and translated, and Mary had baby-sat and tutored English. Patrick had helped build his house with his own hands and borrowed money from Barney to finish it. As long as they could make ends meet, they were happy.

The reviews for *The Chian Wine and Other Stories* came out in the summer of 1974. Most gratifying must have been Helen Lucy Burke's review in the *Irish Press*, which called "The Rendezvous," "On the Bog," and "A Passage of the Frontier" masterpieces. "On the evidence of this collection I would place Mr. O'Brian in the very front of short story writers," she concluded. "His writing is elegant and erudite. His wit is a delight. Without Hemingwayish chest-thumping, he depicts men stretched to the utmost physical limit, or tormenting themselves voluntarily in the cause of sport."

The same could easily have been said about his Aubrey-Maturin tales, but Burke went on. "And with all that," she wrote, "there is this bend, this obliquity in his vision, as disturbing as the flaw in a window-pane which turns a garden vista into a wavering menace." This admiring statement could be applied only to O'Brian's early non-naval stories and books. And perhaps this is at the heart of why critical approval did not come earlier to his "naval tales." Critics of so-called serious fiction perhaps took this absence of an "obliquity in his vision" for a lack of vision altogether. Doubtful reviewers simply overlooked his erudition and his language and writing mastery, or called it showing off. Not until much later did many come to understand that there was an unobfuscated but more complex, universal vision about this work.

That summer, Collins also brought out O'Brian's illustrated *Men-of-War*, a concise look at life in Nelson's navy. The July 5 *Times Literary Supplement* judged it a job well done: "The subject, one often over-dramatized, is treated in a clear and easily read style, whilst still managing to interest and excite by the detail of study. The use of dialogue and anecdote brings to life the fighting ships." O'Brian's combination of elegant prose and encyclopedic knowledge was making him a force in the field of naval history. He soon became an influential book reviewer on the subject as well.

This was probably the same summer that Nikolai Tolstoy, now thirty-nine and a professional historian and writer, read in Collioure his stepfather's copy of Dudley Pope's graphic account of the bloody mutiny on HMS *Hermione* during the Napoleonic wars. Afterward, O'Brian and Tolstoy engaged in a lively discussion about Nelson's navy. O'Brian, himself changing gears from naval history to art history, suggested that Tolstoy consider writing a biography of Thomas Pitt, the second Baron Camelford, a naval officer and would-be assassin of Napoleon. Tolstoy liked the idea, and O'Brian guided him to period sources, such as the *Mariner's Chronicle* and *The Naval Chronicle*, a monthly service journal published from 1793 to 1818 with captains' firsthand accounts of sea actions and shipwrecks and discussions of all naval matters as well as geography and navigation. O'Brian read and critiqued the first three chapters of the book, which Tolstoy titled *The Half-Mad Lord* and published in 1978.

Pitt's phenomenal naval career included a voyage with Edward Riou on board the *Guardian*, which struck an iceberg in the South Seas but miraculously survived. (O'Brian later borrowed the event for his novel *Desolation Island*.) Pitt also sailed with the explorer George Vancouver and with Edward Pakenham, inventor of Pakenham's rudder, a jury rudder made of various ship's parts. Ultimately, motivated by his righteous indignation and perhaps by a touch of insanity, Pitt set out to assassinate Napoleon. In an open boat, he crossed the Channel to France, where he was promptly arrested and locked up in the Temple, the notorious prison in Paris, where Aubrey and Maturin would also be imprisoned in O'Brian's novel *The Surgeon's Mate*.

As usual, O'Brian had set to work on the Picasso biography full throttle, with the gusto he brought to all his books, and with the goal of ferreting out every last important or interesting detail about the artist's life. At least one reliable written work already existed, that of artist and longtime Picasso associate Jaime Sabartes. O'Brian subjected that volume and many others to his usual incisive scrutiny. But his own firsthand research and analysis constituted the greater part of this dense biography.

The fact that Picasso had spent time in Collioure allowed O'Brian to bring a personal aspect to the book. "He [Picasso] was very moody, and if you were to stand up to him, he was quite apt to trample upon you," he later recalled to a reporter. Nonetheless, O'Brian felt that Picasso had respected him—not as an equal, for he was much younger than the artist and naturally less accomplished at that period—but with a "human respect," O'Brian said, adding that he thought it the "correct way."

O'Brian also reported an instance in which a young writer living in Collioure went up to Picasso one day to ask for his assistance. Jean-Marc Sabatier-Lévêque, the brilliant but impoverished author of an autobiographical novel modeled on the form of Bach's Christmas Oratorio, was depressed and had taken to drinking. Although his ambitious novel had merits, it had little chance of gaining an audience, and so no publisher accepted it. However, one had joked that it might have a chance if it were illustrated by Picasso. The author took him seriously and approached

Picasso to plead his case. The artist told Sabatier-Lévêque to come to Perpignan the next day, and there he drew fourteen portraits of the young man. The book was eventually published by the respected French firm of Gallimard.

To begin researching, the O'Brians bought a new car and traveled to Spain, combing the regions of Picasso's childhood, including remote parts of Catalonia, where he had spent his most formative years. Patrick made many contacts and took masses of notes. While exploring, however, he fell and injured his leg in a remote, rocky area. Mary had to hike for several hours to get help.

After recovering, the O'Brians extended their foraging and interviewing to Paris and the south of France. Several photographs show a smiling Patrick, clad in a white jacket and tie, posing on a Paris street with his brother Barney, and Barney's teenage daughter, Elizabeth, in 1974. Mary traveled with Patrick, and they took great pleasure in their sightseeing.

They then widened their circle of inquiry by making trips to the Soviet Union and the United States to see paintings, drawings, and sculptures by Picasso and his contemporaries. O'Brian was enchanted by the Barnes Foundation, an educational institution in a Philadelphia house, which admitted no more than a hundred visitors a day. To his joy, O'Brian found the paintings beautifully hung, and the viewers all properly studious. He and Mary saw such classics of Picasso's early life as *Woman with a Cigarette* (1901), *The Ascetic* (1903), *Acrobat and Young Harlequin* (1905), and *The Girl with a Goat* and *Composition* (both 1906). No doubt, he and Mary also stopped to admire Henri Matisse's *View of the Sea, Collioure* (1906), a warm, colorful scene painted from the shade of the Bois de Py in the hills behind the town. The O'Brians discovered another sublime object in Philadelphia. At the train station, they ate their first American doughnuts.

In the Soviet Union, Patrick and Mary visited the Pushkin in Moscow and the Hermitage in Leningrad, where an incident occurred that amused Patrick. When he asked a docent how to find the post-Impressionist paintings in the vast Hermitage, she responded that it would be too difficult to explain and instructed a young man to show them the way. They walked up an elaborate staircase to get there. When the young man announced that they had arrived, Patrick lifted his eyes to see yet another Matisse painting of Collioure. Delighted, Patrick told the young man, an art student, that they had stopped in front of a painting of his own village. "Yes," replied the young man impassively but obviously not believing him. Patrick was at first astonished and then amused by this insolence. For him, the event came to typify Soviet Russia, where lying was so prevalent that it was difficult to be believed.

While traveling, Mary often wrote postcards to her friend Odette. The O'Brians returned from Russia with gifts for friends in Collioure. Mary had bought a pair of ornate matching bracelets studded with blue stones. One she kept for herself, and the other she gave to Odette.

Among Patrick's best sources for the Picasso book was Matisse's daughter, Marguerite Duthuit, who spent several summer holidays with the O'Brians while Patrick was writing and polishing the book. Duthuit's intimate acquaintance with France's art world was most useful to Patrick, who also enjoyed her "fine disillusioned caustic wit."* She brought Picasso's early days in Paris to life for him.

As a young girl, Duthuit had known Picasso when he was poor, unsung, and living with his voluptous mistress, model, and taskmaster Fernande Olivier. Duthuit never forgot the time she went with her father to Picasso's apartment at the Bateau Lavoir, a seedy apartment building, home to many artists, in Montmartre. Olivier poured cups of coffee and then grabbed a handful of sugar from a cupboard and plopped it unceremoniously on the filthy table for anyone who wanted it.

The result of O'Brian's exhaustive research was a work containing a stupendous amount of factual material and in-depth analysis, so self-assured that it at times bordered on being arcane. O'Brian's geopolitical descriptions of Picasso's world were not of the travel brochure variety, nor even of the travel book kind, but more like those of an obtuse professor racing along on a plane well above his students' heads.

O'Brian once again hand-delivered his typescript to Richard Ollard, and Ollard was forced to read and digest it as best he could before O'Brian returned to the south of France. After wading through the staggering manuscript—all 225,000 words of it—Ollard recognized that the work, erudite, thorough, and penetrating though it certainly was, needed some revising.

---

*O'Brian is quoted here and elsewhere in this chapter, unless otherwise indicated, from his short essay "Second Thoughts: Pleasure and Painting in Spain: Patrick O'Brian Recalls the Easy Path That Led to His Life of Picasso," an article carrying his byline in the January 14, 1995, *Independent*.

It was the first major test of the author-editor relationship. Never before had Ollard needed to deliver more than a scant amount of corrections and a few suggestions, and even then he sensed O'Brian's sensitivity to criticism.

Among the important comments he made to O'Brian—and detailed in his October 7, 1975, editorial report to Chairman Billy Collins—was that he thought the book was too self-indulgent. "Anti-feminism and other quirks are given too free a rein," and "[there is] too much genuflection before everything and everybody French." "There is also too much lecturing on the special needs and tendencies of the creative temperament," he noted. "This will certainly irritate the reader and probably the reviewer, who may well feel that they are being categorized as second-class citizens."

Ollard nevertheless recognized the value of the work, which he strongly supported publishing, "subject to some further work by the author." He continued: "What I want to establish at once is that this is a book of splendid virtues and some rather alarming defects of a type which would certainly provoke any but the best disposed reviewer and might well stop the book reaching its full potential market, which I take to be—and I stressed this particularly to the author—very large indeed."

Ollard delivered his criticism to O'Brian as gently as he could. He provided the author with a list of detailed amendments and suggestions. O'Brian probably returned the revised biography in mid-November, when he and Mary traveled together to London, flying from Orly. Mary reported back to friends in Collioure that the weather was fine and that she and Patrick had settled in to the city comfortably and were busy spoiling themselves.

Whatever his revisions, O'Brian, now sixty, held steadfastly to some dated and even extreme opinions and certainly did not rid the Picasso book of matter that would offend certain elements of the audience, primarily women and those sensitive to women's issues. While Picasso's relationships with women were far from perfect—as Norman Mailer put it in *Portrait of Picasso as a Young Man*, "No man loved and hated women more" (p. 356)—not only did O'Brian fail to comment on Picasso's misogyny in many instances, but his commentary indicated his own. He stated that Picasso was "sucked dry and rendered sterile by women, children, routine" (p. 19), offhandedly mentioned "the sorrow and woe that is in marriage" (p. 231), and described a painting in which "classical figures wrestled, conversed, and raped with wonderful serenity" (p. 245).

It is hard to reconcile misogyny with O'Brian's loving, successful marriage to Mary, yet there is no denying that several passages in *Pablo Ruiz Picasso* are baldly antagonistic to women, for example:

> There are periods when most men hate women, seeing them as eaters of their life, as the enemy.... The toothed vulva is an image to be found in all ages and all countries; and what adolescent boy has not heard tales of lovers being broken, mutilated, or swallowed up entirely? No simple cause can explain the strength of this emotion, the dark side of the sexual drive; but some part of it may have to do with the resentful acknowledgment of the enemy's indispensability, a resentment all the more furious the greater the male's vitality.... Latent homosexuality is often put forward as a deep-lying factor, as well as a host of others, including the fact that in a man's civilization many women are bores out of bed and often in it. (Pp. 261–62)

O'Brian's objectivity also seems questionable when he writes about children. He refers to Picasso and Gilot's son Claude as "Françoise's baby" (p. 389) and their daughter Paloma as "her daughter" (p. 396) and claims that "until babies reach the human stage they are so alike that they can hardly be told apart" (p. 251). About Paulo, Picasso's newborn first child, O'Brian's snide dismissal betrays just how disparaging of children he could be: "And as for the baby," he wrote, "it does not seem to have been markedly less disappointing, troublesome, noisy, selfish, and unamiable than most as it grew to be a child and then a hairy adolescent" (p. 276).

In O'Brian's portrayal, Picasso comes across as besieged by his own offspring. Other biographies paint a different picture. Gilot stated that Picasso "was obviously very fond of [Claude and Paloma], as he always had been of all small children" (p. 336). And in this passage from Pierre Cabanne's biography, the artist's delight in children is evident:

> Claude and Paloma were to come several times for long stays at La Californie. Pablo played with them, dressed them up, dressed himself up, painted them in several pictures, watched them draw, or ecstatically listened to their chatter. One of the

nicest parts of the day for the children was when their father awoke at 11:00 A.M. Paloma recalls how he would have her climb up on the bed and "steal" his extremely frugal breakfast (a bowl of coffee or hot milk and a bit of bread). After which, they all headed for the beach, and he had a high time with the two of them as well as Jacqueline's daughter, Cathy—who called him Pablito—and her little friends, and on occasion Juan, Inéz' son, who had been invited for his vacation. (Pp. 461–62)

Of course, as all biographers must, O'Brian had filtered his subject's life through his own eyes. Throughout his adult life, O'Brian showed discomfort with children, and perhaps to some degree he projected this onto his subject. O'Brian and Picasso had much in common, which may have made it even more difficult for O'Brian to distinguish between their opinions. Both were men of their time—women's suffrage was not achieved in Britain until 1918, four years after O'Brian's birth and nearly four decades after Picasso's; both were creative men, which set them apart from friends and family; and both identified deeply with Catalan culture. One parallel O'Brian could not have known in the mid-1970s: he, like Picasso, would maintain his artistic capabilities to an exceptional degree to very late in life.

The book, *Pablo Ruiz Picasso: A Biography* (Putnam, 1976), was not a great success in the United States, in part, O'Brian believed, because he had scoffed at Gertrude Stein. "I had had the temerity to say that Gertrude Stein's inability to read French and Picasso's to speak it with anything like correctness diminished the value of her reported conversations with him on the subject of painting," O'Brian later said, "and the book was reviewed for the *New York Times* by one of Stein's most fervent worshipers."

Indeed, James R. Mellow, author of *Charmed Circle: Gertrude Stein and Company*, did criticize O'Brian for his treatment of Stein, though not until the end of the review and even then with a light touch, expressing "a few reservations" over some "minor lapses." Mellow otherwise praised O'Brian's book, which he declared "has much to recommend it. It is continuously readable and straightforward; the author is relevant and perceptive in his observations about the artist, his art and his social milieu." He called the book "generally balanced, solid and satisfying" and O'Brian "above all, sympathetic to his subject." Even so, Mellow's gentle criticism stuck in O'Brian's craw. O'Brian rarely forgot a negative remark about his work and often found a way to retaliate, in this case by implying Mellow was biased.

Moderate sales in the United States might have had more to do with the book's daunting length (511 pages) and its beginning. The dense opening geographic, historical, and social background of Málaga (Picasso's birthplace) and Andalusia (where he lived as a child) was not conducive to engaging American readers. Elsewhere, the book sold well and received superlative reviews. Many critics, including the prominent British art historian Sir Kenneth Clark, who was the curator of the National Gallery, considered it to be the best biography of Picasso.

O'Brian's life of Picasso, which the author himself later called a "most conscientious piece of work, the result of intense and loving research," would be translated into many languages, including Spanish, French, German, and Italian. The book was a monument not only to Picasso but to O'Brian's tenacity, sensibility (and its notable lapses), and powers of concentration, and it would remain a pillar of his intellectual reputation.

Part V

DEEP BLUE

17

At Sea Again

1976–1978

> Those authors are successful who do not *write down* to others,
> but make their own taste and judgement their audience. By
> some strange infatuation we forget that we do not approve
> what yet we recommend to others. It is enough if I please
> myself with writing; I am then sure of an audience.
>
> —Henry David Thoreau, journal, March 24, 1842

Following the Picasso hiatus, O'Brian eagerly returned to his Aubrey-Maturin series. This time he chose as the historical basis an intriguing set of actions that had occurred in the Indian Ocean, where French and English squadrons battled for control of the strategic islands of Mauritius (Ile de France, to the French) and Reunion Island (La Réunion). The nearest British naval station to these islands was at the Cape of Good Hope. Since Mary Renault lived in Cape Town, O'Brian, who had never visited the southern tip of Africa, asked her for details of the area. He was most interested in the geographic features visible to a sailing ship from various points at sea. She sent him picture postcards filled with her own impressions. O'Brian, who typically dedicated his books to his wife, dedicated the fourth book in the series, *The Mauritius Command,* to Renault, with a Greek inscription meaning "An owl to Athens."

By September 1976, less than a year after having turned in his revised Picasso manuscript, O'Brian was able to deliver the new novel to Richard Ollard. It must have come as some relief to Ollard, who in 1974 had published his own biography of Samuel Pepys, the famous seventeenth-century diarist and secretary of the navy, to leave the fact-driven and politically turbulent realm of biography for the fictive one to which O'Brian seemed almost preternaturally well suited.

This time there were no reservations or conditions attached to his recommendation: "Emphatically to publish." "This is a first class Jack

Aubrey story, in point of construction perhaps the best we have ever had and with all O'Brian's other gifts showing at their first," he informed his colleagues. Expectation had leveled off somewhat since *Master and Commander*, and whereas he had suggested a printing of more than ten thousand copies for *Post Captain*, this time he proposed seven thousand copies. Each copy could now command a price of £3.95, more than double the price of *Post Captain*. Adding to the financial picture, the Swedish publisher Askild and Karnekull had bought rights to publish *Master and Commander* in Sweden and planned to bring the book out that year.

In June 1977, *The Mauritius Command* hit British bookstores, and at last a voice from the British literary-intellectual establishment spoke up. In the June 24 *Times Literary Supplement*, O'Brian received a watershed endorsement from Oxford don of English literature T. J. Binyon, who observed: "Taken together, the novels are a brilliant achievement. They display staggering erudition on almost all aspects of early nineteenth-century life, with impeccable period detail ranging from the correct mate-rial to grind a telescope lens (superfine Pomeranian sludge) to the subtle points of a frigate's rigging ('he spoke feelingly on the good effect of cat-harpins, well sniftered in'), and at the same time work superlatively as novels."

Indeed, O'Brian had great appeal for scholars. He loved to begin with some solid factual core around which to wrap his tale. He was particularly proud of this novel's plot, which accurately followed the action as reported in historical documents and memoirs.

O'Brian continued to collect and absorb period sources and pos-sessed a singular knack for smoothly incorporating the flavor of these into brisk plots. He drew from the letters or memoirs of the likes of Vice Admiral Cuthbert Collingwood, Admiral James Saumarez, and Admiral Byam Martin. For data on the Pacific, he turned to the writings of Charles Darwin, Samuel Wallis, James Cook, and Joseph Banks. He also consulted Richard Henry Dana, Jr.'s *Two Years Before the Mast*, which contained a superb account of sailing around the Horn. For ship, armory, and forti-fication vocabulary, as well as sailors' slang, he had *Sailor's Word Book*, compiled by Admiral William Henry Smyth, president of the Royal Geo-graphical Society from 1849 to 1851. There were also his old and indis-pensable friends Beatson and James.

Among his most valued tomes was a set of Abbé Prevost's multivolume *Histoire générale des voyages*, as well as many publications of the Naval

Records Society and volumes of *The Naval Chronicle*. Later, when he wanted Maturin to climb in the high Andes, O'Brian opened up Darwin's *The Voyage of the Beagle* for that great naturalist's period description of the Andes.

O'Brian's prized original editions of the era did more than just inform his novels. They carried him viscerally back through time. He liked to read the print that Aubrey and Maturin might have seen and to smell the binding. For him, a newspaper account of Trafalgar, with its surrounding advertisements and quotidian stories, evoked the event far better than a history book. In addition to his naval sources, O'Brian drew from his reading of the classical writers and from such authors as Geoffrey Chaucer, Samuel Johnson, Henry Fielding, Samuel Richardson, Jane Austen, Voltaire, Marcel Proust, and Leo Tolstoy, whose books lined the shelves of the O'Brians' living room.

O'Brian also fed his work by reading about his various passionate interests—medical, literary, ecclesiastical, and naval history, as well as ornithology, viticulture, gardening, and natural history.

In his pivotal review, Binyon noted that "Patrick O'Brian has a gift for the comic which Forester lacks." In the slow shift of the literary sun, this was a discernible tick. Captain Marryat had written with humor, but Forester had lacked it. O'Brian could make one laugh out loud. Although it was not yet high noon for O'Brian, Forester's shadow had begun to recede.

Binyon was a potent ally to have on and off the record. His enthusiasm proliferated like a pyramid scheme. Well before writing his influential review, he had told his friends and fellow Forester enthusiasts John Bayley, also an Oxford English professor, and Bayley's wife, the novelist and philosopher Iris Murdoch, about O'Brian. They had fallen in love with the books and spread the word even farther. One Sunday morning, while visiting the Dorset home of the artist Reynolds Stone, Bayley and Murdoch climbed into their ancient car to go buy a newspaper and to see the local church. A young editor at Chatto and Windus named Christopher MacLehose, also visiting Stone, tagged along. As Bayley sped absentmindedly back to Stone's house along an appallingly curved, high-hedged lane, he called out to the editor sprawled in the backseat with the newspaper tumbling around him, "Will you read out the best-selling list, please?"

In a quavering voice, MacLehose, a lanky Scot from a prominent printing family, read the list.

"It's a disgrace!" Bayley shouted, looking over his shoulder at

MacLehose. "Iris, it's a disgrace," he yelled. "Not to have O'Brian on the list, it's absurd!" Meekly, MacLehose asked who O'Brian was.

"Who is O'Brian?" Bayley chided him, in disbelief. "Patrick O'Brian. You haven't read Patrick O'Brian?"

Monday morning, MacLehose, who would later play a role in publishing O'Brian, went straight to Hatchards, London's oldest and most famous bookstore. He bought the first two volumes in the series. Soon he understood Bayley's disbelief. He was smitten.

MacLehose, in turn, infected Norah Smallwood, the chair of Chatto and Windus and Bayley's and Murdoch's editor, with the O'Brian bug. As soon as MacLehose finished one book, he passed it on to Smallwood. And so the awareness of O'Brian's work spread among the British cognoscenti. But it traveled farther, too. During a trip to New York City, MacLehose met Stephen Becker, an American journalist and novelist, and introduced him to *Master and Commander*. Becker, a former U.S. Marine and a university-level history and English teacher, was astonished at how well this unknown historical novelist wrote. He began to spread the word to literary friends, like Starling Lawrence, an editor at W. W. Norton. Lawrence did not immediately read the books, but he respected Becker's opinion and registered his enthusiasm for O'Brian.

In the United States, after Lippincott bowed out, the Georges Borchardt Agency, O'Brian's U.S. representative, sent the Aubrey-Maturin books to Patricia Day, editorial director of Stein and Day, a small publishing house in Briarcliff Manor, New York. Day loved the books, and she and her partner, Sol Stein, offered O'Brian an advance of $1,000 for North American rights to *The Mauritius Command*. Published in the United States in 1978, the book sold well enough to require a second printing that year.

After submitting the typescript of *The Mauritius Command* to Ollard, O'Brian sat down one day, probably in the winter of 1976, to map out his next work of fiction. With four Aubrey-Maturin books behind him and nothing more than a translation in progress, the ideas flowed. He poured his thoughts out onto twelve sheets of paper, which now rest in the collection of Lilly Library at Indiana University. What he produced was not just a sketch of his next novel but the plots, or at least the germs of the plots, for many of the subsequent novels.

At the top of the page under the innocent heading "Naval Book,"

O'Brian began jotting down ideas, toying with a plot structure: *What if I take a brilliant woman, Pake [a woman's name that O'Brian had used in* Richard Temple*], who has seduced many men, including a schoolmaster or chaplain? JA might marry them and put them on board an American whaler. This schoolmaster might have followed her for love. SM sees a parallel in his own case, uses his influence to get him on board. Or this young man could pursue JA's ship to the Cape as a whaler's surgeon. The tale, other than the nautical part, then turns on SM's passion for this woman, his rivalry with the schoolmaster, and SM's possibly willing defeat.**

O'Brian wondered to himself if this was enough for an entire book. He conjectured that if it was, its length would be between eighty-five thousand and ninety-five thousand words. He then developed a fuller eight-part page-and-a-half outline of the story that proved to be the makings of the fifth book, *Desolation Island*.

As an alternative to that scenario, or for another book, O'Brian continued his thinking: *Aubrey in an undermanned frigate sailing for the West Indies impresses British sailors from an American merchantman. An unhappy affair, with Maturin incensed over the impressment of Irishmen. War with America, new prizes. Aubrey loses battle, becomes imprisoned in America. They meet up with Diana Villiers there. An exchange and passage in* Shannon. Shannon *fights the* Chesapeake.

The last part of this projection came to pass in the sixth novel, *The Fortune of War*, except that Aubrey is not himself defeated by the Americans but taken prisoner while a passenger on board the *Java* after she loses a battle with the *Constitution*, thus adding to the series another historically significant action. O'Brian would describe the action in exact detail, based on the logbooks. In the same novel, Maturin is reunited with Villiers in the United States, and the three are present on board the *Shannon* during her defeat of the *Chesapeake*. As for the part about taking an American merchantman, in the twelfth book, *The Letter of Marque*, Aubrey does take the American merchant schooner *Merlin* and impresses part of her crew. In the book that follows, *The Thirteen Gun Salute*, Maturin has a moral crisis as he weighs whether or not to impede the *Surprise*'s pursuit of a snow (the largest type of two-masted sailing ship in the era) with a United Irishman, whom he recognizes, on board.

---

*O'Brian's notes in this section are paraphrased from his actual notes in the *Desolation Island* file at Lilly Library at Indiana University.

In the momentous brainstorming session, O'Brian then turned his mind to what later provided much of the plot of *The Reverse of the Medal,* the eleventh book in the series: *I could always use Thomas Cochrane's alleged rigging of the stock market. Aubrey could have a friend who actually does engineer such a crime, advising Aubrey to invest but not telling him why. Aubrey makes £10,000 and is arrested. The friend commits suicide. Aubrey averse to blaming a dead man . . .*

This incident would indeed alter the course of Aubrey's career, setting up the long voyage that takes place in novels thirteen *(The Thirteen Gun Salute)* through sixteen *(The Wine-Dark Sea).* O'Brian sketched out what he thought would be another book but, in fact, became incorporated into *Desolation Island.* He placed Aubrey in command of a convict ship headed for Australia. *This could tie into Captain William Bligh [who after his notorious voyage on the* Bounty *became governor of New South Wales and suffered another mutiny]. An eventual rendezvous in the East (Java?) could lead to a wreck on an iceberg. A convict woman could create interesting plot twist.*

As a result of these ruminations, in *Desolation Island* Aubrey is sent on board the fifty-gun *Leopard*—a two-decker infamous in the United States for firing into the not fully armed U.S. frigate *Chesapeake* while impressing men in 1807—to rescue Bligh, who has been imprisoned in New South Wales by his mutinous men. The British government transports convicts on the *Leopard,* giving O'Brian his opportunity to place Louisa Wogan, an American spy and a woman of much sexual experience, on board. She becomes a patient and an intimate of Maturin's, as well as an unwitting intelligence subject.

On the next-to-last page of his notes, O'Brian homed in on the plot of *Desolation Island*: *Why not have the book be about a wreck in frigid southern seas? SM continues to be obsessed with DV and attempts to (& almost succeeds) in seducing Pake, a second DV, perhaps even a girlhood friend (or illegitimate relation) of DV. SM and the stowaway follower of Pake are mirror images.*

O'Brian again had doubts as to whether this was enough to constitute a novel, but he told himself that it might flourish in the writing. He wished he could think of a way for the voyage to bring Maturin closer to Villiers, to make this an element of the longer story of his pursuit of her. Then he pondered over whether the shipwreck provided enough action. *Why not*

Emily Callaway Russ and Christian Carl Gottfried Russ and their children at their home in St. John's Wood

The Russ family in 1893, after the death of Carl Russ, with the executors of Russ's estate. *Standing (left to right):* Albert, Emil, Charles, Edith, Percy. *Sitting:* Schoff (a family friend and maker of chronometers for the Admiralty), Emily, Mühlberg (a family friend and a furrier in the City), Sidney. *Sitting on ground:* Frederick, William, Ernest.

Jessie Naylor Goddard, wife of
Charles Russ and mother of Richard
Patrick Russ, later Patrick O'Brian

Emily Russ with Mary Priestley
on the day of her wedding to
Sidney Russ

Jessie Russ holding the rudder controls of a riverboat

Charles Russ and family (minus Joan) after the death of Jessie. The photograph was taken by Uncle Frank Welch in front of the Russ home in Willesden, in about 1920. *Seated (left to right):* Nora, Barney, Connie, Dr. Russ, Patrick. *Standing:* Olive, Godfrey, Michael, Victor.

Charles Russ

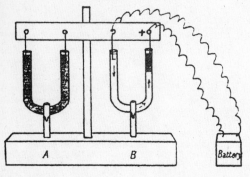

Diagrams accompanying
Charles Russ's article in the
February 14, 1914, *Lancet,*
describing his treatment of
bacterial infections and
gonorrhea using electrolysis

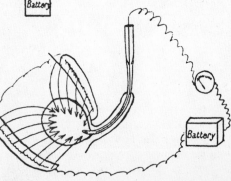

Patrick's uncle Morse Goddard, in the uniform of a lieutenant of the United Kingdom's Royal Naval Reserve

Joan Russ, Patrick's youngest sister and the sibling he was closest to in his youth

Zoe Russ, Patrick's stepmother

Patrick's older brother Mike Russ in Australia

Patrick Russ in his
RAF uniform in 1934

Patrick in Locarno, Switzerland, with eighteen-year-old Londoner Joan Ainsworth in
1937 (*seated*)

(*above*) Patrick Russ striking a pose

(*left*) Elizabeth Jones, Patrick's first wife

(*facing page, top*) Patrick Russ and his son, Richard, walking in a field at Gadds Cottage in 1939

(*facing page, bottom*) Patrick, Elizabeth, and Richard Russ walking on ice at Gadds Cottage

Patrick Russ with his
children, Jane and Richard,
at Gadds Cottage

Patrick's brother Barney
Russ in uniform

Patrick Russ hunting on
snow skis in 1940

(above) Mike Russ after enlisting in the Royal Australian Air Force

(right) Sister Francis, formerly Nora Russ, one of Patrick's older twin sisters

Mike Russ *(right)* with Reginald Cole, the husband of Olive Russ (Patrick's oldest sister), and their two children, John and Daphne *(seated)*, and a friend

Harry Roberts *(left)* and Edgar Williams *(right)* shearing sheep at a neighbor's farm in the summer of 1950

Fron, where Patrick and Mary O'Brian lived after the war, on the edge of Cwm Croesor. In the distance is Cnicht Mountain.

Odette Boutet, on the beach at Collioure

The *vendange* at Ravane (near Collioure) in the fall of 1953. Odette Boutet's Uncle Jean *(right)* and Aunt Fifine *(second from left)* Atxer.

A 1966 snapshot of the O'Brians' quirky little house in the vineyards of Correch d'en Baus, above their recently constructed garden

(*above*) Barney Russ and Patrick O'Brian in Paris in 1974. (*right*) O'Brian and Barney's daughter, Elizabeth.

O'Brian and Stuart Bennett carrying grapes in the O'Brians' vineyard in the fall of 1986. *(Kathryn Bennett; reprinted by permission of Stuart Bennett)*

Correch d'en Baus in 1998, after development has overtaken the O'Brians' hillside

O'Brian firing the evening gun on board HMS *Rose*, with Starling Lawrence and Mary O'Brian looking on, at the South Street Seaport in New York City in the spring of 1995 (*John Liy; courtesy of Book-of-the-Month Club, Inc.*)

use a French or Dutch commerce raider, or even a pirate, which could batter JA's ship, which sinks or burns? Finally, O'Brian hit upon his plot device: *JA flies before a ship of superior force, starts his water (explaining why he needs to go to the iceberg), is overhauled, prevails with superior gunnery.*

O'Brian's idea to have Aubrey start his water (in other words, to empty his fresh water into the sea in order to make the ship lighter and faster) and subsequently seek water from an iceberg was probably sparked by his knowledge of the 1789 voyage of Captain Edward Riou on board the *Guardian.* Although O'Brian did not mention this connection in his brainstorming session, it is especially likely given that Riou's wreck and improbable saving of the *Guardian* served as a model for the shipwreck and escape in the novel.

The ship of superior force O'Brian employed was the fictional Dutch seventy-four-gun *Waakzaamheid.* She became far more than a mere plot device, but a combatant in one of the most dramatic and certainly one of the most admired and talked-about scenes in all of the Aubrey-Maturin canon. Appearing on the horizon one morning, the phantomlike *Waakzaamheid* shadows Aubrey's fifty-gun *Leopard,* always lying between him and his destination, the Cape of Good Hope, and driving the *Leopard* down to the swollen, frigid seas of the lower forties. In a dark storm field of horrific peaks and valleys, the two loft cannonballs at each other, knowing that in these seas one well-aimed shot will probably send the other to the bottom.

O'Brian wrote to the staff of the National Maritime Museum at Greenwich for detailed information about the *Leopard,* which had been a loathed symbol of British oppression in the United States. David Lyon, a Royal Navy veteran and a historian who specialized in ship's plans and armaments, and his friend Conway Maritime Press editorial director Rob Gardiner, both admirers of O'Brian's novels, were only too happy to respond. They sent him a copy of the ship's plans and invited him to Greenwich.

In the spring and summer of 1977, O'Brian worked swiftly on his fifth Aubrey-Maturin book. If he finished it by the end of September, he could work the *vendange* with peace of mind while Mary typed the final version. They would be able to deliver it to Ollard in person in late October when they drove across France and ferried to England in their 2CV to attend the wedding of Philippe Jonquères D'Oriola, the son of their friends Christophe and Claude Jonquères D'Oriola, an old wine-making family living in a Catalan castle, Château de Gorneilla, between Collioure and Perpignan.

O'Brian completed the book on schedule, and Ollard had it in hand just a year after receiving *The Mauritius Command*. "Top class," he called the new 120,000-word typescript in his October 31 editorial report. Ollard considered *Desolation Island* to be O'Brian's most ambitious book yet, with a greater variety of action, more romantic suspense, and "more purely novelistic matter" than in its predecessors—and all of that completely successful. He was moved by O'Brian's atmospheric "description of wind and weather," and he noted that the "majesty and terror of the sea is . . . the best this author has yet achieved and is by any standards remarkable."

Ollard sensed that O'Brian was on the verge of breaking through to at least a new level of popularity, if not to universal critical acclaim. "In my view it . . . is so powerful a piece of writing that we should use this to try and see the author through to a bigger sales bracket, which his work has long deserved," wrote the editor. "This novel is a work of art as well as a thrilling and highly saleable story."

On October 22, Philippe Jonquères D'Oriola married Katherine McWilliam in Billesdon, in the county of Leicestershire. After the wedding reception, Patrick and Mary took off in their 2CV, a very Gallic automobile and something of a curious sight on a country road in the middle of England. Mary was driving. At a blind intersection, she looked the wrong way and pulled out. In that instant, Patrick saw another car coming toward them but too late to prevent the crash. He threw himself across Mary's lap, which helped. But Mary was badly injured in the wreck. She lay unconscious in the hospital for days, with two broken legs, a concussion, and a damaged lung. Trying to bring her back to reality, Patrick, who was also banged up but not so severely, read to her from a Samuel Richardson novel. This, they both believed, helped revive her.

For his own injuries, Patrick had to stay in the hospital for a month. Mary, who lost her lung, was there for two. Finally, an ambulance was hired to drive Mary all the way to Collioure. After crossing southern England and all of France, the ambulance could not make it up the steep drive to the O'Brians' house. Fortunately, Claude Jonquères D'Oriola was there awaiting their arrival, and since Mary was very slight, she and the driver were able to carry her up the road to the house. Claude came every day for a week to nurse her friend and look after the house.

The O'Brians' recovery from the accident would be protracted, especially for Mary. She spent much time recuperating and rehabilitating her crushed legs, which would never be the same again. It was an inward-focused period, a period of both reassessment and looking forward. Nevertheless, out of calamity came renewal.

18

Writing with Stunsails
Aloft and Alow

1978–1984

> In Captain Aubrey's mind there had been a conflict between
> loyalty to his shipmates and loyalty to his ship; the ship had
> won, of course, but a certain guilt haunted his conscience, still
> tender for these things if for little else.
>
> —Patrick O'Brian, *The Far Side of the World,* 1984

In the spring of 1978, while O'Brian was in the thick of writing his next novel, *Desolation Island* arrived in British bookstores. The device that he had employed to carry Aubrey and Maturin down to the iceberg to meet the same fate that Edward Riou had in 1789 was so well conceived that it stole the show. In the June 18 *Observer*, Stephen Vaughn wrote, "For Conradian power of description and sheer excitement there is nothing in naval fiction to beat the stern chase as the outgunned *Leopard* staggers through mountainous waves in icy latitudes to escape the Dutch seventy-four." Christopher Wordsworth, writing in the June 29 *Guardian*, concurred: "Good history, fascinating erudition, espionage, romance, fever in the hold, wreck in lost latitudes, and an action at sea that for sheer descriptive power can match anything in sea-fiction."

If, as George Colman, the Younger, once wrote, Samuel Johnson had hewed passages through the Alps and Edward Gibbon leveled walks through parks and gardens, then Patrick O'Brian was busy taming the sea, sometimes by whipping it into a frenzy. With the publication of *The Mauritius Command* and *Desolation Island* in 1977 and 1978, he now found the wind on his quarter. During the next six years, even as he and Mary recuperated from their devastating car accident, Patrick produced five more Aubrey-Maturin novels. Helping him sustain this remarkable pace was the fact that he now had a clear vision of the length and form of his novels, as well as the process of writing each chapter and structuring the book to maximize narrative tension.

With few exceptions, each new novel in the series would contain ten chapters, just as *The Mauritius Command* and *Desolation Island* did. Each chapter would include ten thousand to twelve thousand words.

While O'Brian carefully regulated the book's structure and diligently maintained a strict work regimen, the creative process remained mysterious and uncontrollable. He often experienced creative bursts during the middle of the night. Waking at two or three in the morning, he drove up the mountain into the vineyards, frequently beneath a dazzling canopy of stars and planets, to an intersection where a military road, marked by distance stones, climbed even higher. He chose a span and then walked steadily, not too briskly, to the designated marker and back. As he paced, the thoughts turned in his mind. His characters spoke to each other, and observations surfaced. He let the ideas flow naturally, not exerting too much control over this mental process. In this way, he relieved his restless mind and was able to return to bed and sleep, allowing his subconscious brain to sort things out.

In the morning, O'Brian had fresh, though hard-earned, material. This was the most vital part of his writing day. To start, he read the previous day's work, edited it, and then pushed ahead. He could see a parallel between his writing and Aubrey's sailing. Like Aubrey, he had a destination to reach, and just as Aubrey had to tack his ship according to wind, course, and current, O'Brian constantly checked his plot markers, as well as his narrative flow, and steered accordingly.

In his sixth Aubrey-Maturin novel, titled *The Fortune of War*, he recreated two significant historical frigate battles in authentic detail, other than the fact that his heroes, Aubrey and Maturin, were present. O'Brian was able to do the research in France thanks to the beneficence of the British Public Record Office and the National Maritime Museum, which copied logbooks and ship plans and sent them to him.

When he reached the end of a chapter, O'Brian pecked it out on the typewriter in his rudimentary fashion. If he was totally in rhythm, the typing might fall on a Saturday, bringing the week's work to a tidy conclusion.

Next, he reread the chapter, making small edits and notations. The typescript of the finished chapter then went to Mary for her reading, while Patrick plowed ahead.

He usually broke for lunch around half past twelve and afterward took time out to work in the garden that sloped down so gracefully behind the house. Or he busied himself in the vineyard. Teatime, at around four o'clock, was an essential element of the day. He felt that the tea lofted his consciousness to a new level, where it was capable of grappling with and articulating the most abstract of matters. Some days he returned to his fiction. Other days, he worked on correspondence, translations, or reviews.

O'Brian planned to submit the new book to Ollard before the *vendange* of 1978. He had been anxious to write about the war with the United States. The prospect of American prizes and battles with heavy American frigates had even elicited a rare moment of unbridled enthusiasm when he laid out his twelve-page plan: "American war. Goody," he had remarked.

O'Brian built his plot around two historic frigate battles. He placed Aubrey and Maturin on board HMS *Java*, which was taken by USS *Constitution*, a devastating blow to the proud sailors of the Royal Navy, who were used to ruling the waves and winning battles even against heavy odds, and especially to Aubrey and Maturin, who become prisoners of war in Boston. Aubrey is hospitalized and loses spirit. Maturin finds Diana Villiers in the United States, living with Harry Johnson, a wealthy Maryland landowner with political interests. Together Aubrey, Maturin, and Villiers escape Boston and board Captain Philip Broke's HMS *Shannon* in time to participate in another of the famous frigate battles of the Napoleonic wars. On June 1, 1813, the *Chesapeake*, under James Lawrence, left Boston Harbor to answer Broke's challenge to battle. The *Shannon* shattered the poorly manned *Chesapeake* with superior gunfire in a battle that lasted only fifteen minutes and did much to revive British naval pride.

On October 19, 1978, Ollard addressed his chairman regarding O'Brian's new 110,000-word novel. Again he felt as if O'Brian was on the verge of reaching a much larger audience, and this time his imagination ran to even grander levels: "It might be well worth, on the basis of this book, approaching a film tycoon to see whether the whole series might not offer a television series," he wrote. "There are so many well defined and established characters who have by now emerged and the variation of incident is extraordinary for anyone working in this comparatively restricted medium."

O'Brian's study of 1813 Boston was impressive, without being pedantic, but Ollard particularly appreciated the development of O'Brian's female characters. Both Diana Villiers and Louisa Wogan played substantial roles in the novel, more substantial than those previously played by any women in the series. Indeed, the author's tales had come a long way from featuring women who, as Ollard had noted in his first editorial report, "appear for strictly utilitarian purposes."

O'Brian had put a shoehorn into the genre and was working back the stiff leather. He was blurring the lines between historic fiction and literary fiction set in history. Ollard was so impressed with the new book that his ambitions for it roamed not only to the movies but to something that would appeal far more to the author, who knew next to nothing about movies and movie stars: "Simply as a novel this [is] very high class stuff and I think we should make some serious effort to have it considered for a literary prize," Ollard wrote. "It is a much richer, more interesting book than J. G. Farrell's *The Siege of Krishnapur* and at least as well written." Farrell's saga, set during the India Mutiny of 1857, had won the 1973 Booker Prize.

Despite Ollard's constant entreaties to push O'Brian's books harder, however, the sales force had apparently grown complacent. Some saw O'Brian as caviar for a limited audience of intellectuals and ex-military men, in which case, selling four or five thousand hardcover copies of each title was not a bad number. O'Brian had not swept England off its feet as Forester had with Hornblower, his nearly mythical hero. So booksellers generally lumped O'Brian with such company as Dudley Pope, C. Northcote Parkinson, and Alexander Kent, whose fiction filled a niche but did not rise above it.

At Collins's sales conference, when the time came to discuss *The Fortune of War*, Deputy Chairman Ian Chapman, who had grown frustrated with the fact that, in spite of the books' quality and critical acclaim, O'Brian's sales seemed to be hitting a glass ceiling, turned to a new editor at Collins for a fresh perspective, "Mr. MacLehose, you say, if you would, what you think about Patrick O'Brian."

Christopher MacLehose, editor of George MacDonald Fraser's witty historical novels featuring Harry Flashman, a self-proclaimed cad and poltroon, knew the genre. Ever since Murdoch and Bayley had introduced him to the Aubrey-Maturin series, he had relished the idea that he might one day work with the author. Before arriving at Collins, MacLehose had once broached the subject with Richard Simon, letting him know that he thought the Aubrey-Maturin novels were woefully underpublished, and that Chatto and Windus would like a crack at them if the opportunity ever arose.

MacLehose now stood up and told the Collins sales force that he thought O'Brian was the best writer on the Collins list, bar none. "He is underrated," he challenged them, "and undersold."

Chapman pounded his fist on the podium. "Look here," he shouted. "There are people outside Collins who believe in Patrick O'Brian! What are we doing?"

Despite the enthusiasm at William Collins and much to everyone's frustration, Stein and Day, after publishing only two books in the Aubrey-Maturin series, now called it quits. Based on the success of the novels in Britain, O'Brian's agent had upped advance demands. But *Desolation Island*, which had hit U.S. bookstores in January 1979, had received only a tepid notice in *Kirkus Reviews*, and sales were not brisk. Stein and Day had no choice but to bow out. It had been an uphill battle for Day, who had struggled to convince her salespeople that she, a woman and a nonsailor, knew anything about books involving the Royal Navy two centuries ago. Borchardt could not find an American publisher for *The Fortune of War*. Ironically, with the *Constitution*'s victory over the *Java* and the scenes in Boston, this was the most America-centric book of the series.

In 1979, O'Brian gained the distinction of being published in Japan, by the publisher Pacifica, which was bringing out *Master and Commander*. But his nautical tales had hit the horse latitudes in the United States. During the long, windless stretch that followed—more than a decade— many notable American editors rejected the series as impossible to revive. Meanwhile, devoted readers had to import British copies.*

In the fall of 1979, *The Fortune of War* reached British bookstores. On that side of the Atlantic, publication of a new Aubrey-Maturin novel now con-

---

*In 1981, Stein and Day would bring out *The Mauritius Command* under their Day Books paperback imprint. This was to be the last Aubrey-Maturin publication in the United States for ten years.

stituted something of a literary event. A growing number of fans hustled into bookshops as soon as word of the book's arrival leaked out. Critics greeted *The Fortune of War* with pleasure, but expectations had grown dangerously high.

T. J. Binyon's February 15, 1980, assessment in the *Times Literary Supplement* was among a new breed of review. With each new book, a reviewer had more to contend with—to summarize and to comment upon—to place the new title in context within the series. Increasingly, reviews had to speak to two different audiences: those who had read previous books in the series and the larger reading public, who had not. In his review, Binyon spoke primarily to O'Brian aficionados, stating that "though Patrick O'Brian writes as brilliantly as ever, his latest novel does not arouse the deep satisfaction engendered by Aubrey's earlier adventures." Unsure why, he reasoned that it might be because Aubrey was often on shore, and when he was at sea, not in command of a ship.

Certainly, another cause is that in setting the novel in the War of 1812, O'Brian was dealing with emotionally more complex material. Napoleon was clearly an evil despot who threatened the sovereignty of Britain and his forces therefore to be proudly opposed. The undermanned navy of the United States occupied a less clear station. In addition, the courageous and determined U.S. Navy frigate commanders scored some bitter triumphs over the Royal Navy.

Although his endorsement of the novel was not always rousing, Binyon concluded with an unequivocal recommendation for the benefit of those not comparing it to others in the series but to all other books: "*The Fortune of War* is . . . a marvellously full-flavoured, engrossing book, which towers over its current rivals in the genre like a three-decker over a ship's longboat."

After submitting the *Fortune of War*, O'Brian had simply carried on with his naval saga. Before the reviews for that novel had even appeared, he had already handed Richard Ollard his next episode, which he had provisionally titled *The Temple*, after the infamous French Revolutionary state prison where Louis XVI was kept and where his son, the Dauphin, was later murdered, and in which Aubrey and Maturin found themselves lodged toward the end of the new novel. While O'Brian had missed with the title—book titles not being his forte—he had not missed with the novel. On October 1, 1979, Ollard reported enthusiastically to his colleagues: "This book has a much broader balance of activity on sea and land and between men and women than in a number of the earlier books. This is an O'Brian [novel] that can be sold right across the whole market, and as soon as we have got a good title for it, we should plan a Jack Aubrey campaign."

O'Brian had set the first two chapters of the novel, which would come to be called *The Surgeon's Mate*—a clever double entendre, since the book is much about Maturin's relationship with Diana Villiers—in Halifax, where the victorious *Shannon* sails with her prize, the *Chesapeake*. He used the town, a British naval station, as a backdrop to return to his exploration of human relationships, in particular the nature of love. Halifax is in a festive mood and plans to celebrate the decisive frigate action with a ball. But Aubrey broods. While a prisoner of war, he lost his promised command of a powerful frigate, the *Acasta*, and grew homesick for Sophie, from whom he received no mail. Maturin, on the other hand, reunited with Diana Villiers, his erstwhile love, is now unsure if he loves her. "Although he still admired her spirit and beauty, it was as though his heart were numb," O'Brian wrote. "What changes in her or in himself had brought this about he could not tell for sure; but he did know that unless his heart could feel again the mainspring of his life was gone" (p. 19).

This theme—the inability to love—O'Brian had explored in his novel *The Catalans*, but now he did so much more gently. Whereas *The Catalans* revealed the stridency and bitter emotion of a young writer caught up in his subject, *The Surgeon's Mate* showed the reflection of a seasoned, mature writer, who handled the material with great finesse.

Likewise concerning Jack and Sophie Aubrey, O'Brian wrote with a flexibility that evoked the emotional complexity of sex and love and of the turmoil that Aubrey was suffering. In one instance, O'Brian wrote: "Their marriage, firmly rooted in very deep affection and mutual respect, was far better than most; and although one of its aspects was not altogether satisfactory for a man of Jack Aubrey's strong animal spirits, and although it might be said that Sophie was somewhat possessive, somewhat given to jealousy, she was nevertheless an integral part of his being" (p. 18).

But a few nights later, when Aubrey is made to feel jealous at the victory ball by an inimical Colonel Aldington, who tells Aubrey he has danced with Sophie at an assembly, Aubrey's mood swiftly turns sour: "Although he was not much given to righteous indignation his angry mind thought of her dancing away, never setting pen to paper, when, for all she knew, he was languishing, a prisoner of war in America, wounded, sick, and penniless," O'Brian wrote. "She had always been a wretched correspondent, but never until now a heartless one" (p. 46). That same night Aubrey drinks heavily and is willingly seduced by Amanda Smith, a tall, buxom young adventuress.

Before this last scene, Aubrey and Maturin are walking down the street and Aubrey is beckoned by a prostitute who calls him husband. Wrote O'Brian: "Jack smiled, shook his head, and walked on. 'Did you notice she called me husband? . . . They often do. I suppose marriage is the natural state, so that makes it seem less—less wrong' " (p. 28).

Maturin responds, perhaps simply for the sake of argument, "On the contrary, as one of your great men of the past age observed, it is so far from natural for a man and woman to live in a state of marriage, that we find all the motives which they have for remaining in that connection, and the restraints which civilized society imposes to prevent separation, are hardly sufficient to keep them together" (p. 28).

Just as Aubrey's marriage seems to be in crisis, O'Brian shows Maturin and Villiers reacquainting themselves with each other, and slowly forming the bonds that will lead to their marriage. Altogether, O'Brian presented a varied picture of male-female relationships in the novel, and he would continue this intricate exploration of love and marriage throughout the series.

Ollard took particular pains to synopsize the fast-moving novel in his editorial report. He explained that, in leaving Halifax:

> Jack and Stephen Maturin and Diana Villiers . . . take passage for England in a dispatch vessel which is hotly and excitingly pursued by two American privateers known to be commissioned by Diana's ex-lover, the rich and vindictive American landowner who is also the key operative of French intelligence in the New World. The chase through the fogs and shallows of the Grand Banks is as good as anything the author has done in this kind, and disaster is only averted at the last minute by the original device of the over-hauling privateer striking a submerged iceberg.

Back in England, Aubrey finds himself blackmailed by his Halifax lover, dogged by his father's outspoken antiestablishment politics, which damage his prospects for a new naval command, and caught in a foolhardy investment with a knavish prospector. As Ollard continued:

> Fortunately for him, Stephen Maturin is invited to undertake a very dangerous mission in the Baltic, which will mean that he will have to be taken through the Narrows in a fast naval sloop, to which of course Jack, in spite of great seniority as a captain, is appointed. The island of Grimsholm, which dominates the Pomeranian coast and thus the supply routes of Napoleon's army in retreat from Moscow, is garrisoned by a Catalan regiment. Since Stephen's entry into the service of British Intelligence is entirely motivated by his Catalan nationalist passions and his desire to overthrow Napoleon, he represents a slender chance of inducing these birds to change sides. This is most excitingly accomplished—O'Brian's skill in making one part of the narrative develop without impeding the main forward motion is very well seen here. Part of the deal is that the Catalan garrison shall at once be put aboard the British transports and taken back to Spain. Stephen and Jack of course are part of the convoy but dirty weather in the Channel separates them and eventually drives them on the Breton coast, where the whole ship's company is made prisoner.
>
> Stephen's past exploits in the last book very naturally lead to him and Jack being whisked off to Paris, where they are imprisoned in the Temple and torture and death seem imminent for Stephen after preliminary interrogation.

Maturin rescued Diana Villiers in the previous novel, however, and now she returns the favor, sacrificing her "Blue Peter," a very valuable diamond that represents her entire wealth, to finance a successful escape just as Aubrey and Maturin are about to make a desperate attempt to break out of the Temple. Ollard liked the way O'Brian tied the novel up neatly:

> The war is fairly obviously lost and Talleyrand, amongst others, is very willing to take out a reinsurance policy by conniving at the escape and flight of the party. The book ends with Stephen and Diana at last being married aboard the vessel that carries them across the Channel. Jack's blackmailing harpy has also been effectively dealt with by matrimony and all is set fair for the next round of adventure.

Collins published *The Surgeon's Mate* in the summer of 1980. One colorful and enthusiastic reviewer, Frank Peters, who had previously declared that Jack Aubrey's "annual appearances are now rated, quite justifiably, a literary event," was so convinced of O'Brian's superiority to Forester that he quipped in his *Northern Echo* review of *The Surgeon's Mate*, "And whaur's your Hornblower noo?" But the ante was about to be upped. The Wadham College, Oxford, professor T. J. Binyon was busy making the case that the Aubrey-Maturin novels should be compared not just to the best naval war novels but to the best of all novels.

Again writing in the *Times Literary Supplement*, on August 1, Binyon hit on an important point at the heart of O'Brian's unique skills: "Here there is nothing of your ordinary historical novel, in which plausibility is vainly sought through a promiscuous top-dressing of obvious contemporary references and slang, which then stand out against the rest as glaringly as the fruit in a naval plum duff. Instead each incident or description is saturated by a mass of complex and convincing detail."

Binyon noted that the detail was effectively buoyed by "the superabundant liveliness of the characters; and by the pace and excitement of the narrative." In fact, the text was so very readable, he asserted that "it is easy to ignore the fact that—largely, though not exclusively, through Maturin—they are, on one level, addressing themselves seriously to questions of human actions and behaviour far beyond the compass of the normal adventure story."

In this unassuming review of three short columns, Binyon had hit on the three sides of O'Brian's effective writing triangle—pace, detail, moral depth—each well measured, each crucial to the whole, and each supporting the other in a symbiotic relationship elevating the work from the confines of its genre, and then some.

Binyon made one last salient point, aimed particularly at series devotees. Readers, like sailors, he reasoned, were basically conservative; they liked their routine, and they wanted to read about the same characters. He lamented the fact that O'Brian too often abandoned his players. While regulars William Babbington, Barrett Bonden, and Preserved Killick each made brief appearances in this book, others whom readers had come to know had unceremoniously disappeared: the earnest master's mate and poet James Mowett had been written out of the plot; Aubrey's eager lieutenant Thomas Pullings, having contracted gaol-fever (a virulent form of typhus), had disembarked at Recife and remained unseen since *Desolation*

Island; and the bungling thief Adam Scriven, a literary hack who tried to rob Aubrey in the novel *Post Captain* and promised to shine under Maturin's stewardship, had vanished almost as quickly as he had appeared.

O'Brian would never become fully hardened to bad reviews, but, conversely, he took joy in positive ones, especially from reviewers he respected. He now wrote Binyon, assuring him that Mowett, at least, would soon reappear in the series.

"Ordinary historical fiction," as Binyon called it, had long had a poor reputation; most of it did not really work. The fact was that in all of literature, and most certainly in this genre, few authors had ever possessed O'Brian's level of concentration, erudition, diligence, and talent. He loved what he was doing, and this allowed him to immerse himself in his subject matter. Spiritually and intellectually he was beginning to exist in his historical period. His language and his tastes, his insistence on formalities, all harked back to an earlier age.

Even Collioure, with its timeless rhythms and ancient stone structures, colluded in transporting him back in time. Isolated by mountain and sea and pride, Roussillon fiercely preserved its Catalan language and customs. The fortresses of earlier centuries still dominated Collioure's landscape. Thick stone walls, rather than air-conditioning, still gave relief to the inhabitants from the region's searing heat. And the locals, including the O'Brians, still produced their wine very much as Catalonians always had.

O'Brian's days had settled into a productive routine of work and relaxation. Awaking before half past seven, he made coffee and toasted the previous day's *pain de campagne*, which made a crusty plank for Mary's homemade orange marmalade. In spring and summer, he often strolled in the garden to see the roses, lilies, or plumbago, which flowered for months, before descending to his narrow gallery for work. He had planned to hang paintings there, but books had taken over, enveloping the room like kudzu, and only one aquatint of frigates in action embellished the walls.

O'Brian preferred a smooth, steady diet of work, a slow hatching of the tale. He rarely wrote more than a thousand words in a day. He now returned Aubrey and Maturin to the Mediterranean, where their adventures had begun and where they remained for two consecutive books. In the Gulf of Lions, O'Brian's home waters, he described the sudden appearance of lightning-streaked western clouds that could turn wicked, "a confused turmoil of water, high, sharp-pointed waves apparently running in every direction" (*The Ionian Mission*, p. 250). To eighteenth-century warships, this sea "threatened not the instant annihilation of the great antarctic monsters but a plucking apart, a worrying to death" (p. 250).

In this book, O'Brian conceived of two principal missions for Aubrey and Maturin, involving an almost impossible confusion of beys, pashas, and sultans. The primary action carried the *Surprise* to the Seven Islands, in the Ionian Sea, where Aubrey, with Maturin by his side, had to choose an ally from among three feuding rulers: Ismail, Mustapha, and Sciahan Bey. Although he crowned the novel with a rousing battle scene, O'Brian cleverly withheld the outcome of Aubrey's mission for the next book, *Treason's Harbour*, and even then he did not give a full description until near the end.

In mid-December 1980, Ollard took pleasure in reviewing for his colleagues O'Brian's latest 110,000-word effort, *The Ionian Mission*, which, he pointed out, "displays the author's virtuosity undiminished." With the eighth book in hand, it was no longer necessary for Ollard to extol the familiar to his Collins cohorts. Instead, he focused on the nuances of working with an author of subtle and sometimes difficult prose, and one who knew his own mind:

> The structure of the story is intricate and I do not think any crude suggestions of bringing in some mayhem and making the scuppers run with blood early in the book would be useful or productive. Where I think the author has indulged his whims rather far is in the use of not only words but expressions so unfamiliar as to present a real difficulty. I have made some notes of these and I will do my best to point out the disadvantages of this kind of thing to the author as tactfully as I can, but it cannot be said that he accepts criticism readily or acts on it often.

Sales had slackened off somewhat since the publication of *Master and Commander*, but they were steady and profitable. The economic recession of the 1970s had not benefited the publishing industry, but O'Brian's sales were of a relatively stable nature. Some readers would have skipped a meal to buy the next installment. Ollard calculated that, taking into account recent library cutbacks, Collins could safely print 4,500 copies of the new book.

Upon publication of the novel in the fall of 1981, O'Brian's reviewers came through with several good notices. Among them, Stephen Vaughn, in the September 13 *Observer*, called O'Brian "one author who can put a spark of character to the sawdust of time" and produced a most memorable line: "Maturin and . . . Aubrey may yet rank with Athos-d'Artagnan or Holmes-Watson as part of the permanent literature of adventure."

In the September 3 *Irish Press*, Helen Lucy Burke added to Binyon's position on the literary merit of O'Brian's work and established a useful frame of reference for argument's sake:

> O'Brian has chosen to set his novels in the early 19th century, and to use the genre of the historical novel to say something important and interesting not only about the times, but about a set of passionate human beings. Those who dismiss the historical novel as a piece of pish-tushery should recollect that Tolstoy's *War and Peace* was also a historical novel. Not that I am drawing a comparison—as easy to compare champagne and port—but I am saying that O'Brian's work should be judged by the highest critical standards.

It was not the last time that the name Leo Tolstoy would be invoked in comparison to O'Brian.

After five consecutive years of an annual Aubrey-Maturin release, 1982 broke the string. Instead, O'Brian's translation of Simone de Beauvoir's *Quand prime le spirituel: Roman* was published in England by Deutsch, Weidenfeld and Nicolson and in the United States by Pantheon Books. *When Things of the Spirit Come First: Five Early Tales*, as it was titled in English, was O'Brian's sixth translation of Beauvoir's work. Soon thereafter, he was enlisted to translate her book *La Cérémonie des adieux, suivi de, entretiens avec Jean-Paul Sartre: Août–Septembre 1974* (in English, *Adieu: A Farewell to Sartre*), and Jack Aubrey had to compete with Simone de Beauvoir for O'Brian's attention during these two years.

In *Treason's Harbour* and subsequent novels, O'Brian enlisted a fictional second secretary of the Admiralty, Andrew Wray, who had once been accused by Aubrey of cheating at cards, to complicate Aubrey's and Maturin's lives. The pair find themselves stranded without a ship in Valletta, Malta, a British naval base for the Toulon blockade but one that is crawling with secret agents from multiple branches of the military and government on both sides. A traitor, Wray manages to have Aubrey dispatched on a fool's errand to the Red Sea. O'Brian ended the book by sending Aubrey to Algeria on another futile mission.

As always, Mary read the manuscript and typed up the book. She laughed out loud at Patrick's attempt at Scottish dialect in his character Professor Graham's dialogue. Though she had forgotten most of it, Mary had once spoken Scots better than the king's English. While her parents were abroad serving in World War I, her nanny had taken her off to Scotland from the time she was an infant to age five, and she had returned to her parents unwilling to speak proper English at first. Mary generally admired Patrick's effort at dialect and his passion for words. He had a gift for remembering particularly colorful ones and producing them at just the right moment. Some even defied definition, such as when Professor Graham mentions the dish "neeps hackit with balmagowry" (p. 74). While "neeps hackit" is mashed turnips, "balmagowry" is untraceable.*

In the spring of 1982, as Britain waged war with Argentina over the Falkland Islands, O'Brian delivered to Ollard his ninth Aubrey-Maturin novel, 85,000 words in length, which he had titled *The Dey of Mascara*. In his June 2 report, Ollard noted that "the author is not averse to our finding a better title though he has no suggestions to offer beyond expressing a wish that we should find a Shakespeare quotation about treachery that is not too hackneyed. All suggestions gratefully received." The eventual title, *Treason's Harbour,* was certainly a play on a line from *Henry VI, Part II* ("and in his simple show he harbors treason," 3.01.54).

Ollard suggested a print run of 5,250 copies and a price of £7.95. At a 10 percent royalty, a standard rate for the first 5,000 hardcover copies, O'Brian could expect to make around £3,500 after the agent's fee, enough for him and Mary to live on in Collioure, but hardly a bounty. Of course, if the book went into additional printings, the O'Brians would benefit accordingly, but by now Ollard was fairly on target with his print-run calculations. Fortunately, O'Brian, whose rare diversions now included outings with the Roussillon Ornithological Society, which he joined that year, worked with great intensity.

In the fall of 1982, he was deeply involved in his two side-by-side

---

*O'Brian later said that he thought he had culled the word "balmagowry" (which he believed meant "slightly sour cream") from the eighteenth-century Scottish poet Robert Burns, but a thorough search of Burns's work reveals no such word.

endeavors, Aubrey-Maturin and Beauvoir. His latest naval tale in progress, *The Far Side of the World,* an *Odyssey*-inspired title of which he was very fond, was advancing regularly. With rueful glee, he was about to strike Aubrey's frigate *Surprise*, sailing on the edge of the doldrums, with lightning. But working on both projects simultaneously began to drain him, and the fiction moved less quickly than he wished.

In the meantime, Simon and Ollard did their best to find O'Brian a new publisher in the United States. A letter from Sol Stein, president of Stein and Day Publishers, dated November 19, 1982, indicates that Stein and Day considered resuming publication of the series, but Stein decided against it, explaining that regardless of O'Brian's merits as a novelist, the genre did not sell well in a country where more than 90 percent of hard-cover fiction was bought by women. He noted that the two biggest chains, representing 25 percent of all book sales, did not even stock such books. There were still no takers in the United States.*

In the summer of 1983, *Treason's Harbour* reached British bookstores to relatively little fanfare. In the July 17 *Observer*, Vaughn called Aubrey "the best thing afloat since Horatio Hornblower," hardly inspiring at this stage. It was easy to top, and Frank Peters did in the London *Times*: "Pope, Kent and Parkinson were all first-class naval constructors, plot-smiths to a man, adept at buckling every swash in sight. But none holed Hornblower below the waterline. Then, suddenly, Patrick O'Brian's Jack Aubrey was hull-up over the horizon and all was changed."

Ollard sent the *Times* review to O'Brian. Although O'Brian found Peters's commentary somewhat baffling, he was sure the intent was kind. Perhaps he was just bored with the Forester comparison, which he did not consider flattering even if he was judged the better writer. However, for practical purposes, all of this mattered little. He was deeply engrossed in his translation and novel and battling off the summer distractions in a land where the sun slowed work to a halt, sending natives into the depths of their thick-walled homes for noontime siestas and tourists sprawling virtually naked on the beaches.

O'Brian hoped to finish *The Far Side of the World* before the end of August, in time to take it to London, to let Mary visit her ninety-three-

---

*According to *Publishers Weekly* (November 4, 1983), in the year 1982, because of a recession in the economy, the book publishing industry suffered one of its worst years in recent memory. The two largest retail booksellers at the time were probably Walden Books and B. Dalton.

year-old mother in Minehead, and to return to France for the *vendange*. But what with the Beauvoir translation, summer guests, and the time pressure of publishing schedules, his usual nighttime creative roving degenerated into severe insomnia. As he grew more and more exhausted, his writing pace became slower than he had hoped. To complicate matters, the grapes, which rarely consulted his schedule, ripened early.

Exhausted and on edge but pleased with his work, O'Brian finished the book on September 15. He had carried Aubrey and Maturin around Cape Horn in pursuit of the frigate *Norfolk*, an episode historically inspired by Captain David Porter's famous (some would say infamous) cruise in the Pacific on board USS *Essex* and his pursuit by the Royal Navy. But O'Brian was feeling the stress a little more than usual. He postponed his five-day visit to London until October 17, after the *vendange*, when he hoped to dine with Ollard and his friends Iris Murdoch and John Bayley, followed by an excursion to see Mary's mother.

Ollard had grown accustomed to working around O'Brian's schedule. The two had, at least in one regard, a relationship not dissimilar to Aubrey and Maturin's in that, though they might bestow favors upon each other, there was no such thing as being in debt to one another.

Professionally and personally, Ollard employed a combination of sensitivity and silence in dealing with O'Brian, who bristled at perceived intrusions into his affairs. A minor point or a mistimed question could grow into a misunderstanding and thus into a conflict. Or O'Brian would snub a valid, subtly delivered suggestion. Sometimes he played the intellectual snob, halting a conversation by growing arcane. One could not be thin-skinned around him. Ollard's editorial mission, as he saw it, was to catch any factual mistakes or anachronisms that might have slipped by O'Brian and, when possible, to deter him from being egregiously obscure. But he could not push the latter point too far, for he knew this about his brainy author: like many who have struggled, O'Brian enjoyed making others, including his readers, struggle a bit, too.

On the other hand, O'Brian could be absolutely charming, especially to publishing staff. Richard Simon's striking young assistant, Vivien Green, to whom O'Brian often brought an orchid when he visited their office at 32 College Cross in the Islington section of London, had recently begun handling foreign rights for Simon. After one sale, she received a tremendous many-stemmed cymbidium orchid in a huge pot, delivered by Moyse Stevens, London's most elegant florist. Simon thought the deliveryman must be mistaken. No, it was O'Brian expressing his joy at the sale. For O'Brian, these pennies from heaven were meant to be dispatched—no matter how needed at home—at least partly with prodigal flair.

Perhaps this feeling of munificence inspired O'Brian to indulge in a book-buying spree as well, for in November, he confessed in a letter to one fan, an alumnus of the Royal Naval College who had written and compared O'Brian's writing to Jane Austen's, that he thought she had no rivals as a novelist and that he had recently indulged himself in buying a first edition of *Northanger Abbey and Persuasion* (published jointly in four volumes in 1818) and an early edition of *Pride and Prejudice*. O'Brian told the writer that few things gave him so much pleasure as discriminating praise, and he generously offered to send copies of *The Unknown Shore* and *The Golden Ocean* for his children.

The publication of *The Far Side of the World* in 1984 marked a passing of the torch at Collins. Ollard, who turned sixty that year, was retiring from full-time publishing to write books. He had written his last official editorial report. Stuart Proffitt, a protégé of editorial director Marjorie Chapman, the wife of Ian Chapman, now Collins's chairman, would take over the responsibility to "look after Patrick." This was more a matter of diplomacy and humoring than anything else, for as MacLehose later put it, "Who is Patrick's editor? He doesn't need an editor." Proffitt was to read attentively, to praise, and to expect not to be listened to except in the correcting of typographical errors. As a Collins consultant, Ollard would continue to read O'Brian's typescripts and comment sparingly.

Despite the absence of Ollard, O'Brian's support at Collins ran deep, in the form of the energetic and eccentric MacLehose, who now oversaw the publishing of O'Brian as an editorial director. Just as T. J. Binyon had passed the Aubrey-Maturin fever to Murdoch and Bayley, who then alerted MacLehose, he too spread the word. On hikes in Europe with his friend Joe Fox, a Random House editor in New York, MacLehose toted along Aubrey-Maturin books or proofs of a new title, from which he read passages to Fox at breakfast. But MacLehose could not get Fox over the threshold of skepticism that exists with any fictional world, especially one so peculiar and so apparently irrelevant. Fox finally told him to lay off. He was not going to publish O'Brian.

At home, MacLehose had a better effect. With piercing dark eyes and a patrician air, the editor was known for his flair. (In one meeting, when an editor could not produce sales figures for a book, MacLehose leaped up, climbed out a window, and scrambled down some scaffolding to the sales manager's window to get them.) With the change of guard at Collins, he decided on a bold show of support for O'Brian. Collins would reissue all of the out-of-print Aubrey-Maturin titles in hardcover. Brimming with satisfaction at the news, Ollard congratulated O'Brian in a letter on December 13: "I cannot think of any better way of showing the world what complete confidence we have that this is a <u>roman-fleuve</u> that will still be flowing when many more voguish works are forgotten."

This good news was much needed in Collioure, where the O'Brians were recuperating from another cruel car accident. While bird-watching with their telescope along the tidal pools of the Camargue, near the mouth of the Rhône River, Patrick had let their 2CV veer off the road. The car rolled over into the water. Mary, who had turned sixty-eight in November, found herself trapped inside the car. Fortunately, a passerby came to her aid, pulling her out. Mary's health had not been the same since their previous accident, and this only compounded her troubles.

In the spring of 1984, *The Far Side of the World* reached bookstores. Although he had not communicated with Tony Gibbs for some time, O'Brian showed that he had a long memory for those whom he respected and who supported his work. He had tracked down Gibbs, who, since working at Lippincott, had become editor of *Yachting* magazine and then executive editor of *The New Yorker*, to tell him that he wanted to dedicate the book to him. After more than a decade, Gibbs was surprised and touched by O'Brian's thoughtfulness. The author inscribed *The Far Side of the World*, "For Wolcott Gibbs, Jr., who first encouraged these tales."

Meanwhile, behind the scenes, MacLehose and Proffitt were orchestrating the rerelease of the first two Aubrey-Maturin novels. They knew that the covers, like every other detail, mattered to O'Brian, and they wanted something special. Ollard pitched in by asking John Bayley and Iris Murdoch if they might consider writing a brief endorsement of the books for use in promoting them.

With the publication of *The Far Side of the World* and the reissue of *Master and Commander* and *Post Captain*, 1984 would be a big year for O'Brian, especially because writing *The Far Side of the World* had presented a particular challenge. Having begun the series in 1800, instead of at the onset of the Napoleonic wars in 1793, he had at last run out of historical maneuvering room for Aubrey and Maturin's adventures. Although O'Brian was proud of his adherence to historical fact, he was not going to let this impediment slow down or end the series. In his preface to *The Far Side of the World*, he confessed to readers that he had been required to create a wrinkle in time to continue the narrative.

Writing in the *Irish Times*, Dublin-based columnist Kevin Myers marveled at how his favorite author was plowing new literary turf: "Patrick O'Brian has now reached the point in his mammoth series . . . where he creates his own laws. Not merely has he openly abandoned the chronological imperatives which are the normal sine qua non of historical dramas simply because they no longer suit his purpose, but he also eschews many of the conventions of novel writing."

Myers had been an O'Brian observer for many years. Following the publication of *The Fortune of War*, in 1979, he had written, "No one else writing in the genre today can match his erudition, humour, inventiveness and flair. Incredibly, he is almost unknown in [Ireland]." Little had changed. This time Myers worked himself into a froth: "Some of you—alas most of you—have never read a Patrick O'Brian novel. I beseech you to start with *Master and Commander*, which should be available in paperback from your nearest bookseller. And if he—or she—does not have a copy then beat the wretched fellow."

In the fall, *Master and Commander* and *Post Captain* would each rise like a phoenix in a splendid new cover with serene vignettes drawn by Arthur Barbosa, who also illustrated the cover of *The Far Side of the World*. Barbosa was a seasoned professional, whose work could be brilliantly evocative and lavishly colorful. He had made his name in the 1940s, illustrating the covers of Georgette Hayers's novels. He was also the illustrator of the bright, stylized, often lusty covers of George MacDonald Fraser's Harry Flashman books.

The new *Master and Commander* cover—Titian red with a decorative gold border, including a hawser motif—featured a finely detailed illustration of a tall Jack Aubrey, an epaulet on his left shoulder, a looking glass in his hand, and a sword by his side, standing above a pale Maturin, seated on a quay, presumably at Port Mahon. The cover was subtle, elegant, literary; it did not advertise "adventure," and Jack Aubrey sported no movie star hairdo, no shimmering white teeth. At last, the book's appearance was worthy of the treasure it contained. On the back cover, it wore its critical decorations proudly, like Nelson.

At the top of the inside back flap of *Master and Commander* was Bayley and Murdoch's quietly powerful endorsement. It had come scrawled in Murdoch's hand on a postcard, and after Ollard's editing, it read:

> We have long been devotees of C. S. Forester and thought that nothing could fill the gap left by the creator of Hornblower. Then we discovered Patrick O'Brian. His series about the British Navy during the Napoleonic Wars are beautifully assembled. In some ways they are more sensitive and scholarly than Forester's tales and every bit as exciting. Captain Aubrey and his surgeon, Stephen Maturin, compose one of those complex and fascinating pairs of characters which have inspired thrilling stories of all kinds since the *Iliad*.

While all of this was happening, O'Brian had, as usual, been hard at work. This time he toiled on one of his more painful novels, *The Reverse of the Medal,* one that plunged Aubrey to the nadir of his naval career, in fact, removed him from the service and the all-important post captains' list, just as had happened to Cochrane in the year 1814.

Once again O'Brian wove an intricate tale on a number of different planes. The story, which climaxes with Aubrey's being framed for financial fraud, tried unjustly, and dismissed from the service, opens forebodingly with the *Surprise* in Barbados and a heavyhearted Captain Aubrey sitting on the courts-martial of captured *Hermione* mutineers, who perpetrated the bloodiest mutiny in Royal Navy history in 1797 and delivered their frigate to the Spanish. With grim inevitability, the accused are convicted, sentenced to death, and promptly hung at the yardarm. Aubrey and the *Surprise* are now free to sail for home. They chase the American-French privateer *Spartan* across the Atlantic but to their great frustration are prevented from capturing her after suddenly encountering the British blockading squadron off France. Aubrey, to his horror, is ordered to report on board the admiral's ship, as his chase escapes unseen by the squadron.

In England, Maturin discovers that, due to his apparent indiscretion with a woman in Malta, his wife, Diana, has left him for a former shipmate, the handsome Swedish officer Jagiello, and is now living in Stockholm. Maturin's letter to Diana explaining the situation and entrusted to the traitor Andew Wray, an Admiralty secretary with a personal vendetta against both Aubrey and Maturin, had never reached her. Distressed, Maturin returns to his unhealthy use of laudanum, while Aubrey is easily duped by Wray's scheme to frame him for rigging the stock market. Aubrey is arrested and imprisoned in the Marshalsea, and Maturin, despite his anguish over his failing marriage and his urgent desire to repair it, springs into action with all his energy and focus to exonerate and protect his guileless friend.

In consultation with Sir Joseph Blaine and Aubrey's attorney, Maturin soon realizes that political forces are at play, and that Aubrey has no chance of winning his case. So he attempts to prepare his friend for the inevitable guilty verdict. Here O'Brian was at his best. Nothing in the novels is more moving than Maturin's anxiety for his friend, his attempts to explain the complex situation to Aubrey, and his efforts to soften the blow. Part of O'Brian's mastery lay in remaining true to his characters in this emotionally charged atmosphere. Visiting Aubrey in prison, the distraught Maturin shows no excessive signs of pity and remains his old irascible self. Arriving late, he fears being scolded by an understandably peevish Aubrey. "In the event, however," O'Brian wrote:

> Jack was playing such an energetic, hard-fought game of fives in the courtyard that he had lost count of the time, and when the last point was over he turned his scarlet, streaming, beaming face to Stephen and said in a gasping voice, "How glad I am to see you, Stephen," without a hint of blame. "Lord, I am out of form."
>
> "You were always grossly obese," observed Stephen. "Were you to walk ten miles a day, and eat half what you do in fact devour, with no butcher's meat and no malt liquors, you would be able to play at the hand-ball like a Christian rather than a galvanized manatee, or dugong." (Pp. 223–24)

Maturin has just come from seeing Sir Joseph Blaine. "Jack Aubrey, dismissed the service, would go stark mad on land," he had confided to Blaine, "and I have no great wish to stay in England either. I therefore think of buying the *Surprise*, since Jack will no longer have the means of doing so, taking out letters of marque, manning her as a privateer and desiring him to take command" (p. 223). Maturin's plan will come to pass, and his influence will to a large degree determine Aubrey's career through the rest of the series.

In the trial of Aubrey, though O'Brian simplified the events, he faithfully reproduced the spirit of that controversial court case, the verdict of which long remained in dispute. Aubrey, like Cochrane, is found guilty of rigging the stock market, fined, and sentenced to be pilloried in front of the Royal Exchange in the City of London.

While Cochrane's sentence also included a year in prison, he avoided the pillory thanks to the intervention of Viscount Castlereagh, Foreign Secretary and leader of the House of Commons. "The reason for such an excess of generosity was their fear of the consequences if Cochrane was forced to undergo such an ordeal," wrote the naval historian Christopher Lloyd in his biography, *Lord Cochrane: Radical, Liberator, Seaman*, which O'Brian considered the best Cochrane biography. "It would have been a signal for a riot" (p. 129). Here O'Brian saw an opportunity to alter history to great effect. The event Castlereagh dreaded was a dramatic show of support for the popular naval officer and against the government.

O'Brian wrote the emotionally charged scene as it might have been, and it became the climax of the novel and one of the landmarks of the series. Throngs of sailors crowd the square in which Aubrey is to be pilloried. They are not there to stone and abuse a helpless officer. On the contrary, they show up to protect him from those who would. These common sailors—many recruited by barbaric means and forced to live in deplorable conditions, under brutal discipline—have plenty of reasons to resent Captain Aubrey, who at sea holds the power of life and death over them. But they do not. Aubrey is one of theirs, a fair and humane captain. Ashamed and bitter over his treatment, especially the loss of his rank, Aubrey cannot savor the poignant moment but remains admirably stoic. However, O'Brian used the crosscurrent of emotions—Aubrey is redeemed even while being publicly humiliated—to create a deep impact on his reader.

O'Brian had foreseen Aubrey's downfall in his brainstorming session before *Desolation Island*, but nothing could have prepared him for the personal impact, the melancholy, of so humbling his beloved fictional character. Perhaps it is no coincidence that the chaplain and surgeon's mate

Nathaniel Martin, the poet-lieutenant Mowett, and Maturin engage in a conversation in this novel on the misery of being an author, citing John Dryden and Edmund Spenser among others who died in poverty, and quoting Tobias Smollett and Ovid.

To add to O'Brian's gloom, his cherished mountain vineyard burned. The summer of 1984 was dry, incendiary, throughout the region. As the sun lashed the maquis in July, fires ignited without warning on inaccessible hillsides. It was as if some evil deity had hurled bolts down from the sky, but these blazes were caused by the carelessness of humans. In August, flames fueled by violent winds consumed more than thirty-five acres near Port Vendres, just to the south of Collioure. Firefighters from those two towns, as well as from Banyuls and Elne, battled the blaze for more than twelve hours. Several days later, fire ravaged forty more acres in the area. On August 22, a midnight flare-up destroyed property near the Collioure train station.

One such fire wiped out O'Brian's 1984 upper vineyard grape harvest. However, green vines do not burn well, and all but about a quarter of the plants would survive. The red-clay vineyard, impossibly rocky and sun-burned in any season, was now bare and ashy in places and bordered by blackened and withered forest.

In early September, not long after the gratifying reissue of *Master and Commander* and *Post Captain*, O'Brian shipped off a typed version of *The Reverse of the Medal* to Ollard. Little could he have known that in taking Aubrey so low he had written the scene—in the pillory—that would carry Aubrey and Maturin to such great heights. Eventually, it would capture the attention of a New York editor, who would gamble his reputation on it, and one day it would even be read on stage in Los Angeles by an admiring actor named Charlton Heston.

In October, Ollard congratulated O'Brian on the new manuscript. The same month, Sir Michael Culme-Seymour, a convivial retired Royal Navy commander and a descendant of the great frigate captain Michael Seymour, who had distinguished himself on board the *Amethyst* during the Napoleonic wars, visited the O'Brians. An energetic seventy-year-old, Sir Michael, whose wife, Lady Faith, daughter of the ninth earl of Sandwich, had died the previous year, took solace by swimming in Collioure's cold October sea.

Sir Michael arrived in time to help out with the melancholy *vendange*.

As a naturalist, O'Brian took a certain grim pleasure in strolling with Sir Michael through the charred remains of his vines, where nature was already capitalizing on the death to build anew.

Even without the wildfire, it would have been a disappointing *vendange* for the soon-to-be-seventy author. His remaining downhill vines had benefited from a good flowering time, only to suffer a cool and ruinous August. He feared the harvest would be reduced by about two-thirds. Not only that, but he doubted whether the quality of the grapes was high enough that year for him to make Banyuls, the area's famous brownish red *vin doux naturel*, a distant cousin of port.

Also that fall, MacLehose informed O'Brian that Norah Smallwood was very ill and probably dying. She was a great admirer of Jack Aubrey. "Why do you waste your time with that thin intellectual?" she had teased MacLehose about his preference for Maturin. "Absolutely characteristic of you. Aubrey's the thing: English, brave, peccable, glorious, lovable. You're young, of course, didn't see England at war."

MacLehose asked O'Brian, who also knew and liked Smallwood, a grande dame of the London publishing set, if he might give her proofs of the latest book. O'Brian agreed, and MacLehose delivered a typescript to her in the hospital. She was delighted. For MacLehose, there could be no greater testimony to the power of O'Brian's roman-fleuve than its ability to please and comfort his friend, so near the end of her life.

19

Singing of Sir Joseph

1985–1986

Nor is it always in the most distinguished achievements that
men's virtues or vices may be best discerned; but very often an
action of small note; a short saying, or a jest, shall distinguish a
person's real character more than the greatest sieges, or the
most important battles.

—Plutarch, "Life of Alexander," c. 110

Collioure's bleak winter of 1984–85 seemed to O'Brian, now in his
seventy-first year, to have simply merged with a cold and blustery
spring. A raging tramontane gusting down from the Rhône Valley
and the Alps besieged the coast of the Gulf of Lions. From December
through March, there was virtually no rainfall, although, as if to spite the
author, who considered the weather "perfectly vile," it snowed on St.
Patrick's Day.

While cooped up, O'Brian read *Thraliana: The Diary of Mrs. Thrale,
1776–1809*, the two-volume diary kept by Samuel Johnson's onetime good
friend Hester Lynch Thrale Piozzi, the mother of Queenie Keith, who in
O'Brian's novels helped raise Aubrey after his mother died and remains a
dear friend and benefactor through her powerful husband, Admiral Lord
Keith. After the death of Piozzi's first husband, according to Thomas
Babington Macaulay, "[Piozzi] was left an opulent widow of forty, with
strong sensibility, volatile fancy, and slender judgement." She married an
Italian music master and shirked Johnson, who, according to Macaulay,
"said that he would try to forget her existence." In Piozzi's diaries, O'Brian
noted in a letter to Ollard, he perceived a high degree of unconscious self-
betrayal.

That spring, O'Brian sent his brother Barney a copy of *The Far Side of
the World* for his seventy-third birthday, but Barney noted in a letter to
Joan that Pat seemed melancholy and increasingly eccentric and unso-

ciable. "I was sorry to see that he continues to indicate that his wife, severely injured in another accident, has suffered psychologically as well as physically," Barney, who had never met Mary, told Joan. "His letters have been short and rare and I take it he is kept very busy tending and fending for his good lady."

This and Collioure's inexorable slide toward modernity, homogeneity, and overcrowding had narrowed the margins of O'Brian's world somewhat. The town's tentacles now reached up the O'Brians' hillside. With more than 100,000 spectators invading Collioure for the mid-August La Festa Major fireworks, condo-mania had struck, and no bit of real estate was to be left undeveloped. Houses had been built at the base of the O'Brians' hill and on the narrow road up to Fort St. Elme, and more were coming.

The arrival of fast-food restaurants symbolized the degradation of Collioure's traditional lifestyle. The young had demanded cheeseburgers, and they had gotten them, along with pop music and electronic games. In summer, it was often impossible to park near the town hall and post office, and bumper-to-bumper traffic through the center of town and even stretching up to the highway above was not unusual.

But O'Brian had the past, in many forms. Several times a year, he and Mary still ate at the Pous family's restaurant. Though they had changed its name to Les Templiers and had long since added hotel rooms, little else was altered. In fact, with paintings hanging from every available space, the place was a time capsule of more than three decades of artists' visits. Recently, Jojo Pous, the proprietor, had invited O'Brian to inscribe the establishment's *Livre d'Or*, its guest book of the talented and famous. Joining the likes of Matisse, Picasso, and Edith Piaf, O'Brian composed a seventeen-line ode to Pauline Pous's fish soup, Les Templiers's friendly atmosphere, and Collioure, which he described as a "tight-packed village like a swarm of bees." At its heart, he placed the café, "where you can eat like a lord or where/you and fishermen and masons may/play most passionately at cards/. . . . while geckos walk upon the wall / and the small owl calls gloc gloc."

The Pouses' refuge was timeless, at least for now, and so was O'Brian's work, which transported him and his readers to a temporal place at once two centuries old and floating magically outside time. This was a comfortable place, where "progress" came slowly. O'Brian's own life having spanned the horse-and-buggy and space-rocket eras, the technological change during the Regency period seemed quaint, almost imperceptible, by comparison. But change was, of course, present, and the fact that O'Brian took such delight in dwelling in the minutiae of the age had the pleasant effect for modern-day readers of counteracting their ennui for subtle change.

For the moment, however, O'Brian had left his imaginary friend Aubrey to stew in his own personal purgatory—neither a member of the Royal Navy, nor a proper, civil being outside it—while he turned his attention to another subject dear to his heart: Sir Joseph Banks, the natural historian and longtime president of the Royal Society, an explorer, a friend of scientists, and a man of letters. O'Brian had several coincidental connections to his subject. Banks had known the scientist Joseph Priestley, an ancestor of Uncle Sidney's wife, and Banks, through marriage, was distantly related to O'Brian's favorite author, Jane Austen.

O'Brian had proved in his novels and in his biography of Picasso that he excelled at painstaking research, and now he basked in it. In writing a life of Banks, the challenge lay not in finding but in culling the material. Banks's own quirky prose ranged from journal descriptions of his explorations to his vast, vibrant correspondence, which one historian calculated amounted to fifty letters a week during his active adult life, more than fifty thousand in all.

Banks was born to a wealthy family, so well positioned that his birth on February 15, 1743, was recorded in the *Gentleman's Magazine*. He had been sent to the public school Harrow at age nine, "pitifully young" (p. 18), commented O'Brian, whose own father had been hustled off to Shebbear at eleven and whose son had gone to boarding school at an even younger age. At thirteen, Banks left Harrow and entered Eton, which O'Brian described using three histories, including Richard Ollard's *An English Education: A Perspective of Eton*, published in 1982. No doubt the intellectual street fighter in O'Brian took pleasure in reminding the many Etonians among his fellow English literati of the colorful, occasionally barbaric history of their institution, albeit founded by Henry VI in 1440.

As O'Brian wrote, during Banks's day the students took part in "badger baiting, bull baiting, bear baiting, cock fighting and—why not?—small boy baiting" (p. 20). One school tradition had the boys beat a ram to death with clubs specially made for the purpose, but the practice had been banned years before Banks's arrival—for fear that the boys might overheat and endanger their health, not for any consideration of the animals.

O'Brian wrote of the "unscrupulous rapacity, not to say the downright dis-honesty, of successive provosts and fellows" (p. 19), who robbed the boys of food and benefits, and of the Long Chamber, where the boys slept, which had not yet but would soon become a "byword for squalor, cruelty, bullying and sexual immorality" (p. 19).

He clearly enjoyed taking the school down a notch, claiming that "there was much to be said against Eton: it lay in low, damp, unhealthy ground rather than upon a salubrious hill; in many respects it was more like an ill-managed bear-garden than a school; and even then there were people who felt that Etonians spent more time than was necessary in thanking God that they were not as other men" (pp. 18–19). O'Brian later took jabs at Eton in the Aubrey-Maturin novels as well. In *The Yellow Admiral*, he reveals that General Aubrey, Jack's disreputable father, is an Etonian, who learned one phrase of Latin there that he often repeated to his young son (as Maturin quotes Pope's translation of Horace): "Get place and wealth, if possible, with grace;/If not, by any means get wealth and place" (p. 204). In addition, Maturin relates that he and a friend were once mugged by Eton students, who were "dressed as Jack Puddings and merry-andrews in antic garments" (p. 204).

It was perhaps a bit audacious of O'Brian to send the Eton section to Ollard to critique. After all, Ollard was not only an old boy but a historian of the school. Ollard's chronicle of Eton, taking in its entire history, was, of course, quite different from O'Brian's brief unflattering portrait. But O'Brian was a competitive man, and part of his gamesmanship was to take the moral high ground by being unquestionably correct and fastidiously courteous, at least on the surface, and then to dunk his opponent—a posi-tion for which anyone with intellectual pretensions qualified.

One of the reasons O'Brian admired Banks was for his lack of such rivalry, evident in a closing he signed in a letter to a colleague: "your ever affect but never emulating/J Banks" (*Joseph Banks,* p. 174). O'Brian found this telling of Banks's nature. "Ordinarily," he wrote, "competition plays such an important part in the relations between men, and is the cause of so much decay in friendship, that a 'never emulating' companion, one who does not feel (as Johnson felt) that all encounters are contests, with evi-dent superiority on one side or the other, must be wonderfully restful" (pp. 174–75). With this characteristic, Banks made many friends and kept them. O'Brian operated more along the Johnsonian model.

But Ollard, whom O'Brian later described in a BBC radio interview as "a sort of pleasant fellow," took it in stride. He was used to and tolerant of O'Brian's ways, no matter how fussy and occasionally condescending. Ollard felt that deep down, at least, their relationship had the same "human respect" that O'Brian had received from Picasso. He understood the weight of O'Brian's talent and his bitterness at not being recognized for his literary genius.

Oxford University, which O'Brian also had not attended, fared a little better than Eton in his hands, though he did quote Gibbon on his time there at Magdalen College ("they proved the fourteen months the most idle and unprofitable of my whole life" [p. 26]). Still, Banks, much to his own credit and industry, thrived there, furthering his deep interest in botany by recruiting the capable teacher Israel Lyons from Cambridge to be his private tutor.

O'Brian was certainly not above a jaundiced view of the iconography of the English educational system and was perfectly willing to tweak the establishment with the evidence that beneath the veneer of these hallowed places—the mere names of which so often served the user with instant credibility, not to mention airs—there lay a human institution, with all the inherent shortcomings.

Once O'Brian carried Banks out to sea, however, the author's spirits seemed to lift. He shook his competitive, Johnsonian edginess and dropped his guard. O'Brian's mastery of the ways of the Royal Navy together with Banks's clear-eyed descriptions of ship life, new flora and fauna, and natives in such places as Newfoundland, Tahiti, Australia, and Iceland made for a read nearly as gripping as fiction. Banks had written more than twenty thousand words on a voyage to Newfoundland at age twenty-three and filled two thick volumes with ten times that during his three years on board the *Endeavour*.

The study of Banks was a chief subtext of O'Brian's book. He steered the reader—as if he were addressing an eager professor—to Banks's journal, "two fat quarto volumes" (p. 70), at the Mitchell Library in New South Wales, to the books Banks acquired on one voyage, kept at the British Museum, and to the lava he returned with, still at Kew Gardens. He complimented at some length Averil Lysaght, who had superbly edited the Newfoundland journal, the original of which, O'Brian noted, lay in a branch of the Royal Geographic Society of Australia. O'Brian praised Lysaght again for uncovering a letter about Banks's relationships with the two important women in his life, his wife, Dorothea, and his sister, Sophia. The letter had escaped the editor of *The Banks Letters*.

Banks's firsthand accounts so impressed O'Brian that he presented the explorer's two early voyages largely by stitching passages of his commentary together. By this means and with evident admiration for an era when natural historians set off wide-eyed into the beguiling world, O'Brian successfully captured Banks's joie de vivre. The voyage Banks made with Captain James Cook to observe from Tahiti the transit of Venus across the Sun was particularly eventful, including amorous interaction with the lovely women of Tahiti, confrontations in New Zealand with fierce Maori tribes, who often had to be pacified by musket shot, and peril along the Great Barrier Reef, which Europeans had never before seen.

But everyday shipboard life could be nearly as colorful. O'Brian quoted a memorable Banks analysis of the ship's "indifferent" bread, which was filled with vermin:

> I have seen hundreds nay thousands shaken out of a single bisket. We in the Cabbin have however an easy remedy for this by baking it in an oven, not too hot, which makes them all walk off, but this cannot be allowed to the private people who must find the taste of these animals very disagreeable, as they every one taste as strong as mustard or rather spirits of hartshorn. They are of 5 kinds, 3 *Tenebrios*, 1 *Ptinus* and the *Phalangium cancroides*; this last is however scarce in the common bread but was vastly plentiful in white Deal bisket as long as we had any left. (P. 108)

O'Brian's only regret was the loss of nuance in the transition from Banks's manuscript to type. "Cold print," he wrote, "differs essentially from a page written by hand, and its inhuman precision makes Banks's way of writing seem wilder and more outlandish than it really is" (p. 41).

For the young Banks, who was healthy, wealthy, courageous, and curious, the natural world really was his oyster. Wherever he roamed, new plants and animals and even human beings waited to be observed and categorized. Banks thought nothing of shooting scores of birds at a time; he served the edible ones—after careful examination and skinning—at mealtime. The sailors, he noted, preferred albatross in savory sauce to fresh pork. Banks and Cook both regretted encounters with fierce New Zealand natives, whom they had to subdue by force, but Banks thought nothing of returning to England with a native for further observation.

For the Aubrey-Maturin audience, reading this section of the Banks biography is something like riding in a Model T, the essence of a car, after driving in a Rolls-Royce, the apotheosis of one. Cook and Banks on some basic levels resembled Aubrey and Maturin. For one thing, despite sometimes conflicting agendas, they coexisted as friends in close quarters for three years (1768–71) on board the *Endeavour*.

Just as Jack Aubrey would do, Cook ran his ship, though a lowly, blunt-bowed collier, built for cargo not speed, "in strict man-of-war fashion, as precise in the little bark of which Cook was the commander as ever it had been in sixty-gun line-of-battle ships in which he had been the master" (p. 73). And like Maturin and his good friend Nathaniel Martin, as scientists on board a naval ship, Banks and his colleague, the Swedish botanist Daniel Solander, suffered the fate of often having contrary desires to those of the crew. They delighted in the sailor's bane known as the doldrums, a fluctuating windless band near the equator, where they fished, collected specimens, and swam. There were also tantalizing misses, like the time Cook agreed to land Banks and Solander on the unexplored island Ferdinand Norronha. When contrary winds made it impossible, the frustrated scientists dolefully watched the fading island, which, O'Brian noted, was not visited until Darwin landed there sixty-four years later. Even worse, on the teeming banks of Rio de Janeiro, the *Endeavour*'s scientists remained shipbound because a suspicious Portuguese viceroy could not be convinced that the ignoble collier was not a pirate or smuggler and so strictly limited traffic between ship and shore.

Somehow, O'Brian made Cook's voyage seem a benevolent way of life. Never mind that during the *Endeavour*'s three-year circumnavigation, one-third of the crew was killed or died of disease.

Upon his return to England, at the age of twenty-eight, Banks was greeted by massive hyperbole. Even Linnaeus called him "immortal." As O'Brian paraphrased Linnaeus's letter: "No one since the earth began had dared so much, no one had been so generous, no one had exposed himself to so many dangers" (p. 148). From such a lofty perch, he was bound to fall. As O'Brian had seen in his own experience and now observed about

Banks, "Going through a war does not necessarily fit men for ordinary life; nor, however horrible their experiences, does it necessarily cause them to grow up" (p. 155). Banks grew vain and squabbled with powerful and wiser men in the Admiralty, and his promising start as an explorer was cut short.

After that, Banks's career, though noble in certain ways, began to falter. Despite his masses of notes, he wilted under the task of writing a book about the great voyage. O'Brian concluded of this writer's block that the "cause, at least to the present writer, is impenetrably obscure" (p. 171). Soon Banks, the intrepid explorer, grew sedentary and obese. O'Brian compared him to the barnacle and the oyster, both of which "have an active free-swimming youth; then when they are still quite young something comes over them—they find a convenient place, settle there, change shape, and never move again" (p. 191).

For all his brilliant, enthusiastic leadership of the Royal Society and Kew Gardens, his well-used influence with King George III, and his humane assistance to scientists and friends around the world, a whiff of dilettantism surrounded Banks. While he had a talent for establishing meaningful acquaintances, "Banks was," as O'Brian noted, "either unluckier than most or . . . in this respect his judgement was not very acute" (p. 236), for he befriended, associated with, or patronized a number of unpleasant men, including the infamous Captain Bligh. Banks was a great benefactor of the sciences, but he was not an innovator as a botanist. He spoke no foreign languages, and, O'Brian admitted, "did not possess . . . the very rare [intellectual] equipment that might have allowed him to strike out a new theory of classification superseding that of Linnaeus, which had already served its time" (p. 175).

Banks was a social lightning rod who capitalized on his wealth and connections. In terms of personality, he couldn't have been more different from O'Brian. Nonetheless, O'Brian admired him and treated him with the gentleness of a friend. Though he had his share of faults and weaknesses, O'Brian found in him "a fund of life . . . a zest and eager intelligent curiosity" (p. 303) and considered him a generous man who was willing to exert his influence and expend his resources for those in need. These qualities provided the foundation of the biography.

O'Brian was confident in the result. After his editor, Stuart Proffitt, sent him several pages of notes, O'Brian wrote back saying, as Proffitt later recalled with a self-deprecating chuckle for the BBC, "Dear Stuart, Thank you for your most sympathetic comments on my typescript, but all I really want is your praise."

However, as with Picasso, O'Brian was perhaps not as exacting as he should have been regarding Banks's relationships with women. Upon the book's publication in the United States in 1993, one unsatisfied reviewer, Linda Colley, wrote in the *New York Times Book Review*:

> There is a harsher side of Banks that Mr. O'Brian neglects. It comes out in his relationships with women, and not just those Tahitian women whom he explored as eagerly as he did any other South Seas artifact. There seems to have been a fiancee, rather brutally paid off. And there were certainly a mistress and a bastard child, discarded along the way. . . . He told his sister, "You women are sad husband killers in your hearts." Yet what Banks meant by that Mr. O'Brian never asks.

O'Brian also glibly reported that Banks, who at thirty-three was openly keeping a mistress, "had not wholly committed himself; nor had he entered upon a regular marriage, which he looked upon as incompatible with natural philosophy, with a life of scientific research, and there was still the possibility that he might become a free-swimming organism once more" (p. 192).

When Banks finally married, at the age of thirty-six, the twenty-one-year-old heiress Dorothea Hugessen, O'Brian could not resist a gratuitous shot at children: "The marriage seems to have been thoroughly suitable and, unencumbered by children, thoroughly happy" (p. 197).

In early 1986, Mary underwent another in a series of operations resulting from her declining health. Her recovery was slow and she lost a lot of weight, but she gradually put it back on and regained her strength under Patrick's watchful eye. Her health would be an ongoing problem as a result of the two automobile accidents. But, though dainty in form, she was a strong-willed and uncomplaining patient.

O'Brian relieved the pressures of writing and helping with Mary's recuperation by indulging in one of his great passions: collecting books. In so doing, he made the acquaintance of an antiquarian bookseller named Stuart Bennett. Bennett, an American based in London who specialized in seventeenth- to nineteenth-century literature and who was reading the Aubrey-Maturin series, had sent O'Brian a catalog of eighteenth-century English libertine literature. All of the books had been purchased by a Texas collector, but Bennett thought that O'Brian might take an interest in the bibliographical information.

O'Brian wrote back to see if Bennett could help him acquire early editions of Jane Austen. Most of those published in her lifetime were printed in the classic Regency three-volume format. O'Brian already owned those that were not: a two-volume third edition of *Pride and Prejudice* (1817) and a first edition of the four-volume *Northanger Abbey and Persuasion* (1818), though the latter had been rebound in inferior material. He hoped Bennett might find him other early editions at good values, but they had to be in durable condition because he wanted to read them. He loved to read a book produced when it was written. The physical object, from the binding and cover, to the pages, to the typeface, acted as a time capsule to transport him to the period of the story. Though early editions were pricey, he had no use for the less-expensive Bentley editions of Austen, which became the standard when published in the mid–nineteenth century. Spellings had been modernized and type regularized; these books felt Victorian, anachronistic.

Bennett responded with discouraging news. Austen novels had been the subject of a recent buying frenzy, particularly by Japanese universities and trophy-book collectors. But he would be on the lookout for volumes satisfying O'Brian's demands and within his means. This he proved to be very good at.

In the spring of 1986, Bennett produced an unusually nice copy of the second edition of *Sense and Sensibility*. At £400, the book was a relative bargain. When O'Brian received the three leather-bound volumes published in 1813, he was elated; they were finer than Bennett had described. That May, Bennett and his wife, Kate, were vacationing in France and arranged to spend a night in Collioure. O'Brian, wearing a dapper white linen jacket, picked them up at their hotel to take them home for dinner. The Bennetts presented him with a jar of Gentleman's Relish, a highly seasoned anchovy paste, which had been O'Brian's only request when Bennett pressed him to name something he wanted from England. They also gave the O'Brians a bottle of Chambolle-Musigny, the Burgundy served by Aubrey to the Bristol merchant Canning at a feast on board the *Polychrest* in *Post Captain*.

Urbane, intelligent, and unassuming, Stuart and Kate Bennett, both in their midthirties, hit it off with Patrick and Mary. Patrick was particularly charmed by Kate, a museum curator who was elegantly mannered, soft-spoken, and conversant in all areas of art. She was also a beauty of Nordic and Italian descent, with fair hair, slightly olive skin, and blue eyes. They ate a feast that Mary had magically produced from her tiny kitchen, drank Patrick's red wine, which tasted of the fragrant hills around them, and finished off with his sweet Banyuls. The talk meandered agreeably. When Stuart referred to Jane Austen's mysterious suitor, with whom she had an intense relationship until he died within a year of their meeting, both Patrick and Mary pounced on the bibliophile with passionate interest. "What is your source for this?" they wanted to know. "Tell us more." And when Stuart mentioned the Augustan publisher Jacob Tonson, the first to publish Alexander Pope, Patrick rose to the occasion, breaking into John Dryden's famous lampoon of Tonson: "With leering looks, bullfac'd and freckled fair,/With two left legs, and Judas-coloured hair,/With frowzy pores, that taint the ambient air." Laughter filled the house.

"Of course, you will come for lunch tomorrow so we can have a walk around the vineyard," O'Brian insisted at the end of the evening. The Bennetts ended up staying for two days, and a friendship was forged.

In June, O'Brian received in the mail a second edition of *Mansfield Park*, rebound in the mid–nineteenth century. Bennett had bought the book at Philips Auctioneer and sent it to O'Brian on approval. The relatively inexpensive book (£250) again pleased O'Brian. Bennett next provided him with the modern scholarly edition of *The Trial of Jane Leigh-Parrot*, about Jane Austen's aunt's conviction for shoplifting in 1799, an event that traumatized the Austen family. The original, a scandal sheet, was unobtainable.

In the fall, the Bennetts returned to Collioure, staying in the O'Brians' small house with them for three days. They tried to time their visit to help with the *vendange*, and although O'Brian was concerned that they might have arrived too early, he decided to proceed anyway, while he had the help.

Of all the Jane Austen books, *Emma* was the most difficult to acquire under O'Brian's requirements. The others had all been reprinted during Austen's lifetime, but *Emma* had not. Bennett had previously managed to buy a copy at Sotheby's for £1,000, however. One evening, he casually offered to swap his first edition of the book for one of O'Brian's manuscripts. Then, recalling the price, he quickly reconsidered aloud: "Gosh, maybe I should ask you for two manuscripts for the book?" O'Brian shot Bennett a chilling look. Bennett realized his mistake but could not unsay what was said.

Although O'Brian remained pleasant, he grew more reserved with Bennett, withdrawing into the shell he maintained for most of humanity. Bennett knew that he had to do something. Two nights later, he found O'Brian alone. "Patrick, I owe you an apology," he said. "I made a flippant remark, and it was never my intention to seriously suggest such a thing. I would be honored to trade, if you are still willing to consider it, my first edition of *Emma* for one of your manuscripts."

Now that Bennett had broken the ice, O'Brian admonished him for having reduced something between friends to horse-trading, but he accepted the apology. The set look in his face relaxed. He retrieved the manuscript of *Master and Commander*, two worn spiral notebooks, from his basement studio and handed them to his guest.

Bennett said, "But you haven't seen *Emma* yet."

"I'm sure *Emma* will be fine," O'Brian replied.

The two couples, the young and the old, labored happily together in the sunny vineyard. The hut where Patrick sometimes wrote sat at the edge of the vineyard on the crest of a hill with a magnificent view of the coast. Downhill, the ruins of a stone house evoked the past but also a hint of promise since, in France, where building restrictions flourish, one always has the right to build on old foundations. Red and white grapes intermingled randomly, and the pickers tossed one and all into the bins, which Bennett and O'Brian lifted together and loaded into the O'Brians' 2CV. O'Brian, now approaching his seventy-second birthday, pointed out where he had planted clippings of vines and sprigs were emerging through the charred earth. "The experts tell me that in twenty years they will be more susceptible to the phylloxeral beetle," he told Bennett, with an impish grin, "but I don't care what happens in twenty years."

They picked the grapes in three mornings, taking the afternoons off. Kate could do no wrong, and Patrick, who had once declared he loathed being photographed, even relaxed enough to pose for her pictures in the vineyard. Mary, despite her frailty, seemed always on the move. Even after working in the vineyard, she would be the hospitable hostess, fixing meals and making sure her guests were comfortable.

Picking the grapes and carrying them back to the house was only part of the work. O'Brian then had to press the fruit and seal the juice in barrels. Bennett helped him with this, but when the novice twisted the much adored wooden wine press too tightly, causing it to groan in protest, O'Brian firmly put an end to the experiment.

Contrary to the vintners' careful calculations, the O'Brians had picked at just the right time. The next week bad storms followed the fine weather. That fall while reading his new first edition of *Emma*, O'Brian could do so with the added comfort of knowing that he had fared better than many vintners with the 1986 vintage. And when the covers of *Emma* fell off in his hands, he had confidence that Bennett would do the right thing. He mailed the fragile book back to England. Bennett—amid profuse apologies—had it rebound and returned it to him in France.

20

Sailing in
the Trade Winds

1987–1990

The artist . . . speaks to our capacity for delight and wonder, to
the sense of mystery surrounding our lives; to our sense of pity,
and beauty, and pain; to the latent feeling of fellowship with all
creation—and to the subtle but invincible conviction of
solidarity that knits together the loneliness of innumerable
hearts, to the solidarity in dreams, in joy, in sorrow, in
aspirations, in illusions, in hope, in fear, which binds men to
each other, which binds together all humanity—the dead to
the living and the living to the unborn.

—Joseph Conrad, from the suppressed preface to
The Nigger of the Narcissus, written 1897, published 1914

O'Brian now happily returned to his friends Jack Aubrey and
Stephen Maturin. But he must have paused to wonder what kind
of impact his eleven-book series, this still expanding opus, was
actually having. Would it be remembered? Reviews of *The Reverse of
the Medal* had been less than overwhelming, in fact, barely existent. It
is somewhat shocking, in retrospect, that one of the seminal novels of
the Aubrey-Maturin series received notices but went and remains essentially unreviewed. The April 10, 1986, *Times* lumped it in with novels by
Alexander Kent and Bernard Cornwell, noting that the "gallant Captain
Aubrey and his friends never fail to entertain."

A brief *Times Literary Supplement* notice in July was of a type that
O'Brian would have to learn to live with: the "disappointed" review, usually from a kindly-disposed critic who allows that the current book is a bit
of a letdown. "Perhaps not the best of the celebrated Aubrey books," the

reviewer mildly lamented, "being concerned for nearly half its length with the recapitulation of past adventures and scene-setting."

In March 1987, John Bayley handled *The Reverse of the Medal* for the *London Review of Books* in an omnibus article called "The Matter of India," which barely mentioned O'Brian's treatment of India and, instead of commenting on his latest novel, assessed the series as a whole. Bayley produced memorable lines, among them that Aubrey "is Lord Jim without the author's philosophic pretension, and in his context far more convincingly contrived." But the end result was that *The Reverse of the Medal,* not published in the United States at the time and unreviewed there when it eventually was, was almost entirely neglected from a critical standpoint.

Nonetheless, as Bayley noted, O'Brian was "in full swing as a novelist." What O'Brian had in mind at this point was even more ambitious than anything he had yet accomplished with his two characters. The series had been called one extended novel. The next eleven hundred pages would bear out that judgment.

Meanwhile, O'Brian himself reviewed books for the *London Review of Books*, where he established himself as an expert on nautical literature. His reputation was growing, not just as a novelist but as a scholar. The reviews of *Joseph Banks* in the spring of 1987 also enhanced his profile as an able historian. The April/May *London Magazine* noted that the "leisurely and witty biography brings this 'genuine' Englishman to life." In the May 7 *London Review of Books*, Peter Campbell wrote: "The book, like Reynold's picture of Banks in his twenties, which O'Brian much admires, is an attractive portrait. It is continuously interesting and coloured by the cheerfulness of a lucky subject."

The April 12 *Observer* took a slightly more critical view: "It's all very amiable—O'Brian believes that 'sailors are friendly creatures upon the whole'—but it makes no pretense of interpretation. . . . Nor can O'Brian register the underside of his cheery hero's activities." Perhaps, for reasons of his own, O'Brian simply believed it better not to judge the man too harshly.

O'Brian was now writing *The Letter of Marque*, a novel that would restore some of Aubrey's luster, thanks to Maturin. On board Maturin's *Surprise*, Aubrey captures the heavy privateer *Spartan*, which had evaded him in the previous novel, and retakes some of her very valuable prizes, earning a small fortune in the process. As the *Surprise* prepares for a secret political mission to South America, she boldly strikes the coast of France, cutting out the French frigate *Diane*, which was to carry Napoleon's political operatives to South America. Finally, Aubrey's father, General Aubrey, dies, apparently causing Jack little grief and removing another obstacle to his reinstatement in the Royal Navy. When Jack's cousin offers him his father's Parliamentary seat of Milport, Aubrey's influence at the Admiralty becomes even stronger. Maturin, meanwhile, travels to Stockholm and reunites with Diana, after nearly killing himself in a fall while on laudanum.

A fortuitous epistolary conversation took place that spring between O'Brian and Bennett, who happened to be rereading the Aubrey-Maturin series. Bennett was preparing a catalog description for an item he was about to offer for sale called *The Battle of Trafalgar: A Heroic Poem*, which had been published in 1806 by a Belfast priest named William Hammond Drummond. Reading the overwrought verse, Bennett thought of O'Brian's versifying lieutenant, James Mowett. He transcribed part of the poem and sent it in a letter to O'Brian. O'Brian read it with amusement and interest. He had just the place for it in his new novel. He wrote back to Bennett saying that he wanted to use the verse and asking him if he would send him more. Bennett did.

Although it is unacknowledged in the novel, when Mowett recites his battle poetry at dinner at Pullings's insistence (*The Letter of Marque*, p. 62), he is actually speaking the lines of the Reverend Drummond.* The verses come from *The Battle of Trafalgar*, book 1, lines 219–26 (though O'Brian omitted line 223):

> *Swift o'er the deep with winged speed they flew*
> *And nearer now the frowning squadrons drew.*
> *"Quick, clear the decks," the shrill-voiced boatswain cries.*
> *"Quick, clear the decks," each hollow ship replies.*
> *The dread command comes tingling on the ear.*
> *Pale grows each cheek, with strange unwonted fear:*
> *All stand a moment, lost in fixed amaze,*
> *In awful silence, and unconscious gaze.*

After a brief interruption, he continues with lines 198–201 from book 2 of *The Battle of Trafalgar*:

---

*In other instances, Mowett's poetry sometimes derives from the sailor-writer William Falconer, author of "The Shipwreck" (1762) and other poetry as well as of the famous *Universal Dictionary of the Marine* (1768).

Death strides from ship to ship with sweeping scythe;
On every poop damned fiends of murder writhe,
Demons of carnage ride th'empurpled flood,
Champ their fell jaws, and quaff the streaming blood.

In the fall of 1987, O'Brian finished *The Letter of Marque*, a pleasant task on the whole, for the book to a large degree righted the wrongs to Aubrey that had occurred in *The Reverse of the Medal*. *The Letter of Marque* was also a transitional book, one that now propelled Aubrey and Maturin into a lengthy circumnavigation of the globe. In that sense, *The Letter of Marque* was a prelude, setting up this extended voyage and foreshadowing certain events that would not come to fruition, or at least reach closure, until four books later, in *The Wine-Dark Sea*. This twelfth novel took the pair to parts of the world they had not yet visited and brought the series to a new level of continuity and cohesion.

In September, the Bennetts, who were vacationing on the Costa Brava, in Spain, drove up to Collioure for a visit. O'Brian asked Bennett if he would mind delivering the typescript to his agent, Richard Simon, in England. Bennett agreed, and his effort was not without reward. Not only did he get to read the draft on the way to London, but he returned to England with a five-gallon jug of wine from the 1986 harvest. The typescript had a successful journey; the jug, unfortunately, shattered during the flight.

Collins now decided to abandon the highly stylized Arthur Barbosa covers and try a new, more nautical look for the Aubrey-Maturin series. Paul Wright, the illustrator of O'Brian's paperback covers, was a capable nautical painter, but he was already the illustrator for Dudley Pope's Ramage series, which Collins also published.

When Geoff Hunt, a Wimbledon-based nautical scene painter and former art editor of *Warship Journal*, heard that Collins was looking for an illustrator for its Patrick O'Brian books, he told his agent, Dom Rodi, "Please get me that one." Hunt had painted hundreds of nautical book covers, everything from pleasure yachts to square-riggers to submarines, including Conway Maritime Press's well-known Anatomy of Ships series. But this opportunity was something special. He had read and admired the Aubrey-Maturin novels and was eager to illustrate the covers.

Not only was Hunt a masterful painter, but he was also an accomplished sailor. In 1979, he and his wife had sold their house and sailed to and around the Mediterranean for nine months on their twenty-six-foot yacht *Kipper*, a sloop-rigged Westerly Centaur. Hunt's knowledge of the sea and his painstaking attention to detail endowed his paintings with the same degree of accuracy and evocativeness as O'Brian's writing. It was a perfect match.

During the week before Christmas 1987, Hunt and Rodi had lunch with John Munday, the Collins art director. Munday gave Hunt free reign to create new cover works for all of the previous Aubrey-Maturin books in paperback and the new hardcover, *The Letter of Marque*. His only instruction to Hunt was to leave space for a lettering cartouche on either the left or right side of the illustration. It was a dream come true.

Hunt spent the next month drawing thumbnail sketches of the new covers. His approach was to create close-up pictures of actions, rather than ship portraits. This concept proved to be right on target. Collins accepted the illustrations without change. In February 1988, Hunt executed studies for approval and began painting the cover of *The Letter of Marque*.

While the Aubrey-Maturin books got something of a fresh start, the surviving Russ siblings slipped deeper into old grooves. Like Patrick, they pursued their various intellectual and creative interests. Nora, having long ago left the convent, now lived in Canada near Barney. She gardened, kept bees, and made her own mead. Joan, a mother of eight, wrote poetry and painted. Barney, who had divorced the mother of his two children and remarried, also wrote verse and planned to write an autobiography to capture some of the family history. They had all reached the age where they were prone to reflect on life. Patrick remained a puzzle to Joan and Barney and consequently a frequent topic of conversation. In December 1987, Barney wrote to Joan: "Nora and I noted that it was Pat's birthday—his 73rd—on Saturday, 12th December. It is amazing to think that he has survived so long, considering his frail health and weak chest, bronchitis, etc. in early life." Barney speculated that he would soon hear from his eccentric brother, "as I usually get a copy of his latest book and at least greetings and news in his own style."

The following June, Barney reported to Joan that Pat had recently grown more communicative. In the letter, Barney reflected on earlier days, showing just how indelible the pain of their childhood was. He confessed that he did not like to think about the time in the "unhappy abode" in London, which he thought was particularly hard on the twins. He regretted that Pat

Bombay (HMS Surprise)   Leopard (Desolation Island)

Geoff Hunt's thumbnail sketches drawn in 1988 for the covers of the paperback reprints of the Aubrey-Maturin series. (Courtesy of Geoff Hunt)

had changed his name. Regarding Pat, Barney lamented, "I do wish he would think of himself as a part of the family and that he had not copied Mike in taking the name of O'Brian." As much as Barney wanted to press Patrick on the issue, he knew to let it lie or he would only deepen the rift.

"We ought to keep in touch with one another," Barney concluded, rather wistfully. "Our original team of nine is down to five and it is pretty good to have five of 70 years of age or more still going strong."

For his part, Patrick, having overcome his fear of putting himself under an obligation, had recently asked Barney if he would send him an eagle feather. He wanted to write with a quill and ink. Delighted by the request, Barney found out that it was illegal to export eagle feathers from Canada, so, instead, he sent his brother a set of Canadian goose feathers, along with a formula for making ink. Pat thanked him and reported that the goose feathers worked splendidly.

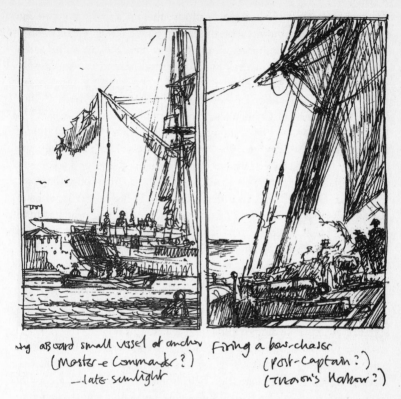

...ny aboard small vessel at anchor
(Master-e Commander?)
—late sunlight

Firing a bow-chaser
(Post-Captain?)
(Treason's Harbour?)

O'Brian's reasons for detaching himself from his family were complex. As much as fending off the pain and anger of what he considered to be an extremely unhappy childhood, isolating himself allowed him the time and focus to write, an activity that now more than ever defined him. He was wary of making commitments to anyone, not just his relatives. His work came first. Yet it is hardly surprising that his family members, with the most reason to expect some attention, felt severely treated. They shared many interests—not to mention their fractured childhoods—in common with their well-known brother, who barely acknowledged them privately, and certainly not publicly. A few well-placed words from Patrick could have gone a long way in smoothing over familial relationships.

But O'Brian was not predisposed to reconciliation, and his work currently demanded all of his powers. He had outlined books thirteen and fourteen of his series and had begun writing thirteen in July 1988. From that year to 1993, between the ages of seventy-four and seventy-nine, he would publish five more Aubrey-Maturin books, 1,435 pages' worth. Making it even more impressive, in both 1989 and 1990, he wrote half a dozen book reviews, most dealing with nautical history, for the *London Review of Books*. He also translated a 615-page abridgment of Jean Lacouture's *Charles de Gaulle: La Rebelle, 1890–1944*, which both Collins Harvill (an imprint of Collins) and Norton published as *De Gaulle: The Rebel, 1890–1944* in 1990. Though *The New Yorker* called O'Brian's translation of the first volume of Lacouture's two-part biography "mediocre," his publishers wanted him to translate the second volume as well. O'Brian had to refuse because it was simply too time-consuming.

Indeed, O'Brian sounded a desperate note in his July 1988 letter to Barney, who had written to say that Elizabeth, his daughter, who had fond memories of her Uncle Pat from their first meeting fourteen years before in Paris, was hoping to see him on her upcoming visit to France. O'Brian wrote back to deter the visit and, it appears, to deter further contact of any sort. He complained of ill health that had depleted both physical and spiritual resolve. He also protested that he had overcommitted to book contracts before discovering the seriousness of the illness and that he would suffer financially if he did not fulfill his obligation.

Barney was disturbed by his brother's cryptic letter, which neither named the illness nor said whether it was he or Mary who was afflicted, making it clear that he wanted no help from Barney. He sent a copy of Pat's "mysterious, gloomy, and thoroughly uncommunicative" letter to Joan. "I have offered to help him," Barney wrote, sounding confused and upset, "but he has declined any form of assistance and as you see, in his final sentence, he talks about 'her affectionate, intelligent family.' Very well, I take it that is his wife, but he does not make it clear and I just wonder whether I am simply being a bother and all I am trying to be is a brother."

Joan, who had long since grown sour and often belittled Patrick's work in her letters to Barney, replied with evident bitterness: "The best thing to do in the face of such persistent rudeness is to maintain an unequivocal silence. He has been consistently blocking all communication with one and all, so why bother?"

Even though Barney strongly discouraged the idea, Elizabeth, her husband, and their two children did stop in Collioure while touring the Pyrenees that summer. Patrick relented. But he did not ask them to the house because, he claimed, Mary was too sick. Instead, he invited Elizabeth alone for lunch at a village café. He brought her a bottle of his home-made wine as a gift and spoke of his pleasure that his novels were being newly promoted. As usual he was circumspect in his conversation. When Elizabeth, who was keen on family history, asked him if he had a son in England, he flatly denied it. Although she had heard differently, she let the subject drop.

In the winter of 1988–89, a rare hawfinch came to O'Brian's window, and a robin, to his delight, nested in the orange tree in the garden. Another cause for joy was a significant new weapon that he had added to his arsenal of period sources, thanks to the efforts of Stuart Bennett, and to his and Mary's willingness to make sacrifices and extend their budget. In September 1988, Bennett had spotted the twenty-volume 1810 *Encyclopaedia Britannica* for sale at Christie's South Kensington. O'Brian had given him the go-ahead, and Bennett had bought the set for £300.

The arrival of the volumes in Collioure had been aggravatingly delayed by a strike of customs officials in France. Nevertheless, by the end of November, they were in O'Brian's hands, and he was able to slowly peruse the velvety pages contained between dark calf covers. He marveled at the wealth of information, all of which, of course, fit the epoch of his novels.

In London, Collins published *The Letter of Marque* at the end of 1988. The book was well received in the January 5, 1989, *London Review of Books*. Taking his cue from the novel's final, joyful scene, in which the characters sing lines from Mozart's *The Marriage of Figaro*, Peter Campbell called the book "both serious and light-hearted, true and sentimental, as comic opera can be."

O'Brian loved the distinctive new look for the series that Collins established with Geoff Hunt. He had executed a remarkable illustration that fit *The Letter of Marque* in both style and tone. From the fore-masthead of the *Surprise*, two sailors examine a potential prize on the horizon. Beneath them a topgallant sail billows in the wind. The scene is dramatic but not melodramatic, beautiful but real, as vivid as a jewel. Hunt credited O'Brian's brilliant writing for inspiring his art. He found exhilarating that moment when an account of a chase or a battle or a storm burned into his mind an image for a painting. "The true magic, the incandescence when something far off in time or space seems suddenly real, is to be found in the subject itself," he later explained. "For nothing can quite match the electrifying instant when historical research jumps into life." A vivid captain's log or a description in James's *Naval History* could do it. But O'Brian could do it best of all. Stated the artist: "[He] possesses in a high degree the magic . . . to hot-wire the past directly to present life."*

Even O'Brian was impressed by the precision of Hunt's ship. In fact, Hunt had read not only O'Brian's book but many of the same sources O'Brian used in writing. Whenever Hunt painted a historical ship, he researched every detail, from the tonnage and beam to the heights and rakes of the masts and special distinguishing details of sail, armament, ships' boats, and sailors' dress. His goal went beyond evocative representation. He wanted to get each line, each spar exactly right. Hunt and O'Brian were cut from the same cloth.

With this twelfth book, O'Brian finally teamed up with the artist who would put the face on the Aubrey-Maturin series. Hunt's paperback covers all lived up to his first one. Collins approved the studies with little more than a pat on the back. The only glitch was that they decided after the fact that the title cartouche would always be on the left-hand side of the cover. Hunt had already painted scenes with a right-hand space for *H.M.S. Surprise* and *The Fortune of War*. So Collins had to print them in reverse. This created a few inaccuracies: a minor error in the rigging and a city on the wrong bank of the river in the former, and a marine on the gundeck, firing his musket left-handed, which, according to Hunt, never would have happened, in the latter.

O'Brian praised the illustrator without reserve. The choice of Hunt, he later said, was a stroke of brilliance. In Hunt's paintings he could see a play of light and shadow that reminded him of the work of the great eighteenth-century Venetian painter Canaletto. With seamen dwarfed by ships and by nature, the scenes were infused with awesomeness. In the cut of an angle, a gleam of light, an expanse of sea, sky, or sail, Hunt communicated tension and much more, including the mood of O'Brian's books. O'Brian appreciated the spirit of the work, and so did his readers.

The Letter of Marque was not published in the United States until two years later, when it received high acclaim in a pivotal retrospective review by Richard Snow in the *New York Times Book Review*. While O'Brian remained all but forgotten in the United States, in Collioure, he busily finished up his next book.

*Quotations taken from Geoff Hunt's essay "Geoff Hunt RSMA," in *The Tall Ship in Art*, pp. 90–92.

In *The Thirteen Gun Salute*, he delayed Aubrey and Maturin's voyage to Chile and Peru due to Spain's having learned of their mission to subvert these Spanish territories. Instead, he carried the pair to the South China Sea, where they escort the British envoy and orientalist Edward Fox in the frigate *Diane* to a fictional equatorial island called Pulo Prabang. On the way, they pass through the Sunda Strait and stop at Batavia, Java, where they meet an actual historical figure, Stamford Raffles, who served as Java's lieutenant governor–general from 1811 to 1816 before going on to found Singapore in 1819. The *Diane* heads north from Batavia to Pulo Prabang, where Fox is to negotiate a treaty with the sultan to ensure the safety of East India Company ships along the east Sumatran coast. However, on Pulo Prabang Aubrey and Maturin confront their old nemeses Andrew Wray and Ledward, who, it turns out, are homosexual lovers, like the notorious so-called Cambridge spies Guy Burgess and Donald Maclean.

Burgess and Maclean defected to the Soviet Union in 1951; Ledward and Wray, their fictional counterparts, having been tipped off to their impending arrest by a third traitor, the highly placed duke of Habachtsthal, have fled to France. Now openly French agents, Ledward and Wray are on Pulo Prabang to sway the sultan to the French side, but with the help of Maturin, Fox prevails in gaining the alliance for Britain. In so doing, he apparently arranges the assassination of Ledward and Wray (Maturin's participation is unclear, but his sentiment is certain). If ever any doubt existed about what O'Brian, the former intelligence agent, felt about traitors such as Burgess and Maclean, he made it clear here: to dispose of the bodies of the two spies ("Burgess and Maclean in wigs and knee breeches," as one reviewer would describe them), Maturin and his associate Cornelius van Buren quite happily dissect them.

O'Brian finished *The Thirteen Gun Salute* in late February and dispatched to London what he confessed was a rather messy typescript, one not up to Mary's usual standards, perhaps because of her poor health, which might have caused Patrick to peck out the story in his rudimentary fashion. Ollard promptly sent back his comments on another very agreeable work, never mind its appearance. He had only one reservation: O'Brian had again sprung off into the realm of fantasy when he sent Maturin on a walk through a preternaturally peaceful valley on Pulo Prabang to a Buddhist temple at Kumai, where wild animals eat from the palm of his hand. Like the episode in *Post Captain* in which Aubrey trekked hundreds of miles through France dressed as a bear, this one stretched the limits of credibility, but it was less integral to the plot than the earlier device had been. To Ollard, it was clearly O'Brian's fancy, and the editor might have been tempted to invoke the advice of Samuel Johnson's college tutor: "Where ever you meet with a passage which you think is particularly fine, strike it out." Instead, he tactfully suggested that perhaps the scene was structurally out of place. O'Brian shrugged off the advice. The scene was dear to his heart, and Mary had approved it. End of conversation.

The scene was perhaps a bit self-indulgent on O'Brian's part, but then, for all intents and purposes, as he had shown with *Testimonies*, after he had written a book and incorporated Mary's suggestions, he listened to only one critic—himself. While his occasional flights of fancy did stand apart from the rest of his writing, they were entertaining. They were also useful in undercutting the tendency of readers and critics to become prepossessed with the books' high degree of historical accuracy.

The year 1989 was one of upheaval for the aging O'Brians, both personally and professionally. With Patrick turning seventy-five, his career was outlasting those of his editorial colleagues, many of whom would soon retire. But this was also a breakthrough year for O'Brian.

In the spring, Patrick and Mary arranged a two-week trip to England. The plan was to arrive in London on April 2, stay at the Challoner, an inexpensive old hotel in central London, for several days, and then travel down to Burnham-on-Sea in Somerset, which Patrick jokingly referred to as Burnham-on-Mud, to see Mary's mother, Frieda, at her nursing home. Patrick intended to meet Ollard, who now lived in the coastal town of Bridport, at a convenient pub between the two towns.

While they were in England, however, Frieda Wicksteed suffered a stroke. Mary rushed to the nursing home, where she and her relatives kept a vigil during the ninety-nine-year-old's last days. Naturally, it was a time when old family wounds were revisited. One evening she met her nephew, Peter, there. "Does Granny realize what happiness Patrick has given me all these years?" she asked him in a flash of insecurity, suddenly acutely aware of the effects of her husband's foibles on the family. Taken aback, Peter quickly realized that this troubling, pent-up doubt over whether Patrick was appreciated by everybody had surfaced in her distress. "Of course," he reassured her. "Everyone realizes what a good husband Patrick is."

Frieda died on April 15. Among her last wishes were that her nurse be given a wedding present upon her upcoming nuptials and that the family's old cook should continue to have her coal cellar filled every September. For herself she wanted no flowers, no mourners, and her family to have a good lunch after a private service.

Before the sad news of Frieda's death, there had been some cause for celebration. Simon had finalized a deal with W. W. Norton to publish the Aubrey-Maturin series in the United States. *Master and Commander* and *Post Captain* would appear in paperback in the spring of 1990 and *The Letter of Marque* in hardcover in the fall. This was in essence found money because it involved an advance payment and no additional work. But, though there was cause for optimism—Norton was a substantial and prestigious publishing house—O'Brian could not allow his expectations, based on past experience in the United States, to rise too high.

For the Collins editors, the deal marked the end of more than a decade of frustration at trying to bring O'Brian back to the U.S. market, but poor timing sullied the moment. Rupert Murdoch took over the firm in 1989, merging it with Harper and Row to form HarperCollins and bringing on a new era of uncertainty and shifting personnel, including the departure of Ian Chapman.

As well, Richard Simon retired that year. He had been suffering from bouts of debilitating fatigue for some years and was finally diagnosed with myalgic encephalomyelitis (better known as chronic fatigue syndrome in the United States and as ME in Britain). He needed rest and rural life. Vivien Green, Simon's longtime assistant, had taken on a greater share of the work as his illness progressed. Popular with publishers and authors but tough when necessary, Green now became O'Brian's agent. As the old guard faded out, O'Brian, now seventy-five and the oldest of them all, was about to find the widespread recognition so long denied him, as well as the spotlight of literary fame.

For now, life continued in Collioure as usual. In the evenings, O'Brian had long taken great pleasure in listening to music and reading, primarily his time-worn companions, Chaucer, Proust, Gibbon, Johnson, Austen, the Russian writers, which he preferred to read in French translation rather than English, as well as Virgil, Horace, and Catullus. In the summer of

1989, he read all of Homer, in Chapman's translation, often on the warm evenings outside under the stars.

He also learned that Barney, now living very comfortably as a retired barrister, was writing an autobiography that mentioned him. Infuriated, he fired off a stern letter to his brother. His reprimand so upset Barney that the latter wrote to Joan, complaining about it:

> I have had the most fearful letter from Patrick. I really think he thinks he is not my brother. I do not know why he took on the name of O'Brian, copying Mike . . . but I have his birth certifi-cate anyway and whether he likes it or not, I claim him as my brother. He is frightfully anxious that the book I am putting out about the family should make no reference to him, as far as possible. I cannot help having him in the family group, but I do not show him as Patrick O'Brian, I just show him as Pat and that ought to satisfy him. . . . He scolds me for referring inces-santly to my helping him financially to build his house. . . . The tone of his letter is so violent that I think we have to call an end to friendly correspondence.

Patrick and Barney ceased writing to each other.

With his translation of the massive de Gaulle book safely behind him, O'Brian was now swimming along in his next naval tale, but he had a second project going as well. He still wanted to write a novel outside his tried-and-true series. On his desk, he had what he considered to be an excellent start for a Gothic tale, inspired in part from a stay with friends in a southern Austrian castle with a Romanesque chapel and a bear pit, through which the servants once had to carry meals, or so he liked to jest. This was the setting for the unfolding of a series of emotional crises based on his own life and the experiences of some friends. He was excited about the possibilities, perhaps even more so because it involved the risks inherent in stepping off his well-worn track.

While the Gothic novel turned in his mind, so too did *The Nutmeg of Consolation*. On Aubrey and Maturin's return to Batavia following their mission to Pulo Prabang, O'Brian marooned them on a deserted island. To envision this setting, where Maturin, the best shot on the ship, hunts boar to feed the crew (and to indulge Aubrey's delight in soused pig's face),

O'Brian sketched a map of the oval island, elongated east to west, with a point jutting out from the southwestern edge. He roughed in cliffs on the north side. A cruel reef lies to the south, and the landing beach is on the island's southern rim, with a makeshift cricket pitch just to the west. He jotted down the dates of the monsoons for Sarawak, on the western end of the northern coast of Borneo, which he figured were valid for his island. He completed the first two chapters by late July.

O'Brian could now savor the coming release of the Aubrey-Maturin series in paperback in the United States. That market was like a Manila galleon lying halfway around the world, strange, unfathomable, immensely rich. But success was still a longshot. From his vantage in rural France, what was about to happen there was almost unthinkable.

That fall, southern France produced one of its most spectacular grape harvests, and the O'Brians' haul was half a ton of luscious fruit. O'Brian also allowed himself to be profiled in the *Sunday Times Magazine*'s column "A Life in the Day," coincidental with the publishing of *The Thirteen Gun Salute*. The profile, about his workday, appeared on November 5, 1989. A photograph showed him, white hair combed neatly back and to the side, prominent ears flanking his gaunt face, a thin, unaffected smile, looking confident and amiable. Wearing a blue checked dress shirt, with rolled-up sleeves, and khaki pants, the expatriate writer in the sunny south of France was, for his age, the picture of health. Deep grooves under his eyes and from his nose to his chin gave him a distinguished air, and the otherwise smooth tanned skin on his face belied his seventy-five years.

He looked like the moderately successful, midcareer writer that he had become, albeit at a more elevated age than most. In the profile, O'Brian even dropped his characteristic reserve, happily revealing details of his closely guarded private life: "When I go to bed, and I'm listening to some tricky contrapuntal music, one part of my mind follows it closely, while another part carries on with the book I am writing," he confessed. "That's when the dialogue takes fire—and I laugh, or cry 'God damn your eyes!',—angering Mary, because it wakes her up. So I may go into the next room and write down a snatch."

Peter Campbell's review of *The Thirteen Gun Salute* in the January 25, 1990, *London Review of Books* was kind without approaching hyperbole: the book was, he noted, "as entertaining as its predecessors." Campbell's best insight was his assertion that part of the novels' effectiveness lay in "the escape they offer from present anxiety into past discomfort. . . . when wildernesses were challenging, not fragile." These discomforts and challenges being met by able bodies, "the final escape for the reader is into a fantasy of competence."

Following the release of *The Thirteen Gun Salute* in the United States, Thomas Flanagan, author of *The Year of the French* (1979), the highly regarded historical novel about the Irish Uprising of 1798, would write in the August 4, 1991, *New York Times Book Review,* "These eccentric, improbable novels seem to have been written by Patrick O'Brian to please himself in the first instance, and thereafter to please those readers who may share his delight in precision of language, odd lands and colors, a humane respect for such old-fashioned sentiments as friendship and honor. Like Aubrey and Maturin playing Mozart duets beneath a Pacific moon, he works elegant variations on the tradition of the seafaring adventure story."

Indeed, O'Brian did write his naval tales for himself and Mary. They delighted in the nine lives of his jokes, the lavish recapitulation of plots in the manner of a master storyteller rekindling his epic saga, and the occasional flights of fancy, such as Maturin's recent visit to a peaceable kingdom. He had created a realm that enchantingly existed outside time, and that provided balm for the soul and spiritual courage to face a less ideal world. His readers found the same solace and strength in these transcendent tales.

O'Brian's own life was anything but tranquil. From the death of his mother-in-law to health concerns at home, from turmoil in the Russ family to the turnover at his publisher and his literary agency, his life spun out of control. To take it to a nerve-racking extreme, his stepson Nikolai Tolstoy, accused of libel by Lord Aldington, who as Brigadier Toby Low was the chief of staff to the commander of V Corps in 1945, lost his case in court, and record damages of £1.5 million were awarded against him.

Tolstoy had written a well-received book, *The Secret Betrayal (Victims of Yalta)*, which made a case for the guilt of British officials who, he claimed, at the Yalta Conference in February 1945, sent seventy thousand Cossacks and Yugoslavs to death at the hands of Joseph Stalin and Tito. The book altered public opinion on an important historical event, and a memorial to the victims was even erected in London. However, Tolstoy also associated himself with a defamatory pamphlet written by one Nigel Watts that claimed Aldington had "the blood of 70,000 innocent men, women and children on his hands" (*Daily Telegraph,* October 14, 1997). Aldington sued Watts. Tolstoy, sure that he could prove his claims, demanded to be included in the suit. It was an act that would haunt him.

There were appeals, and the litigation dragged on, casting a pall over Tolstoy's household. And so O'Brian could later write on solid authority in *The Yellow Admiral,* "There is nothing worse for children than a house with lawsuits hanging over it—threats they do not understand—universe crumbling—parents nearly always sad or cross—perpetually anxious" (p. 21). Losing the trial left Tolstoy virtually penniless, his seventeenth-century Oxfordshire estate massively encumbered. With four children in school, Nikolai and his wife, Georgina, struggled to pay tuitions. The O'Brians contributed what they could. In Collioure, the financial Cerberus reared its heads once again.

O'Brian did all he could do: he kept writing. In early March 1990, he finished *The Nutmeg of Consolation.* In this, the fourteenth Aubrey-Maturin episode, he turned to the famous wreck of the *Alceste* in 1817 for historical inspiration. Under the command of Captain Murray Maxwell, the *Alceste* had left England in February 1816 with Lord Amherst and his embassy to China. They were to present a list of grievances that English subjects had suffered under the rule of the emperor of China. But Amherst was not allowed to meet with the emperor because he refused to kowtow to him. His mission failed. The *Alceste* carried Lord Amherst away, only to wreck on an uncharted reef in the Straits of Gaspar, off Sumatra.

The event is described in *Narrative of a Voyage in his Majesty's Late Ship Alceste* by John M'Leod, the ship's surgeon, and in the ship's log, held by the Public Record Office in London. O'Brian certainly read one of these sources and probably both. After the ship wrecked, Lord Amherst and his delegation were put on board the ship's barge, and they sailed for Java. Captain Maxwell and the rest remained behind on a marshy island infested with ants, scorpions, and snakes and having no fresh water. The shipwreck attracted a Malay war party, who came to plunder her. A tribe of cannibals, the Battas, finally burned the wreck, ending any hope that the crew would be able to escape by its own means.

O'Brian took certain liberties with the story. For one, he dragged it back in time to the Napoleonic War. For another, he changed the diplomatic delegation, its mission, and its result in a way that spiced up the plot.

Finally, O'Brian carried Aubrey and Maturin and their stranded ship-mates to Batavia on board a Chinese merchant junk. The amiable Governor Stamford Raffles lends Aubrey a new command, the freshly dredged-up twenty-gun *Gelijkheid*, which Aubrey renames the *Nutmeg of Consolation*, after one of the sultan of Pulo Prabang's titles. After pursuing the French frigate *Cornélie*, the *Nutmeg* reunites with the *Surprise* at sea, and Aubrey and Maturin transfer over to renew their voyage to South America. But first they sail to Australia to resupply, stopping en route at Sweetings' Island, where Maturin rescues a pair of native girls, the only survivors of a smallpox epidemic. This was to be one of his defining noble acts, made all the more moving because O'Brian downplayed it—though the girls appeared throughout the rest of the series—and because it was clearly a moment of personal redemption for the author and for his wife.

But O'Brian was too clever to let Maturin get away with such a beatific act scot-free. In Sydney, Maturin makes the layover anything but peaceful, quarreling and fighting a duel with a Captain Lowe and plotting the escape of his former servant Padeen Colman, now an abused convict in Australia. Both of these actions create tension between Maturin and Aubrey, who has promised the governor that there will be no stowaways on board the *Surprise* when she departs.

To O'Brian's great delight, he was able to use a little-known fact about the duck-billed platypus, the animal that his brother Michael had poached during the Depression, as a resolution to the conflict. The species had just been discovered in 1797 in New South Wales and was considered the most unusual mammal known. Maturin aches to encounter one; however, he does not learn until too late that the male platypus's spur has a venomous barb. Although O'Brian had to exaggerate the result of such a sting considerably, he did it persuasively and to good effect. When Colman carries the unconscious Maturin on board, thus saving him, Aubrey relents and lets Colman join the ship.

O'Brian toted the typescript over to England himself, arriving on March 28 for a week's stay. Ollard, who had retired with his wife to their Dorset country home, Norchard Farmhouse, to write, would still read O'Brian's typescripts, primarily to offer moral support and the occasional grammatical and historical point. This time, O'Brian officially presented the book to his new editor, Stuart Proffitt, with whom he also discussed his future plans. After another Aubrey-Maturin book, O'Brian thought he might at last write his Gothic novel, for which he had high hopes. The diversion from Aubrey-Maturin made Proffitt uncomfortable, but he allowed himself to be convinced.

While in England, O'Brian traveled up to Leicestershire to visit Michael Saunders Watson, a retired Royal Navy commander, at Rockingham Castle, which had passed down to Watson from his uncle and O'Brian's friend Sir Michael Culme-Seymour, who now lived in Dorset near Ollard. O'Brian had recently joined Brooks's, a prestigious London men's club established in 1764, where Culme-Seymour, Watson, and Ollard were all members. Watson represented the family's sixth generation of naval officers, and O'Brian had come to see the family naval artifacts, including the log of the second Sir Michael Seymour, who commanded a frigate in the South Atlantic in the 1830s. His father had commanded the frigate *Amethyst* in two famous frigate battles in 1808 and 1809.

O'Brian took pleasure in his social connections, which now reached very high levels. He and Watson, chairman of the British Library, were also part of the informal Naval Historians Dining Club, organized by the naval historian Tom Pocock and meeting at the Garrick Club in London. More and more, O'Brian engaged in a social life through the connections his naval fiction provided him, at a level and in settings that Jack Aubrey and Stephen Maturin were privy to in his fiction. Quite remarkably, the creative current, which usually moves from a writer to his fiction, was showing signs of reversing itself.

By mid-April, Ollard had written an admiring letter to O'Brian with a few notes and corrections. He questioned the historical likelihood of a passage in which Aubrey feels that it is wrong to target an opposing commander in chief. O'Brian had been extrapolating from the duke of Wellington's sharp message to Napoleon about cannonballs falling quite close to him. This time Ollard's point won O'Brian over, and he altered the passage.

For a brief interval, however, O'Brian stretched his legs and relaxed a little. This year, like the previous one, was shaping up well for grapes, and he busily attended to the garden and vineyard, which had been unfortunately neglected during his press to finish the last novel. He read and reviewed Deirdre Bair's biography of Simone de Beauvoir. That O'Brian reserved extra skepticism for American scholars and journalists was obvious to those who knew him. His review of Bair's book ran in the June 9, 1990, *Independent,* and although he called it "the definitive life . . . required reading for anyone concerned with Simone de Beauvoir and the history of feminism," he seemed impressed only by the research, which included interviews with Beauvoir over six years. He criticized Bair's negative attitude toward Beauvoir in the later chapters, implying that they betrayed Beauvoir, who was unable to see them (she had died). He faulted Bair's portrayal of almost everyone in the book as unlikable and unhappy.

O'Brian felt that Bair, like many Americans, played too fast and loose with the language. He called her writing "pedestrian." Bair, a National Book Award winner for her 1978 Samuel Beckett biography, used, he complained, "a mixture of the academic, the folksy colloquial, and American slang, so that we have a 'negative role model', 'a tiny bit miffed', 'gypped' or 'running interference'." Finally, Bair's grasp of French cultural nuances seemed insufficient to O'Brian. In reading the book, he observed, "After a while one begins to realise how very wide the Atlantic is."

However, the United States would not go away. In mid-June, O'Brian was in London, where he met and dined with Charlton Heston and his son Fraser, who were there for the debut of the movie *Treasure Island*, which Fraser had written, produced, and directed and in which his father had acted. O'Brian found the elder Heston a friendly companion and gratifyingly familiar with Aubrey and Maturin.

In Heston, O'Brian made an exception to his general dislike of America and Americans, a prejudice, although not entirely untested, that he had lived with since perhaps World War II. Then professional rivalry might have colored his view, as British intelligence officers had considered their U.S. counterparts inferior and resented their upper hand due to American military dominance. O'Brian had later somewhat haughtily declined aiding the promotion of *Master and Commander* in the United States, and the dark decade when his Aubrey-Maturin novels were not published there had added weight to this ill feeling.

However, conditions were about to change dramatically for O'Brian in the United States. A bright, determined editor was about to support his work, an enthusiastic journalist to lionize it, and the public to embrace him. He would have to reconsider his feelings.

Part VI

GOLD

21

The Best Writer
You Never
Heard Of?

1990–1992

A man in pursuit of his living will immerse himself in any
number of difficult tasks required of him, but when it comes to
reading novels nothing will induce him to attempt anything
difficult; a publisher who thinks he will induce a public or find
a readership for novels that have never achieved popularity, is
of course a mad philanthropist, a self-righteous lunatic if he
thinks he can influence or change general taste.

—Herbert van Thal, *The Tops of the Mulberry Trees,* 1971

Just why the Aubrey-Maturin novels had never caught on in the United
States is hard to say, but following the dismal experiences of Lippincott
and Stein and Day, U.S. publishers for years had not dared pick up the
series again, no matter how positive the reviews in Britain. Still, as in the
early days there, O'Brian's books had found some fertile soil in the New
World. Throughout the O'Brian-less decade, a small, potentially influential group doggedly followed his work. They prevailed upon English
friends or American expatriates living in England to mail over each volume
in the series, or they relied upon book dealers to mysteriously produce the
coveted work, almost as if it were contraband.

Among these devotees were New York City writers Mark Horowitz
and Richard Snow. They and their friends devoured each new novel—
bootlegged from England—like a brotherhood of monks anxiously

awaiting the next gilt-lettered scroll. "We would show the books to our publisher friends," recalls Horowitz. "But they wouldn't get it. No one would publish him here."

As O'Brian's reputation increased in Britain, however, friends of a New York City editor named Starling Lawrence urged him to take a look at the books. A 1965 Princeton graduate, Lawrence had done stints at Cambridge and in the Peace Corps, where he taught English to French-speaking Cameroonians, before becoming a reader for Evan Thomas and Eric Swenson, prominent editors at W. W. Norton, one of the more staid and cerebral Manhattan publishers. Lawrence had proven his good eye when he plucked James Grady's *Six Days of the Condor* (1974) from the slush pile. The spy thriller became a best-seller. Around the same time, he became involved with another of Norton's major successes, Vincent Bugliosi's *Helter Skelter* (1974), the prosecutor's story of Lawrence's Charles Manson murders.

Lawrence, a tall, gangly man, with deep-set eyes and a boyish sense of humor, had a knack for pushing the boundaries at Norton and scoring big. One of his lucrative discoveries was Dr. Martin Katahn, whose third diet book, *The Rotation Diet* (1986), sold 800,000 copies. The year 1989 would be the most momentous of Lawrence's editorial career. He published *Liar's Poker*, a colorful exposé of greed, gall, and testosterone on Wall Street by the former Salomon Brothers bond trader Michael Lewis. The book quickly became a best-seller. Lawrence's other big discovery that year could not have been more diametrically opposed in subject matter to the cynical, money-loving world of Wall Street.

While in London scouting for books, the editor happened to be in the offices of the literary agency Sheil Land, which had bought Richard Simon's agency upon his retirement. There Lawrence saw Vivien Green, who had joined Sheil Land and oversaw Simon's clients. Lawrence noticed several paperback copies of O'Brian's books on a shelf. He remembered the words of his cousin: "How can you call yourself a publisher and allow this man to remain unpublished in the U.S.?" And he recalled Stephen Becker's enthusiasm for the books. A sudden, fortuitous impulse overcame what Lawrence later laughingly called his "deep abiding aversion to boats of every sort," a condition he had acquired after one distressing summer of sailing lessons at Fisher's Island, where he came in last in every race.

Green gladly gave Lawrence the books. On the flight home, he opened *The Reverse of the Medal* and fell into the rhythm of O'Brian's prose. He had virtually no background in nautical history, and he simply let the language wash over him, he later recalled in *Publishers Weekly*, like "the high sea off the side of the deck," feeling fully satisfied that this author "wasn't talking through his hat."

"It was a slow fuse," he said later, "but it took hold." Slow for a New York publisher perhaps; a quarter of the way through the book, he decided that he wanted to publish O'Brian. This was not Hornblower redux, he had discovered, much to his delight, but a subtly written, multi-textured novel of manners that gained energy and appeal by being set during Nelson's age. Unlike so many Forester copycats, it did not owe its existence simply to the action of that era and to Britain's nostalgia for the days when its empire stretched around the globe.

But it was the climax of the novel, where Jack Aubrey is pilloried for rigging the stock market, a crime of which he is innocent, that convinced Lawrence of O'Brian's greatness. O'Brian had brilliantly tapped the emotional potential of that moment to create a heartrending scene. If it wasn't clear before that O'Brian was looking deeply into the human soul through his naval stories, then it was now.

Lawrence was under no illusions. Relaunching the series would not be easy. Taking over a mature author in midstream was hard enough, but when it was one whose work already had the taint of failure, it was almost a no-win situation. Just convincing his own sales staff to put their hearts into selling books that had already proven to be nonstarters in the marketplace was a daunting task. He would be sticking out his neck, and if he lost credibility on this seemingly perverse and personal mission, it could damage his influence for the rest of his authors. Nonetheless, convinced that O'Brian's writing was extraordinary, he was willing to give it a try. From a business standpoint, the fact that thirteen titles existed and O'Brian was still writing meant that even with marginal sales, the potential upside was meaningful.

Deciding to give O'Brian another chance was perhaps the highest hurdle to leap, but there were plenty more. As Lawrence set about persuading financial and marketing executives at W. W. Norton to revive the series in the United States, the world's biggest book market, there were many ponderous questions: Should they launch the series in hardcover or paperback? Should they start at the beginning or with O'Brian's new novel? If the latter, how would they bring the readers up to speed on what had already transpired in the series? If the former, were they risking a repetition of failure? (Lawrence felt that *Master and Commander*, though, of course, the natural place to enter the series, was one of the more difficult books.) How would they create a fresh image for the series?

Adding pressure to complication was the fact that the launch needed to happen quickly if Norton wanted to capitalize on the publication of O'Brian's upcoming book, *The Nutmeg of Consolation*. Reviewers, after all, would be far more likely to write about this new hardcover book than paperback rereleases of old books. Despite some skeptics at Norton, Lawrence convinced the publishers to make a big play.

The editor negotiated through Anne Borchardt, Vivien Green's corresponding agent in the United States, for a package of rights, including new releases and the backlist, meaning that if Lawrence's instincts proved correct, Norton stood to benefit greatly from O'Brian's revival. When Norton finally published *Master and Commander* and *Post Captain* in paperback in August 1990, it became evident that many lessons had been learned since the days when Lippincott and Stein and Day had groped in the dark to convey to readers that these books were the rarest of species: well-written page-turners.

Norton had a tradition of publishing good-quality nonfiction books about the sea and had taken the high road, where it was clear from the critical acclaim in Britain that there should be some appeal. The cover of *Master and Commander* carried a beautiful painting by Geoff Hunt of the tiny brig *Sophie* in port at Minorca. Inside, an elegant nineteenth-century illustration from marine painters to the Crown Dominick and John Thomas Serres' *Liber Nauticus* named the sails of a square-rigged ship. On the back cover was a thoughtful quote from Stephen Becker: "O'Brian is literature, and I read and reread him with awe and gratitude. . . . If I could keep only half a dozen contemporary writers O'Brian would be one of them."

It was just the right touch, sophisticated but not too heavy. Norton's tactics worked. Compare *Publishers Weekly*'s original review of *Post Captain* in 1972 ("overwritten for so little plot") to its enthusiastic July 6, 1990, review of *The Letter of Marque*: "The early-19th-century locutions are fascinating, as are the evocation of period shipboard life (including ship-provisioning and naval lingo), Whitehall politics (rotten boroughs, etc.) and drug addiction (coca leaf-chewing as well as opium-eating). Seafarers and landlubbers alike will enjoy this swift, witty tale of money and love."

However, on October 7, 1990, the bottom appeared to fall out of

Lawrence's courageous effort to revive O'Brian's series. In the *New York Times*, Newgate Callendar, a pseudonymous reviewer, sneeringly reviewed *The Letter of Marque*. "Most likely Patrick O'Brian snarls with rage every time a reviewer points out that his sea stories are derived from C. S. Forester's Horatio Hornblower series," he wrote. "But it is true, and never truer than in *The Letter of Marque*."

Callendar must have skimmed the book, and he certainly had not read the rest of the series, for he continued: "[O'Brian] does not have Forester's flair. His Capt. Jack Aubrey has none of Hornblower's complexity and charm. And Mr. O'Brian's writing is rather long-winded, even turgid. . . . [Aubrey] does pull off a brilliant coup, and it's a shame that it's hard to grow interested in so colorless a figure." It is difficult to imagine anyone truly acquainted with the series calling Aubrey colorless. Bluff, absolutely; insensitive and imprudent, yes; simple-minded, certainly, at times; but Aubrey—whose face had "the mark of a cutlass-slash from one ear right across the cheek-bone and another scar, this one from a splinter, along the line of the jaw to the other ear"(*The Surgeon's Mate*, p. 49)—was anything but colorless.

One can easily sympathize with O'Brian's pain at seeing his opus, so long underrated, assassinated so glibly. Callendar's comparison of O'Brian to Forester hardly needs to be addressed now. By contrast, consider Oxford don John Bayley's far better informed assessment of the Aubrey-Maturin novels in the *London Review of Books* in 1987: "These are emphatically not adventure stories, or the sort of mechanical marine thrillers which sprung up in the wake of C. S. Forester. Smollett and Marryat are being re-written less for the excitement than for the feeling."

But the damage, in the most influential newspaper in the United States and in the publishing industry, was done. O'Brian's hopes of redemption, so near, seemed to be dashed. How terribly ironic it was to have had his book *Testimonies* praised in a comprehensive review at the expense of Evelyn Waugh, Angus Wilson, and Ernest Hemingway, and now, some forty years into his career, to have *The Letter of Marque* denigrated beside the novels of Peter Tonkin, Bernard Cornwell, and Paul Bishop.

O'Brian was heartsick. For a while, he found it impossible to work, and he set aside the manuscript of the next book. In this dark moment, it looked as if the idea to revive the series in the United States had been a mistake. The dread of having to suspend publication of the series halfway through had haunted Lawrence from the very start. It would be like abandoning an orphan on the street. It would be a public embarrassment. In fact, ever since he had convinced his colleagues to publish the series, Lawrence later confessed, he had been motivated to succeed more by the fear of failure than by the potential of selling thousands of copies.

Callendar's review aside, some inexplicable barrier to commercial success seemed to thwart O'Brian's novels in the United States. Perhaps it was the crossing of genres. It was, and remains, an axiom of publishing that a book needs to fall into a specific, nameable category to sell. Publishers want to know exactly which bookstore shelf a title will be sold on before they will commission it. The Aubrey-Maturin novels were too well written, too nuance-laden, and too challenging to be classified as adventure-genre stories. They certainly weren't for children or even for any but the most advanced young adults. But could historical fiction, a genre generally shunned by critics and scholars, make it in the literature section? At this point, it looked as if the answer was no.

Come what may, Lawrence had no doubt that he could bear up; however, he worried about O'Brian, whom he deemed to be the most deserving author he knew. It distressed him that O'Brian quite likely would have to suffer the humiliation of failing all over again in the United States.

Fortunately, Mark Horowitz, now living in Los Angeles, had already set other wheels in motion. He had not forgotten the many years of reading bootleg copies of Aubrey and Maturin and the rebuffed suggestions to publisher friends. When he had found out that there was an editor brave enough to give O'Brian another shot, he decided to help out. He called his old friend Richard Snow, who had since become editor of *American Heritage* magazine. "You have to do something," Horowitz told Snow, who had not yet heard the news of O'Brian's rerelease in the United States. "O'Brian has an American publisher for five minutes." Snow said he would see what he could do.

Meanwhile, Norton busily played catch-up. The company had made a commitment to the author, and it was not going to cave in at the first signs of adversity. It still planned to issue the next four titles—books three to six—in paperback in 1991.

Urged on by Horowitz, Snow took advantage of this opportunity. Hence sprang O'Brian's, and indeed Lawrence's, redemption—in the form of a lucid, unequivocal statement about O'Brian's work. In his front-cover essay, "An Author I'd Walk the Plank For," in the January 6, 1991, *New York Times Book Review,* Snow not only praised *The Letter of Marque* but also stated that the Aubrey-Maturin novels constitute "what I continue to believe are the best historical novels ever written." This clean assessment sliced through the usual book babble like an arrow through straw, and it lodged fast in the consciousness of the nation's fiction readers.

Snow went on to say, "On every page Mr. O'Brian reminds us with subtle artistry of the most important of all historical lessons: that times change but people don't, that the griefs and follies and victories of the men and women who were here before us are in fact the maps of our own lives." Snow's eloquent endorsement pierced, if only for a moment, the stigma associated with historical fiction. And if these works were, as he claimed, the best ever written, they had the potential of elevating the genre, perhaps even changing it. Now even literary snobs could afford to give O'Brian a chance. And they did. Positive word of mouth began to flow.

While Snow's watershed review was seeping into the minds of American book readers, *The Nutmeg of Consolation,* book number fourteen in the Aubrey-Maturin series, arrived in British bookstores. T. J. Binyon's February 23 review in the *Independent* contained another powerful and emphatic statement in support of the author:

> On 1 April 1800, during a performance of Locatelli's C major quartet in the music-room of the Governor's house in Port Mahon, Minorca, a penniless Irish physician drives a hostile elbow into the ribs of a naval lieutenant without a ship. It is perhaps the most productive affront in fiction since April 1625, when d'Artagnan, rushing headlong down the stairs of M de Treville's house on the rue Vieux-Columbier in pursuit of the Chevalier de Rochefort, accidentally insulted the three musketeers.

Binyon went on to make a favorable comparison with Leo Tolstoy.

Shortly before Binyon's critique, fittingly on February 14, the anniversary of the Battle of Cape St. Vincent (where Admiral Sir John Jervis, with the help of Captain Horatio Nelson, defeated the Spanish in 1797), British author and 1990 Booker Prize–winner A. S. Byatt had reviewed the book with great enthusiasm for the *Evening Standard*. Byatt had begun reading the series on the recommendation of her friend Iris Murdoch; Murdoch had recommended O'Brian's books several times to her, but she kept forgetting his name. Finally, she had tried *Master and Commander* a few times and had given up. It was too complicated and moved too slowly. But another writer friend, Francis Spufford, had brought her a copy in France, where she did much of her creative work and where her library was dominated by the likes of Nietzsche and Freud. She had taken O'Brian to bed with her one night. This time the mood had been just right, and off she had sped into a deep romance with the series.

Praising the wide-ranging plot of *The Nutmeg of Consolation*, Byatt concluded: "I experienced desolation on reaching the end of this, O'Brian's 14th book—but am told that the next is half written. I can hardly wait."

Since O'Brian was now in his late seventies, Byatt wasn't the only reader to find the author's progress with the saga—not just completing the next episode but moving toward some grand, or otherwise, conclusion—a topic of speculation. How would he end the series? He couldn't possibly leave his readers hanging, with Aubrey and Maturin halfway through some remote mission for the Admiralty. Or could he? Certain important events in Aubrey's life and career were based on the life of Thomas Cochrane, the legendary frigate captain. Would O'Brian turn to historical events to find a conclusion? Following the stock market scandal that destroyed his reputation, Cochrane found vindication by leading the navies of Chile and Peru in overthrowing Spanish colonial rule. Here he displayed his intrepidity and leadership abilities on a grander scale than he could have as a cog in the Royal Navy, and he was restored subsequently to the post captain's list.

But while O'Brian might have felt some pressure to push to a grand conclusion, he was ambivalent about neatly tying up the series. After all, life is rarely endowed with tidy endings. Besides, his writing output had not fallen off, nor had his reviews begun to suffer. As Byatt, herself a capable literary technician and a shrewd critic, wrote in her review of *The Nutmeg of Consolation*:

> O'Brian's narrative pace is always gripping: it shifts its speed
> and provides endlessly varying shocks and surprises—comic,
> grim, farcical, and tragic. An essential of the truly gripping
> book for the narrative addict is the creation of a whole, solidly

living world for the imagination to inhabit, and O'Brian does this with prodigal specificity and generosity.... The writing is as strong and delightfully various as the people and plots. And everything—skies and seas and ports and creatures—is vivid and sensuously present.

Prodigal specificity and generosity! There was no condescension here, no kindly comments suggesting that the tales were nice for a writer rapidly approaching his ninth decade but not what they used to be. In fact, the voyage that began in *The Thirteen Gun Salute* had, to many minds, revitalized the Aubrey-Maturin epic.

Indeed, perhaps by necessity from his own frail youth, O'Brian had set an enviably mellow pace for his life, ripening slowly and fully. As a writer he was a methodical craftsman who gave everything to that craft and received in return the satisfaction of knowing he did a job well, the only reward he could ultimately expect. This is not to say that he did not crave popular and critical recognition. However, such recognition was beyond his control. His greatest accolades would come very late in life. His mind and body were still telling him that he had many more miles to travel with his beloved characters. But perhaps, also, O'Brian did not plan any great crescendo for the series.

In fact, he intimated just this in chapter 9 of *The Nutmeg of Consolation* in a discussion on the endings of novels. There, Maturin's close friend and fellow natural philosopher, the chaplain turned surgeon's mate Nathaniel Martin, questions the importance of endings, citing one Bourville, who he says defined the novel "as a work in which life flows in abundance, swirling without a pause: or as you might say without an end, an organized end" (p. 256). Maturin agrees, quoting an unnamed Frenchman: "*La bêtise c'est de vouloir conclure.** The conventional ending, with virtue rewarded and loose ends tied up is often sadly chilling; and its platitude and falsity tend to infect what has gone before, however excellent" (p. 256).

Those who knew O'Brian well did not expect him to tie off the series in a neat bundle. So inextricably interwoven was his life with his fictional characters and their world that for him this would be tantamount to saying: "Right, I've had a long wonderful life. It's time to end it now." Indeed, as he later approached that seemingly unattainable twentieth

---

*In English, "The absurd thing is the desire to come to a conclusion."

novel, the one that for many years he held out as the carrot, the one that would take Aubrey full circle in his naval career, the one that he had predicted would probably wrap up the series, he began to back off his prediction: "I'm not sure whether I shan't take him a bit beyond full circle, with one or two incidents at the very height of the Royal Navy's glory," he later told *Time* magazine. "I should like simply for my own amusement—and because I don't really see how I can bear easily to live without writing—and at least for my own pleasure—to write one more, or perhaps two."

In the winter and spring of 1991, while U.S. book sales began to mount beyond anything O'Brian had ever seen, he worked on a new Aubrey-Maturin novel, *Clarissa Oakes* (*The Truelove,* in the United States), a largely self-contained episode in the series, which may have drawn its inspiration from U.S. Navy captain David Porter's battles with natives on the South Pacific island of Nuka Hiva. The beginning of the novel saw Aubrey irritable and frustrated, not the least reasons for which were that Maturin had gotten into a bloody duel in Sydney, leading to a distinct lack of cooperation from port officials, and that he had helped a convict escape on board the *Surprise.* "Profound attachment to Stephen Maturin," O'Brian wrote, from Aubrey's point of view, "did not preclude profound dissatisfaction at times: even lasting dissatisfaction" (p. 11).

O'Brian had long since settled on a pattern of reintroducing the characters and updating readers on their recent exploits in the first twenty pages. This also eased him back into the flow of his fictional world. As he wrote, using a detailed outline, he numbered the pages in each chapter separately so that he could carefully control its length. Upon his request, HarperCollins's editorial assistants helped with minor historical research, allowing O'Brian to write without interruption.

But O'Brian was in no hurry to bring Aubrey and Maturin back to the Atlantic. Their eventual arrival in South America to conduct the political mission with which Maturin had been charged so long before in *The Letter of Marque* would be put on hold for another 256 pages while O'Brian took them on a sudden detour through the Pacific. He had contrived a special assignment, involving two cannibalistic tribes warring on a remote fictional island named Moahu: Aubrey simply needed to make sure the victor in the struggle remained loyal to the Crown.

But first O'Brian planted a stowaway on board the *Surprise*, an escaped female convict named Clarissa Harvill, who has been hidden in the cable-tier of the frigate by her lover, the rather hairy but very popular mid-shipman Oakes.* Aubrey, who discovers that the entire crew, including Maturin, has kept her presence a secret from him, is irate. "Everyone knows how I hate a woman aboard," he erupts to Maturin. "They are worse than cats or parsons for bad luck. . . . It will be the lower deck full of Portsmouth brutes next, and a Miss in every other cabin—discipline all to pieces—Sodom and Gomorrah" (p. 33). But Maturin counters, "It is perfectly well known throughout the ship that when you were Oakes' age you were disrated and turned before the mast for hiding a girl in that very part of the ship. Surely you must see that this pope-holy sanctimonious attitude has a ludicrous as well as a most unamiable side?" (pp. 33–34).

Aubrey threatens to turn the couple ashore as soon as he can, and in a droll turn, Maturin orders Aubrey, whom he happens to be treating for a stomach disorder, to bend over a chest for an enema. From his "position of great moral advantage," Maturin lectures his patient in a mutinous manner. "Damn you, Stephen Maturin," Aubrey finally responds, pulling up his pants. "And damn you, Jack Aubrey," Maturin retorts. "Swallow this draught half an hour before retiring: the pills you may take if you do not sleep, which I doubt" (p. 34).

The scene was vintage O'Brian, capturing the complex Aubrey-Maturin relationship like time in a bottle. The two are best friends, but O'Brian never let that friendship grow flabby. Instead, it feeds on its own tension, the pair sometimes struggling to abide each other, to communicate, to convince, pushing the limits of tolerance, but above all tolerating. This last was a commodity the O'Brian family, particularly Patrick, had often been short on. He was certainly not one to suffer a fool. But in this fictional relationship he could demonstrate how friendship should work, and by infusing the scene with his slightly absurd sense of humor, he was able to do it without a heavy hand. It was precisely such passages that his increasingly large devoted readership had come to expect and cherish.

In resolving the matter, Midshipman Oakes marries Clarissa Harvill, and Clarissa Oakes became an important new character for O'Brian, in some ways a female counterpart of Maturin. Oakes, as she later confesses

---

*While O'Brian probably derived the name "Harvill" from Jane Austen's character Captain Harville, "Clarissa" was inspired by Clarissa Harlowe, the heroine of Samuel Richardson's second novel, a cautionary tale against the misconduct of parents and children in relation to the latter's marriage and one that ends in tragedy.

to Maturin, was a sexually abused orphan, who consequently cannot experience sexual desire as an adult. (She is yet another O'Brian character struggling with an inability to love.) Oakes and Maturin form a strong attachment. While they are perhaps too similar to fall in love (not to mention the fact that Maturin is married), their relationship has the tension of a courtship and is the subject of speculation on board ship. O'Brian was pleased with his new character, who allowed him the rare opportunity to explore platonic love between the sexes, and he was anxious to find out how convincingly he had portrayed this unusual female character.

In his notes, O'Brian mapped out Moahu, hourglass-shaped, standing north to south and not too tightly cinched at the waist. He drew five rows of hash marks to indicate hills dividing the island in half, and a circle to denote an old volcano. In the southern half lay the territory of Puolani. A stream ran from the hills to a bay on the south coast, called Eeahu, protected by semicircular shoals to the east and west. The northern half of the island was controlled by the ruler Kalahua. The inlet Pabay, around which this tribe lived, lay to the northeast and was protected by a single bar of shoals. Beneath his map of Moahu, O'Brian drew an inset of Pabay with the path a ship would take in tacking into the harbor.

As he had done in *The Nutmeg of Consolation*, O'Brian created a land battle that proved he was as effective there as he was at sea. The battle occurs offstage. Maturin, who is stationed, as is the reader, downhill from the action, learns of the victory only after two natives come running down the path, each gripping a human head by the hair. Aubrey then relates the ambush and the effect of ten rounds of case shot on a surprised enemy in a narrow jungle lava cleft.

In the spring of 1991, Barney contacted Patrick again. They had not corresponded since 1989, when Patrick reacted so peevishly to Barney's autobiography. Barney had recently been diagnosed with cancer. Patrick sent a sympathetic letter and his two latest books, which greatly pleased his brother. Their relationship, though far from perfect, was restored, which was fortunate since Barney did not have long to live.

Mary's health was very fragile too. She was weak and taking an array of pills and drafts prescribed by a Perpignan doctor. Patrick fretted about her health all summer, but still he finished *Clarissa Oakes*. He found he was proud of his new character Clarissa, but he also knew that he had walked a fine line in pulling her off successfully. Mary assured him that he had.

Ollard read the manuscript and concurred, though he once again warned O'Brian about excessive arcaneness. As a concession, O'Brian agreed to define a Pyrenean "desman," which he did as "that rare ill-natured cousin to the shrew" (p. 185). But as for the Latin phrase *"foeda est in coitu et brevis voluptas"* (p. 165) (meaning, there is a filthiness in sex and only brief pleasure), readers were still on their own.

Now that O'Brian was becoming an established name in less rarefied literary circles, the *Washington Post* asked him to review Tom Clancy's 798-page *The Sum of All Fears*. The behemoth novel clearly caused O'Brian some consternation. In his July 28 review, he even resorted to public self-reference, a rarity for him: "To be sure my first introduction to the book was unpromising: an ill-printed set of pages that would not hold together, an inept blurb and a curiously authoritarian note from the publisher." Despite a slow start, he had read the proof until midnight one night, keeping running notes. He was impressed by Clancy's skill in recounting a series of complex events involving the CIA, the FBI, the Vatican, Arab terrorists, East German intelligence, Israelis, and even a disgruntled Sioux, all leading up to the brink of world war. But he found Clancy's inability to effectively inhabit his characters and to make them come alive disappointing. Each new character, he complained, arrived on the scene with an "artless but interminable interior monologue."

O'Brian presented a theory regarding Clancy, who, he wrote, was "by nature a storyteller, like those sennachies who used to recite genealogies, history, legends and tales in the great Irish houses." Oral storytellers speak primarily of events, O'Brian reasoned, and their characters are revealed by statements and inferences. The storyteller comes at his characters mainly from the outside. On the other hand, the capable novelist has far greater freedom and can come at his characters from the inside, even to the point of presenting streams of consciousness. O'Brian admired Clancy's descriptive powers, just as he admired Forester's, but, he wrote, when Clancy "deals with his people from within it seems to me that he is out of his element, that he labors too hard, that he becomes verbose."

In August, the American reviews of *The Nutmeg of Consolation*, no less approving than the British, rolled off the presses. In the *Washington Post*, Jonathan Yardley wrote that "all of O'Brian's strengths are on parade," although he deemed the book "primarily for insiders—many of whom no doubt will pepper me with missives taking exception to that judgement." In the *Boston Globe*, Robert Taylor called O'Brian's novels

much trickier and more complex than Forester, and less farci-
cal than [George MacDonald] Fraser. . . . O'Brian's off-slant
techniques, his renunciation of big bow-wow scenes—even amid
a cannonade, Aubrey pauses for "a cold collation in the gunroom"—require close attention, likewise the far-ranging web
of wit and allusion. Consider the odd title here, the name of
Aubrey's ship, which is derived from a Malayan phrase. The series
is idiosyncratic and, once you've found your sea legs, captivating.

After all these years, O'Brian was winning an audience in the United
States on his own terms, and soon this exuberant nation, in so many ways
the antithesis of his beloved eighteenth-century England, would do its best
to win him over. The advance on royalties in America now gave way to
royalties, money in the bank. Although neither he nor Mary were at all
avaricious, there were many pleasant ways to employ the new funds.

Among them for Patrick was setting himself up as a proper gentleman in London, much in the fashion of Aubrey and Maturin. In October
1991, he attended a dinner at Brooks's, the St. James's club where he was
a proud new member and which became his home base in that city. At
the dinner, Richard Ollard introduced him to John Saumarez Smith, a
member of the club's library committee and managing director of the
noted Curzon Street bookshop G. Heywood Hill, where Nancy Mitford
worked during World War II.

The next day, O'Brian and Smith ate lunch together in the informal
Spencer Room at Brooks's. Smith mentioned to O'Brian that there were
book dealers who seemed to be making a living selling the relatively rare
first editions of the Aubrey-Maturin novels.

"I am afraid I am going to spoil your lunch," O'Brian responded. "The
publisher is always very generous with copies. But I don't like to give them
to friends because I feel like it puts them under an obligation to read them.
So there they are. They stack up, gather dust, take up space . . ."

"How many books?" asked Smith, his eyebrows arching.

"I should think thirty or forty," replied O'Brian.

"What exactly did you do with the books?" asked the bookseller, a
chagrined smile creeping across his face.

"Just in the last two or three weeks, I took them to the local tip,"
O'Brian said.

Toward the end of lunch, during coffee, O'Brian looked squarely at Smith and said softly, "Tell me, how much are my books worth?"

"Well, it would be very unusual for them to go for less than thirty or forty pounds," Smith said.*

"Now you've spoiled *my* lunch," replied O'Brian.

Coming on top of the laudatory reviews of *The Nutmeg of Consolation*, O'Brian had a new honor in which to bask. In December 1991, he received an invitation to become a fellow of the Royal Society of Literature. He strongly suspected that his friend Richard Ollard, himself a member, had something to do with his election, and he was right. O'Brian joyfully accepted the invitation to join this august group, and he felt special gratitude toward Ollard.

Meanwhile, O'Brian worked on his next installment in the series, *The Wine-Dark Sea*. He at last carried Maturin to South America, where he had been bound since *The Letter of Marque*, four novels earlier. But things do not go well for Maturin there, and he is forced to march through the High Andes to escape. O'Brian had never been to the Andes himself, but he used his copy of Abbé Prévost's *Histoire générale des voyages*, which collected accounts of many early voyages of discovery, as well as the 1810 *Encyclopaedia Britannica*, to provide him with the descriptions of flora, fauna, and landscape that he needed to see the ever-observant Maturin through the trek. Although O'Brian had disparaged Prévost's book in the foreword to his anthology *A Book of Voyages*, over the years it had proven to be an indispensable tool in writing the series.

In December, O'Brian, celebrating his fortunate autumn and the accumulating royalties, replaced his eleven-year-old Citroën 2CV, which had a hole in the floor under its rubber carpet. The 2CV was no longer manufactured, so he bought a long, gray, fin-backed Citroën BX, more car than he actually wanted, though he valued its power for climbing the steep, rutted road to the high vineyard.

It was holiday time, and the O'Brians planned a stay in England, which they usually visited about twice a year. These days, travel constituted O'Brian's starkest exposure to the twentieth century, and he loathed it. In a 1990 book review, he summed up in a single sentence his feelings on

---

*Today they sell for ten times this amount.

modern-day travel: "Anyone who has travelled even as far as Paris, threading with more or less success the Kafkaesque corridors of Heathrow or God preserve us Gatwick, will agree that a man's soul has to be riveted to his body to survive it."

Once in London, however, he could in many ways still buffer himself from the twentieth century. He banked at Coutts, an ancient institution, now part of NatWest but nevertheless maintaining something of its own identity. He shopped for books at the venerable Hatchards, at 187 Piccadilly Street, which had opened in 1797. He bought his hats from James Lock and Company, the hat shop of Nelson and the duke of Wellington, located at 6 St. James's Street. Collins, his publisher, had occupied a number of buildings along St. James's Place before moving to Mayfair in 1983. All of these establishments were in the vicinity of Buckingham Palace, and none was far from Brooks's, which had changed little in more than two centuries.

It was the rarefied halls of Brooks's (fictionalized as Black's in the Aubrey-Maturin series) that truly and most benevolently anachronized London for O'Brian. There he was attended to by the always helpful but never too personal staff. There the throbbing anonymity of London's depressing multitudes was reduced to a village of distinguished gentlemen; he could bump into fellow members Richard Ollard and Philip Ziegler (another Collins editor and biographer of Lord Melbourne, King William IV, and King Edward VIII) or the likes of Max Hastings, the editor of the *Daily Telegraph*, Roy Jenkins, chancellor of Oxford and president of the Royal Society of Literature, and Cambridge don Sir John Plumb, a biographer of Sir Robert Walpole. Although the club's membership had recently grown to 1,400 after hovering in the 600-to-850 range in all the years up to 1960, the makeup of its members had hardly changed; all were either wealthy, powerful, intellectual, or from England's first families, and usually a combination of these.

On this trip, however, the O'Brians stayed not at Brooks's but at nearby Boodle's, whose "ladies' side," with its spacious rooms, was open to Brooks's members and their wives. Brooks's remained resolutely opposed to admitting women. This was fine by O'Brian, who much respected the club's traditions.

He had recently contributed an essay on the notable World War I members of Brooks's to a collection called *Edwardian Brooks's: A Social History*. The book was edited by Ziegler and historian Desmond Seward. In his essay, O'Brian used as his departure point the club's entrance hall, with its fireplace and mantel clock, where members, relaxing in comfortable chairs, frequently waited for their guests to arrive. On the walls hung a marble plaque commemorating the members and club servants killed in the two world wars of the twentieth century.

No fewer than forty were killed in the First World War, O'Brian related in the essay, from a membership of just 609, only two-fifths of whom were of an age eligible to serve. O'Brian estimated that including wounded, the casualty list for the club would have included about 134 of the 244 age-eligible members, a remarkably high percentage, which he attributed to the fact that the members were far better off than most of their fellow citizens and "took it entirely for granted that they should pay for these privileges."

He was unapologetically proud of Brooks's and the values it stood for. "Varied as their backgrounds were," he concluded his elegy of the most noted members to be killed at war, "they were all clubbable men and they all shared a liberal attitude towards the world: not so much Liberal in the party sense—indeed, many of them may scarcely have been politically-inclined at all—but liberal as one says the liberal arts or a liberal education, which surely encourages a certain openess and candour."

For O'Brian, to step into the hallway at Brooks's was to enter another world, "a wholly traditional place untied to any of the set periods and surviving them all." Founded in 1764 by William Almack and known for its high-stakes gambling, Brooks's later became the Whigs' club and had as members the prime minister William Pitt the Younger, the actor and dramatist David Garrick, the man-of-letters Horace Walpole, and the philosopher David Hume. As John Campbell, later Lord Campbell, the lord chancellor, wrote of Brooks's in 1822, when elected a member despite recently losing his estates: "To belong to it is a feather in my cap. . . . The Club consists of the first men for rank and talent in England."

Brooks's was, indeed, physically and in spirit a manifestation of what O'Brian had now spent the greater portion of his life capturing on paper. When one enters the halls of Brooks's, he wrote—and one could apply the statement as easily to O'Brian's fiction—one steps "into a timeless way of life, a material and spiritual civilization that has almost vanished." His membership in the club was also the most obvious manifestation of what he had ardently desired and become: accepted by the wealthy and intellec-tual upper crust of England. Now in his seventy-seventh year, he was immensely proud of this status and took pleasure in throwing lavish dinners there for his friends and editors. He was also proud that his books were on the shelves there and that they were often borrowed by his fellow members. He distanced himself from his past poverty and especially did not like to talk about having built his house, at least in part, with his own hands, which he now thought made him look vulgar.

At Brooks's, O'Brian, ever wary of the media, could also host interviewers at great advantage, as he did in late February 1992. There was no confusion about whose ground rules applied; the interviewer was officially a guest and so had to mind his manners. Not only that, but in these hallowed Old World halls, a nonmember, no matter how determinedly iconoclastic, was smothered by the member's moral superiority. It was an intimidating place, and a humbled inquisitor was far less likely to probe in sensitive spots.

Francis Spufford, a soft-spoken Cambridge graduate and freelance literary critic, who was writing a profile of O'Brian for the Sunday edition of the *Independent*, was unlikely to do that anyway. As a child of twelve, he had read *The Golden Ocean*, beginning a long devotion to O'Brian's work, and when O'Brian, out of the blue, had written him a postcard admiring a narrative poem he had published in the *London Review of Books*, Spufford was grateful beyond words. He had had to work hard to convince the *Independent* to commission the piece on O'Brian, and he was crestfallen when an IRA bomb threat delayed his train and made him three hours late for lunch at Brooks's with the author.

Much to Spufford's relief, however, O'Brian was not aggrieved. In fact, he could not have been more gracious. Other than the fact that he had arrived too late for lunch at the club, it was as if Spufford had been perfectly punctual. The two walked to an upscale pub hidden in a nearby lane, ate steak and kidney pie while perched on bar stools, and then returned to the club's library, where they sat on either side of a death mask of Napoleon (whom O'Brian, Spufford later wrote, called in his "accentless patrician English ... 'the ogre' "). The impeccably dressed author, who was scheduled for a photo session later that afternoon, was relaxed and conversational. Spufford, who was all too aware of O'Brian's pronouncement against question and answer in his new novel *Clarissa Oakes*, behaved well, needing from the chat only a little flesh to add to his well-reasoned theories regarding O'Brian's work. The two parted company on the best of terms, with Spufford promising to send him a copy of the story before it was published.

In March, *Clarissa Oakes* reached bookstores in Britain, and in April the same book, renamed *The Truelove*, hit bookstores in the United States. Norton's print run quadrupled that of just two years earlier for *The Letter of Marque*. Indeed, O'Brian was on the verge of becoming a modern-day publishing phenomenon, a literary phoenix. Through Norton he now had 250,000 copies in print, and the publisher sensed that this was merely the beginning. Norton planned to revive O'Brian's short stories and to print calendars featuring Geoff Hunt's cover art. Another publisher, David R. Godine, however, had wrestled away and just brought out O'Brian's Banks biography, which had appeared only in England in 1987.

On March 15, Spufford's profile, "Navigating Through Stormy Genres," appeared in the *Independent*. As promised, he had previously faxed the story to O'Brian at Brooks's for review. O'Brian had telephoned to inform Spufford that he was satisfied with the piece and suggested only a minor revision. However, subsequently the editors at the *Independent* insisted that Spufford spice the piece up a bit. The young journalist complied with a somewhat smug jab at O'Brian's supporters—"John Bayley, Iris Murdoch and the old guard of literature lining up to back an escape into fantasy and politesse"—only to turn around and defend O'Brian. Spufford had thought the ribbing innocuous enough. However, O'Brian felt betrayed by the changes. He was irate. When Spufford heard of this through a HarperCollins friend, he was shocked at O'Brian's extreme sensitivity and upset that he had unwittingly violated O'Brian's code. Thus crashed before it even got rolling a promising relationship based on respect for each other's work.

O'Brian took such interviews very personally, scrutinizing them as if under a microscope. Although he still fed reporters his enigmatic version of his past, if any, he lacked the modicum of cynicism it took to give an insincere interview for the sake of publicity. He was usually polite and endearing while artfully dodging questions. But he was unforgiving when he felt crossed, and even the faintest criticism from a journalist infuriated him.

Not all interviews ended badly. In the August 2, 1992, *Washington Post*, Ken Ringle wrote in his feature story about O'Brian and his novels titled "Is This the Best Writer You Never Heard Of?" a memorable assessment of the author: "To compare even the best of his predecessors to him is to compare good straightforward table wine with the complexity and elegance of Bordeaux. . . . Though each book is essentially self-contained, the Aubrey-Maturin series is better thought of as a single multi-volume novel, that, far beyond any episodic chronicle, ebbs and flows with the timeless tide of character and the human heart." A sailor himself—he once even served a brief stint on a square-rigged schooner—Ringle had not run afoul of O'Brian during a phone interview for his story. The two talked of sailing, and Ringle reported that O'Brian had "shipped out on square-rigged ships as an adventurous youth 'on long vacations and that sort of thing,' " an idea that would creep into the scant body of information about O'Brian and be often repeated. Never mind that in his "A Life in the Day of Patrick O'Brian" essay in the *Sunday Times Magazine*, O'Brian had already said, "I am acquainted with most fore-and-aft rigs, but only once alas was I ever in a square-rigged ship."

On a whim, Ringle decided to send O'Brian a book, about the speedy sailing vessel known as a Baltimore Clipper. He also slipped in a copy of a letter from a former colleague, who had turned to the Aubrey-Maturin books based on Ringle's story. O'Brian received the package at a low point. He had bogged down toward the end of his current manuscript, *The Wine-Dark Sea*. Mary was ill and needed attention, and he was drained. He wondered if perhaps his creative fire had been doused. However, he was much taken by the Baltimore Clipper, and reading about the craft, much used for blockade running and privateering during the War of 1812, gave him a fresh spark. Lo and behold, Aubrey's good friend Heneage Dundas finds adrift off Cape Horn an abandoned vessel—an "American contraption" (p. 259), as Aubrey calls it—a Baltimore Clipper.

O'Brian was grateful for the inspiration. To show his appreciation, he dashed off a postcard to the reporter. Would you mind very much if I named the vessel the *Ringle*, after you? he asked. And so she took the journalist's name. In the years to come, O'Brian and Ringle continued to correspond and even traded visits.

O'Brian was now on the verge of a financial windfall; however, in the fall of 1992, he could not yet fully feel the relief either monetarily or literarily. He worried about his ability to provide for his extended family. O'Brian had never met his two granddaughters, Richard's children, and they played no role in his life. But he was involved with Mary's grandchildren, of whom he was proud. His step-grandson, Dimitry Tolstoy, attended Eton, a fact that pleased O'Brian, for both its social and intellectual implications. However, Eton cost £3,800 a term, an expense that the O'Brians had agreed to bear after Nikolai's bankruptcy.

Dimitry was happy at school and especially delighted with Rugby football, but O'Brian disagreed with his academic decisions. The boy planned to give up Greek because he did not like the master and because he was doing better in history, but O'Brian felt that Greek was best learned at an early age and, if necessary, as his son had discovered long before, under an uncompromising master. History, O'Brian believed, should be tackled once the mind was better fed. A more concrete reason for his concern was financial. Proficiency in Greek, he thought, would give Dimitry the best shot at one of Eton's scholarships. With his books selling well in the United States, O'Brian could continue to pay Dimitry's tuition for now, but after so many years of struggling, he was reluctant to depend on this run of good fortune. A scholarship would put that question to rest.

The author was wary that fall, perhaps the more so for his recent taste of fame and good fortune. Could it possibly be so? Would it last? Or would it vanish like a genie after granting three wishes? He was on guard, and in his September 10 review of *The Oxford Book of the Sea* in the *London Review of Books*, he seemed testy and protective of his turf. He picked apart the book and the editor's unrealized intentions before begrudgingly admitting that "although the ideal Book of the Sea . . . has yet to be written, this foretaste of it makes a very agreeable companion."

In fact, there was some history behind this review. The book was edited by the popular English travel writer and novelist Jonathan Raban, who was edited by Christopher MacLehose. While Raban, an expatriate living in the United States, was editing the book, MacLehose urged him to use a passage by O'Brian. Though not convinced by what he had read (he found O'Brian's books a little too bluff), Raban respected O'Brian's reputation and agreed to include a passage by him if the right one could be found. He asked MacLehose to suggest an excerpt of about a thousand words that focused on the sea. MacLehose in turn asked O'Brian. This was perhaps ill-advised, since the excerpt still had to pass Raban's approval and had to suit the specific needs of the anthology, creating a situation ripe for misunderstanding.

A suggestion was made. But Raban felt it did not fit and decided that he would not be able to include a passage by O'Brian. "You must," MacLehose, in his own good-humored way, urged him, "and if you don't, not only will you infuriate me but your anthology will be much less good." However, Raban never did find a suitable passage.

In his review of the anthology, when he wasn't subtly damning Raban, O'Brian took the opportunity to anoint certain of the writers: Richard Walter's account of Commodore Anson's voyage in the Le Maire Strait he deemed "very fine—this was a true seaman's sea"; William Cowper's "Castaway" was "prodigious"; and the American biologist Rachel Carson's "splendid" *The Sea Around Us* (1951) was "deeply informed, lucid, accessible." O'Brian had recently reappraised Coleridge's *Rime of the Ancient Mariner*, which was also excerpted. The poem had been spoiled for him as a schoolboy when he had been forced to memorize it, later by so often being parodied and by his eventual realization that the poet had gotten his facts wrong. Having read Richard Holmes's book *Coleridge: Early Visions*, however, O'Brian revisited the poem and now felt a qualified awe for it, for while "the sea, the ship, and her company may not belong to this world in any literal sense," he commented, "at times they blaze with a most uncommon splendor."

Although he had reconciled with Coleridge, O'Brian was not yet ready to forgive Raban. The second paragraph of the review began: "Before ever I began my heart felt for the editor. Pope had not gone far into his Homer before he hoped that somebody would hang him, and the same wish may well have filled Mr. Raban's bosom." O'Brian was shedding crocodile tears. (He was no fan of Pope's Homer either.)

In October, Alan Judd, unlike Raban a devotee of O'Brian's work, also experienced some public discomfort at the author's hands. As part of the promotion of *Clarissa Oakes*, the novelist and biographer of Ford Madox Ford, a former paratrooper and still a foreign office operative, interviewed O'Brian on *Third Ear* for English radio. In several amusing bits of repartee, O'Brian, just shy of seventy-eight, complained that he had a "wretched memory" but showed just how keen his intellect and focus remained. When Judd brought up the fact that O'Brian had met Picasso in Collioure, O'Brian responded that Picasso, who liked the sea, had looked like "a turtle swimming in the bay."

Judd said, "Yes, you have a beautiful description of him. Is it like a bald-headed turtle swimming . . . ?"

"I don't think I could have said bald-headed turtle," chimed in O'Brian impishly, "because turtles are so rarely really hairy."

"Was it round-headed then?" asked Judd.

"I suppose it was," O'Brian deadpanned, hanging Judd out to dry.

A little later, O'Brian praised Joseph Banks's courage for landing on New Zealand, where in those days one was likely to be cooked for dinner by unfriendly natives. "Licking their lips, as it were, and sharpening their knives," Judd responded innocently, only to be corrected by the author: "They did not have them, but they had frightful clubs. They did have some obsidian knives, it's true. But they essentially bashed your skull in."

It was a fine demonstration of how the gentlemanly O'Brian kept his intellectual counterparts on their toes. Challengers—even if they did not view themselves as such—had to be prepared, for the author would ever so precisely pull the rug out from under them. It paid to have a sense of humor when interviewing O'Brian because inevitably he cornered you, and, more often than not, you became the butt of the joke—much to the audience's howling delight.

Back in Collioure, the *vendange* was just under way. Over the years, O'Brian had developed his own formula for a full-bodied red wine. He grew primarily black, gray, and white Grenache grapes, but also some Carignan and a small amount of muscat. He found it made a very fine *vin nouveau*, which turned into an acceptable wine for four or five years. With even more aging, it showed significant and steady improvement.

With the banner 1988 and 1989 vintages safe in the bins, 1992 was not a make-or-break year, and that was a good thing. O'Brian had little hope for the year's wine. Bad weather had led to a great deal of decay and damage by wild boars, which lived in the maquis above the vineyard and in the cork-oak forest below. And despite twice as much spraying— grapevines are highly susceptible to diseases and insects—he estimated that the vineyard would yield half as much wine as usual, and that of inferior quality.

The boars did not actually eat the grapes, but their young knocked ripe bunches from the vines as they scampered about and wreaked havoc with the dry-stone walls protecting the vines from harsh Mediterranean storms. The adults, on the other hand, grubbed up O'Brian's stone-pine seeds, which he had planted in the hopes of a grove to yield piñons, the prized nutlike seed in the tree's reddish brown cones. They also rooted up the earthworks he had built to protect his stone writing house and its path from foul weather.

As much as he liked to complain about the exasperating boars, O'Brian secretly loved them and all the wildlife of his mountain terraces, where golden orioles, bee-eaters, eagles, ocellated lizards, badgers, and genets foraged. In the spring, the northward flight of the honey buzzards to the south of France, thousands of the big gray bee-eating birds darkening the sky at a time, filled him with joy and admiration. But O'Brian liked to walk here and think in all seasons.

His brother Barney had died in British Columbia that summer, on July 26, at the age of eighty, leaving O'Brian with only two sisters alive. He was approaching seventy-eight himself, and Mary had grown frail. In his quiet vineyard, these facts had an added poignancy. O'Brian could see over the unchanging hills to the Spanish border on the south and a thirteenth-century watchtower to the west, reminding him of the gyre of humanity upon which he was lofted and in which he would soon be absorbed.

He often retreated to his stone writing house, especially in the summer, to escape the hordes of loud, fleshy vacationers who created a great din in Collioure from July to September. A thousand feet above the fracas it was considerably cooler, stiller, and, despite the exposure to nature's occasional violent outbursts, a far more reasonable place to be. As summer merged into fall and the *vendange*, here, a little closer to God and a little farther from humanity, O'Brian's inexorable work, physical and mental, the wellspring of his youthful energy, carried on. The vines would always be there, and more and more he had the conviction that what he put down on paper would be too.

That fall, O'Brian polished up *The Wine-Dark Sea* and sent it to Ollard. He was particularly pleased with a passage he had derived from Garcilaso de la Vega, the Peruvian-born Spanish soldier and chronicler who wrote an account of Hernando de Soto's expeditions (1605) and a two-part history of Peru (published in 1609 and 1617). In the passage, Maturin tells those assembled at Captain Aubrey's dinner table about the magnificent golden chain that Huayna Capac, the Great Inca, ordered to be made for a ceremonial dance to celebrate the birth of his son Huascar. The chain was as thick as a man's wrist, seven hundred feet long, and so heavy that it required two hundred men to lift it.

In December, O'Brian dispatched *The Wine-Dark Sea* to Norton and checked his three-month-old vintage, bemoaning the fact that every week his seven wooden barrels greedily absorbed a liter and a half of the fermenting wine. It was especially irksome given 1992's meager and sad-looking crop. But, much to his surprise, the beverage was clear, fragrant, and had an excellent taste. It was already round and potent, and, although he wondered how it would age, the taste of the fruit juice raised his spirits. The weather, too, had taken a notable turn for the better. The winds were unusually subdued; the air was warm and pleasant. The season's grapefruit were already ripening.

These fruit were especially dear to Patrick because Mary had grown the tree herself, grafting a grapefruit pip to the trunk of a Spanish tangerine tree, some thirty years before.

22

The Wages of Fame

1993–1994

The mind of an author is complex, and his emotions bubble at times like the contents of a witch's cauldron.

—Fredric Warburg, *An Occupation for Gentlemen,* 1960

By February 1993, 350,000 Aubrey-Maturin books (including 50,000 hardcovers) had been sold in the United States in about two years. In one particularly good summer week, Norton shipped 18,000 books to booksellers. O'Brian's sudden renaissance was quite extraordinary. Surprisingly, word filtered back from booksellers that as many women were buying the Aubrey-Maturin novels as men.

Once again Stuart Proffitt had been impressed by the pristine state of O'Brian's typescript. Other than to correct the rare typographical error, he had done virtually nothing to *The Wine-Dark Sea*. Richard Ollard, too, had made only a couple of minor points. One change that O'Brian did accept was to alter the name of a seaman being treated for venereal disease from Douglas Hurd to Douglas Murd. The original name happened to be that of a British foreign secretary who had been indirectly involved in the Tolstoy-Aldington affair, which had financially ruined Tolstoy.

With O'Brian poised on the brink of best-sellerdom in the United States, Mark Horowitz convinced the *New York Times Magazine* to let him write a profile of the author. Norton prevailed upon O'Brian to cooperate: This was the only way to achieve the next step in sales. Despite his misgivings about publicizing his private life, O'Brian relented.

Horowitz arrived in Collioure in early February during one of the heaviest rainstorms in decades. O'Brian picked him up at the airport in his long gray Citroën, but Horowitz spent his first evening in the village—

dinner with the O'Brians was a washout due to impassable roads—pacing his bamboo-furnished hotel room, reviewing the day's interaction. A perceptive journalist, he had instantly tuned in to O'Brian's wavelength on the drive from the airport to Collioure. He sensed an ego of iron beneath a surface of humility. O'Brian had pointed out the château of the Jonquères D'Oriolas, "one of the oldest and still richest families in the region," with whom, he said, he and Mary had "struck up a very intimate friendship, rare for these parts." Horowitz asked how they had managed that, and O'Brian replied, "Genius and beauty." He also discoursed on Catalan culture, painting, architecture, wine, and Catalonia's "manly" language.

As they pulled into Collioure, O'Brian had declaimed on the hilltop Fort St. Elme, built by King Charles V of Spain, and his and Mary's house, the highest on the hill but well below the castle. Horowitz began to joke, "Though you don't command the town as Charles V did . . ." But before he could finish, O'Brian interjected, "We command it morally."

That O'Brian would have the upper hand was clear. Nevertheless, by the time he dropped off Horowitz at his hotel, the journalist was relieved. O'Brian was talkative and friendly, if enigmatic. Horowitz's expectations had deteriorated in the previous week in England during his disheartening talks with O'Brian's editors, who had known shockingly little about his background and much about his testiness, but now he felt sure that he was going to get along with the author.

The next day, O'Brian showed Horowitz his book collection, which became the touchstone of their discussions: the first edition of *Emma*, Chesterfield's letters, Chekhov in French, Johnson's dictionary, the 1810 *Encyclopaedia Britannica*, which O'Brian could not display without an exultant grin. These said much about his life, what he valued, how he spent his time, what inspired him to write, and through them he was comfortable talking. Saint-Simon, Gibbon, Richardson, Voltaire, Burton's *Anatomy of Melancholy*, Boswell's *Life of Johnson* and *Trip to the Hebrides*—they all held a special place in his life.

As the three ate rillettes, pâté, and various cheeses for lunch and drank wine, a light red from O'Brian's vineyard, O'Brian quizzed Horowitz about Los Angeles. At one point, he ventured on an ill-fated joke about the smog killing off the male population of L.A. The punchline, relying on the idea that there were so few real men there, revealed that he had confused Los Angeles with San Francisco. Horowitz's polite laughter did not betray that it was at the author's expense.

After lunch, O'Brian and Horowitz walked through the vineyards up the cool, cloudy mountainside, where O'Brian became particularly animated. His pale, observant eyes shone clear and alert, Horowitz observed, like a hungry young bird of prey's. O'Brian mimicked the shrill laughter of an objectionable woman he once met and pranced like a fairy in the fashion of a peculiar "sodomite" who lived in one of the nearby villages. He pointed out birds and boar tracks. He plucked a stem of the flowering plant euphorbia, disserting, not without a certain perverse admiration, on the plant's toxic juice, which, he said, if rubbed into the eye would cause sudden, permanent blindness. For a moment, Horowitz could have mistaken him for Stephen Maturin.

O'Brian talked lovingly about his vineyard, and, in an endearing way, he griped to a sympathetic listener: the village was quarrelsome—if you were friends with one person, you couldn't be with another; he found his books on tape disagreeable, and he wanted to know how to record over them; he preferred the book title *Clarissa Oakes* to *The Truelove*, the one Lawrence had chosen. Horowitz himself was not immune; biographical criticism, O'Brian felt, was foolish. "Not who but what," he said, citing Homer as a great author about whom little is known. He knocked Alan Judd for having used information picked up during a dinner conversation in a *Daily Telegraph* article. He laughed heartily, recalling how Judd, in turn, showed up at a black-tie dinner at Brooks's dressed informally, no one having forewarned him.

That evening before dinner, O'Brian broke out the Veuve Cliquot to welcome Horowitz. Mary served jugged hare, and O'Brian liberally poured wine from a decanter commemorating Admiral Rodney. As the evening progressed, O'Brian's competitive nature kicked in. An American with literary claims was irresistible, and he began to pepper Horowitz with arcana. But Mary gracefully came to their guest's rescue, parodying O'Brian when she offered Horowitz the bread basket. "Here's a test of your knowledge," she mimicked. "Do you know what that's made of?"

Horowitz laughed, thankfully. "No, do you?" he asked.

"Oh, yes," Mary replied sarcastically, "banana leaves."

She often provided balm to a humiliated party. The couple had confided in Horowitz that the secret of their long marriage was shared values and a love of books, wine, and the aesthetic things. Add to that Mary's ability to soften O'Brian's edge and a healthy sense of humor on both parts.

Chocolate mousse and strong coffee followed dinner. Not feeling well, Mary retired, leaving the men at the table.

During Horowitz's stay in Collioure, O'Brian sometimes spoke openly of personal matters not for print. He seemed to warm to the journalist. Still, Horowitz sensed he was getting a carefully presented persona. He was frustrated by the rigidness of their discussions and his need for extreme discretion in asking questions. At one point, feeling low, he called his wife and despaired that he might not be able to do the story.

In fact, Horowitz was in the position of an insect hitting a window-pane, doomed by something he couldn't see and powerless to overcome it even if he could. O'Brian never wavered from the illusion he had con-structed of his early years. His cover was nearly foolproof, and his casual, leading lines led the inquisitor nowhere. When Horowitz asked how he learned to speak French, O'Brian responded, "Of course, I had a gover-ness, and my mother spoke French, and there were often French people in the house. It was taken for granted that one learned French."

When Horowitz asked O'Brian if he should be called an Irish writer, he said, "Of course," acting amused that Horowitz would ask. Later, for good measure, he disclosed that he was from the west of Ireland and described the breathtaking cliffs plummeting to the sea there. He wrote his name in Irish in a lovely script and explained the Irish form of his name and how he had anglicized it.

"My childhood was colored by the Irish Troubles, the Irish Civil War," he told Horowitz. The English should be gone, he said, the country uni-fied, and those who could not stand the idea allowed to move elsewhere. The rest of the Protestants, he continued, would, no doubt, be as well treated in the north as they were in the south.

But none of this was to be mentioned in the article, O'Brian cautioned the journalist. He feared that the IRA might target him or his family for reprisals. After all, he was an Irishman who had worked for the hated British intelligence. O'Brian played this card to perfection, disarming Horowitz and casting his Irishness in stone.

In the spring and summer of 1993, O'Brian spent many a pleasant Collioure evening under the stars rereading all of Chapman's Homer, though he had to displace a redstart from her favorite night spot, and she vainly attempted to remove him by flapping around his head. O'Brian could now read the ancients with a deep sense of satisfaction, knowing that he was about to take his own place in literary history. The British Library was in the process of creating a critical bibliography of his work, its first of a living author, an unprecedented and monumental recognition. In addition to cataloging his fiction and nonfiction publications and his translations, the book would carry tributes by Richard Ollard, naval historians Brian Lavery and N. A. M. Rodger, Oxford professor John Bayley, Charlton Heston, and Jolyon West, a UCLA professor of psychiatry and a friend of Heston's with whom O'Brian had been corresponding for several years. O'Brian was shaping an autobiographical essay to be included, and he had sent his scrapbook of four decades of reviews to Stuart Bennett, who had been enlisted to select excerpts from them.

In August, A. E. Cunningham, the head of publications at the British Library's National Bibliographic Service and editor of the bibliography, sent O'Brian a proof copy. After examining the book, O'Brian wrote to Jolyon West in early September expressing his gratitude for West's praise of the medical history in the Aubrey-Maturin series. He also mentioned that he hoped he would be able to see West on his upcoming trip to the United States to promote *The Wine-Dark Sea*. Among other things, O'Brian looked forward to discussing with the doctor his views on Sigmund Freud's *Coca Leaf Papers*, which he was reading. Freud, in "Über Coca" (1884), his first essay on the coca plant, had described the history of its use in South America and praised the therapeutic uses of its extract, cocaine. Freud had hoped that cocaine would cure a friend's addiction to morphine, just as Maturin would use the drug to wean himself from laudanum.

For a while, O'Brian added to two piles on his desk: the next Aubrey-Maturin novel and the Gothic novel, a work that had haunted him for some time and that continued to interfere with his vision of the former. Although he had been able to steer a meandering course with Aubrey and Maturin over the years, seizing on the random nature of life and fiction to digress and turn plots, the Gothic novel allowed him to say things that simply did not fit into that context. Still, O'Brian found that he could not have the same affection for this book that he had for his roman-fleuve, and finally Aubrey and Maturin won out.

In June 1993, HarperCollins published *The Wine-Dark Sea*, the first Aubrey-Maturin book to be released since O'Brian's popularity had soared in the United States and was now boomeranging back to the United Kingdom. For the cover, O'Brian had suggested to Hunt that he imbue the scene with a hellish red hue. Hunt painted a somber but powerful scene, with a smoldering volcano on the horizon, the *Surprise* heeled over in a swollen, frothing sea, shadowy figures on deck and at the fore-masthead, all enveloped in an eerie umber-orange sky. He had achieved almost impossibly fine detail, but with the restricted, somewhat garish coloring it was dangerously close to an action scene.

As fine as the painting was, O'Brian felt, the result underscored the degree to which Hunt, left on his own, with his usual brilliant palette and subtle dramatic power, was on target. A change, even in color, could shift the look of the cover toward melodrama. O'Brian considered Hunt to be the best marine painter since Nicholas Pocock, the famous painter of battle scenes during the Napoleonic wars, and he credited his illustrations with having helped elevate his books from the disreputable precincts of the historical fiction genre. He decided never again to meddle in the process.

Proffitt had timed the publication of the book for maximum impact. June was a good time to publish, before the summer exodus of reviewers to vacation retreats and apart from the crush of new books in the fall. Reviewers now leaped onto the bandwagon. In the June 27 *Sunday Telegraph*, Jessica Mann complained that there was not one woman in the cast of *The Wine-Dark Sea* but still called the series "one of the great achievements of contemporary fiction." William Waldegrave, a member of Parliament, a government minister, and a recent convert thanks in part to Iris Murdoch, wrote: "This is not just storytelling of the highest quality; it is something more. There is a depth of scholarship in the natural history, the cultural history, and of course the naval history which is itself a phenomenon." Dubbing the book "a homeric achievement," T. J. Binyon produced an elegant appraisal in the *Evening Standard*:

> O'Brian's language is an immensely flexible instrument, which can describe with equal felicity the boarding of a ship, a snowstorm in the Andes or a dinner in the gun room, never offending with a lapse into modernity or self-conscious archaism.
>
> The sheer excitement of the narration, its wit and humour, obscure the fact that these are not mere novels of adventure. They concern themselves seriously with questions of human

nature, of motivation, of relationships far beyond the scope of their apparent genre.

There was one dissonant voice in the chorus, however. The *Spectator* found a reviewer who dared to look the rest in the eyes and say he did not get it. Although freelancer Byron Rogers called the book "the most extraordinary work I have read by a contemporary," conceded to O'Brian a "wonderful first sentence," and cited "one amazing scene," he concluded, "I have to record that it took me four weeks to read the book, and in the course of this I did not detect the genius the London chattering classes are now agreed on. I found Mr O'Brian a curiosity."

In any case, the real excitement for *The Wine-Dark Sea* was reserved for the fall when the book would reach stores in the United States. Expectations were justifiably high. The advance galleys, distributed to reviewers and bookstore buyers, boasted a forty-thousand-copy first printing and an advertising and promotion budget of $50,000.

Lawrence and Norton's publicists had urged the author to make his first American tour to support the book. O'Brian, who had once, to Wolcott Gibbs, Jr., scoffed at the idea of promoting *Master and Commander* in the U. S., agreed to make the trip. Dates were scheduled in New York, Philadelphia, Washington, D.C., and Boston in November 1993.

Patrick and Mary flew to the U.S., where he received star attention. *CBS News Sunday Morning* interviewed him for a profile to be shown in 1994. The segment showed the author admiring a narwhal tusk at the Academy of Natural Sciences in Philadelphia and regarding a scarlet ibis at the Bronx Zoo. O'Brian found American television far less invasive than he expected. In fact, his television appearance, with its respectful treatment, was not unpleasant at all.

However, O'Brian continued his rancorous relationship with print journalists. He complained of overly personal interviews. Horowitz's flattering profile had run in the May 16, 1993, *New York Times Magazine.* But, as he had with Spufford's friendly essay, O'Brian found reasons to be annoyed. One unnamed source had said that he could be "a bit of a snob, socially and intellectually," and another had said that his personal history "over the years . . . had varied a bit." O'Brian took offense at these faint censures—of a type commonly used by journalists to round out a profile and that almost every modern media figure knew to be standard—and severed his correspondence with Horowitz. Horowitz, who following his Collioure visit had harbored a notion that he might become O'Brian's biographer, suddenly found himself persona non grata at the events celebrating the publication of *The Wine-Dark Sea*.

Although Horowitz accepted this reaction from the subject of an article as a professional hazard, in this instance, he was stung by the bitter irony. For two decades he had read and loved and talked about O'Brian's work; he had laughed and cried with O'Brian's characters; and he had identified with O'Brian's sharp moral judgments. Horowitz had embarked on the story about O'Brian to bring the author his deserved renown, and he had used his connections to land one of the best venues in the United States for that purpose. He had spent five mostly enjoyable days with the O'Brians cheerfully enduring Patrick's intellectual browbeating and including a warm farewell from Mary. "We will miss you," she had said. Yet now, because of a perceived slight, he found himself rejected by the author.

Spufford had suffered a similar fate. Stuart Bennett nearly did, too, over a disagreement on his selection of reviews for the British Library's critical bibliography. "Your name," O'Brian said, when Bennett called to mend fences, "was mud." Other friends also fell by the wayside. O'Brian was exceptionally acute and quick to take offense, and he had a cold-blooded streak. He was as swift to shrug off friendships as he had been to sever familial ties.

Reviewing *The Wine-Dark Sea* in the *Washington Post* on November 7, 1993, Princeton professor of politics and Bertrand Russell biographer Alan Ryan nicely captured the O'Brian paradox:

> It is astonishing that until Norton gambled on bringing [the Aubrey-Maturin novels] out in the United States only a few years ago, almost nobody in this country had heard of them, while even in England they had until then appealed to a small if passionate following. It still remains somewhat mysterious that in the age of the Brat Pack and *American Psycho*, and at a time when the novel of domestic disappointment, racial unkindness, and the unsuccessful search for missing fathers dominates the scene, these unabashedly romantic and improbable stories should suddenly find their audience.

Just how pervasive and diverse that audience was was beginning to become apparent. *The Wine-Dark Sea* was cheered in the conservative *Wall Street Journal* by John Lehman, secretary of the navy under President Ronald Reagan, and O'Brian's next novel would prompt lengthy praise in the traditionally liberal *New Republic* from the English novelist James Hamilton-Paterson.

O'Brian packed the Princeton Club in New York City and the National Archives in Washington, D.C. "Neither . . . had ever drawn such numbers to a lecture, and the Boston Athenaeum [a historic downtown library] was filled to capacity as well," Starling Lawrence, who accompanied his aged author at his appearances, later wrote in Norton's *Patrick O'Brian Newsletter.* "We have never known anything like this in trade paperback publishing." At a Washington-area book signing at Crown Books, the line stretched outside the store. One man had driven all the way from South Dakota to be there.

O'Brian found the trip exhausting but rewarding. Above all, he and Mary seemed to have developed a genuine fondness for America and Americans. "We came away with an impression of freshness, of far greater friendliness, hospitality, and general kindness, a world with much less dust, formality and constraint," O'Brian later wrote in Norton's newsletter. For a positive start in favorably impressing the O'Brians, America can thank an anonymous woman who at the airport guided a tired and befuddled British couple to the proper luggage carousel and even put coins into the luggage cart dispenser for them, refusing reimbursement. "This is on me; welcome to America," were her parting words, O'Brian reported.

In Washington, *Washington Post* reporter Ken Ringle hosted a dinner party for the O'Brians. In New York, the O'Brians met Dr. Jolyon West, the UCLA psychiatrist, and Kathryn, his wife, at dinner. O'Brian and West had been corresponding since 1990. Their conversation on such topics as the death penalty (of which they were both strong opponents) and left-handedness had convinced them that they would like one another, and they did.

Patrick and Mary filled every minute, savoring Boston's cod and clam chowder, shopping for a piece of eighteenth-century silver for Patrick's collection of antique silver, and sightseeing. On the morning of their flight out of Boston's Logan Airport, they explored Plum Island, where 270 species of birds nested on dunes and salt marshes amid wild beach plum trees. They saw yellowlegs, black duck, Canada geese, and horned larks, but, sadly, not O'Brian's much-anticipated loon.

While America made its impact on the O'Brians, they had their own conquest. *The Wine-Dark Sea* made best-seller lists, including that of the *New York Times*, a milestone for any author. Like the Little Engine That Could, the seventy-nine-year-old author had kept plugging away, confident in himself and in Aubrey and Maturin, and now his achievement was being recognized, not just by scholars and critics but by a large adoring audience. O'Brian's growing presence could even be felt on the Internet. The WELL, a hip West Coast computer bulletin board, hosted an O'Brian forum, where Aubrey-Maturin readers discussed everything from the politics of the Napoleonic wars to navy grog. In addition to producing a *Patrick O'Brian Newsletter* and a 1994 O'Brian calendar, Norton started a Web page, which would eventually have many links to O'Brian-related Web pages around the Internet.

For many American readers, O'Brian made a profound impact on the way they looked at their lives and at modern life in general. His novels championed civility, and reinforced such basic principles as the importance of self-discipline, respect for authority figures (and even for adversaries), love of the arts, and admiration for nature and knowledge. Turn-of-the-millennium America—with its vapid television culture, urban sprawl, and road rage—seemed to have rejected these tenets.

O'Brian's generally well heeled and well educated fans were notoriously ardent. They cornered family and friends and read favorite passages in an effort to hook them on this new Old World they had discovered. So outspoken were O'Brian's adherents that in his August 21, 1991, *Washington Post* review of *The Nutmeg of Consolation*, Jonathan Yardley had felt compelled to clarify his status as "one who admires the Aubrey novels a great deal but hasn't reached the heights, or depths, of fanaticism." Yardley, a Forester admirer, had somewhat reluctantly acknowledged that "the numbers of Aubrey devotees are steadily growing on this side of the Atlantic." By the fall of 1996, he would describe O'Brian's American audience as "substantial and loyal; its members take their O'Brian seriously and in some cases solemnly, reciting chapter and verse not merely about past naval adventures in the Napoleonic wars but also about Aubrey's taste in music and Maturin's botanical explorations."

O'Brian was now a celebrity of sorts on both sides of the Atlantic, albeit a reluctant one. In the end-of-the-year best-book lists, Max Hastings, editor of the *Daily Telegraph*, chose *The Wine-Dark Sea*. He had picked up the series just that summer and read all of the novels in four months. "O'Brian, who is 79, possesses the literary grace so often lacking in younger British novelists," he noted. "Also unlike those of many modern novelists, his books have beginnings, middles and ends."

Under Hastings, the *Daily Telegraph* became O'Brian's biggest supporter in the British media. In a December 27, 1994, article suggesting worthy recipients for a new year's Honours List that served the purpose of "cheering up society by showing that merit is recognized," the paper would recommend O'Brian for an Honorary Knighthood (honorary because the staff incorrectly assumed he was not a British citizen). "Few of the names listed . . . are likely to feature in the list you will read on Saturday," the paper wrote, "but they might help prod the pen-pushers and ministers who wield the patronage of Honours for next time around."

As the dust settled from the O'Brians' intense two-week tour of the United States, Patrick continued to work on his next novel, *The Commodore*. He had laid out the plot in a lengthy outline, complete with math jotted in the margins to calculate the strength of Aubrey's squadron. For some historical details involving a discussion between Aubrey and Maturin about sodomy in the navy (in chapter 9), O'Brian turned to *The Nagle Journal*, which he had reviewed for the *London Review of Books* in 1989. This diary of an American sailor who fought against the Royal Navy during the American Revolutionary War and then for it during the Napoleonic wars, supplied O'Brian with the particulars of a demoralizing incident in which the first lieutenant of the frigate *Blanche* accused his captain of making blatant homosexual passes at the crew. Nelson himself had to restore order on board the frigate.

For the navy's regulations on dealing with slavers, O'Brian turned to W. E. F. Ward's *The Royal Navy and the Slaves* (1969). While writing the novel, he also consulted ship models, which he assembled himself and kept in his writing studio, and he created impromptu seating diagrams to keep dinner conversations straight.

O'Brian pushed to finish the book by May 1994, in time to relax and enjoy Jolyon (now "Jolly") and Kathryn West's visit. The O'Brians took them for a drive and walk up to the mountaintop tower of La Massane for a memorable view of the vineyards and coast and a distant view of Spain, where the publisher Edhasa had the previous month produced a Spanish edition of *Master and Commander*.

This was also a time to catch up on mail from readers, most of which was answered by a tactful note from the publishers. To others, Patrick wrote polite postcards, chosen for their generic views of ships and the sea, never of the famous Collioure church tower. He feared that fans might come visit the town.

Among the letters that passed his publisher's screen, one from Joe Ditler, development director for the San Diego Maritime Museum, stood out. Charlton Heston had introduced Ditler to O'Brian's novels while they were on a sail on the museum's 1863 jute-trader bark *Star of India*. Since then, Ditler, like Heston, had seized his chances to read the books aloft in the *Star* with sea salt blowing in his face. He had been infatuated with the series when his pregnant wife went into labor in January 1994. He sent O'Brian a belaying pin made from the timbers of *Star of India* and a fond description of the impact of the Aubrey-Maturin novels at the museum:

> The carpenter keeps a copy in his work apron, the ship modeler keeps one beside his model-to-be of *Cutty Sark*, the librarian has collected the entire series to make available to members on a check-out basis, and cannot keep enough books in supply to meet the demand. The woodcarver cannot often find his book, as it is covered with wood chips and sawdust much of the time . . . but it is always near. And volunteer docents cannot be found on their shifts because they are snuggled up in the mizzen staysail on board our 1863 barque, deep in imagination with your books, presumably in tropical latitudes aboard the privateer *Surprise*.
>
> I too have been moved by the relationship between these two characters. So much so that I named my new born son Jack Aubrey Ditler. . . . One day, no doubt, my son will share his father's passion for Aubrey.

O'Brian could not help but be moved by such enthusiasm. He wrote a letter to Ditler, saying that he was wonderfully flattered by the news of a flesh-and-blood Jack Aubrey on the far side of the world.

In the summer of 1994, HarperCollins brought out O'Brian's *Collected Short Stories* (published in the fall in the United States as *The Rendezvous and Other Stories*). His reputation now had its effect, and reviewers handled his stories with more respect than they once had, though in less depth.

"It is easy to see why the critics of the Fifties, Sixties, and Seventies might not have been drawn to these apparently old-fashioned short stories," Godfrey Hodgson wrote in the July 23 *Independent*. "Yet their quality is unmistakable. To take a single example, in 'On the Bog,' O'Brian paces to perfection the reader's introduction to the idea that what the narrator feels for his ostensible friend is in fact murderous hatred." Hodgson went on to speculate about why such a talented short story writer went so long unnoticed. "Is the answer perhaps not just that critics have for three generations turned up their noses at realism, but that readers, too, 'cannot bear too much reality'?"

In the July 24 *Sunday Telegraph*, an impressed Jane Shilling wagged her finger:

> Young writers who insist on sharpening their milk teeth on short stories ought, before lurching into print, be obliged to learn by heart at least one of Patrick O'Brian's *Collected Short Stories*. . . . There is nothing showy in O'Brian's writing. Nothing conscious, or clever. . . . O'Brian writes like a man to whom writing comes as easily as breathing: precisely, fluently, economically. He writes of angels and devils as familiarly as he writes of foxes and hounds, in prose whose perfect cadences are as chastening to a would-be writer as a bucket of cold water first thing in the morning.

O'Brian surely had a laugh at the idea that his writing came as easily as breathing—at times in his life breathing had come none too easily—but to be held up as a master and example to the younger generations must have pleased him.

Also that summer, on both sides of the Atlantic, came the British Library's *Patrick O'Brian: Critical Appreciations and a Bibliography*, all the more impressive for being the institution's first such work about a living author.* For a man who had been so thoroughly ignored by the

---

*The U.S. version, subtitled "Critical Essays and a Bibliography," was printed in England but published by Norton.

bestowers of literary awards, O'Brian was receiving the highest accolades. The parallel to Picasso would not have been lost on O'Brian: in 1971, the Louvre had honored the innovative painter with its first exhibition of the work of a living artist. O'Brian had a glimpse now of the height to which his reputation might rise.

However, for the most part, while his stature and his fame soared, he changed very little. He stayed at home with Mary, taking great pleasure in the writing of his tales and entertaining the occasional guests. Most mornings he walked down to buy his copy of *Le Monde* at the newsstand, where he sometimes appeared with an entire appliance to have the vendor replace the batteries for him. During the day, there was the garden, the vineyard, and the sea. Once competitive at chess, he and Mary now settled for daily backgammon games and sometimes bridge with friends.* At night, they tuned in to a radio program called *France Musique*, on which they had come to depend for Locatelli and other interesting selections.

Many opportunities now presented themselves for O'Brian to speak to the media or to his readers. He wrote an essay for the *Weekend Telegraph* to coincide with the publication of *The Commodore*. In "Just a Phase I'm Going Through?" he discussed his career and reflected on his recent good fortune. He confessed that he found a "moderately heavy purse more agreeable than one so light that the first breath of crisis would blow it away" but promised that this would not affect his writing. And he ruminated on the fact that "the books now praised are exactly the same as those which were scorned." Perhaps it was a matter of phase, he concluded:

> To take ludicrous examples: Cézanne and van Gogh said little to most of their contemporaries; our grandfathers could have bought an El Greco for a hundred guineas or less; and my early *Encyclopædia Britannica* does not even mention Monteverdi. They were out of phase: the phases, ruled by who knows what laws, now coincide. Perhaps on a miniature scale the same thing may have happened here.

---

*This change, interestingly, is echoed in *The Truelove*. O'Brian explains that Aubrey and Maturin have abandoned chess, where they are evenly matched but overly competitive, for backgammon, "a game in which a mere throw of the dice played so large a part that it was not shameful to lose, but in which there was still enough skill for pleasure in victory" (p. 113).

O'Brian's "ludicrous" self-comparisons to Cézanne and van Gogh, as well as to Homer and Proust elsewhere, were perhaps a bit disingenuous, but many would have considered them just.

That year, over the course of several months, Stephen Becker, the American novelist whom MacLehose had turned into an ardent O'Brian fan, interviewed O'Brian by correspondence for the *Paris Review*. "What is it like to fall into the past?" Becker asked him.

O'Brian responded, "The sensation . . . is not unlike that of coming home for the holidays from a new, strenuous, unpleasant school, and finding oneself back in wholly familiar surroundings with kind, gentle people and dogs—inconveniences of course, such as candlelight in one's bedroom (hard to read by) but nothing that one was not deeply used to."

Cyclists, hikers, and, most intrusively, an automotive train carrying tourists and blaring pop music now worked O'Brian's hillside like ants at a picnic. Oblivious to the fact that one of the best-loved living writers in the English language resided there, they came to see the fortress at the top and the view of Collioure and the sea. Like a hermit, O'Brian retreated to the stone hut in his vineyard higher up in the hills. Thanks to steep slopes and the rugged maquis, the vineyard still belonged to the lizards, wild boars, eagles, and eagle owls. For fun, he still sometimes wandered around the mountain observing the flora and fauna and looking for boar tracks. O'Brian's fascination with wild boars dated back to his boyhood. In *Caesar*, to protect his sounder of pigs, an enormous boar disembowels a tiger with his long tusks.

But the vineyard was a physically demanding place, exposed to the elements, and O'Brian's time there would soon have to be greatly cut back. At home, while reaching for a book from a high shelf in his library, he fell from a ladder, narrowly dodging a harpoon that hung on the wall. It was a blow that gave him a taste of his own mortality. He crushed two vertebrae and was in extreme pain. However, like Mary, Patrick proved to be remarkably resilient in body and spirit. Certainly the many years of walking, of working in the vineyard, of physical exertion, and the mental acuity he had maintained through his writing now paid off. It was almost as if O'Brian's call to work, the tug of his awaiting fictional friends, would not tolerate any prolonged convalescence, least of all a downward spiral of his emotions or health. There were miles to go yet.

The bad news for O'Brian was that he could not work in the vineyard that fall, or perhaps ever again. So he made an arrangement with a young man from the village, who would do it for him. By not selling, he kept his writing hut, where he continued to work in peace and enjoy the dramatic view of mountain, coast, and sea, and now with contentment he watched the young man tend the vines that he himself had looked after for so many decades. His connection to this beloved swath of mountainside, which had provided him over the years with so much honest physical toil to complement his mental gymnastics, and which had produced so much fruit for his table, would be unbroken.

Fortunately, he had laid by an ample supply of some excellent vintages in the cellar. On that he and Mary could coast for some time, and he could always have grapes if he wanted them. As for Aubrey and Maturin, there would be no coasting, but awkward breezes in which to tack, storms to weather, and crises necessitating that the *Surprise* "crack on like smoke and oakum." O'Brian could not live any other way. An aging captain survives not by reflex and strength but by resourcefulness and cunning, the years a plus as much as a minus.

On September 5, 1994, HarperCollins published *The Commodore* in England. While it covered some interesting historical terrain, and Aubrey's stature advanced with his victory over a French squadron bent on fomenting rebellion in Ireland, the novel did not move the Aubrey-Maturin saga toward any grand conclusion. *The Commodore* was more of a self-contained bridge between the long voyage of books thirteen to sixteen and some next phase.

O'Brian had dearly enjoyed his digression into the episode of Aubrey versus the slave trade. He had stationed Aubrey's squadron off Africa as a feint to lure the French out of Brest and into their planned expedition to Bantry Bay, Ireland, of which the Admiralty had been informed in advance. But Aubrey made the most of his short stay by temporarily devastating the odious slave trade. The actions against the slavers, occupying some eighty pages, stole the show, while the climactic pursuit and battle against the French squadron bound for Ireland was relegated to the novel's concluding twenty pages. O'Brian's original title for the novel was *The Middle Passage*. Although he was persuaded to abandon that, he was rightly pleased at having written what the *Guardian* later called "one of the best descriptive analyses of the slave trade in fiction."

In the *Daily Telegraph*, editor Max Hastings, an author of many highly praised histories, claimed for himself the now plum assignment of reviewing the latest Aubrey-Maturin book and wrote: "All the familiar virtues of O'Brian are here: effortless command of period dialogue, seamanship, culture and manners; intimate understanding of a small floating world dominated by the vagaries of the wind; droll observation of human idiosyncrasy."

In the *Spectator*, James Teacher noted that *The Commodore* was "a quieter and more reflective book than the rest. The bruising conflicts are more domestic than naval and there are enough loose ends for us to hope that somewhere in Roussillon a grand old man of English letters is doing his 1,000 words a day." In the United States, where *The Commodore* would be published in the spring of 1995, *The New Yorker* agreed: "The most arresting moments in this installment come not in battle but in dramas of parenthood and marriage far from the sea," wrote an anonymous critic, adding: "O'Brian acknowledges Jane Austen as one of his inspirations, and she need not be ashamed of the affiliation."

In the *New Republic*, James Hamilton-Paterson observed that "loose ends are the hallmark of O'Brian's originality, which often deals cavalierly with usual expectations of adventure narratives. Climaxes are sometimes deliberately sidetracked or frittered away, yet without seeming anticlimactic."

Irish Times columnist Kevin Myers, now a friend of O'Brian's, though under the illusion that Irish was O'Brian's first language, was unconcerned about the author's recent walk in the wilderness regarding overall plot. To those clamoring for a grand finale to what he deemed "the greatest continuous work of literary endeavour in the English language since the Waverly novels," Myers had this to say in his September 14 "Irishman's Diary" column:

> It is clear some reviewers think it is now Saturday night. And on the sabbath he will rest. I doubt it. The man is so full of energy, of vigour, of mental sharpness that although he is 81 years old there is no reason to believe that his creative qualities will be blunted or reduced by the immediate years. . . . He is far, far sharper, far cleverer, far more inventive still than P. G. Wodehouse was in his spritely sixties and Wodehouse wrote on until he was into his nineties.

But O'Brian's fall and confinement had intensified his thinking on how to close the series. He had in mind bringing the tales full circle in some manner. His own comparison, which, in modesty, he again termed ludicrous, was the way Marcel Proust brought *A la recherche du temps perdu* (*In Search of Times Past*) full circle in *Le temps retrouvé* (*Time Regained*). Though, in truth, O'Brian was deeply ambivalent about concluding the tales in any way, he claimed to have mapped out two possible routes to the end. The path he would navigate would be determined by his physical and mental strength, or as he put it, "on how well I seem to be lasting."

He did not produce another book until the fall of 1996, a quick pace by normal mortals' standards but a slow one for O'Brian.

23

The Commodore's Second Triumphal Tour

1995–1996

> You young people who are frightened at the thought of
> growing old must learn that there is no happier condition than
> that of an aged man. Faust was a half-wit who changed his state
> for yours, and little good it did him. To begin with, let me—I
> who shall be seventy-five before this book is finished—tell you
> a secret: it is not really a fact that you grow old at all. . . . The
> immaterial being that gives our threatened building all its life
> does not show a single wrinkle, nor will it ever do so.
>
> —Maurice Goudeket, *The Delights of Growing Old*
> (translated by Patrick O'Brian), 1966

In the United States, O'Brian's popularity took on a life of its own.
With an upcoming presidential election, one bumper sticker read
"Aubrey-Maturin in '96." Starling Lawrence, now editor in chief at
Norton, was incredulous at the level of O'Brian worship. He recalled his
only similar experience, which was as an early admirer of Tolkien. "The
Tolkien cult was a bit much," he confessed to one reporter. "If you were in
on the early going, all that was a little distressing. I finally had to give up
when I saw the Hobbit cookbook. And when there's an O'Brian cookbook
I may have to resign."

Lawrence's bravado did not last long, however. He was soon helping O'Brian search for an author for an official companion book to the
series. In the September 1994 newsletter, O'Brian's article "Thoughts on
Pudding" sparked a chain reaction leading to the forsworn cookbook as
well. Two compact discs of the music played in the series, mostly by
Aubrey and Maturin, followed. Norton's Internet discussion group would
burgeon into a virtual literary salon, nicknamed the Gunroom, where jour-

nalists, scholars, professionals, and college students from around the world congregated to talk about the Aubrey-Maturin series and related history and literature, in disciplines ranging from botany and zoology to music and the culinary arts. The Gunroom even took up a collection and bought O'Brian two bottles of Bordeaux as a Christmas present.

As O'Brian's popularity increased—his books now sold nearly 400,000 copies a year in the United States—so did the demand for appearances. To celebrate the publication of *The Commodore* on April 10, 1995, Norton again encouraged O'Brian to make a publicity tour, this time for two weeks and encompassing more cities, including some on the West Coast. As a sweetener, Lawrence invited Patrick and Mary to his family home in Charleston, South Carolina. The O'Brians had not been to the South on the previous tour, and Charleston, one of America's oldest ports, active with privateers during the War of 1812, offered both historical and ornithological interest. Both Patrick and Mary had serious medical concerns. Patrick's back still troubled him and could make traveling painful. Nevertheless, he lined up medical support on both coasts through Jolyon West and accepted the invitation.

O'Brian left the first three chapters of the next book on his desk in Collioure. The first third of the book was set on land in England, one of the longer land segments in the series. In it, he staged a boxing match between Aubrey's loyal coxswain, Barrett Bonden, a former boxing champion of the Mediterranean Fleet, and a hard-faced hired bruiser in the service of an inimical neighbor of Aubrey's. The bare-knuckles fight on the Dripping Pan, a salt pan, whose name O'Brian conjured up from his days in Lewes, brought to a head Aubrey's struggles on land and set the scene for Aubrey and Maturin's departure to the Brest blockade.

The spring tour in the United States began inauspiciously when the O'Brians missed their connecting flight from Washington's Dulles Airport to Charleston. No other planes were flying to their destination that night, so O'Brian hailed a taxicab. Could you please take us to Charleston? he asked the Turkish-born cabdriver. The cabbie radioed headquarters and answered in the affirmative.

Not long thereafter, O'Brian figured out that they were heading in a westerly direction. He leaned forward and reminded the driver that Charleston was in South Carolina. The driver gave him a blank look. "South Carolina?" he exclaimed. "Where him?"

"It is below North Carolina," O'Brian replied, but not knowing much more than that, he recommended that they pull over at the next gas station for more detailed directions.*

This they did, and the driver, who had been steering toward Charleston, West Virginia, tacked and headed south for the overnight drive to South Carolina, as intrepidly as Cook might have with Banks on board. At one stop for coffee, in the wee hours of the morning, O'Brian paused outside a convenience store and listened to the call of a black-billed cuckoo. The Lawrences' country home hove into sight at dawn, many, many hours from Collioure.

After recuperating from the ordeal, the O'Brians, accompanied by Lawrence, went in search of winged wonders. In addition to woodland birds, such as Carolina wrens, cardinals, and pileated woodpeckers, O'Brian spotted the coastal green-backed heron, blue-winged teal, and pied-billed grebe. He saw a long-necked anhinga and a skimmer, both species he had much hoped to glimpse. But the highlight came at Four Hole Swamp, where—after the birders had abandoned all hope—two baby bald eagles, black from head to tail feather, finally alighted on their nest.

After a few restful days, the O'Brians began their migration north. Patrick was dependent upon Mary and his handlers for traveling. Although he could still read Latin and quote Johnson with apparent ease, he had a hard time recalling his schedule for the next day, and city names often escaped him.

The first stop was the U.S. naval base in Norfolk, Virginia, where the O'Brians toured USS *Hampton*, a nuclear submarine equipped with the Tomahawk cruise missile system. Their escort, Vice Admiral G. W. Emery, commander of the U.S. Atlantic Fleet submarine force was, O'Brian calculated with satisfaction, the world's most powerful sailor, and the *Hampton* his most powerful ship. Emery had read the Aubrey-Maturin novels in the isolation of a submarine circumnavigating the globe and had been deeply moved by their humanity and their truths, which applied equally to wooden ships and nuclear submarines. He had written O'Brian a passionate letter, and a correspondence had sprung up, as well as an invitation for a visit. O'Brian sensed a sincere harmony among the officers of the *Hampton* and felt certain that she would be most effective at war.

In nearby Newport News, at the Mariners' Museum, O'Brian held a letter from Lord Nelson in his hands and examined a French artillery

---

*From "The United States, 1995" in the *Patrick O'Brian Newsletter*, September 1995. O'Brian also told the story to great effect at the New York Public Library on April 12, 1995.

manual. A sold-out audience of 350 jammed the hall to hear him discuss his work with John Hightower, the museum's president. Another hundred fans showed up on the evening of the program but had to be turned away. "I don't sleep well at all, you know," O'Brian confessed to the appreciative crowd. "I do much of my writing at night, walking the far mountain round. This is how I compose." This was the first of an intensive series of public conversations.

The next day, en route to New York City, O'Brian stopped in Washington to eat lunch at the Pentagon and talk with admiring admirals. At six in the evening, while Manhattanites rushed for subways and vied for taxis, inside the regal domed forum of the New York Public Library, O'Brian and Richard Snow, the editor of *American Heritage* magazine and the critic who had finally launched O'Brian in the United States, began a relaxed discussion before another packed house. The crowd was brimming with goodwill, and the rapier-sharp author proved that he had not lost his edge. In a soft, lyrical voice, his wit crackled, and his self-deprecating humor and agreeably stifled laughter at his own jokes charmed the audience. O'Brian could amputate a lesser writer's reputation with a butter knife, as when he praised Forester's action scenes but not his characters. The audience members frequently roared with laughter at the repartee on stage, and their questions proved they knew his work. One woman asked O'Brian if he would drum on the desk "The Roast Beef of Old England," the call to mess on board Royal Navy ships, but he candidly confessed that he did not know it.

The next night at the South Street Seaport, Norton threw a publication party on board HMS *Rose*, a replica of an eighteenth-century Royal Navy frigate very similar to Aubrey's favorite command, the *Surprise*. On board the square-rigged sail-training ship (whose prototype was scuttled by the British off Savannah, Georgia, during the Revolutionary War), O'Brian emerged from below deck to fire the evening gun at the city's spring drizzle.

Starling Lawrence introduced Patrick and Mary to Anne Chotzinoff Grossman and Lisa Grossman Thomas, an American mother-daughter team who had proposed writing the culinary companion book to the Aubrey-Maturin series and whose lobscouse recipe was being sampled that night. Delighted with his gift from Thomas—the words and music to "The Roast Beef of Old England"—Patrick humbly served visitors from the tray of lobscouse, with his hearty recommendation. Grossman, a musician and opera translator, and Thomas, a stage manager and computer consultant, who could quote long passages of the Aubrey-Maturin novels, had much to talk about with the O'Brians. Among other topics the four discussed was a detailed analysis of the making of drowned baby, a suet pudding. "Never chop the suet in a meat grinder!" O'Brian advised.

O'Brian enjoyed his time on the frigate. Later, as he sipped Irish whiskey with Captain Richard Bailey in the great cabin, he couldn't resist making a suggestion. "Have you ever considered the Nelson checker?" he hinted. By May, the twenty-four-gun frigate sported Nelson's famous yellow-and-black checker pattern.

Before heading to the West Coast, O'Brian participated in a panel discussion on historic fiction with Mary Lee Settle and George Garrett at Manhattan's 92nd Street Y. All three read from their work. O'Brian chose the first chapter of *The Commodore*. As usual, he credited his early reading of the *Gentleman's Magazine* for imbuing him with the language and mentality of the period. Also as usual, he elicited the greatest applause and the heartiest laughter of the event, this time when the moderator asked him what the word "idoneous" meant. O'Brian said, "Oh, you mean *idoneous*. It means suitable. You are an *idoneous* moderator."

Earlier that day, Neil Conan had interviewed O'Brian live on National Public Radio's *Talk of the Nation* program. The first caller made the mistake of asking him if *Post Captain* was his most tightly edited book. O'Brian, who was nervous about being on national radio, bristled: "I've never put up with any editing at all at any time." After this crankiness, he warmed up, however, telling the imperturbable caller, who also asked how many books he would write, that he thought twenty would allow him to "bring the wheel around full circle." To the host, he confessed that he felt very deeply for Aubrey and Maturin and, in a rare hint at the series' outcome, that he hoped he "may eventually provide for them."

The most telling subject of discussion, one that never failed to betray O'Brian's innocence of all things modern, was movies. He mentioned that he was flying to San Francisco the next day. "And then I'm going to the city that always escapes me . . . somewhat of the south, near Mexico."

"San Diego?" suggested Conan.

"Not quite. It's where they make films."

"Los Angeles," Conan said.

"Just so. Exactly," replied O'Brian. He then suggested that Charlton Heston, seventy at the time, might make a "capital Jack Aubrey" (who was shy of thirty in *Master and Commander*).

"A later Jack Aubrey, though?" offered the caller, forcing O'Brian to admit that although he had met Heston, he had no clear idea of his age. Nothing could better underscore the difference in the worlds occupied by O'Brian and his readers.

The next day, the O'Brians flew cross-country to San Francisco, where they were scheduled to have dinner with Samuel Goldwyn, Jr., who had bought the film rights to *Master and Commander* and had optioned the rest of the series.

On April 19, O'Brian appeared on stage at the Herbst Theatre with Robert Hass, who had just been named poet laureate of the United States. The sold-out audience of nine hundred fixated on the small, soft-spoken author, responding like a hair-trigger to his supple humor. As the conversation rambled from the derivation of O'Brian's characters to Jane Austen's exquisite use of the semicolon to the beauty and conservative nature of Irish English, O'Brian's comments elicited howls of laughter. Hass quickly realized that his role was to be the straight man. O'Brian sparkled, diverting one discussion on *War and Peace* to puddings.

When the floor opened up for questions, O'Brian remained jovial, referring to his publisher as an "unscrupulous creature" and noting that he had read Hornblower "at the express recommendation of Winston Churchill, an English statesman." The only time O'Brian appeared out of sorts was when he was asked about his childhood. He replied bluntly that it had little to do with his writing.

Toward the end, the audience asked O'Brian to read the first paragraph of *The Commodore*. This provided the evening's emotional culmination. O'Brian's voice deepened and strengthened as if for a vow. In his accent, a combination of Old World England and France, he delivered the words slowly and rhythmically, hanging on to endings as in poetry. The slight quaver, the pause for breath, the resonance of his many decades transcended mere sound, stirring up the emotions of the audience. He seemed to draw life from his words. One could have heard a pin drop in the hall.

The O'Brians took the next day off. They crossed the Golden Gate Bridge to see the redwoods and the birds. At Point Reyes, in Bolinas Lagoon, a mudflat where a host of chubby seals frolicked, their guide, a young woman, identified marbled godwits, western grebes, western gulls, and, fittingly, a Bonaparte's gull.

Following a brief excursion to Portland (which O'Brian later described as a "northern settlement"), the O'Brians flew to Los Angeles, where they lodged among the jacaranda and hummingbirds in Beverly Hills. *San Diego Union-Tribune* critic Welton Jones sought out the author at his hotel. O'Brian stuck to his public persona, but Jones was an inspired observer, capturing O'Brian at the moment: a "compact, wiry gentleman, gracious but distant, insulated from the jostling of a reality not exactly his. His hair is white and his face lined, but the piercing eyes under the dark brows have the combination of innocence and wisdom, of vision and madness found only in the highest of priests."

Despite his busy schedule, O'Brian was not to be denied an excursion to the Mojave Desert, an undulating landscape with little to break the monotony but rocky outcroppings, some wildflowers born of a recent rain shower, and the occasional Joshua tree, which O'Brian later called "that grim vegetable . . . of two minds whether it wants to be a cactus or a scaly pine." He studied gopher holes and tracks and an ant colony. A defiant prairie dog returned his glare. But the rattlesnake and the burrowing owl that he longed to see never appeared, and other birds disappeared before he could raise his binoculars. The party was mocked by crows. Mary trod up an imposing sandy slope and returned exhausted and dehydrated. After their return to the city, she did not bounce back. She was eventually diagnosed with pneumonia and, with the help of Jolyon West, admitted to the UCLA hospital.

The main event in Los Angeles was a discussion between O'Brian and Charlton Heston on the UCLA campus. A delightful exchange preceded the event. At Heston's invitation, Joe Ditler and his wife, Eva, had driven from San Diego to Los Angeles with their children to meet O'Brian. At a reception before the talk, Ditler introduced his family. His four-year-old daughter, Chelsea, gave O'Brian a homemade tape titled "Music to Read Patrick O'Brian By." O'Brian kneeled down and kissed her cheeks. Ditler then introduced baby Jack Aubrey to the author. A great smile crossed O'Brian's owl-like face. He reached out, took the boy in his arms, and said, "Oh, Jack Aubrey, I have waited so long, and traveled so far to meet you."

A standing-room-only crowd of four hundred turned out for the discussion and reading. Of the many dramatic moments in the novels, Heston chose to read the pillory scene in *The Reverse of the Medal*, the same scene that had so impressed Lawrence on that fateful flight home from London. Heston's gruff delivery suited it perfectly, and hardly a dry eye remained in the audience by the time he was through. Even Heston had a hard time keeping his composure.

America had opened up its arms and heart to O'Brian, and he found that its generosity could be staggering. Tom Perkins, a wealthy Silicon Valley venture capitalist, offered him a fortnight's use of *Andromeda la Dea*, his 154-foot sailing yacht with a crew of seven and an excellent chef. It was a thank-you, Perkins told O'Brian, for having so enriched his life. O'Brian sensibly abandoned his reserve and accepted, choosing a sail in the Mediterranean. He would be picked up at Port Vendres, the deep-water port near Collioure, a month after his return. He fairly bubbled at the thought of making twenty knots under sail on board one of the world's largest sailing yachts.

His feeling did not soften, however, for American reporters, who relentlessly sought personal information. They often encountered a cold glare and a rapid end to the conversation. O'Brian was sensitive to formalities, and a journalist who was overly familiar also received his disdain. Furthermore, reporters had to stay on their toes because O'Brian's lashes could be administered at any time. In an interview with the *Atlantic Monthly*, during a perfectly admissable discussion of the rhythm of his prose, O'Brian quoted as an example of superb prose rhythm Samuel Johnson's famous rebuff of Lord Chesterfield:

> Is not a Patron, my Lord, one who looks with unconcern on a man struggling for life in the water, and, when he has reached ground, encumbers him with help? The notice which you have been pleased to take of my labours, had it been early, had been kind; but it has been delayed till I am indifferent, and cannot enjoy it; till I am solitary, and cannot impart it; till I am known and do not want it. (Boswell, *Life of Johnson,* p. 185)

True, the passage was illustrative of eloquent rhythm, but O'Brian's double entendre certainly reflected his somewhat unjustified contempt for his literary reviewers. A close examination of the reviews shows that over the decades he was by and large treated well by American reviewers, notwithstanding some notable lapses and the fact that the public did not catch on at first. But to O'Brian, who had his true identity to protect, every journalist was a potential enemy. They hovered around him as thick as flies.

Back in Collioure, where pictures of Mary's grandchildren lined the living room and Patrick's eighteenth Aubrey-Maturin novel awaited him, the complexities of the twentieth century as well as the quirks and fads of literary critics vanished like a mountain stream in August. The sun and the wind, the mountains and the sea were the only masters of this place, and O'Brian's mind was a private garden to be tilled and harvested as he saw fit. If the tour of the United States was like the victory lap of a marathoner, O'Brian still had a surprisingly spry step. Other than Mary's illness, all had gone exceedingly well. The crowds were adoring, largely civilized, and his popularity continued to rise.

In May, Patrick and Mary sailed with friends on board the luxurious *Andromeda la Dea* in the Mediterranean. Perkins had been true to his word. O'Brian was allowed to chart the ketch-rigged yacht's course for two weeks. In addition to Mary, O'Brian had invited Richard Ollard, Stuart Proffitt, and Vivien Green, as well as his host, whom he had taken a liking to in San Francisco and who now explained the functions of the modern sailing instruments on board. Although O'Brian's dream itinerary, which had included stops in Sicily and Greece, had to be reined in because it was not feasible, the high-tech, computer-controlled yacht, much to the author's satisfaction, did enter the challenging harbor of Port Mahon under sail alone. She checked into other Minorcan ports and then sailed for Majorca and Ibiza, where she stopped for birdwatching. Thanks to some incorrect Spanish charts, she even briefly ran aground while trying to sail between Minorca and a small island. Perkins ran a hawser astern, grappled it to a large rock, and hauled the yacht into deeper water using a windlass. No serious damage was done, and Patrick was exhilarated by the unplanned show of seamanship.

At night, O'Brian and Ollard continued their ongoing, occasionally cranky literary discussions, some three decades old. When O'Brian revealed that he intended to destroy his diaries, Ollard expressed shock and urged him to reconsider. He reminded O'Brian that his Picasso biography was so good precisely because he had had access to much personal material; however, O'Brian insisted that he wanted his novels read without reference to his own life.

But during the day such heavy matters disappeared. Life at sea and the sailing of *Andromeda la Dea* spurred Patrick's creative juices, and each afternoon, he borrowed Perkins's charts of the waters off Brest and worked for several hours on his new novel, much of which was set on the Brest blockade. Afterward, he would emerge from below and blithely show Perkins his progress. Mary, as used to her husband's writing routine as he was himself, was astonished that Patrick had grown so carefree.

Shortly after returning from the magical voyage, O'Brian received glorious tidings from England. On June 17, in the Birthday Honours of the queen, he was appointed Commander of the Order of the British Empire (CBE) for services to literature. He was to be invested with the honor at a ceremony at Buckingham Palace in the fall. This well-established tribute preceded a brand-new one. At the end of June O'Brian was awarded the first Heywood Hill Literary Prize, for "a lifetime's contribution to the enjoyment of books," at a luncheon on the lawn of Chatsworth, the great house of the duke of Devonshire. The eleventh duke of Devonshire, a part-owner of the old-school London bookshop, G. Heywood Hill, had helped found the award, along with John Saumarez Smith, the director of the store. Smith and two cojudges, Oxford chancellor and president of the Royal Society of Literature Roy Jenkins and Mark Amory, literary editor of the *Spectator* and Lord Dunsany's biographer, had chosen O'Brian to be the first recipient of the £10,000 prize by unanimous decision.

Before the presentation, they revealed their choice only to O'Brian and a very few others who had to know. Among the many noteworthy writers on the train from London to Chatsworth was Alan Judd. In the July 1, 1995, *Spectator* he described the scene: "The sun shone, the bands played cheerfully, the literati were littered and the gliterati glittered— though not as brightly as the chains adorning the assembled mayors of Derbyshire. The RAF laid on a timely unintended fly-past, the Chatsworth dogs proved that if you're handsome enough you can scrounge any number of free lunches."

The playwright Tom Stoppard, himself a great fan of O'Brian's novels, presented the eighty-year-old author with the award. O'Brian had previously warned Smith that he was not much of a speechmaker. He was assured that as little as "thank you" would do just fine. But, instead, he proceeded, in his own proud but diffident way, to endear himself to the assembled with his confession that—despite sixty-five years of writing— this was the first prize of his adult life and his first literary award ever. The other prize he had been given by the headmaster of a prep school he had attended in Paignton, he told the guests. In a long-distance foot race, he had been left far behind and gotten lost, and after the others had finished, the headmaster found him still running. He awarded Patrick a fine double-bladed penknife for his perseverance, for his bold heart.

Toward the end of the festive day, a friend of the duke, a redheaded sculptress of bronze busts, danced the Charleston on a table, encouraged by a former ambassador. Although he did not participate in the dancing and although Mary was unable to attend the event, O'Brian could not help but be pleased at the celebration on his behalf. In his article, Judd observed of O'Brian that "it was clear at the prize-giving that the pleasures of literary recognition do something to render tolerable the passing inconveniences of fame."

O'Brian now counted the duke of Devonshire among his friends and was elected a member of Pratt's Club, an exclusive bastion of upper-class males owned by the duke. Keeping with tradition, at Pratt's, where only fourteen could sit for dinner at the dining room's one table, all the servants were known as George.

Collioure's sea of concrete and red tiles had many years since rumbled past the O'Brians' humble house, slinging condos up the coast for fashionable sun worshipers. The balcony of an apartment building across the alley looked down into their garden. (O'Brian, in a fit of extravagance, eventually had a helicopter airlift in an adult magnolia tree to block its view.) Real privacy no longer existed. The O'Brians' house, however, remained the highest on their part of the hill for now, and thus they could still look out on and walk amidst grapevines, cork trees, and sun-baked hilltops. Patrick had cut back on his moonlight treks, instead keeping a pen beside the bed to capture any midnight epiphanies. He even described his creative experience more placidly now: "You know that little state of beatitude, when you've slept well enough and you lie perfectly relaxed in bed—then large parts of books will pass through my mind," he told a reporter. Still, he occasionally ventured up the quiet road near his vineyard to let his muse dance beneath the Northern Cross and Boötes.

Aided by the three chapters of his eighteenth Aubrey-Maturin novel that he had left on his desk before the U.S. tour, plus the pages that had accumulated since then, in July O'Brian slipped back into his fictional world. He kept a rigorous schedule. By early October, when it was time to put the year's wine into barrels—he had not given up wine making altogether—he had finished chapter 5. Aubrey, who is himself showing some signs of aging—his eyesight is no longer what it once was—had just landed Maturin in France on a dark night for a clandestine meeting, and there Maturin would remain for some time while O'Brian tended to other business.

Following the wine making, Patrick and Mary went to London for two weeks. The combined effect of the summer's travel and the intensive writing had exhausted Patrick. He looked tired. But the anticipation of having the queen personally decorate him with the CBE put him in high spirits. Mary had butterflies, just as she had had half a century earlier when presented at court as a teenager. Then, she had feared that her knees would knock during her curtsy; now she feared that they might buckle. The October 25 event was graced by sunshine. A photograph of the occasion shows Patrick looking as neat and proper as usual, and grinning like a hyena.

O'Brian, who would be eighty-one years old in December, returned to his novel, and though recent events might have had him floating on clouds, his current manuscript was not one that brought Aubrey, flawed man, much joy. In fact, O'Brian ratcheted up the tension. The first third of the novel takes place at Aubrey's estate, Woolcombe House. His slave-trader prizes are being successfully contested in court, and he is on the brink of financial ruin, yet again. Aubrey compounds his problems by campaigning in the House of Commons against naval abuses, harming his own allies, and by resisting the enclosure of the common lands near Woolcombe, antithetical to Admiral Stranraer, commander of the Brest blockade, where Aubrey is stationed.

But what really worries Aubrey is that he is approaching the top of the post captain's list and that he might fall victim to the Admiralty's increasing practice of promoting post captains to rear admirals but not assigning them to a ship. In the navy vernacular, by not being assigned to one of the three squadrons—red, white, or blue—he would then be "yellowed," essentially retired out of the service.

The outlook was grim for Aubrey, and O'Brian complicated his life even more by providing Sophie Aubrey with irrefutable evidence of her husband's affair in Halifax with Amanda Smith, which O'Brian had described eleven books earlier, in *The Surgeon's Mate*. Although Jack, a man of his era, regrets having saved the woman's letters, he finds it impossible to feel remorse for the infidelity. At about the same time, Admiral Stranraer accuses him of having allowed French ships to evade the blockade on his watch. To top it off, Aubrey imagines a slight from Admiral Lord Keith, his supporter, and Keith's wife, Queenie, who has been his friend since childhood.

By contrast, Maturin is in good form in *The Yellow Admiral*. More than ever, he seems at peace personally. Living at Woolcombe House with the Aubreys, he, Diana, their daughter Brigid, and Clarissa Oakes have settled into a happy domestic arrangement. Admiral Stranraer consults with Maturin for medical reasons, giving the doctor influence there, though only to the slightest degree when it comes to Aubrey. Maturin also negotiates a pact with Chilean leaders and English ministers, providing for Aubrey's future at the same time.

Toward the end of *The Yellow Admiral*, with Napoleon exiled to Elba and Aubrey indefinitely detached from the service, the *Surprise* sets sail for South America, where, as Maturin has arranged it, Aubrey will serve as an admiral in the Chilean navy—as did the historical Thomas Cochrane—during Chile's struggle for independence from Spain. In an aberration for the series, Aubrey and Maturin bring their families on board for the sail to Madeira. Through seventeen books, O'Brian had used the ship's departure as a symbolic and actual escape for Aubrey and Maturin from domestic strife, particularly for Aubrey, who finds family life chaotic and constraining, and his role at home insignificant compared to serving his country and his career. An obvious parallel is Patrick and Mary's own departure from London to Wales and France, places where they lived away from their families and, in a sense, within wooden walls. Though, like Aubrey and Maturin, the O'Brians periodically gravitated back to England, they lived more fully, more effectively away from their country. But now O'Brian united the families in a blissful peacetime cruise. One reviewer, writing for the *Christian Science Monitor*, would call the tranquil voyage to the island of Madeira, with the happy Aubrey and Maturin families on board, "as lovely a piece of writing as anything in O'Brian's work."

O'Brian endowed the novel with yet another cliffhanger ending. Aubrey and Maturin get no farther than Madeira, where an urgent letter from Admiral Lord Keith informs them of the shocking news that Napoleon has escaped from exile and returned to Europe. Keith orders Aubrey to take command of the Royal Navy ships in Madeira and to return with all haste to Gibraltar.

O'Brian finished the book in mid-February 1996 and mailed it to England. *The Yellow Admiral* was something of a teaser, a prelude to grander events, and a rather dark novel. Much as *The Reverse of the Medal*, another dark novel, set the scene for *The Letter of Marque*, a bright one, *The Yellow Admiral* paved the way for more glorious days in book nineteen. Some reviewers criticized *The Yellow Admiral* for a lack of action, while many regular readers applauded the glimpse of Aubrey's domestic life at Woolcombe House and with his family at sea.

Some cracks in O'Brian's armor, consisting of minor memory lapses and confusion about names, were beginning to show. On the Internet, e-mail flew back and forth: O'Brian had called two different characters—the first lieutenant of the *Bellona* and a stable hand—by the name of Harding, and he had named a new minor character General Harte, duplicating for no apparent reason the name of Aubrey's nemesis of earlier novels, Admiral Harte. Sophie mentions an admiral named Craddock, perhaps muddling the name of Admiral Haddock, who lives at Grope in Hampshire in *Post Captain*. (Another Craddock, the secretary of Admiral Stranraer, appears later in the novel.) Some complained that he had not worked in the information about enclosures and boxing as smoothly as he had inserted other factual passages in earlier novels, and others wanted more naval battles. Such was the fate of an author in the Internet age. Every reader could be a published critic.

Although *The Yellow Admiral* raised some questions among reviewers as to whether O'Brian's powers as a plot spinner were waning, for Patrick and Mary, that no longer seemed to be the point. Aubrey and Maturin were entwined with their own existence. They were like the seasons, to be enjoyed, to be anticipated, sometimes to be fretted about, often to be missed, but never—as long as they could help it—to cease. As always, sending off a book was a time of mixed sadness and relief, something like dropping off a child at boarding school. Aubrey and Maturin now receded from their lives, and the eighteenth century reverted to the twentieth overnight.

Snow covered the mountaintop visible from the O'Brians' window, and it was icy cold in Collioure. At such a time, reflection was inevitable for the aging pair, with a century and a half of memories between them. Though neither Patrick nor Mary liked cold weather anymore, Mary had many fond remembrances of winters at her school in Switzerland. Each morning, a luge pulled by a gallant St. Bernard had arrived with fresh milk for the girls. During the day, they had skated, played ice hockey, and tobogganed over an ice-covered run lined with feathery, freshly shoveled snow to soften any falls.

As usual after finishing a book, Patrick and Mary rekindled their epistolary conversations. Mary handled queries regarding the culinary companion book to the series, *Lobscouse and Spotted Dog*. Her own cooking depended upon fresh ingredients and old standby recipes. One of the few advantages of the development around them was the installation of a butcher, a greengrocer, and a cheesemonger, all excellent, nearby. Although for lunch she often served Provençal pâtés and cheeses—they had grown very fond of Pyrenean sheep's cheese—supper was frequently more elaborate and English. It was in Switzerland that Mary had developed a love for food. Her school had employed a Parisian chef, whose wife, like Mary, had been sent by doctor's orders to the mountains to restore her health. The chef doted on the girls, making them all sorts of treats, including, on special occasions, confectionery animals and even a coach with horses.

Mary dispensed advice to Grossman and Thomas on making dishes such as the suet pudding known in the navy as drowned baby, and she loaned them her secret cooking mainspring, a battered old copy of *Radiation Cookery Book*, written by Justina Fox, with whom she had driven ambulances during the war. In return, Patrick and Mary received progress reports with photographs of their culinary creations.

The cold weather soon passed, and one of the more glorious Collioure springs in recent memory followed. Patrick and Mary now paid special attention to their garden, enchantingly guarded by a tall cypress hedge, like a castle wall. By mid-March, the small magnolia had blossomed with its fragrant, velvety flowers, and the lemon and grapefruit trees were laden with fruit. In the court just outside their front door, a winter robin lived in the orange tree and perched on an orange each day until Patrick or Mary gave him his crumbs. By the end of March, the swallows and the crested hoopoes, the couple's favorites, had arrived, and Mary had turned the oranges into marmalade.

O'Brian was now an elite author. His books had been translated into more than a dozen languages, including Danish, Greek, German, and Russian, and had sold more than two million copies. In the United States, Norton estimated that more than seventy thousand readers had read the entire series since its relaunch in 1990. Forty thousand had signed up for the *Patrick O'Brian Newsletter*. O'Brian exercised a good deal of influence in his field. A foreword or promotional blurb by him could make a book that might have gone unnoticed receive considerable attention. One book that he praised was Dava Sobel's *Longitude*, about John Harrison, who invented a chronometer that remained accurate at sea, allowing seamen to calculate their longitude. The book became an unlikely best-seller in the winter of 1995–96.

In the summer of 1996, O'Brian wrote to his friend Jolly West. In the past, West had served as the chairman of the University of Oklahoma psychiatry department, and he had returned to Oklahoma City to help in the aftermath of the bombing of the federal building. He had recently undergone triple bypass heart surgery, and O'Brian, no stranger to medical problems, asked matter-of-factly if he thought his operation was connected to the stress he faced in Oklahoma. He also thanked West for the news that he had bought out one bookstore's stock of O'Brian's Picasso biography.

That summer, Presses de la Cité, a Paris publisher, released the French translation of *Master and Commander*, titled *Maître à bord*. The works of C. S. Forester and Alexander Kent had already been published in France, despite the fact that their British heroes specialized in drubbing Napoleon's navy. According to Renaud Bombard, O'Brian's French editor, "Perhaps twenty-five or thirty years ago these defeats were still a touchy subject, but now they are just ingredients in excellent historical novels."

Even in France, even after all this time—half a century after World War II and four decades after the death of his father—and even as more and more journalists probed deeper, O'Brian did not backtrack on his claim that he was born in Ireland. This piece of biographical misinformation ran on the inside flap of the French edition. Perhaps O'Brian had become so used to this version of his life story that it now felt real and comfortable.

If the release of an Aubrey-Maturin book had been an English publishing event in 1979, as one reviewer declared, it was now something of an American spectacle, employing the full array of late-twentieth-century marketing techniques. Norton scheduled the on-sale date for *The Yellow Admiral* for October 21, Trafalgar Day. To whet readers' appetites, the publisher offered the first chapter of the book on its Patrick O'Brian Internet site. For those less technologically savvy, the September 1996 issue of the *Patrick O'Brian Newsletter* also contained an excerpt. Norton advertised the book everywhere, from the *Boston Globe* to the *Seattle Times*, from *The New Yorker* to the *Wall Street Journal*. They even produced a gold-stitched yachting cap touting the book.

However, this year something else even more spectacular was afoot, in England. Friends of O'Brian, under the aegis of the *Evening Standard*, had decided to throw a special event for him in the fall. It would turn out to be a fitting salute and a most memorable occasion.

24

A Night of Honor

October 11, 1996

It did not need much imagination to feel that it was an evening
when ghosts walked among the vastness of the Painted Hall at
the Royal Naval College at Greenwich; the ghosts of Jack
Aubrey and Stephen Maturin and the myriad of other
characters brought to life by the pen of Patrick O'Brian.

—Valentine Low, *Evening Standard,* October 14, 1996

"I t is as though, under Mr. O'Brian's touch, those great sea-
paintings at Greenwich had stirred and come alive," the naval historian Tom Pocock once wrote about the Aubrey-Maturin series.
On Friday, October 11, 1996, a week before the publication of *The
Yellow Admiral* in the United States, Patrick O'Brian made much more
than the paintings come alive. The previous summer, Max Hastings, now
at the helm of the *Evening Standard*, and A. N. Wilson, the paper's literary editor, had dreamed up the Greenwich celebration. They felt that
O'Brian—though made a CBE by the queen, celebrated at a dinner
hosted by the sea lords in the Old Admiralty, and awarded the first Heywood Hill Prize—had still not been accorded the status merited by his
body of work.

Two years previously, in his September 3, 1994, *Daily Telegraph* article
"Will They Set Sail Again?," Hastings had called O'Brian "the most amiable of men" and admired his "great gentleness of spirit." He noted that
O'Brian's work possessed "a pervasive serenity, a generosity towards
human frailty" that attracted readers around the world. "If some aspiring
young novelists take O'Brian as their model, rather than the likes of
[Salman] Rushdie or Amis fils [Kingsley Amis's son Martin]," he concluded, "there will be fewer remaindered books on the shelves of Water-
stone's and Smiths in the 21st century."

The banquet he and Wilson dreamed up had an air of fantasy fulfillment for this group of Aubrey-Maturin buffs. Military bands would play. The chefs would serve naval food chosen by O'Brian, along with Bordeaux and port, and notable guests would salute O'Brian. It would all take place in Christoper Wren's ornate Painted Hall of the Royal Naval College at Greenwich, where Nelson had lain in state after Trafalgar, from December 23, 1805, to January 8, 1806, before his burial at St. Paul's.

Invitations went out on *Evening Standard* letterhead. Hastings suggested to Starling Lawrence that he notify Americans through the newsletter. But Lawrence decided against it, afraid that it might create too great a demand for seats in the hall, which accommodated fewer than 375 people. He also did not want to appear to be publicly hawking seats, which cost £55 per head. However, he did send invitations to a small group of guests whom he thought O'Brian would particularly appreciate having there.

Guests, decked out in evening dress or military regalia, began to arrive at 8 P.M., filing past naval cadets in the vestments of a jolly-boat crew posted at the door. In the Queen Mary Ante-Room, they mingled and drank champagne, as members of the Orchestra of the Age of Enlightenment played a Bach trio sonata, Boccherini, and other music that Aubrey and Maturin were in the habit of entertaining themselves with in the captain's cabin during long evenings at sea.

O'Brian's readers made an impressive group. Among them were armed forces minister Nicholas Soames, sea lord Admiral Sir Michael Boyce, cabinet secretary Sir Robin Butler, former British ambassador to the United States Sir Robin Renwick, permanent secretary at the Department of National Heritage Hayden Philips, artist Sir Alistair Grant, writers Danielle Steel and Rose Tremain, and musician Mark Knopfler. William Waldegrave, a distinguished member of Parliament and chief secretary to the treasury, who would give the keynote speech, was accompanied by his wife, Caroline, and daughter, Katie.

Among the Americans represented in addition to Steel were her future husband, the yachtsman Tom Perkins, Starling Lawrence, and Admiral William J. Crowe, Jr., the former chairman of the Joint Chiefs of Staff and U.S. ambassador to the Court of St. James, London. In all, 343 O'Brian admirers showed up that evening for one simple reason: to toast the author. It was a joyful, selfless evening, and spirits ran high.

Once guests were seated at the massive oak tables lining the Painted Hall, there remained only one arrival to kick off the festive dinner. When O'Brian made his entrance, the assembled—who had taken reading pleasure in Aubrey and Maturin, hour upon hour, year after year—rose en masse in a thunderous greeting.

Impeccably dressed in a black tuxedo and black bow tie, flush from the Collioure sun, O'Brian—followed by a camera crew—proceeded to the front of the Painted Hall. This evening was an improbable affair indeed, more so than anyone there realized. Throughout life, O'Brian had been a consummate outsider: an intellect who had not gone to Eton or Oxford; an elite who was not from the upper classes; a citizen of the twentieth century who was more at home in the eighteenth. O'Brian was an Irishman who was not Irish; an Englishman who lived in France; a brilliant author in a spurned genre. He had even given up his family name and abandoned his family ties.

Tonight, O'Brian was the ultimate insider. Tonight his family of readers—many of them highly accomplished people—had gathered for the one purpose of honoring him. O'Brian made his way to the tables flanking the dais, where Mary, his beaming wife, sat beside Perkins, with whom Patrick and Mary would continue their celebration at a house party in Patrick's honor at Plumpton Place, Perkins's manor house in southern England. The cheering died down, and dinner was served. O'Brian's memory had grown more selective of late. He did not recognize the man seated across from him. "I looked at him with a perfectly blank face," he later confessed, and then realized to his embarrassment that it was Britain's second sea lord, with whom he was staying.*

Pea soup fit for seamen made hungry by furling water-soaked canvas or shoving on capstan bars preceded a hardy meal of salt beef, turnips, potatoes, and sauerkraut. The 1988 Château Beaumont that washed it down was a good deal more refined. For dessert, or "pudding" as the English call it, Patrick had requested figgy-dowdy, a West Country suet pudding with raisins. The less adventurous could opt for custard. Then, for anyone who could eat or drink more, the waiters brought cheese and ship's biscuits and port—Cockburns 1970. The orchestra of the Band of the Royal Marines performed nautical tunes, followed by a violin, cello, and harpsichord recital played by the Orchestra of the Age of Enlightenment.

*From "The Giant O'Brian," an interview with Amazon.com in 1998.

Hastings welcomed the guests. Actor Robert Hardy read passages from the Aubrey-Maturin books, including the much revered account of their first meeting during a private concert in Port Mahon, Minorca, and a selection from *The Yellow Admiral*.

Standing erect, clad in white helmets and gloves, the Corps of Drums of the Royal Marines pounded out the Beating of the Retreat, which reverberated like a cannonade in the lofty hall and set a sober stage for the keynote address by the Right Honourable William Waldegrave, whose official responsibilities included being chancellor of the Duchy of Lancaster (part of which is the Liberties of the Savoy, once a semiautonomous region in London where Aubrey often sought refuge from his creditors). "We have gathered here tonight . . . to celebrate and to honour one of the greatest storytellers in the English language," he began, igniting a great roar of approval.* Just as the storytellers of Argos, Thebes, and Sparta told their tales of Troy at court in return for hospitality, so those gathered this night, he proclaimed, were in a small way compensating their great storyteller: the man who had created from the grand history of Nelson's navy a universal story whose lessons and examples of heroism would speak to the ages.

"If Kipling wrote the epic of British India and if Conrad did it for the worldwide mercantile empire of steam and iron, then Patrick has done that service for the navy of St. Vincent, the Nile and Trafalgar," Waldegrave declared, adding that in Maturin, O'Brian had created a hero to whom the intelligence community could look for verisimilitude and inspiration. He wondered whether there were some of that community present in the audience, a certain if subtle indication from this London insider that there were.

Finally, Waldegrave said of O'Brian, "We celebrate him tonight above all . . . for the extraordinary care which founds every reference on the rock of scholarship; for his love of nature and the sea; for his celebration of courage, honour, and humanity." Waldegrave thanked Mary for her support of O'Brian and offered a traditional seated naval toast to the guest of honor: "May we drink to you in three times three."

How far O'Brian had come, how steadily he had marched, bouncing back from life's setbacks, tramping on again, as his career and reputation ascended in great spurts and languished in long valleys. Like Thoreau's

*Waldegrave's speech is quoted from the British paperback edition of *The Yellow Admiral*, 1997.

slow-growing tree, he was not made of a soft and perishable timber, but through contending with difficulties, he had persevered splendidly, advancing to a ripe old age, looking fit and far younger than his years.

What odds he had overcome. As a boy, he had dreamed of attending the Royal Naval College at Dartmouth, but not having a heart of oak, he was rejected. Now, at the age of eighty-two, sound of mind and strong of heart, he was the toast of admirals. He had not been admitted to their institution, and that had turned out for the best, for, without the demands and restrictions of a naval life, he had been able to bring the Royal Navy's proudest era to life—better than anyone else—in words so noble they did the service immeasurable honor.

As he stood at the podium before those who had come to honor him, the next naval tale was more than just a glimmer in O'Brian's pale hawk-like eyes. Jack Aubrey and Stephen Maturin coursed through him like his own blood, bringing him courage, defining him, and in many ways defining his readers as well. As long as a pulse still beat in O'Brian, Aubrey and Maturin would ride the waves.

Aglow, the author, a humble speech maker but a commanding, almost transcendent, presence nonetheless, thanked those assembled for bestowing such an honor on him and proposed his own toast: "To the Royal Navy, that glorious service."

Epilogue

A s was his usual habit, Patrick O'Brian had begun his next novel, the nineteenth in the series, shortly after finishing his previous one, *The Yellow Admiral*. Although he had now scaled the pinnacles of literary appreciation, he would not win one battle terribly important to Mary and him. When the undeveloped land on the uphill side of the O'Brians' house came up for sale, they attempted to buy it but were denied the right by the local housing authority. Instead, a French family was allowed to purchase it and began building a house abutting the O'Brians' terrace. The noise, dust, and loss of the wild landscape that the O'Brians so cherished aggravated Mary's already poor health. Her condition spiraled downward.

In March 1998, Mary died in a hospital in Perpignan. She was buried in a private ceremony in Collioure in a tomb built for the couple. O'Brian was distraught at losing his soulmate, the woman who took care of him and who was the only person whose creative input he took seriously. Although Patrick often acknowledged that Mary was his most trusted reader, the extent to which they collaborated was a secret she took to the grave.

In October, O'Brian published *The Hundred Days*, a novel that postpones the *Surprise*'s voyage to South America, carrying Aubrey and Maturin instead to the Mediterranean to prevent a Muslim plot to aid Napoleon, who has returned to the Continent from exile on Elba. The novel is most notable for the shocking death of Diana Maturin, in a carriage wreck, certainly an expression of the pain O'Brian felt as Mary's health failed and she died.

That fall, the BBC aired a much publicized documentary about O'Brian and the publishing phenomenon surrounding his Aubrey-Maturin series. The show raised questions about O'Brian's identity and led to an exposé in the *Daily Telegraph*, which revealed that he was not Irish. O'Brian was deeply distressed at this revelation, particularly because he had recently been awarded an honorary doctorate from Trinity College in Dublin under the belief that he was Irish. The provost nonetheless remained supportive of O'Brian, who lived in rooms at the college that winter while working on the twentieth Aubrey-Maturin novel.

O'Brian dedicated *Blue at the Mizzen*, which was published in November 1999, to his friends at Trinity College. In this novel, Aubrey and Maturin sail to South America in the guise of preparing a hydrographical survey of the Strait of Magellan and the southern coast of Chile. Prior to arriving there, Maturin, recovering from the loss of Diana, proposes marriage to Christine Wood, an anatomist living in Africa. In Chile and Peru, Aubrey wins several key battles, helping to assure the independence of Chile, much the way Thomas Cochrane once had.

As he had in 1993 and 1995, O'Brian visited the United States for various publicity and honorary events, including a conversation onstage with Walter Cronkite at the New York Public Library. He refused to answer personal questions and continued to make references to his Irish background, despite the public evidence to the contrary. The trip ended on a sour note when O'Brian, during a dinner in his honor at the New York Yacht Club, unwittingly made a disparaging comment about his dinner guest to her husband, who then reported the remark on the Internet. This ignited—unbeknownst to O'Brian—a fiery discussion on the topic of his alternately charming and disdainful personality.

Feeling weak, O'Brian cut short his stay in the United States. He returned to Collioure, where, belying his self-effacing public persona, he was sitting for a Perpignan sculptor who was creating a clay model for a bronze bust of him. He then traveled to Dublin, where he intended to lease a flat, in part to take advantage of Ireland's generous tax laws for artists and writers.

Three chapters into his twenty-first Aubrey-Maturin novel, O'Brian died in the Fitzwilliam Hotel in Dublin, Ireland, on January 2, 2000. In a final ironic twist to his life, he died on the island where he claimed he had been born. At his request, his death was kept secret while his body was transported to Collioure. On January 11, he was buried next to Mary during a private ceremony attended by Nikolai and Natasha and their families, the mayor of Collioure, and a few close friends.

In the three decades since O'Brian wrote *Master and Commander*, the Aubrey-Maturin novels ascended from their sleepy literary-naval niche to acclaim as some of the best fiction of their time. By October 1999, according to *Publishers Weekly*, more than three million novels in the series had been sold.

O'Brian's son, Richard Russ, now sixty-three, lives in London with his wife, Mimi. A mechanical engineer by training, Russ owns a company called London Screen Printing. They have two daughters, Victoria Russ, a corporate executive, and Joanna Hubbard, a schoolteacher.

Selected Bibliography

Adrian, Jack, ed. *Detective Stories from the Strand.* Oxford: Oxford University Press, 1991.

Baker, John F. "Starling Lawrence: Editor to Spare-Time Novelist." *Publishers Weekly,* August 4, 1997.

Barr, Donald. "Substance and Shadow." Review of *The Walker and Other Stories,* by Patrick O'Brian. *New York Times Book Review,* August 14, 1955.

Bayley, John. "The Matter of India." Review of *The Reverse of the Medal,* by Patrick O'Brian. *London Review of Books,* March 19, 1987.

——. "Glorious Pictures of Life on the High Seas." *Evening Standard,* October 14, 1996.

Binyon, T. J. "Ship-shape." Review of *The Fortune of War*, by Patrick O'Brian. *Times Literary Supplement,* February 15, 1980.

——. "Fore and Aft." Review of *The Surgeon's Mate,* by Patrick O'Brian. *Times Literary Supplement,* August 1, 1980.

——. "The Man with His Eye on the Mast." Review of *The Nutmeg of Consolation*, by Patrick O'Brian. *Independent,* February 23, 1991.

——. "Taken by Surprise." Review of *The Wine-Dark Sea*, by Patrick O'Brian. *Evening Standard,* July 1993.

——. "A Life on the Ocean Wave." Review of *The Yellow Admiral*, by Patrick O'Brian. *Sunday Times,* January 5, 1997.

"Bogged Down in Vietnam." Review of *The Quicksand War*, by Lucien Bodard, trans. Patrick O'Brian. *Times Literary Supplement,* May 16, 1968.

Boswell, James. *Life of Johnson.* 3d ed., ed. R. W. Chapman. London: Oxford University Press, 1970.

"Broken Marriages." *Times,* July 17, 1945.

Brown, Beatrice Curtis. *Southwards from Swiss Cottage.* London: Home and Van Thal, 1947.

Byatt, A. S. "Salts of the Earth." Review of *The Nutmeg of Consolation*, by Patrick O'Brian. *Evening Standard,* February 14, 1991.

———. "At Sea in the Brothel of Life." Review of *Clarissa Oakes*, by Patrick O'Brian. *Evening Standard*, March 26, 1992.

Cabanne, Pierre. *Pablo Picasso: His Life and Times*. Trans. Harold J. Salemson. New York: William Morrow, 1977.

"Character and Motive." Review of *Three Bear Witness*, by Patrick O'Brian. *Times*, May 10, 1952.

Chesterfield, Earl of (Philip Dormer Stanhope). *Chesterfield's Letters to His Son*. New York: Tudor, 1937.

"Clash with Convention." Review of *Three Bear Witness*, by Patrick O'Brian. *Times Literary Supplement*, May 16, 1952.

Colley, Linda. "A Curiously Impersonal Man." Review of *Joseph Banks: A Life*, by Patrick O'Brian. *New York Times Book Review*, March 28, 1993.

"Coming to the Point." Review of *Lying in the Sun*, by Patrick O'Brian. *Times Literary Supplement*, May 11, 1956.

Cunningham, A. E. *Patrick O'Brian: Critical Appreciations and a Bibliography*. Boston Spa: The British Library, 1994. Subsequently published as *Patrick O'Brian: Critical Essays and a Bibliography*. New York: W. W. Norton, 1994.

Davey, Richard. *Furs and Fur Garments*. London: International Fur Store; Roxburghe Press, 1895.

Dening, Greg. "Around the Natural World." Review of *Joseph Banks: A Life*, by Patrick O'Brian. *Washington Post*, August 8, 1993.

De Quincey, Thomas. *Confessions of an English Opium-Eater, and Kindred Papers*. Vol. 1. Boston and New York: Houghton, Mifflin, 1876.

Ditler, Joseph. "The Commodore." Review of *The Commodore*, by Patrick O'Brian. From manuscript, April 19, 1995.

Doe, Bob. "Maritime Master." *Times Educational Supplement*, January 24, 1997.

Dunlea, William. "Men and Nature." Review of *The Walker and Other Stories*, by Patrick O'Brian. *Commonweal*, September 23, 1956.

"Dust of Battle." Review of *The Golden Ocean*, by Patrick O'Brian. *Times Literary Supplement*, May 11, 1956.

Fairchild, Tony, ed. *A School Apart: A History of Shebbear College*. Guildford and King's Lynn, England: Old Shebbearians Association, [1987?].

"Family Failings." Review of *The Frozen Flame*, by Patrick O'Brian. *Times Literary Supplement*, September 18, 1953.

Fenton, Ben. "The Secret Life of Patrick O'Brian." *Daily Telegraph*, October 24, 1998.

———. "Brotherly Love Behind a Hero of the High Seas." *Daily Telegraph*, October 29, 1998.

Fisher, Margery. "Books for the Children." Review of *The Road to Samarcand*, by Patrick O'Brian. *Housewife*, June 1955.

Fitz-Gibbon, Constantine. *London's Burning*. New York: Ballantine Books, 1970.

"Foul-weather Jack." Review of *The Unknown Shore*, by Patrick O'Brian. *Times Literary Supplement*, July 24, 1959.

Gaunt, William. *Chelsea*. London: B. T. Batsford, 1954.

Gibson, Wilfrid. "Six New Novels." Review of *Hussein*, by R. P. Russ. *Manchester Guardian*, April 22, 1938.

Gill, Brendan. "Small Towns." Review of *The Catalans*, by Patrick O'Brian. *New Yorker*, October 24, 1953.

Gilot, Françoise, and Carlton Lake. *Life with Picasso.* New York: McGraw-Hill, 1964.

Goudeket, Maurice. *The Delights of Growing Old.* Trans. Patrick O'Brian. Pleasantville, N.Y.: Akadine Press, 1996.

Great French Paintings from the Barnes Foundation: Impressionist, Post-impressionist, and Early Modern. New York: Alfred A. Knopf in association with Lincoln University Press, 1993.

Grossman, Anne Chotzinoff, and Lisa Grossman Thomas. *Lobscouse and Spotted Dog: Which It's a Gastronomic Companion to the Aubrey/Maturin Novels.* New York: W. W. Norton, 1997.

Guttridge, Peter. "A Landlubber Beneath the Stuns'l Boom Iron." *Independent,* July 3, 1993.

Hart-Davis, Rupert. *Halfway to Heaven: Concluding Memoirs of a Literary Life.* Thrupp, England: Sutton, 1998.

Hastings, Max. "Books of the Year." Review of *The Wine-Dark Sea,* by Patrick O'Brian. *Daily Telegraph,* November 27, 1993.

———. "Will They Set Sail Again?" *Daily Telegraph,* September 3, 1994.

———. "The Great Adventurer." Review of *The Hundred Days,* by Patrick O'Brian. *Evening Standard,* August 10, 1998.

"Hidden Powers." Review of *Hidden Powers,* by Charles Russ. *Lancet,* August 1, 1931.

Hobbs, Harry. *The Romance of the Calcutta Sweep.* Calcutta: H. Hobbs, 1930.

"Hopefull Travellers." Review of *A Book of Voyages,* by Patrick O'Brian. *Punch,* November 12, 1947.

Horowitz, Mark. "Down to the Sea in Ships." *Los Angeles Times,* September 8, 1991.

———. "Patrick O'Brian's Ship Comes In." *New York Times Magazine,* May 16, 1993.

Hough, Richard, and Denis Richards. *The Battle of Britain: The Greatest Air Battle of World War II.* New York: W. W. Norton, 1989.

Hunt, Geoff. "Geoff Hunt RSMA." In *The Tall Ship in Art,* by Roy Cross et al. London: Blandford, 1998.

Hutchison, Percy. "Elephant Boy." Review of *Hussein: An Entertainment,* by R. P. Russ. *New York Times Book Review,* May 8, 1938.

"In Three Dimensions." Review of *Richard Temple,* by Patrick O'Brian. *Times Literary Supplement,* June 1, 1962.

Jones, Welton. "Virtual Reality, 19th-Century British Navy Style." Review of *The Commodore,* by Patrick O'Brian. *San Diego Union-Tribune,* May 2, 1995.

Judd, Alan. "Writer on the Crest of a Wave." *Daily Telegraph,* February 3, 1992.

———. "Men of War." Review of *Clarissa Oakes,* by Patrick O'Brian. *Sunday Times,* March 15, 1992.

———. "The Winning-Post at Last." *Spectator,* July 1, 1995.

Kazin, Pearl. "Outsider in the Valley." Review of *Testimonies,* by Patrick O'Brian. *New York Times Book Review,* August 24, 1952.

Keene, Frances. "Xavier the Cold Fish." Review of *The Catalans,* by Patrick O'Brian. *New York Times Book Review,* October 11, 1953.

Kerr, David. "Repelling all Boarders." *Daily Telegraph,* September 26, 1998.

———, prod. "Close Up: Patrick O'Brian, Nothing Personal." BBC 2, September 30, 1998.

Kludas, Arnold. *Great Passenger Ships of the World.* Vol. 2, 1913–23. Cambridge: Stephens, 1975–77.

Korg, Jacob. *Dylan Thomas.* Boston: Twayne, 1965.

La Farge, Oliver. "That Motherly Land." Review of *Testimonies,* by Patrick O'Brian. *Saturday Review,* August 23, 1952.

———. "Frenchmen from the Pyrenees." Review of *The Catalans,* by Patrick O'Brian. *Saturday Review,* October 17, 1953.

Lambert, J. W. "New Novels." Review of *The Frozen Flame,* by Patrick O'Brian. *Sunday Times,* September 27, 1953.

Laski, Marghanita. "First Time Lucky." Review of *The Frozen Flame,* by Patrick O'Brian. *Observer,* September 13, 1953.

Levin, Martin. Review of *Master and Commander,* by Patrick O'Brian. *New York Times Book Review,* December 14, 1969.

Lewin, Tamar. "Hooked on Boy Books." *New York Times Magazine,* July 23, 1995.

Lockhart, Sir Robert Bruce. *Comes the Reckoning.* London: Putnam, 1947.

Low, Valentine. "The Master Takes Command at Greenwich." *Evening Standard,* October 14, 1996.

Macaulay, Thomas Babington. *Select Essays of Macaulay.* Ed. Samuel Thurber. Boston: Allyn and Bacon, 1891.

Mailer, Norman. *Portrait of Picasso as a Young Man: An Intrepretive Biography.* New York: Atlantic Monthly Press, 1995.

Mann, Jessica. "A Man from a Better Age." *Sunday Telegraph,* December 15, 1996.

McGrath, Charles. "The Long Journey." Review of *The Wine-Dark Sea,* by Patrick O'Brian. *New Yorker,* October 18, 1993.

Mosley, Leonard. *Backs to the Wall: The Heroic Story of the People of London During World War II.* New York: Random House, 1971.

Mosley, Leonard, and editors of Time-Life Books. *Battle of Britain, WW II.* Alexandria, Va.: Time-Life Books, 1977.

Murdoch, Iris. *Under the Net.* New York: Viking Press, 1954.

Myers, Kevin. "An Irishman's Diary." *Irish Times,* January 16, 1997.

"Nature Books." Review of *Beasts Royal,* by Patrick Russ. *Times Literary Supplement,* November 22, 1934.

"New Fiction." Review of *The Frozen Flame,* by Patrick O'Brian. *Times,* September 12, 1953.

Niall, Ian. *Portrait of a Country Artist.* London: Gollancz, 1980.

Nolen, Barbara. "Of, by and for Children." Review of *Caesar,* by Patrick Russ. *New York Herald Tribune,* August 9, 1931.

"Novelties in Fur." *The Queen, The Lady's Newspaper.* London: Horace Cox, October 30, 1880.

O'Brian, Patrick. *See also* Russ, Patrick.

The Aubrey-Maturin Novels:

———. *Master and Commander.* Philadelphia: J. B. Lippincott, 1969; London: Collins, 1970; New York: W. W. Norton, 1990.

———. *Post Captain.* London: Collins, 1972; Philadelphia: J. B. Lippincott, 1972; New York: W. W. Norton, 1990.

———. *H.M.S. Surprise.* London: Collins, 1973; Philadelphia: J. B. Lippincott, 1973; New York: W. W. Norton, 1991.

————. *The Mauritius Command.* London: Collins, 1977; New York: Stein and Day, 1978; New York: W. W. Norton, 1991.

————. *Desolation Island.* London: Collins, 1978; New York: Stein and Day, 1979; New York: W. W. Norton, 1991.

————. *The Fortune of War.* London: Collins, 1979; New York: W. W. Norton, 1991.

————. *The Surgeon's Mate.* London: Collins, 1980; New York: W. W. Norton, 1992.

————. *The Ionian Mission.* London: Collins, 1981; New York: W. W. Norton, 1992.

————. *Treason's Harbour.* London: Collins, 1983; New York: W. W. Norton, 1992.

————. *The Far Side of the World.* London: Collins, 1984; New York: W. W. Norton, 1992.

————. *The Reverse of the Medal.* London: Collins, 1986; New York: W. W. Norton, 1992.

————. *The Letter of Marque.* London: Collins, 1988; New York: W. W. Norton, 1991.

————. *The Thirteen Gun Salute.* London: Collins, 1989; New York: W. W. Norton, 1991.

————. *The Nutmeg of Consolation.* London: Collins, 1991; New York: W. W. Norton, 1991.

————. *Clarissa Oakes.* London: HarperCollins, 1992; subsequently published as *The Truelove*, New York: W. W. Norton, 1992.

————. *The Wine-Dark Sea.* London: HarperCollins, 1993; New York: W. W. Norton, 1993.

————. *The Commodore.* London: HarperCollins, 1994; New York: W. W. Norton, 1995.

————. *The Yellow Admiral.* New York: W. W. Norton, 1996; London: Harper-Collins, 1997.

————. *The Hundred Days.* New York: W. W. Norton, 1998; London: Harper-Collins, 1998.

Other Works:

————, ed. *A Book of Voyages.* London: Home and Van Thal, 1947.

————. *The Last Pool and Other Stories.* London: Secker and Warburg, 1950.

————. *Three Bear Witness.* London: Secker and Warburg, 1952; subsequently published as *Testimonies*, New York: Harcourt, Brace, 1952.

————. "Song." *Poetry Ireland,* April 1952.

————. "The Green Creature." *Harper's Bazaar,* December 1952.

————. *The Catalans.* New York: Harcourt, Brace, 1953; subsequently published as *The Frozen Flame*, London: Hart-Davis, 1953.

————. "Samphire." *Harper's Bazaar,* March 1953.

————. "The Walker." *Harper's Bazaar,* October 1953.

————. *The Road to Samarcand.* London: Hart-Davis, 1954.

————. "The Slope of the High Mountain." *Harper's Bazaar,* January 1954.

————. *The Walker and Other Stories.* New York: Harcourt, Brace, 1955; subsequently published as *Lying in the Sun and Other Stories*, London: Hart-Davis, 1956.

————. "Lying in the Sun." *Harper's Bazaar,* August 1955.

————. *The Golden Ocean.* London: Hart-Davis, 1956; New York: W. W. Norton, 1994.

————. *The Unknown Shore.* London: Hart-Davis, 1959; New York: W. W. Norton, 1995.

————. *Richard Temple.* London: Macmillan, 1962.

———, trans. *Papillon,* by Henri Charrière. London: Rupert Hart-Davis, 1970.

———, trans. *Banco: The Further Adventures of Papillon,* by Henri Charrière. New York: William Morrow, 1973.

———. *The Chian Wine and Other Stories.* London: Collins, 1974.

———. "A Sung Landscape Remembered." *Cornhill Magazine,* summer 1974.

———. *Pablo Ruiz Picasso: A Biography.* London: Collins, 1976; New York: W. W. Norton, 1994.

———. "In Upper Lesson Street." *Irish Press,* March 5, 1977.

———. *Joseph Banks: A Life.* London: Collins Harvill, 1987; Boston: Godine, 1993.

———. "A Life in the Day of Patrick O'Brian." *Sunday Times Magazine,* November 5, 1989.

———. "Great Encounters." Review of *The Price of Admiralty,* by John Keegan. *London Review of Books,* January 11, 1990.

———. "Das Boot." Review of *The U-Boat War in the Atlantic, 1939–1945,* by Günter Hessler, and *Business in Great Waters: The U-Boat Wars, 1916–1945,* by John Terraine. *London Review of Books,* August 30, 1990.

———. "The Great War." In *Edwardian Brooks's: A Social History,* ed. Philip Ziegler and Desmond Sewald. London: Constable, 1991.

———. "What Boswell Didn't Tell Us About Johnson." Review of *The Life of Samuel Johnson,* by James Boswell. *Daily Telegraph,* August 22, 1992.

———. "Just a Phase I'm Going Through?" *Weekend Telegraph,* August 27, 1994.

———. *The Collected Short Stories.* London: HarperCollins, 1994; subsequently published as *The Rendezvous and Other Stories.* New York: W. W. Norton, 1994.

———. "Second Thoughts: Pleasure and Painting in Spain." *Independent,* January 14, 1995.

———. "The Clockmaker's Prize." Review of *Longitude: The True Story of a Lone Genius Who Solved the Greatest Scientific Problem of His Time,* by Dava Sobel. *Sunday Telegraph,* August 11, 1996.

———. Foreword to *The Drake Manuscript in the Pierpont Morgan Library: Histoire Naturelle des Indes.* London: André Deutsch, 1996.

Conversations with Patrick O'Brian

"Third Ear." Interview by Alan Judd. *BBC Radio,* October 3, 1992.

Interview by Neil Conan. *Talk of the Nation.* National Public Radio, April 17, 1995.

Panel discussion. 92nd Street Y. New York: April 17, 1995.

"Patrick O'Brian in Conversation with Richard Hass." Hosted by Maya Angelou. City Arts of San Francisco, April 19, 1995.

Interview by Neute Berger. Portland Arts and Lectures, April 21, 1995.

Interview by Charlton Heston. UCLA Friends of English, April 24, 1995.

"Author Chats." Interview by Richard Snow. Barnesandnoble.com, 1998.

"The Giant O'Brian." Amazon.com interview, 1998.

O'Connor, Philip. *Living in Croesor.* London: Hutchinson, 1962.

Paris Universal Exhibition of 1878—Official Catalogue of the British Section. Published by direction of His Royal Highness the Prince of Wales KG, etc., etc., president of the royal commission for Great Britain and Ireland. London: George E. Eyre and

William Spottiswode, printers to the queen's most excellent majesty. For Her Majesty's stationery office, 1878.

Poland, F. Rexford. "A Short History of the British Fur Trade." *British Fur Trade Year Book.* London: Hutchinson, 1933.

"Poor Painter Analysed." Review of *Picasso, 1881–1972,* by Patrick O'Brian. *Irish Press,* December 15, 1973.

Powers, Katherine A. "An Eighteenth-Century Voice." Review of *The Commodore,* by Patrick O'Brian. *Atlantic Monthly,* July 1995.

Pratter, Frederick. "Battling Slavers off the West Coast of Africa." Review of *The Commodore,* by Patrick O'Brian. *Christian Science Monitor,* May 2, 1995.

Prial, Frank. "The Seas of Adventure Still Beckon a Storyteller." *New York Times,* October 19, 1998.

Ranger, Sir Douglas. *The Middlesex Hospital Medical School Centenary to Sesquicentenary, 1935–1985.* London: Hutchinson Benham, 1985.

Ringle, Ken. "Is This the Best Writer You Never Heard Of?" *Washington Post,* August 2, 1992.

Review of *Caesar,* by Patrick Russ. *Saturday Review of Literature,* September 5, 1931.

Review of *Hussein,* by Patrick Russ. *Times Literary Supplement,* April 23, 1938.

Review of *Hussein,* by Patrick Russ. *Saturday Review of Literature,* July 9, 1938.

Rothnie, Niall. *The Baedeker Blitz: Hitler's Attack on Britain's Historic Cities.* Shepperton, Surrey: Ian Allan, 1992.

Rothwell, Robert L., ed. *Henry David Thoreau, An American Landscape: Selected Writings from His Journals.* New York: Paragon House, 1991.

"Round the Christmas Shelves." Review of *Caesar,* by Patrick Russ. *New Statesman,* December 6, 1930.

Russ, A. B. *Lady Day Prodigal.* Victoria, British Columbia: A. B. Russ, 1989.

Russ, Charles. "Further Results in the Electrolysis Treatment of Cystitis." *Lancet,* October 31, 1914.

Russ, Emily Callaway. Daybook, 1893–1906. Courtesy of John Russ.

Russ, Patrick. *Caesar: The Life Story of a Panda Leopard.* London and New York: G. P. Putnam's Sons, 1930. Subsequently published under author name Patrick O'Brian. Boston Spa: The British Library, 1999.

———. "Skogula—the Sperm Whale." *Chums,* October 24, 1931, 314–15.

———. "Wang Khan of the Elephants." In *The Oxford Annual for Scouts*, ed. Herbert Strang, 107–12. London: Oxford University Press, 1933.

———. "A Tale About a Great Peregrine Falcon." *Great-Heart: The Church of Scotland Magazine—for Boys and Girls,* March 1933, 50–52.

———. *Beasts Royal.* London: Putnam, 1934.

———. "The White Cobra." In *The Oxford Annual for Scouts*, ed. Herbert Strang, 66–70. London: Oxford University Press, 1934.

———. "Cheetah." In *The Oxford Annual for Boys*, ed. Herbert Strang, 144–52. London: Oxford University Press, 1935.

———. "Noughts and Crosses." In *The Oxford Annual for Boys*, ed. Herbert Strang. London: Oxford University Press, 1936.

———. "Two's Company." In *The Oxford Annual for Boys*, ed. Herbert Strang, 5–18. London: Oxford University Press, 1937.

———. *Hussein: An Entertainment.* London: Oxford University Press, 1938. Subsequently published under author name Patrick O'Brian. Boston Spa: The British Library, 1999.

———. "One Arctic Summer." In *The Oxford Annual for Boys*, ed. Herbert Strang, 88–96. London: Oxford University Press, 1938.

———. "No Pirates Nowadays." In *The Oxford Annual for Boys*, ed. Herbert Strang, 5–22. London: Oxford University Press, 1940.

Sacks, Captain John C. *Furs and the Fur Trade*. London: Sir Isaac Pitman and Sons, 1923.

Schwartz, Delmore. "Long After Eden." Review of *Testimonies*, by Patrick O'Brian. *Partisan Review,* December 1952.

Simson, Maria. "Patrick O'Brian: Full Speed Ahead at Norton." *Publishers Weekly,* October 26, 1992.

Smith, Constance Babington. *Rose Macaulay*. London: Collins, 1972.

Smith, Stevie. "New Novels." Review of *The Frozen Flame*, by Patrick O'Brian. *Spectator,* September 18, 1953.

Snow, Richard. "An Author I'd Walk the Plank For." *New York Times Book Review,* January 6, 1991.

Snyder, Marjorie. "Love Encounters Weird Perversion in Welsh Valley." Review of *Testimonies*, by Patrick O'Brian. *Washington Post,* August 31, 1953.

Spufford, Francis. "Navigating Through Stormy Genres," *Independent,* March 15, 1992.

"Stories and Anecdotes." Review of *The Last Pool,* by Patrick O'Brian. *Times Literary Supplement,* September 1, 1950.

Strawson, Galen. "The Habit of Victory—in the Year 1815b." *Independent,* December 29, 1996.

Sugrue, Thomas. "Regional Novels, War, and Tales of India." Review of *Hussein*, by R. P. Russ. *New York Herald Tribune Books,* May 8, 1938.

Teacher, James. "Incidents of the Seas." Review of *The Commodore*, by Patrick O'Brian. *Spectator,* December 3, 1994.

Tolstoy, Nikolai. *The Half-Mad Lord*. New York: Holt, Rinehart and Winston, 1978.

———. *Tolstoys: Twenty-four Generations of Russian History, 1353–1983*. New York: William Morrow, 1983.

van Thal, Herbert. *The Tops of the Mulberry Trees*. London: George Allen and Unwin, 1971.

Waldegrave, Rt. Hon. William. "Speech at the Painted Hall, Greenwich." In *The Yellow Admiral*, by Patrick O'Brian, 265–68. London: HarperCollins, 1997.

Warburg, Fredric. *An Occupation for Gentlemen*. Boston: Houghton Mifflin, 1960.

———. *All Authors Are Equal*. New York: St. Martin's Press, 1973.

Warner, Oliver. " 'Are We Alone?' Adventure Stories New and Old." *Time and Tide,* April 23, 1955.

Whately, Rosaleen. "An Anti-hero Takes His Chance." Review of *Richard Temple*, by Patrick O'Brian. *Liverpool Daily Post,* June 6, 1962.

Wheatley, Keith. "The Long Life of O'Brian," *Financial Times,* January 11, 1997.

Williams, L. F. Rushbrook. Review of *Hussein*, by R. P. Russ. *South Asian Review,* vol.34, 1938.

Wood, Derek, and Derek Dempster. *The Narrow Margin: The Battle of Britain and the Rise of Air Power, 1930–40*. New York: McGraw-Hill, 1961.

Wordsworth, Christopher. "Worldly Box of Tricks." Review of *Desolation Island*, by Patrick O'Brian. *Guardian,* June 29, 1978.

Yardley, Jonathan. "Beat to Quarters." Review of *The Letter of Marque*, by Patrick O'Brian. *Washington Post,* August 26, 1990.

———. "Capt. Aubrey, Making Waves." Review of *The Nutmeg of Consolation*, by Patrick O'Brian. *Washington Post,* August 21, 1991.

———. "A Test of Your Sea Legs." Review of *The Yellow Admiral*, by Patrick O'Brian. *Washington Post,* November 6, 1996.

Zaleski, Jerome A. "An Evening with O'Brian." *Philadelphia Lawyer,* fall 1994.

Ziegler, Philip. *London at War: 1939–1945.* New York: Alfred A. Knopf, 1995.

Acknowledgments

Without the assistance of many kind and generous people, this book would not have been possible. Several people made invaluable contributions for which I am deeply grateful. *New York* magazine editor Mark Horowitz made available interview transcripts and notes from his research for his 1993 *New York Times Magazine* story and encouraged me. Barney Russ's children, Charles and Elizabeth, supplied family stories and photographs, as well as permission to excerpt from Barney's privately published autobiography *Lady Day Prodigal* and his letters. Sidney Russ's son, John Reginald Russ, lent me his (and Patrick O'Brian's) grandmother's day book; Richard Ollard gave me permission to quote from his editorial reports; Jean Yves Goëau-Brissonière allowed me to examine his father's World War II files; and lovely Odette Boutet opened up her heart and home to my wife, me, and our daughter, Willa, in Collioure, and shared her memories of her good friend Mary O'Brian.

To Patrick O'Brian's intelligent and thoughtful son, Richard Russ, who spent dozens of hours in conversation with me reconstructing elements of his first thirty years, I would like to acknowledge my admiration. Although his early life was tumultuous at times, he emerged the stronger for it, became a successful husband, father, and businessman, and never soured. Special thanks to Richard's wife, Mimi, as well.

For sharing their time, knowledge, and memories with me, I am most grateful to antiquarian bookseller Stuart Bennett; Brigadier Walter Greenway; Croesor, Wales, residents Edgar Perry Williams and Owen Tudor Owain; former William Collins chairman Ian Chapman; literary agent Richard Scott Simon; former Lippincott editor Wolcott (Tony) Gibbs, Jr. My thanks to Geoff Hunt for his account of how he became the cover illustrator for the Aubrey-Maturin novels and for his permission to show his cover sketches. For his soothing advice and guidance, my kindest regards to Dublin genealogist Harry McDowell.

I would like to thank all the members of the Russ family who helped me to assemble the history of several generations of their family. In England, Joan Russ Russell's children

Acknowledgments

Harold Russell, Gwen Russell-Jones, James Russell, and Mary Russell Morton were particularly generous with their time and effort and allowed me to quote from their mother Joan's wonderful letter written at Crowborough during World War II, as were Olive's son, John A. Cole, and Connie's daughter, Linda Green. Thanks also to Brenda Russell, Charles V. J. Russ, and Dorothy Russ Collins. In Canada, my appreciation goes to Barney Russ's widow, Fifi Russ, for her memories and anecdotes and, on the Goddard side of the family, to Morse and Jane Goddard. Finally, in Australia, Mike Russ's son, Stanley Charles Russ, Sr., unknown to the rest of the family, stood up to be counted after the first printing of this book.

Also after the publication of the first edition of this book, I had the pleasure of corresponding with and talking to Mary's brother, H. F. S. Wicksteed, and his wife, Dorothy, as well as their children Peter, Jane, and Joanna. This allowed for a number of very useful emendations and additions. I would like to express my deepest gratitude to each of them. Many others provided me with publishing information and personal recollections, including, in England, former Rupert Hart-Davis editors Nicholas Barker and Richard Garnett; Peter Barnett (of Melbury Lodge); Wadham College, Oxford, don T. J. Binyon; G. Heywood Hill bookseller John Saumarez Smith; Patrick O'Brian cover artist Paul Wright; Royal Air Force veterans R. Noel Smith, Herbert Pinfold, and Gerald Bell. Also, Michael Clark, Stephen E. Clark, David Kerr, Tanya Ilingworth, Charles Latimer, Christopher MacLehose, Tom Pocock, James Puckridge, Francis Spufford, Lu Wanklyn, Commander Michael Saunders Watson, Beryl Richardson, and Joan Bonnor-Moris; in Wales, Commander Naish and Primrose Roche; in France, Jojo Pous, Mimi Atxer, Joseph Hiard, Jean Yves Goëau-Brissonnière; in the United States, Deirdre Bair, Joe Ditler, Anne Chotzinoff Grossman, Tom Perkins, Jonathan Raban, Roslyn Targ, Lisa Grossman Thomas, John West, Judge Jerome Zaleski; in Ireland, Michael Dolphin; in Canada, John Harland; and in Australia, Jeanette Mary Egan, Gregory William Egan, and Peter Jeans. A number of contributors wished to remain anonymous, and I offer them a silent thank-you.

As for my family and friends, I owe them a great deal. First, I would like to express my everlasting gratitude to my wife, Jessica King, whose editorial insight, moral support, and cheerful companionship both abroad and at home buoyed me throughout the process of researching and writing this book.

For their invaluable readings of the manuscript, thanks to Jessica King, David Sobel, Charlie Slack, Ben and Lila Fenton, Andy Smith, Stuart Bennett, Mark Horowitz, and Vicki Haire, each of whom contributed in his or her own way to the shaping of this book. They certainly prevented me from making numerous mistakes. Any errors that still exist are, of course, my own. I'd especially like to thank William R. Cline Jr. for making his perhaps unequaled collection of Patrick O'Brian and Richard Patrick Russ first editions available to me and for his good company during my research in England and Wales, and Andy Smith, who assisted me while researching in Ireland and whose enthusiasm for the detective work at least matched my own. I'd also like to express my gratitude to my editor, David Sobel, and my agent, Jody Rein, for their much-valued guidance and encouragement, to my foreign rights agent, Agnes Krup, and to Henry Holt assistant editor Anne Geiger.

Along the way, many friends, old and new, contributed to this book. I send my thanks to John Hattendorf, Robert and Jane Mocatta, Geoffrey Morris, Eléonore Renié,

Phillip and Hydrox Turner, and Logan Ward for helping me in various ways with research and/or logistics.

Finally, a hardy thanks to all the researchers, whose tireless fact-finding helped me tremendously, especially Nancy Steed (my able assistant), Jane Hines and Kristin Ellis (in England), Sylvie Deroche (in France), and genealogists Duncan Harrington (in England), Sherry Irvine (in Canada), and André Schmidt (in Germany).

The following individuals and institutions were particularly helpful with my research: in England, Michael Bott at the University of Reading, Ian Thurman at the Office of National Statistics, Mrs. J. Knapman and David Hart at Shebbear College, Humphrey Osmond at the Dean Close School, Jenny McMorus at Oxford University Press, Leigh Aspin at BBC Proms, David Harris at the Crowborough Town Council, Sister Margaret McVoy of the Franciscan Sisters of Mill Hill, Steve van Dulken at the British Library Patents Office, the Commonwealth War Graves Commission, the Public Record Office, the London Metropolitan Archives, the Family Records Centre, the British Medical Association, the Royal College of Surgeons of England, the Westminster Reference Library, the British Library, the Colindale Newspaper Library, the Chelsea Library, the National Arts Library at the Victoria and Albert Museum, the Lewes Library, the Lewes Tourist Information Centre, the Sussex Past/Sussex Archaeological Society, and the Worcester Library.

In the United States, Nicholas King at the Barnes Foundation, Steve Speigel at the 92nd Street Y, the Virginia State Library, the Richmond Public Library, the James Branch Cabell Library at Virginia Commonwealth University, Saundra Taylor and Sue Presnell at the Lilly Library at Indiana University, the University of Richmond Library, and the University of Virginia Library. In Australia, David Wilson and Anthony Staunton for research on the Royal Australian Air Force.

Index

(A-M novels *refers to Aubrey-Maturin novels*.)